A COOK'S TOUR OF ITALY

A COOK'S TOUR OF ITALY

More than 300 Authentic Recipes
from the Regions of Italy

JOE FAMULARO

HP Books

THE BERKLEY PUBLISHING GROUP
Published by the Penguin Group
Penguin Group (USA) Inc.
375 Hudson Street, New York, New York 10014, USA
Penguin Group (Canada), 90 Eglinton Avenue East, Suite 700, Toronto, Ontario M4P 2Y3, Canada
(a division of Pearson Penguin Canada Inc.)
Penguin Books Ltd., 80 Strand, London WC2R 0RL, England
Penguin Group Ireland, 25 St. Stephen's Green, Dublin 2, Ireland (a division of Penguin Books Ltd.)
Penguin Group (Australia), 250 Camberwell Road, Camberwell, Victoria 3124, Australia
(a division of Pearson Australia Group Pty. Ltd.)
Penguin Books India Pvt. Ltd., 11 Community Centre, Panchsheel Park, New Delhi—110 017, India
Penguin Group (NZ), Cnr. Airborne and Rosedale Roads, Albany, Auckland 1310, New Zealand
(a division of Pearson New Zealand Ltd.)
Penguin Books (South Africa) (Pty.) Ltd., 24 Sturdee Avenue, Rosebank, Johannesburg 2196,
South Africa
Penguin Books Ltd., Registered Offices: 80 Strand, London WC2R 0RL, England

Copyright © 2003 by Joe Famularo
Text design by Tiffany Estreicher
Cover design by Ben Gibson

PRINTING HISTORY
HP Books hardcover / November 2003
HP trade papeerback edition / November 2005

HPBooks is a registered trademark of Penguin Group (USA) Inc.

The Library of Congress has cataloged the original HPBooks hardcover paperback as followed

    Famularo, Joseph J.
      A cook's tour of Italy : more than 300 authentic recipes from the regions of Italy /
    by Joe Famularo.—1st HP Book, ed.
        p. cm.
      Includes index.
      ISBN 1-55788-418-8
      1. Cookery, Italian. I. Title.

    TX723.F35 2003
    641.5945—dc21

                                    2002192182

PRINTED IN THE UNITED STATES OF AMERICA

10 9 8 7 6 5 4 3 2 1

CONTENTS

● ● ●

III. The Italian Riviera: Liguria and the Northeast Corner of Italy, Piemonte and Valle d'Aosta   71

● ● ●

Contents

● ● ●

● ● ●

VI. Emilia-Romagna's Star Cities: Bologna, Parma and Modena, and Others Along the 125-Mile Roman Road, the Via Emilia 141

● ● ●

VIII. Naples and Its Bay: Bari and the Adriatic South   196

• • •

GRAZIE MILLE

● ● ●

I wish to thank the many friends, chefs, restaurant owners and workers in Italy who always found time and patience to inform and instruct me. Many of their names have been included in the text or as part of a recipe title. In addition, I would like to thank Tizania and Francesco Antonini (Bevagna), Ermenegildo Baggio at Hosteria Ca'Derton (Asolo), Walter and Emanuele Ascani (Bevagna), Rosalba Balestrazzi (Ostuni-Apulia), Bruno Boggione at Il Vicoletto (Alba), Gianrodolfo Botto (Palermo), Giovanni Cappelli (Panzano in Chianti), Pina and Marco Carli (Naples), Paola Cavazzini and Maurizio Rossi (Parma), Corrado Costanzo

(Noto-Sicily), Agata Parisella and Romeo Caraccio (Rome), Monseignor Divine (The Vatican), Piero and Pina Fassi (Asti), Luca Garrone at Ristorante Universo (Vignale Monferrato), Giovanna Gradassi and her son, Andrea Scotacci (Spoleto), Giorgi Intelesano (Taormino), Mariuccia at the Fiaschetteria Toscana (Venice), Fauto Monti (Florence), Emanuele Monzeglio and William Perrotta (Asti), Gabriele Moscati and her sons, Giuseppe and Filippo Saladini (Doglie-Todi), Georgianna and Armando Orsini, Fabio Picchi (Florence), Cristina di Piovani (Mantova), Jim and Warrie Price (Lucca), Angelo Ricci (Bari), Cinzia Ricci (Lucca), Nicoletti Ruggieri (Siracusa), Pietro and Angela Santi and Carmensita Poggianti of Hotel Brunamonti (Bevagna-Umbria), Antonio and Nadia Santini at Dal Pescatore (Canneto sull'Oglio-Mantova), Clotilde Treves (Monteporzio-Rome) and Benedetta Vitali (Florence).

I want to especially thank AnnaMaria and Maurizio Mancioli di Montefano for their invaluable help with the Italian recipe titles and other Italian expressions; Tina Redecha for her recipes, inspiration and understanding; Marylin Bender Altshul for long-term support; Lauren and Brendon McAloon at the Waterfront Market in Key West, Florida, for sharing their knowledge of fish; John Duff, my publisher, Jeanette Egan, my editor, and Stacey Glick, my agent, without their help and faith, you would not be holding this book; Bernie Kinzer and other friends, Louise and John Imperiale and other family members, for joining me on many trips to Italy, to visit, sightsee, study and most of all, to cook; Eileen Canzoneri for her steady support and help with the manuscript, and, without a doubt, to Cristopher Laus, my assistant, for accompanying us to Italy on several major trips and whose good help in testing these recipes was simply wonderful and indispensable. To all of you, I dedicate this book.

INTRODUCTION

Going to Italy always reminds me of how we should be eating (and living) in the United States. Italians seem to be more passionate about their food. They market daily, talk about food all the time, spend time in the kitchen, even close their shops to devote three hours a day to eat lunch. For them, eating is a simple pleasure, and eating the Italian way delivers a better quality of life. No one expects our lunchtime to increase, but I think there is agreement that most of us want (many crave) the Italian eating experience at home.

My love for Italian food began before my first visit to Italy. Growing up in New York in an Italian household taught me to appreciate homemade pastas and breads, fresh vegetables, delicious soups, fish in simple preparations and meats and stews in all their guises. I am an American-Italian, proud of his Italian roots, its history, culture and food. I love eating Italian food. When I did get to Italy, the food seemed better, the flavors were clearer, the perfume of the fresh fruit was outstandingly noticeable. Eating in the trattorias and in friends' homes clearly showed how the various foods melded together, as in perfect harmony. Every time I returned from Italy, my goal was to recreate these food experiences. Along the way, I learned that the Piemontese cook their way, the Umbrians their way, the Neapolitans their way, and so it is for all Italian regions. I learned, in fact, that each Italian has his or her own style. In spite of these differences, there is a fundamental truth that ties the various cuisines together: careful selection of ingredients, treating them separately and purely, striving for flavors that at the same time are both natural and powerful. This makes Italian cooking unique, and to recreate it outside Italy, one must have excellent-quality ingredients to make the same dish. Italians market every day, sometimes two times a day; they inspect asparagus spears and artichoke leaves for freshness, and imprint their thumbs on eggplants, snap green beans and pierce pea pods with their thumbnails, all in search of freshness. If an Italian doesn't have or can't get the ingredient it takes to make a dish, they'll move on to something else.

In our family kitchen, the message on a Florentine wall tile, painted in shades of blue and yellow, and sprinkled with years of kitchen duty marks, reads: "*Il padrone di casa sono io, chi comanda e mia moglie!*" (I am the master of my household, but it is my wife who commands.) No one in the family disputed Mama's authority and it was witnessed in many ways. What I remember most of all was the way she rattled off the day's supper menu, the next day's lunch menu or a dinner menu for the upcoming Sunday. We knew, as she did, what she was going to cook and serve, from start to finish, day in, day out. She was a fabulous cook, with an uncanny sense for menu planning. I've been writing about food for fifteen years, have traveled across the country promoting my books and have taught at several cooking schools. I am always asked this question: "If I prepare veal scaloppini (or linguine, or risotto), what should I serve with it?" I believe most Americans need some help in designing a meal and this is especially true for Italian food. This is exactly what this book is all about.

Americans love Italian cookbooks. Yet few of them tell the reader how to compose the meal. I'm talking about Italian food on American tables, food more consistent with American eating habits, yet tasty, chic, easy-to-prepare lunch, supper or dinner menus, Italian in spirit and taste, from start to finish. In answer to this need I have written a book of menus—Italian menus that come from all over Italy. Italians rarely consider a dish by itself; it is always set in the context of the meal as a whole, except perhaps when it is time for a one-dish meal (with a salad, of course). The meal has a pattern, if you will, designed to see that each dish is congenial to the others, and complementary in taste, color, texture and, of course, substance. *Piatti alla buona,* everyday food, is included if for no other reason than they're easy, quick, simple family preparations. *Piatti domenicali,* Sunday food, is also included because it is more special and out of the ordinary.

Most of the recipes included here are souvenirs of my "working" trips to Italy; enjoying food there and writing about it is never work, whether I'm in well-known cities or in remote villages. The recipes have been tested in Italy and America. But let me assure you that the talented, imaginative cooks of Italy have their own way of sharing a recipe: it is always a "little of this, some of that" (in the same way they give directions; it is always *"sempre diretto,"* always go straight even if there is a T in the road, or roads that go left and right.) Sometimes when I returned home to the United States, the recipe did not work for the American table. It was necessary to translate the "little of this and some of that" to get a good replication of the Italian dish. Flours, water and many fish are only a few examples of the differing ingredients.

One must recognize that *la nuova cucina* was a disaster in Italy. Ties to family and land are so entrenched that trattorias, restaurants and food at home are unabashedly antiurban. *Mamma e Nonna* are still stirring the polenta. In Montefalco, just north of Spoleto in Umbria, at the charming restaurant Coccorone, and in fact all over the Italian boot, lamb and other meats are still slowly roasted in a wood-burning hearth, as it has been for hundreds of years. We all know the beauty of Italian cooking is startling simplicity and honest, direct flavors. At times, it seems Italy is light-years away from the concept of altacasual dining. Culinary time seems languid and foodwise, anything too far ahead of its time has to fight for a generation to be born. On many trips over the last several years, however, I have felt a breeze floating through their kitchens. New cooks and others are defining the future by celebrating the past. In the countryside, particularly, younger cooks are creating small revolutions by redefining their own regional tastes. An example in Asti, a short distance from Turin, at the splendid restaurant Gener Neuv, I enjoyed a dish of a half roasted red pepper wrapped around an ethereal tablespoonful of tuna mousse. Grilled peppers and tuna antipasti have always been traditional, but Gener Neuv was showing its concept of this "updated" cooking in Italy. Another example farther south in San Remo on the Ligurian Sea, at the highly regarded Paolo e Barbara: the traditional *stoccafisso* (air-dried cod with potatoes) is given a major lift by the addition of the thinnest slivers of candied lemon peel. One has to taste it to appreciate this unpredictable touch.

These updated, upscale, new wave recipes—call them what you will—are included here if they meet the test of simplicity, and honest and direct flavors. Many traditional recipes are adapted for American use by reducing portions, substituting easier-to-get ingredients, improving presentation and garnishment of the dish.

MY TRAVELS IN ITALY

I have traveled to Italy many times. I recently returned from a home in southern Tuscany. We shopped in Pienza, Montalcino, Sienna, Asciano, Montepulciano, Sarteano and Chiusi and a host of other fabulous villages and towns. Last year, I lived in Lucca and spent time in Viareggio, Pisa, Pietrasanta, Camaiore, Empoli, Montelupo and Florence. On several other trips, I concentrated on the hill towns of Tuscany.

Before that I traveled from Monteporzio (a suburb of Rome) to Rome (for the twentieth time), to Frascati, Tivoli, Castel Gandolfo, Velletri and more. One spring, I traveled through Umbria. I have been to La Spezia, S. Margherita, Rapallo, Portofino and others in Liguria on the Italian Riviera. Of course, I've spent time in Torino, Milano, Asti, Alessandria and the Italian towns bordering Switzerland, such as Bellinzona. Several trips were to Venice, to Padova, Verona, Treviso, Conegliano, Asolo (oh, beautiful Asolo), Bassano (sad for the trees planted there in memory of deceased Italian war heroes), Vicenza and Bergamo (*alta* and *basso*—high for the old town and below for the new town), and Como, too. Longer stays were in Bologna, Modena, Parma (for one of the most delicious meals at La Greppia) and Ferrara. Another time: along the Adriatic coast visiting Ravenna, Rimini, Pesaro, Fano, Ancona, Pescara, Vasto (for a special homemade brodetto), and Brindisi (the end of the Appian Way).

Many trips were made to Napoli, Capri and Ischia, and spending time in the southern towns of Potenza, Matera, Taranto and Lecce (a true melting pot location of the different Mediterranean people). I've circled Sicily, loving Siracusa, Agrigento and Erice. La Puglia, the region of Italy's seventh largest city, Bari, was explored foodwise; another time, there were Monopoli, Molfetta, Trani, Barletta, Conversano and Alberobello—villages and towns surrounding Bari.

Thirty years ago, on my first trip to Rome, I looked out of my hotel window and saw the local outdoor market. I was intrigued at the sight of the panorama of fruits and vegetables, the hustle of business, the view of Italians engrossed in their daily shopping. Although I was jet-lagged and needed a nap, I had to visit the market first, which proved to be a timeless experience. The month was May and the *primizia,* the produce of the season, was deliciously displayed. The freshly picked local fare was set up in architectural splendor: mounds of fresh green peas, layered paler green arugula, rectangles of light green asparagus, baskets of field greens, cornucopias of fragrant strawberries set on fern leaves, tubs of yellow and red peppers, pyramids of long-stemmed green and purple artichokes were everywhere. Italians were doing their daily marketing for the day's meal, exchanging recipes with vendors and sharing family gossip. In the U.S. markets, I now see more and more vegetables without plastic wrap, which was the only way to pack fresh vegetables a few years ago. Might this be Italian influence?

It may seem frivolous to say that Italian cooks emphasize color and contour in addition to flavor and texture, but it is not. The Italian sense of color and shape dominates their lives in many ways: the planning of a garden, the arrangement of vegetables and fruit in the open markets all over Italy, the way a meal is presented in the trattorias and restaurants and in their homes.

ITALIAN COOKING IN THE UNITED STATES

Italian cooking in this country has made major advances. Americans now know a lot more about the range of the Italian kitchen, well beyond spaghetti and meatballs and manicotti swimming in a bland tomato sauce. The food revolution of the '70s, thanks to Craig Claiborne, Julia Child and Alice Waters helped tremendously to create food awareness. Specific Italian food awareness by outstanding teachers and food writers Carol Field, Lynne Rossetto Kasper, Marcella Hazan, Biba Caggiano, Giuliano Bugialli and others has helped make Italian food the number one cuisine preferred by Americans. I believe the appearance of fresh greens in markets across the country, the importation of many more Italian foodstuffs and the enlightened marketing practices of U.S. supermarkets, which now feature a greater variety of Italian olive oils, cheeses, vegetables, herbs, condiments and more, give the entire realm of Italian cooking a major push forward. Just look at the fresh portobello and cremini mushrooms, Italian eggplant, broccoli rabe, radicchio, curly endive, escarole and arugula in the supermarket bins (mostly sold fresh and loose, not shrink-wrapped). All of these mean the full joy of Italian home-cooking is within one's reach.

ABOUT THE BOOK

There are twenty regions in Italy, each with many provinces, cities, towns and villages, each with a cooking style of its own. I've taken the liberty of grouping them into nine chapters in a way that makes sense to me. Also, it is the way I've traveled them. There are a variety of typical dishes of each area, others not as well known, presented in a group of menus plus several one-dish meals in each of the chapters. If you've been to Italy, this book will help you re-create some of your eating experiences there and hopefully offer you some others. If you've not traveled there, read the introductory material before each menu, and hopefully, you will be transported there as you cook an Italian meal, here in your kitchen in the United States. The goal of this book is to present simple Italian pleasures, fresh, fragrant and flavorful food from the joyful Italian table to yours in America.

Joe Famularo
Key West, Florida

joefamularocookbooks.com

IMPORTANT
ITALIAN
INGREDIENTS

● ● ●

Wherever possible, an ingredient of a specific dish, such as cheese, has been written about in more detail in the text, where it applies to what is being prepared. The following list, however, is a brief overview of most of the key ingredients used in cooking Italian. Hopefully, it will give the reader an opportunity to appraise the contents of his or her pantry to see what might be added to it.

Almonds (Mandorle). There are sweet and bitter types; the sweet are for cooking and baking and the bitter for flavoring liqueurs, such as amaretto.

Anchovies (Acciughe). Those imported from Sicily and packed in sea salt are preferable to those packed in oil but they need to be split open, cleaned and boned. Or use those, also from Sicily, that are preserved in olive oil.

Artichokes (Carciofi). Mostly available in the United States as globe artichokes: large, round and with a choke that must be discarded (before or after cooking). Small artichokes are starting to appear in the markets.

Arugula (Rucola). Now sold in most supermarkets. Use small young leaves, as older ones are more bitter and peppery. The young leaves are wonderful in salads and can be chopped when fresh and added uncooked to sauces for pasta.

Asiago is a cheese from the Veneto. Actually there are two kinds: one for the table called *grasso di monte* and one for grating, *Asiago d'Alliero*.

Basil (Basilico). There are numerous varieties, but sweet and bush basil are the most common. Use fresh whenever possible.

Beans (Borlotti). Dried beans from the same family as red kidney beans, always speckled in appearance, they range in color from pink to ruby-red. They need to be soaked in water, usually overnight. Canned beans can be substituted but they must be rinsed well to rid them of brine. Cannellini beans, used almost always dried, require soaking and are used more in Italy than any other bean. Dried white navy beans can be substituted. Canned cannellini beans must be rinsed well to rid them of brine.

Bel Paese is a cheese from the beautiful countryside of Lombardy (thus its name). It is soft, mild and creamy, and used as a table cheese; it melts easily and well and is used in cooking, often replacing mozzarella.

Bread crumbs (Pangratto). It is best to make your own with fresh or stale bread; this is easy to do in a processor. Herbs and spices of your choice, or those called for in a recipe, can be added. See page 7.

Broth (Brodo). Italians use water as much as they do broth in soups, but a good broth is essential in making risottos. Several broth recipes are included; see pages 7–10. Canned broths are handy, especially when there is not enough time to create one. Dilute canned broth with water to reduce sodium and overpowering flavor.

Butter (Burro). All the butter used in recipes in this book is unsalted. Use fine quality sweet butter. To my knowledge, all butter used in Italy is unsalted.

Cabbage. There are two Italian cabbages. The first, Tuscan Black (*cavolo nero*) is now available in some shops in the United States. It has long, dark green curly leaves that look like kale. If you can't find the Tuscan Black cabbage, use kale. Savoy cabbage (*cavolo verza*) has crinkled, dark and light green leaves, filled with more flavor than any other cabbage. For a good recipe, see pages 88 and 92.

Caciocavallo is a cheese from Calabria; the best-known type is provolone. The name means "on horseback" because it is sold strung together in pairs, and perhaps it was carried astride a horse.

Capers (Caperi). These are small, immature flower buds that grow on wild Mediterranean shrubs, preserved in brine or pickled in white wine. Capers from Sicily are packed in whole salt, which means they must be rinsed. They are used as a condiment or garnish, but more importantly to add a zing to salads, seafood and other fish dishes, pizza toppings and in sauces.

Capocollo *(Capocolla)* is a salted raw ham cut from the shoulder instead of the leg. The best coppa ham is Coppa di Zibello from the city near Parma.

Cardoons *(Cardi)* look like overgrown celery stalks but have an artichoke flavor. They belong to the thistle family. The stalks must be thoroughly peeled and it is best to use the inner medium and smaller stalks. They are not easy to find in the United States, but do appear in some farmers' markets, from May through November.

Cornmeal. *See* Polenta.

Cotechino is a fresh pork sausage from Emilia Romagna with a spicy flavor. It is served with lentils or mashed potatoes. To cook it, prick holes all over with a wooden skewer, wrap the sausage in cloth and boil for 3 hours. Slice it. Cooked, sliced and served with lentils is a traditional dish in Rome on New Year's Eve.

Cream. *Panna* is heavy cream, or half-and-half, as called for in the recipe. *Panna* is used often in Italy in sauces, cooked dishes and in desserts. Avoid ultra-pasteurized because of its nondescript flavor.

Escarole *(Scarola)* is now available in all supermarkets and greengrocers in the United States. Outer leaves are dark green, inner leaves are pale, light green, yellowish and white. Either may be eaten raw or cooked. The inner leaves are truly delicious in salads.

Fava beans *(Fave secche)* are like dried broad or lima beans used in soups, antipasti and mashed with potatoes, oil and cooked greens.

Fennel *(Finocchio)*. The bulb is cooked in many ways as a vegetable dish and eaten raw or cooked in salads. Fennel seeds are used as a spice in sausage, and wild fennel stems and leaves are used to flavor sauces.

Fontina is one of the most famous of Italian cheeses made in the Val d'Aosta; it has a sweet, nutty flavor and creamy texture. It's a table cheese, but used frequently in cooking because it melts easily and well.

Garlic *(Aglio)* is used all over Italy, especially in pesto, *bagno caoda,* cooking meats, poultry and fish and some pasta sauces. Purple-skinned varieties are less strong in flavor and are sweeter. Buy fresh heads, unpackaged, and do not store for longer than one month.

Ginger *(Zenzero)* is used mainly in southern Italian dishes. Fresh ginger is used in certain pasta and other dishes, and candied in some desserts.

Gorgonzola is blue-veined, and one of the most famous cheeses worldwide, from the town with the same name, in Lombardy. It is creamy, used in salads, cooked dishes, including pasta sauces, and it is also a table cheese.

Grana Padano is the name of a group of hard cheeses used for grating. This name applies also to the cheese from the Lombardian Plain. There are other types of grana; only the grana made around Parma can be called Parmigiano.

Hazelnuts *(Nocciole)* are used in many confections, such as nougat, or in Perugina's famous "Baci" (kisses). They are also used in fillings and stuffings for pasta and poultry. They make an ideal tart shell; see page 150.

Honey (Miele) has been used for years in Italy in a variety of ways. There are several hundred types of honey; remember that the darker the color, the greater the flavor.

Lentils (Lenticche). Italians use brown lentils, grown in Umbria. The brown ones do not break up in cooking. There is no need to soak; just sort and rinse. See Stewed Lentils with Duck on page 153.

Mortadella is a very famous Italian sausage from Bologna; the best is made of pure pork. Spices and peppercorns and pistachios are added. Serve it in thin slices (with pickled pepper slices) or dice it for cooked dishes.

Mozzarella is a perfect cheese for many Italian dishes, and the best is made from buffalo's milk in the Naples area. It is a moist, white cheese, oval shaped (large and small), has a springy texture and melts easily and well. There is also cow-milk mozzarella that sometimes comes braided and both types are available smoked.

Mushrooms, dried (Funghi) are used mostly when fresh mushrooms are not available, or as a "boost" to fresh mushrooms when some extra flavor is needed. They require soaking and draining, are then chopped and used in many ways, from frittatas to soups to stews. If a recipe calls for dried, don't use fresh ones or the flavor will be lost.

Nutmeg (Noce moscata) is used in both sweet and savory dishes. Buy whole nutmegs to grate directly into the dish being prepared.

Olive oil (Olio d'Oliva) is the main basis for cooking in Tuscany, Liguria and the south, including Rome. The finest is from Lucca (Tuscany) but some say oil from Umbria is better. Cheap olive oil is a waste; always use extra-virgin or pure olive oil. For frying, use a vegetable oil or a combination of some good olive oil with either corn or peanut oil. Many recipes call for sautéeing with good olive oil and butter.

Oregano (Origano). Also called wild marjoram, oregano is an important herb for many dishes. It is best known for its use on pizzas. Sweet marjoram (*maggiorana*) can be substituted.

Pancetta is salted raw belly of pork used as a fat basis for many Italian dishes. It is used as bacon is in the United States, especially when it is sautéed with onions, carrots and celery to begin cooking a dish. It is sold rolled, by slices. Further dicing is usually required.

Parmesan cheese (Parmigiano Reggiano) is the most famous of all the grana cheeses. It takes two years to come to maturity and improves with age. Always buy it in a large piece and grate as needed. Packaged grated Parmesan cheese should be avoided. Cooking Italian is nearly impossible without this cheese, for the American table or any other.

Parsley (Prezzemolo) refers to the flat-leafed, fresh Italian parsley that is used throughout this book, as it is in Italy. It is used in cooking to flavor dishes rather than as a garnish.

Pasta. There are two basic types: dried (*pasta-sciutta*) and fresh (*fresca*). If eggs are added, it becomes *pasta all'uova;* with spinach added, it's *pasta verde,* or with squid ink, it's *pasta nero.* There are four basic shapes: ribbon and long strand, such as pappardelle and spaghetti; short pasta, such as farfalle and penne; flat pasta, such as that used in lasagna; and filled pasta, such as ravioli and tortellini.

Pecorino is a country cheese that matures quicker than Parmesan cheese; there are *pecorino Romano,* one of the best, *pecorino Sardo,* made in Sardinia, and *pecorino pepato* with black peppercorns, also made in Sardinia. Both grate well and can be used in cooking and as table cheeses.

Pepper *(Pepe).* Black peppercorns should be freshly ground at time of cooking or eating. Ready-ground should not be used, as much of its peppery flavor is lost.

Peppers *(Peperoni).* There are several kinds of peppers. Bell peppers are available everywhere and Italian fryers, sometimes called *Cubanelles* or *Italianelle* are more flavorful, but they seem more seasonal in the markets than are the bells. Red chili peppers, small and pointy, are definitely hot. It might be easier to use red pepper flakes, as they are always available in jars.

Pine nuts *(Pignoli)* are the seeds of pine cones and are indispensable in Italian cooking. Toast them by sautéeing for a minute or two in a small, dry skillet to bring out their flavor.

Pistachios *(Pistacchi)* are nuts grown in Sicily, used in desserts and are studded in mortadella. They are also eaten raw as a snack.

Polenta is a grainy yellow flour, a type of meal made from ground corn, usually sold in coarse or fine varieties. Its versatility is seen in first courses, vegetable dishes, main courses, cookies and cakes. American-made polenta is quite satisfactory for the dishes in this book (Arrowhead Mills and King Arthur both have good yellow cornmeal. See Sources, pages 269–270).

Prosciutto is sold as Prosciutto di Parma, boned and unboned, and Prosciutto di San Daniele. All the Parma hams come from around Parma; the San Daniele comes from Fruili. It is one of the best known cured meats in the world, used as thin slices in antipasti (with figs, pears and several condiments) and in cooked dishes.

Provolone. There are two types: *dolce,* which is mild and young, and *piccante,* which is strong and older.

Radicchio is now available in most U. S. supermarkets and greengrocers in two varieties (Italy has about twelve): *radicchio di Verona,* with small, rounded heads with deep red crinkled leaves, and *radicchio di Treviso,* with pink to dark red elongated leaves. California is now a major producer of radicchio.

Rice *(Riso).* There are three basic types of Italian rice: *Arborio, Vialone Nano* and *Carnaroli,* all ideally suited for making Italy's most famous rice dish, risotto. Rice comes in different sizes; for risotto, *superfino* should be used.

Ricotta is one of the most used cheeses in Italy and the United States. It is soft and crumbly, made from sheep or cow milk whey. It is extremely versatile in filling lasagnas, ravioli, pasta shells, mixed with pasta as part of a sauce, in cheesecakes, tarts and other pastries. It is often a filler for vegetables such as eggplant, peppers and tomatoes, and makes a fabulous dessert by itself; see page 180.

Rosemary *(Rosmarino)* is used everywhere in Italy, especially to flavor lamb and pork, stews and soups. Be careful not to let its distinctive flavor overtake other ingredients. A special use of it with shrimp is on page 212.

Saffron *(Zafferano)* is used often in Italian cooking especially in fish soups and stews. Use saffron threads instead of powder. Steep them first in warm liquid.

Sage *(Salvia)* is an important herb in Italian cooking especially with veal, liver and some pasta sauces (butter and sage, for example).

Salami *(Salame)*. Each region has its own specialty and not all of them are sold in the United States. But you can buy salami from Milano, Naples, Genoa and Varzi (near Parma).

Salt *(Sale)*. In this book, salt is not usually listed as a specific amount; unless otherwise specified, salt to your taste is the guide. Please use sea salt throughout as cooks do in Italy. Buy coarse sea salt and use it rather than table salt. Kosher salt is fine.

Sausage *(Salsicce)***,** or *Luganega* as it should be called, is long, thin, spiced sausage sold by the pound. In our supermarkets you may find it this way or surely tied in links, which may be used in place of the untied, long, thin one. It can be fried, baked, boiled, grilled. It is often removed from its casing to play a role in stuffings, fillings, sauces and so on.

Soppressata is a sausage specialty of Basilicata and Apulia, sold whole with meat coarsely pressed instead of ground as in other salami. It is popular in the United States and in Italy.

Squash blossoms *(Fiori di Zucca)* are easy to find in Italy but fairly difficult in the United States except at certain farmers' markets from May to September. They must be used the day they are bought. They are battered and fried in olive oil or stuffed with bread crumbs, anchovies, olive oil, chopped parsley and black pepper, or simply stuffed with a little anchovy and cubes of mozzarella.

Strutto is Italian lard, a shortening, usually sold in tubs. It is difficult for most people to find it so I have used other fats as substitutes.

Taleggio is a cheese named after a valley near Milan. It is a *stracchino*-type cheese, soft and creamy. Some say it does not export well, but it is available in specialty cheese shops.

Tomatoes *(Pomodori)*. Italians use fresh tomatoes in the summer and canned ones in the winter. Though never matching the fresh ones (if really red and ripe), canned tomatoes nonetheless are a very satisfactory substitute in cooked dishes. Everyone seems to agree that the canned tomatoes from San Marzano (near Naples) are the best, but there is considerable competition with American-made brands.

Vinegar *(Aceto)*. Use a wine vinegar in all the recipes in this book calling for vinegar unless another type is called for. A good wine vinegar label will show the name of the wine it is made from, and it should be made 100 percent from that wine. Balsamic vinegar *(Balsamico)* must be at least ten years old before marketed to be good, but by far the best are twenty-five to fifty years and older. Most of what is available in the United States is mass-produced and varies greatly in strength. Because so little is used in most recipes, it pays to buy the better quality.

Wine *(Vino)*. Over the last 20 to 30 years, sweeping changes have been made in the history of Italian wine that have surely put Italy on the wine map. In spite of this recent renaissance, for centuries there has been a culture of grapes and vines that goes back to Romans, Greeks and Etruscans. Italy now produces more types of wine from more grape varieties than any other country.

For many years, Italian wine producers were wary about the use of official appelations (and many still are) and sold wine as "table wine" *(vino da tavola)*. But now many qualify as IGT (typical wines from a specified territory), *indicazione geografica tipica*. The higher rating is DOC *(denomizione di origine controllata),* which are identified by the name of a place, or the grape variety, or the type (dry, sweet), by age or may even be called superior. The highest rating is DOCG, which is the same as DOC but the "G" stands for guaranteed, a rating imposed by experts before being so labeled. DOCG wines are sold with a pink strip seal at the top of the bottle. Wine selections have been suggested for each of the menus presented in this book, but they are anything but sacrosanct. There is fun and enjoyment in finding a new wine and breaking some of the rules sometimes is the path to discovery.

A FEW NOTES ON KITCHEN UTENSILS AND EQUIPMENT

The Italian kitchen does not depend on or need the most sophisticated, most modern or highly complex machinery to produce a good, tasty, healthy meal. Most of the work in the Italian kitchen is done with good knives, earthenware vessels, a good cutting board and the indispensable (for me, at least) *mezzaluna* or *lunetta,* the half-moon cutter. Americans love kitchen tools and probably have many of the following; any or all of them will make life easier in the kitchen.

Cheese grater. I would be lost without my stainless-steel box graters, large and small; use the smallest holes for nutmeg, medium holes for grating hard cheeses and large ones for softer cheeses, such as mozzarella for pizzas. Some people prefer the rotary cheese grater and that is fine, but it doesn't do more than what the box grater does, because you can grate cheese directly into a dish with either.

Colander. A stainless-steel one with large holes is essential for draining pasta and for use with many vegetables (especially for salting eggplant slices).

Dough scraper. The blade should be stainless steel and the handle wooden. It helps in preparing bread and pastry doughs.

Food mill. This is one of the most important kitchen utensils in Italian cooking. Spend a few extra dollars and seek out the stainless steel variety. It is perfect in processing tomatoes, as it keeps the skin and seeds from getting into the puree. A regular processor or blender will process skins and seeds with the puree, so don't use either of these for this. You can use a foodmill with other vegetables also, and you might consider a ricer especially for mashing potatoes or chestnut puree.

Knives. Most chefs prefer carbon steel blades because they can be sharpened more easily than stainless steel, and some say they have cleaner edges. Many of the manufacturers these days emphasize high-carbon stainless steel for long-lasting sharpness and durability. The important thing is to have the straight-edged chef's knife, more than one paring knife and the *mezzaluna,* or half-moon cutter. Chopping parsley and anything else is quite easy with this half-moon genius.

Meat mallet or pounder. I have a brass one that I bought years ago from Bridge Kitchenware in New York and it seems as if it will last forever. I use it to pound veal scalloppine, chicken breasts and beef slices. I am not so interested in the ones that attempt to tenderize meat; the pounder is needed to flatten the meat.

Parchment paper. For nonstick baking and lining pans for conventional ovens, it is also ideal for cooking *al cartoccio.*

Pasta machine. I have tried the machines that mix pasta ingredients and extrude pasta out of their sides, but I find the best pasta is made with a roller-type machine, which is inexpensive and beautifully engineered. Keep it dry and always work a little flour through the rollers. It is sold across the United States. The hand-cranked ones are fine; no need to electrify for automatic rolling (it takes the joy out of making pasta).

Pastry wheels and boards. For those who like to make sheets of pasta, a fluted-edge wheel can be helpful to make ravioli look more attractive, or to cut pappardelle. Straight-edge wheels can be used for cutting pizza and most of the flatbreads, such as focaccia. If you are going to make pasta by hand and want to roll it out, I suggest a sturdy wooden pasta board. My grandmother and mother never washed theirs—they simply scraped it clean with a dough scraper, wiped it clean with a cloth and stored it carefully. It was treated as an important piece of antique furniture. I remember a visitor once watching my mother's pasta rolling technique inadvertently placed a burning cigarette on the edge of the board. Need I say more? Which makes me think that a rolling pin is also needed.

Pots and pans. Earthenware pots are used for many dishes, such as the bean dish called *tofeja* on page 91. They should have covers; several of these pots are in well-equipped kitchens. However, I like using the enameled cast-iron pots, because they transmit heat more evenly, are pretty enough to bring to the table and they are flame-proof and oven-safe. They come in all shapes including square and oval. Most manufacturers have designed special lasagna pans of this material.

Skillets with nonstick coatings are essential in several sizes and will be used more than you can imagine.

An asparagus cooker is handy, but as I've written elsewhere in this book, I have used a coffeepot to achieve the same results.

Most important is to have a pot large enough in which to cook pasta; this must be either 6 or 8 quarts in size.

Then there is the pizza pan for pizzas and jelly roll pans for baking cookies and all kinds of bread.

Salad spinner. This is the best way to dry out salad greens to prevent diluting salad dressings.

Spatulas. I refer to spatulas in my writing almost more than any other utensil, especially the rubberized spatula, which I use in almost every preparation of food. I really don't know any other way to clean a bowl without one, or to transfer food, or to fold one ingredient into the other, or on which to sample something you are cooking; the only exception to this might be in tasting a strand of pasta and its state of *al dente,* in which case a fork is more helpful.

Spoons and forks. Wooden spoons of varying lengths, a large ladle for soup, a mesh one for extracting pasta and other food from boiling water, a slotted spoon for retrieving food from deep-fryers are all important. A wooden fork is helpful when cooking pasta; that is, a simple wooden fork, not one with separate parts meant to retrieve spaghetti, as inevitably one of the parts will end up in the pot of boiling water.

Other nice things to have. A baking stone, good scissors (especially if you don't have a *mezza-luna*), a great variety of glass bowls, several balloon whisks for zabaglione, a Kitchen-Aid stand mixer with an extra stainless steel bowl, a food processor and grill equipment, which I am sure you have.

THE BASICS:
BREADS, BROTHS
AND PASTA

BREADS

Bread is always served to accompany food in Italy. In fact, it often consti-
tutes one of the dishes of the meal in the form of a *bruschetta* or *crostini*,
toasted bread canapés, or *pancotta*, a bread soup, or *panzanella*, a bread
salad, or a pizza. In some parts of Italy, such as in Florence, an appetizer
called *fettunta* plays a more important role than pasta. *Fettunta* is grilled
or toasted bread, rubbed with garlic, painted with olive oil and sprinkled
with coarse salt. It becomes *bruschetta* when a topping is added, such as
roasted bell peppers, chopped olives or chopped fresh tomatoes and basil.

Bread is toasted, buttered and jammed for breakfast, added to soups or used to absorb tasty sauces. It serves as a base for anchovies, tomatoes, tuna, salamis, mushrooms, olives, beans, artichokes and chicken liver. It is used as stuffings for vegetables, meats, fish and poultry. It is gratinéed for toppings on pasta and oven-baked vegetable dishes. I like it best when it is used as a device to mop up any Italian sauce.

Each region of Italy has a style of bread, and the repertoire goes beyond focaccia, flatbread, pizzas and ciabattas. It doesn't matter what they are called really; the ingredients (and shapes) in making these breads is nonending. In Maremma (Tuscany), for example, there is *schiaccia di ricotta*, an oval-shaped flatbread made with sheep's milk ricotta and dried fennel seeds. Farther south, there is the same dough studded with pork cracklings. And still, there are breads made with raisins, olives, figs, nuts, marjoram, mascarpone, basil and so on. There are large batches of bread dough used to make cheese focaccias and braided breads scented with rosemary. The cheese breads may use taleggio, stracchino, fontina, fresh mozzarella or almost any other cheese.

On a daily basis, almost everyone in Italy buys or bakes bread. The country Tuscan bread is made without salt, since it is always served with salty cured meats. Southern Italian breads not only contain salt, but also have olive oil as an ingredient, a perfect combination with tomatoes. One of my favorites is *pane integrale*, a whole-wheat bread, cooked classically in a wood-burning oven. All Italian breads are firm-textured with real crusts. The texture and flavor will of course depend on the type of flour and seasonings used, but nowhere will you find the soft, cottonlike-textured white sandwich bread one finds in U.S. supermarkets.

Because bread is so important to the Italian table and needs to be replicated for the American table, I have chosen to include four basic breads: a generic country loaf; the popular smaller loaf called *ciabatta* (meaning slippers, which can be cut into slices or cut across its length and stuffed with all kinds of foods as one might do with focaccia; focaccia, not only popular all over Italy but in other countries, especially the United States; and a crisp, scented flatbread that is easy to make if one has the roller-type pasta machine.

Notabene:

Measuring flour: It is important to aerate the flour before measures are made. This simply means to transfer cupfuls of flour from its sack to a large bowl and then lightly stir the flour with a spoon to break up any clumping or packing of flour that occurs after packaging. After the flour is "fluffed," spoon it into the measuring cup and level it off with a straight edge.

Testing for the rise: Put two fingers into the dough, if the indentations remain, the dough is properly risen. If the indentations disappear, the dough needs more time to rise properly.

COUNTRY LOAF

Pane casereccio
MAKES 1 (2-POUND) LOAF

This is the typical bread one sees all over Italy although let me assure you that the variations are many. This is a basic loaf that can be eaten with soups, used in soups, used to make bruschetta, dipped into peppered oil, and eaten with pasta, which is not uncommon in Italy. This is one of the breads that is always brought to you in a restaurant for which you are charged on your bill under the listing *coperto*. You will use it in these ways, but you will also toast it for breakfast, laden with butter and jam and you will make sandwiches with it. It requires a starter, or sponge, or as they call it in Italy, a *biga*. I like to make this in an electric mixer but it can be done by hand.

FOR THE STARTER (BIGA)

1 cup warm water (105F)

1 teaspoon sugar

2 (¼-ounce) envelopes plus 1 scant teaspoon active dry yeast

1½ cups unbleached all-purpose flour plus 2 tablespoons for dusting

FOR THE DOUGH

1 cup warm water

4 cups unbleached all-purpose flour

1 tablespoon coarse salt or sea salt

1 tablespoon good olive oil for the bowl

1. *To make the starter:* Pour the warm water into the large bowl of an electric mixer that has a paddle attachment and add the sugar. Sprinkle the yeast over the water and blend on low speed until the yeast is dissolved.

2. Add the 1½ cups flour and on low speed, stir until smooth. With a rubber spatula, scrape down the sides of the bowl. (It is best to stop the machine while doing this and start again immediately after scraping.) Beat until the mixture is blended, 2 or 3 minutes; remove the bowl from its stand. Sprinkle the 2 tablespoons of flour over the top and cover with a moistened cloth kitchen towel. (Take a clean dry cloth towel, wet it completely with water, squeeze it dry and shake it out.) Let this rest at room temperature for a minimum of 1 hour or refrigerate overnight. Before proceeding to make the dough, the mixture should be bubbly and feel tacky.

3. *To make the dough:* Add the warm water to the starter. Combine 1 cup of the flour with the salt, mix well and add it to the bowl. On low speed, stir with the paddle until mixed. Add another cup of the flour and mix on low speed

until blended. Add another cup of the flour and mix on low speed until blended, for a total mixing time of 2 or 3 minutes. The dough will be quite sticky and tacky.

4. Put the remaining cup of flour on a flat work surface and make a large well in it. Turn out the dough with the help of a rubber spatula and start kneading the bread, bringing in a little of the flour from the well until all the flour has been absorbed by the dough. You will notice that midway through this procedure, the dough becomes easier to knead. The kneading should take about 8 minutes. Form the dough into a ball.

5. Use the olive oil to coat a large bowl and place the ball of dough in it, moving the ball around to coat all sides with oil. Cover with a moist cloth kitchen towel and let the dough double in size, up to 60 minutes.

6. Lightly flour a work surface. Turn out dough (it should fall out in one piece without the help of a rubber spatula, but if the spatula is needed, use it.) Punch down the dough and knead it for 2 minutes. Shape the dough into a 15-inch elongated loaf, gently rolling it with the palms of your hands to the desired length. Line a large jelly roll pan with parchment paper and transfer the loaf to it, laying it diagonally across the pan to gain the longer length of the pan. Again, cover with a moist cloth kitchen towel. Let the loaf rise until it about doubles in volume, up to 60 minutes.

7. Preheat the oven to 500F. (If using tiles or a baking stone, preheat for a minimum of 30 minutes before adding the loaf. Make 3 or 4 diagonal slashes on top of the loaf using a razor blade or very sharp knife, cutting almost ½ inch deep. Put the loaf into the oven, and immediately spray liberally with water; repeat the spraying after 3 minutes, and again after 6 or 7 minutes. Bake for 10 minutes. Lower the temperature to 425F and bake until the bread is browned and sounds hollow when tapped on its backside, 40 to 45 minutes.

8. Cool the loaf on a rack and then wrap in a large dry kitchen towel to keep it fresh.

●ITALIAN ●SLIPPER BREAD

Ciabatta
MAKES 2 LOAVES

Ciabatta in Italian means slipper, and this bread is shaped more or less like a slipper. The bread is made with olive oil and often flavored with herbs, sun-dried tomatoes or olives. The whole loaf can be cut from one end to the other and filled with meats, cheeses, tomatoes, olive oil or whatever else you wish to make a delicious sandwich. It is delicious sliced, toasted or not, for breakfast, and if warmed, it is a perfect accompaniment to cheese.

The starter will make a little over 2 cups. Use what you need and keep the remainder in the refrigerator, covered, up to 3 days.

FOR THE STARTER (BIGA)
1/4 teaspoon active dry yeast
1 teaspoon sugar
1/4 cup warm water
1 cup water, room temperature
2 1/2 cups unbleached all-purpose flour
Olive oil for the bowl

FOR THE DOUGH
1/2 teaspoon active dry yeast
3 tablespoons warm milk
3/4 cup water, room temperature
2 teaspoons extra-virgin olive oil, plus extra for the bowl
1 cup starter or *biga*, (see headnote above) made the day before
2 1/2 cups unbleached all-purpose flour
2 teaspoons coarse salt or sea salt

1. *To make the starter:* Stir the yeast and sugar into the warm water in the large bowl of an electric mixer and let stand until the mixture becomes puffy, about 8 minutes.

2. Stir in the remaining water and then the flour, 1 cup at a time.

3. Mix at low speed 2 minutes using the mixer attchment.

4. Remove to a lightly oiled bowl, cover with a moist cloth kitchen towel, and let rise at room temperature, 6 to 24 hours. *Biga* will triple in volume and still be wet and sticky when ready. Cover well and refrigerate until needed.

5. *To make the dough:* Stir the yeast into the milk in the large bowl of an electric mixer with a paddle arm. Let stand until foamy, about 10 minutes.

6. Add the water, oil and starter and blend with the paddle arm. Combine the flour and salt and add to the bowl. Stir with the paddle for 2 to 3 minutes.

7. On low speed, knead the dough with the paddle for 2 minutes. Increase to medium speed and knead 2 minutes more. Transfer to a lightly floured surface (adding as little flour as possible) and knead by hand to make a smooth, springy dough.

8. Form a ball and place it in an oiled bowl, cover with a moist cloth kitchen towel and let rise until doubled, about 1 1/4 hours. The dough will be bubbly and sticky.

9. Fit parchment paper into a baking sheet large enough to hold two loaves. Cut the dough in half. Pat each half into a small flat rectangle, then stretch each into a large rectangle, about 5 × 10 inches. Place the 2 loaves on the lined baking sheet and make dimples in each with your fingers. Cover with a moist cloth kitchen towel and let rise until puffy, almost 2 hours (the dough will not quite double but shall in the oven).

10. Preheat the oven to 425F. Bake until done, 20 to 25 minutes, spraying the oven with water 3 times during the first 10 minutes of baking. Cool the loaves on wire racks.

FOCACCIA WITH
FRESH SAGE, OLIVE OIL
AND SALT

Focaccia col salvia, sale e olio
MAKES 1 (14-INCH) ROUND LOAF

This seasoned focaccia bread showcases sea salt, sage and extra-virgin olive oil. In Florence, it's called *schiacciata*, in Bologna *piadina*, in America, *focaccia*. No matter the name, this lightly seasoned pizza dough bread makes an especially delicious change from grilled bread. It is put on the table and eaten with and without other food. In Italy, a whole loaf from a bakery weighs several pounds and is sold by weight, cut into manageable pieces. Various ingredients can be worked into the dough or served as a topping: cheese, ham, olives, onions, oregano, pancetta or rosemary. Compare the one presented here with the one served on Good Friday in Apulia, *focaccia del Venerdi Santi*; it is topped with anchovies, capers, chicory, fennel and olives. For other occasions, it may be flavored with sun-dried tomatoes or herbs, but one of my favorites is the simple one with sea salt, an herb and extra-virgin olive oil.

It seems to me that no one in Liguria eats regular bread. Focaccia reigns here and it is present everywhere in this region, almost always herbed, or with olives, or just plain. This is a basic recipe and feel free to change the herb to one you wish. There is one made with marjoram on page 72.

1 (¼-ounce) envelope active dry yeast
1 teaspoon sugar

1 cup warm water
3 to 3½ cups unbleached all-purpose flour
26 fresh sage leaves, 20 finely chopped, 6 left whole
¼ cup plus 2 tablespoons extra-virgin olive oil
2 teaspoons coarse salt

1. Sprinkle the yeast and the sugar over the warm water and stir. Let stand 10 minutes.

2. Place 3 scant cups of the flour in a large bowl and make a well in the center. Add the yeast mixture, the chopped sage leaves, ¼ cup olive oil and 1 teaspoon of the coarse salt. Work in the flour until a dough forms, then turn the dough out onto a floured work surface and knead until smooth and elastic, about 10 minutes, adding more flour as needed. Place the dough in a clean bowl, cover with a moist cloth kitchen towel, and let rise until doubled in volume, about 1 hour.

3. Punch the dough down, shape in a ball and put back into the bowl. Let rise again until doubled in volume, about 1 hour.

4. Brush a 14-inch pizza pan or an 11 × 17-inch jelly roll pan generously with olive oil. Gently punch down the dough fitting it in the pan, and brush all over with the remaining olive oil. Arrange 6 sage leaves in a decorative fashion to express your creativity. Sprinkle with the remaining 1 teaspoon salt. Let rise for 30 minutes.

5. Preheat the oven to 450F. Bake the focaccia about 15 minutes, until nicely browned. Serve warm.

SEMOLINA FLATBREAD WITH ROSEMARY

Schiacciata
MAKES 12 (3 TO 5 × 12 TO 16-INCH) STRIPS

These thin slices of crispy bread will keep in a crisper for up to two weeks. They can be served with antipasto, soups and main courses. Some say the bread originates from the Greek phyllo, others from the Sardinia sheet music bread; no matter, these are now so easy to make because of the pasta machine and can be made days ahead.

2 cups semolina flour
2 cups unbleached all-purpose flour
1½ teaspoons sea salt plus extra for dusting
2 tablespoons finely chopped fresh rosemary
1 cup plus 2 tablespoons water
5 tablespoons extra-virgin olive oil plus extra for
    brushing

1. Combine the flours, salt and rosemary in the bowl of a food processor. Pulse four or five times.

2. With the motor on, pour the water and oil through the feed tube and stop just as a ball of dough is formed. Rest 2 minutes and pulse on and off for about 30 seconds, only until the dough is smooth. Do not overwork the dough.

3. Remove the dough from the bowl. Shape into a ball, cover with plastic and refrigerate for 60 minutes.

4. When ready to bake, preheat the oven to 450F. Divide the dough into 12 even-size pieces. Keep them well covered. Lightly flour your hands and flatten a piece of dough just enough to get it through the widest opening of the pasta maker. Run it through the rollers again and then decrease the opening size by 3 notches; roll the dough through and repeat once again. (Think of making large lasagna strips.) As each strip is rolled out, lay it on a lightly oiled baking sheet. Repeat until all pieces are rolled. Bake flatbreads about 8 minutes. The flatbread should appear lightly browned at the edges, with one or two blisters. Remove from the oven.

5. Cool for 1 to 2 minutes and lightly brush with olive oil and sprinkle lightly with coarse salt.

BRUSCHETTA

Brushetta
MAKES 4 SLICES

Once a poor man's dish, grilled garlic bread has become even more popular now that it is called by its Italian name, *bruschetta*, which comes from *bruscare*, meaning to roast over coals. I still like to grill the bread over a charcoal fire or a gas-fired grill, though it is much easier to broil it. Bruschetta is always made with fresh garlic, even when the bread is not roasted over coals. Ideally, bruschetta should be made with *pane integrale* (Italian whole-wheat bread), which is now available in many specialty food shops, not just Italian bakeries.

4 (1-inch-thick) slices Italian bread, preferably
    whole-wheat
2 large cloves garlic, peeled and cut in half
2 tablespoons extra-virgin olive oil
Coarse salt, to taste
Pepper, to taste

1. Preheat the grill or broiler.

2. Place the bread slices on the grill or broiler rack and grill until crisp and golden brown, 1 to 2 minutes per side.

3. Rub the cut side of the garlic over one side of each piece of toast, preferably the side that last faced the heat source.

4. Carefully brush the oil liberally over the garlic side of the toasts. Sprinkle with salt and pepper and keep warm until ready to serve, no more than 1 hour.

Notabene:

Crostini are smaller, thinner pieces of bread, that are used for canapés. They may be fried in butter (and oil, if you wish), or put on a baking sheet and baked at 350F until dry, 12 to 15 minutes. They can be broiled also, but you have to carefully watch the entire time to be sure they do not burn. These dry pieces of bread can be spread with various toppings such as shrimp butter, truffles, olive pastes or liver pâté for a canapé. They can also be cut into various shapes—rounds, squares, triangles, ovals and stars.

FRESH BREAD CRUMBS

Pangrattato
MAKES ABOUT 2½ CUPS

Although supermarket shelves are filled with Italian-style bread crumbs, it is best to use homemade crumbs. If you don't have Italian bread, use a rich white bread and crumb it in a food processor. You can vary the herb and spice flavoring to your liking and if you're not going to use them in the next week or two, freeze them.

> 4 (½-inch-thick) slices Italian bread, crusts
> removed
> 2 tablespoons finely chopped parsley
> Sea salt and freshly ground pepper
> 2 tablespoons extra-virgin olive oil
> 2 tablespoons butter

1. Cut bread into 1-inch pieces and put in a food processor. Pulse on/off for about 1 minute to make fine crumbs.

2. Add parsley, salt and pepper to crumbs. Toss well. Set aside.

3. Heat oil and butter in a large skillet over medium heat. When bubbly and hot, add the crumb mixture and sauté, stirring frequently, until the crumbs take on some color and become crisp, 10 to 12 minutes.

4. Use immediately, or cool before using. Crumbs can be stored in an airtight jar, refrigerated, until needed.

BROTHS

Making a good broth is important in Italian cooking because it serves as a base for creating sauces, soups and risottos. As a rule, pork and lamb are not used as ingredients because their flavors are too pronounced. There are as many ways to prepare broths as there are Italians, but here are basic broths of meat, poultry, vegetables and fish.

To save time, canned broths may be used if they are diluted with water to reduce their sodium content. Or use low-sodium broths, which have become popular on grocery shelves.

One Italian chef I know recently said to me, "I'm for flavor, and I get it with a good broth." But these chefs do not fuss over broths and stocks the way some cooks do in other countries. In Italian cooking, simplicity and subtlety are the keys.

BASIC MEAT AND POULTRY BROTH

Brodo Misto
MAKES ABOUT 3 QUARTS

When Italians use broth, they will usually combine meat and poultry to achieve a more complex and richer taste. In Italy, this is sometimes considered a holiday broth. It may be used in soups, stews, pasta sauces and for risotto. Keep in mind however, that Italians will often use water as the primary liquid in making a dish. For example, in Naples they add water to vegetables to make a vegetable soup or minestrone. At one time I asked a Neopolitan why water, and his reply was that nothing is to interfere with the taste of the vegetables.

4 pounds beef and veal bones including some beef shank, beef or veal marrow bones and neck bones
1½ pounds chicken legs, thighs and other parts
4 quarts water
5 onions, each cut into 8 pieces
5 ribs celery with leaves, coarsely chopped
5 carrots, coarsely sliced
1 (14-ounce) can Italian plum tomatoes, drained and chopped or 3 large tomatoes, coarsely chopped
¼ cup coarsely chopped Italian parsley
3 teaspoons coarse salt
2 teaspoons freshly ground pepper

1. Rinse the meat and poultry with cold water and put it into a large stockpot with the water. Bring to a boil over medium-high heat and cook uncovered, 20 minutes. As foam comes to the top of the pot, skim it off.

2. Add the vegetables, parsley, and the salt and pepper and return to a boil. Reduce the heat and simmer, partially covered, until the meat falls off the bones, 3½ to 4 hours.

3. Let the broth cool, remove the meat and bones and strain the broth through two or three layers of dampened cheesecloth. Discard the bones and meat and refrigerate the broth overnight. The fat will congeal during the night; in the morning, remove the top layer of fat. (It will come off in large pieces like broken thin chocolate.) Refrigerate for several days or freeze for several months. Always bring the broth to a boil before using it in a recipe.

CHICKEN BROTH

Brodo di pollo
MAKES ABOUT 2½ QUARTS

Italians do not always agree on broth-making techniques; perhaps this is why there are so many recipes. But they do agree that a soup bone should be cracked before it goes into the soup pot and that parsley stems are more important to the broth than their leaves.

3 pounds chicken parts including wings, backs, gizzards, necks and other bones
1 pound veal marrow bones, cracked
3½ quarts water
2 carrots, sliced coarsely
1 large leek, including green parts, washed carefully, cut into thin slices
8 parsley stems without leaves, chopped coarsely
1 large sprig fresh thyme or 1 teaspoon dried
1 teaspoon each coarse sea salt and freshly ground pepper

1. Put the chicken parts and veal bones into a large stockpot, add the water and bring to a boil over medium-high heat. Boil for 10 minutes, skimming off the foam as it appears.

2. Add the carrots, leek, parsley, thyme, salt and pepper. Bring to a boil, uncovered. Reduce the heat, partially cover and simmer for 2 hours.

3. Cool slightly and strain the broth through two or three layers of dampened cheesecloth. Discard the bones, meat and seasonings. Refrigerate the broth overnight. The fat will congeal, making it easy to remove the next morning. Keep refrigerated for several days or freeze for 4 months. Always bring the broth to a boil before using.

VEGETABLE BROTH

Brodo vegetale
MAKES ABOUT 2¹/₂ QUARTS

A Neopolitan chef (who prefers to be called a cook) working at the famous L'Ortica restaurant in Rome said that only water should be used to make vegetable stock, and the vegetables must be fresh, and simmered a long time (over an hour). Do not be tempted as some cooks are by adding a light chicken- or other meat-flavored broth to make a vegetable one.

> 1 pound cremini or other mushrooms, wiped clean and coarsely chopped, including stems
> 4 ribs celery with leaves, thinly sliced
> 4 large carrots, trimmed, thinly sliced
> 2 medium boiling potatoes, rinsed well, cut into 1-inch pieces with skins on
> 1 large leek, carefully rinsed, thinly sliced
> 4 cloves garlic, unpeeled, cut in halves
> ¹/₄ cup chopped Italian parsley stems (without leaves)

> 1 teaspoon freshly ground pepper
> 3¹/₂ quarts water

1. Put all ingredients in a large stockpot and bring to boil over high heat. Reduce the heat and simmer, uncovered, for 1¹/₂ hours.

2. Cool slightly and strain the broth through two or three layers of dampened cheesecloth. Discard the vegetables. Refrigerate the broth for several days or freeze for 1 to 2 months. Bring the broth to a boil before using.

FISH BROTH

Brodo di pesce
MAKES ABOUT 6 CUPS

The addition of uncooked shrimp shells in making a fish broth can add lots of flavor. This is especially useful if the fish dish being prepared includes shrimp such as stews, *brodettos* and soups. Reserve the shrimp shells and add them as in the recipe. However, if you do not want the flavor of shrimp in the broth, simply eliminate the shrimp shells and double the non-oily fish ingredient by making it 2 pounds instead of 1 and continuing with the recipe.

> Shells from 1 pound uncooked shrimp
> 1 pound fish bones from non-oily fish (heads should be included but the gills should be removed), cut into small pieces
> 1 medium onion, coarsely chopped
> 2 ribs celery, including leaves, coarsely chopped
> 8 whole black peppercorns
> 2 small bay leaves
> 7 cups cold water
> 1 cup white wine
> 1 fish bouillon cube (optional)

1. Put all the ingredients in a saucepan and bring to a boil over medium-high heat. Reduce the heat and simmer, uncovered, for 30 minutes.

2. Cool slightly and strain the broth through two or three layers of dampened cheesecloth. Discard the bones, shells and seasonings. Refrigerate for up to 3 days or freeze for 1 to 2 months. Always bring the broth to a boil before using.

Notabene:

I try not to use bouillon cubes because of their high-sodium content. I have seen, however, many Italian chefs add a touch of bouillon, be it chicken, beef, mushroom, fish or vegetable. Italians seem to like salt more than Americans. If you want more flavor in the broth, add a half bouillon cube first, then add more if needed.

PASTA: HOW TO MAKE IT, COOK IT, SAUCE IT AND EAT IT

How to Make Pasta

This is about homemade pasta, *pasta fatta in casa*, as contrasted to the factory mass-produced kind. It is only recently, the last twenty years or so, that pasta shops have opened, making fresh pasta daily. People also began making fresh pasta at home, especially since the roller type, inexpensive pasta machines came on the market. Fresh pasta and dried pasta may seem to be similar, but they are not and are used in different ways in Italian cooking. Rarely would someone sauce dried pasta such as spaghetti with the Bolognese ragu sauce; such a sauce is more suitable to freshly made lasagna. Neopolitans prefer their pasta dried and they manufacture it for distribution all over Italy, and also all over the world. In the United States Gia Russo pasta is imported from Naples, as are other brands. Of course, there are other places in Italy besides Naples where excellent dried

pasta is made (Del Verde in Abruzzo, De Cecco in Fara S. Martino, also in Abruzzo, and Barilla in Lombardy, just to mention a few of them). On most packages of factory-made pasta the words *pasta di pura semola di grano duro* will appear, and this means that the pasta is made from the fine flour of the cleaned endosperm, or heart of the durum (hard) wheat grain. When buying pasta, it is best to purchase brands with this claim.

Italians in Emilia-Romagna show a preference for fresh pasta, which they cut into *tagliatelle*, or roll it out for tortellini.

ONE-EGG PASTA

MAKES ABOUT 1/2 POUND, ENOUGH FOR 2 FULL SERVINGS

In making fresh pasta, experience will count because formulas do not always fit exactly when the flours differ (they absorb eggs differently), and eggs vary in size. There is a general guideline, however, and my basic rule in making pasta is for every egg, add 3/4 cup flour. Basically, just use flour and egg with pinches of salt. Many of my friends in Italy, especially those living in rich olive oil–producing areas, such as Lucca, will add several tablespoonfuls of their oil, and more. Because many of the sauces include olive oil, I don't often include it. However, you may add 1 to 2 teaspoons of olive oil to one- and two-egg pastas, and 1 tablespoon to three- and four-egg pastas. You should try making pasta with and without the olive oil and make your own determination about ease of kneading, rolling, cutting, cooking and eating it.

3/4 cup all-purpose unbleached flour
1 egg
1/4 teaspoon sea salt
1 teaspoon olive oil (optional)

1.   Put the flour on a flat surface and form a well deep enough to hold the egg. The sides should be kept high enough to prevent the egg from running out. Break the egg into the well, add the salt and with a small whisk or fork, beat the egg lightly and, in so doing, begin to pick up a little of the flour from inside the well with the whisk or fork. Incorporate the egg into the flour until no longer runny. A good technique for doing this is to hold the wall of flour with one hand, while whisking with the other.

2.   When all the flour has been incorporated, make a ball with the dough. Put the ball on a flat surface and start kneading. With the heel of your hand, push down firmly into the center, giving the dough a slight turn and pushing down again. Dust your hands with flour as you knead, especially if there is some stickiness. A one-egg recipe will take 5 minutes of kneading. (Four-egg pasta requires about 10 minutes and others somewhere in between.)

3.   The dough should rest for a minimum of 15 minutes. Cover with a cloth or turn over a bowl. (You can roll out a ball of dough made with 2 eggs if you have a large flat work surface or a large pasta board. For larger amounts, cut the ball of dough in two.)

4.   To roll by hand, lightly flour the surface on which the rolling will take place. Flatten the dough with a rolling pin by rolling first forward toward you and then backward, away from you. With each roll, turn the dough by one-quarter. Try to keep the dough as round as possible. The finished sheet of pasta should be about 1/8 inch thick. Don't flour the dough too much, as it will toughen it.

5.   To make any of the string pastas, such as *tagliatelle* or fettucine, roll up the pasta as you would a jelly roll. Hold the roll with one hand and slice with the other hand into the thickness

of pasta you wish. Open out the cut pasta with both hands and put them on a lightly floured towel to dry for several minutes. Cornmeal may be used in place of the flour.

Variations

Two-Egg Pasta: Double all ingredients. Makes about 3/4 pound serving 3 or 4.

Three-Egg Pasta: Triple all ingredients. Makes about 1 pound for 5 or 6 servings.

Four-Egg Pasta: Quadruple all ingredients. Makes about 1 1/2 pounds for 7 or 8 servings.

Spinach Pasta

To make green, or real spinach pasta, cooked finely chopped spinach thoroughly squeezed dry is added to eggs. The spinach and eggs are carefully beaten together and then added to the flour to make a dough. The amount of cooked, and squeezed spinach is:

One-Egg Pasta: Add 1 tablespoon spinach.
Two-Egg Pasta: Add 2 to 3 tablespoons spinach.
Three-Egg Pasta: Add 3 to 4 tablespoons spinach.
Four-Egg Pasta: Add 4 to 5 tablespoons spinach.

How to Roll Pasta with a Pasta Machine

The smooth rollers of a pasta machine will produce several thicknesses of pasta by turning a knob to widen or narrow the opening between the smooth rollers. Most machines have six settings. Run each ball of dough (a three-egg pasta after resting should be cut into six pieces, which are to be formed into balls and put through the rollers) through the opening two times without folding it. Some people fold the dough but that seems to distort the shape. It is not necessary to put each piece of dough rolled out through each of the openings. On a 6-notch machine, roll the dough through opening 6, then 4 and then 2. For very thin pasta, roll through the thinnest opening, number 1. Very lightly flour each strip of dough after it is rolled, preferably with a brush.

How to Cook Pasta

The rules are simple:

1. Use 4 quarts of water for each pound of pasta. The water should come to a rolling boil before adding anything.

2. Add 1½ tablespoons coarse salt for every 4 quarts of water.

3. Add the pasta all at once immediately after the salt. Stir with a wooden fork.

4. Cook to *al dente* stage (firm to the bite). Remember that fresh pasta cooks in a matter of 2 to 4 minutes.

5. Drain the pasta in a colander, and shake it to remove as much water as possible (some recipes call for reserving 1 or 2 cups of the boiling liquid, so be sure to check this out before pouring it down the drain) and return the pasta to the pan in which it cooked or follow the specific directions of the recipe. (Never run the cooked pasta under cold water unless making pasta salads.)

Many recipes call for returning the cooked pasta to a skillet with sauce in it to marry the pasta and sauce. (If the pasta is to be held, add 1 tablespoon good olive oil or butter and stir; this will help keep the strands from sticking together.)

6. Most Italians combine part of their sauce with the just-drained pasta, toss it well and then add more sauce on top. Rarely is pasta put on a plate with the sauce spooned over it.

How to Eat Pasta

Italians use forks but no spoons to eat pasta. However, table settings do include the spoon (and fork) but that is for tossing the pasta and sauce at the table, not for eating it. Put the fork into a few strands of spaghetti. Let the tines of the fork rest against the curve of the bowl or the curved indentation of the plate, and twirl the fork around giving it brief, quick lifts to prevent too much pasta from accumulating. If pasta is cooked properly, it will twirl easily around the fork and some of it will dangle, but not much of it.

Bread is always on the table in Italy with pasta and other food, and there is always more cheese in a bowl. As for putting cheese on pasta with fish sauces, it is a matter of taste. I think you should do what pleases you.

I

ROME

THE ETERNAL CITY, ITS SEVEN HILLS,
ITS OLD GHETTO AND THE COUNTRYSIDE
TO THE NORTH, EAST AND SOUTH

My love affair in Rome began about forty years ago and it remains a passion. The city is like a movie star past her prime but still alluring because she exudes all the confidence and personality of someone who knows she has nothing left to prove. Neither age nor years of decadent excess can wither her.

To watch the light change during the magical hour between day and night, when ochre-tinted buildings turn from mellow to an inspiring shade of fiery red, to wander around my pivotal point, the Spanish Steps, buying mozzarella at DeLucchi, olive bread at Palombi, lunching at Nino's or Al 34, of these small pleasures is contentment born. It is a city of human scale, in spite of its magnificence, pomp and sense of history. The heart of Rome is easily crossed by foot. For those whose passion is cooking, Campo dei Fiori is one of the most picturesque open markets. Mounds of oranges, piles of artichokes and baskets of lemons perfume the air. Cut flowers are at one end of the market, fish are on the other. Specialty shops surround the piazza offering meat, sausages, cheese, fresh pizza and bread and homemade pasta. I also enjoy going to Piperno's in Rome's ghetto, two blocks from the synagogue, where families enjoy fried artichokes, cured meats and "grandfather's balls," deep-fried, chocolate-filled balls of ricotta for dessert.

All roads lead to Rome and one road to get to is the famous Via dei Fori Imperiale for one of the most impressive walks in this ancient city. You will walk straight through the middle of this legendary street in a direct line from the Piazza Veneziana, where Mussolini once gave speeches from his residence there, to the Coliseum. Your eyes will open to Rome's grandeur and history: the monument to Victor Emanuele II, the first king of unified Italy, the ancient forums built by the emperors from Augustus and Caesar to Trajan, the Arch of Titus, which commemorates the Roman conquest of Jerusalem and the Arch of Constantine, the largest arch built in Roman times. After all that walking, you will be hungry, and if you are Roman, you are a robust eater and hearty drinker. The Roman breathes deep, and attacks life with gusto. When he or she cooks, serves and eats, it is to enjoy. And he or she enjoys roast lamb (*abbacchio*), roast pork (*porchetta*), veal and prosciutto ham cooked together with sage (*saltimbocca*), oxtail cooked in wine and tomato sauce (*coda alla vaccinara*), flattened chicken grilled with hot pepper (*pollo alla diavolo*), noodles with butter (*fettucine al burro*), artichokes (*carciofi*), and soups, more pasta, fish, fruit and

sweet desserts (*crostati e zuppe ingles*). The best way to get to know a Roman is to meet at dinner.

A ROMAN LUNCH FOR 6 ON A ROOFTOP OVERLOOKING THE SPANISH STEPS

MENU

Artichokes Cooked in a Saucepan
Carciofi al tegame

Sweet Macaroni with Cheese
Maccheroni con la ricotta

Roman Sour Cherry Tart
Crostata di visciole

Every traveler to Rome will visit the Spanish Steps, the *Piazza di Spagna,* so named in the seventeenth century when the Spanish ambassador to the Vatican lived there. At one time, it was considered Spanish territory and the Italians still joke about this, saying that if you enter the piazza or any street leading to it, you might be drafted into the Spanish army. The Spanish Steps themselves are breathtaking. Their design, a combination of baroque style and *trompe l'oeil,* creates the illusion of three successive flights of steps, some narrower, some broader. The most beautiful view of Rome is from the upper terrace, especially at dusk when a golden glow suffuses the city's seven hills. This piazza is filled with good restaurants ad infinitum and glorious good food.

Wine Selection

A favorite wine choice for this meal is a white wine, Frascati. When leaving Rome by the via Tuscolana, the village of Frascati is only a few miles away. Along with other villages and towns, such as Monteporzio, Grottoferrata, Velletri and Castel Gandolfo (where the Pope has a summer residence), they form the area of Castelli. In fact, there are thirteen towns, each one producing a famous wine, the noted *vine dei Castelli*. Frascati is as popular in American wine shops as Chianti wine.

Preparation Advice

This is simple, tasty, Roman food that is easy to prepare.

1. The artichokes may be cooked ahead several hours and left at room temperature or cooked a day ahead and refrigerated overnight. If refrigerated, they must be taken out of the refrigerator at least 30 minutes prior to serving.

2. The tart may also be made ahead several hours and left to cool at room temperature. If made the day ahead, it can be left out, covered with plastic or foil wrap overnight.

3. The pasta dish is extremely simple and can be brought together in 30 minutes or less before mealtime.

ARTICHOKES COOKED IN A SAUCEPAN

Carciofi al tegame
MAKES 6 SERVINGS

Artichokes are a part of the most typical Roman meal. I particularly like this preparation because of its simplicty and taste. This recipe was given to me by an Italian woman who sells artichokes at a vegetable stand in the Campo dei Fiori, where Roman chefs go early in the morning to do some of their major food shopping.

> 12 baby artichokes, without chokes, trimmed
> ½ cup finely chopped fresh mint leaves plus 12 whole mint leaves
> ¼ cup finely chopped Italian parsley
> 3 cloves garlic, minced
> Sea salt and freshly ground pepper
> ⅔ cup extra-virgin olive oil plus 6 teaspoons
> 2 cups water

1. To prepare the artichokes, tear off the outer leaves and remove the stalk. Press down on each artichoke with the palm of your hand, adding a little pressure to open it up. Immediately plunge into water mixed with lemon juice to keep them from turning dark. When ready to cook them, drain well and dry.

2. Combine the mint, parsley, garlic, salt and pepper in a small bowl and mix well. Open the center of each artichoke and put in some, dividing the mint mixture equally.

3. Arrange the artichokes side by side in a heavy saucepan with a cover. Pour the oil over all the artichokes, and then slowly add the water. Cover the pan and simmer over medium-low heat for 1 hour. Remove the cover, and continue to cook, over high heat, to reduce the liquid, about 10 minutes.

4. Place 2 artichokes on each plate, pour 1 teaspoon oil onto the plate crisscrossing the artichoke. Add 2 mint leaves to the side for garnish. Pass more salt and pepper.

SWEET MACARONI WITH CHEESE

Maccheroni con la ricotta
MAKES 6 SERVINGS

It is rare in Italian pasta dishes to add sugar and spices but that is exactly what gives this Roman dish a special appeal. Romans cannot help but express their character in their cooking, where their inspiration bursts forth. Romans love newly born lamb and Pecorino cheese, but there is something else they love from sheep and that is ricotta cheese. The macaroni/ricotta preparation below is as simple as the combination can get, but Roman individuality offers other ways of pairing these two foods. No other city in Italy has as many restaurants, *trattorie* or inns as Rome. *Alta cucina* didn't fare well in Rome because Romans stick loyally to their traditions. Because this particular dish is so simple, there's no need to prepare it ahead. Your family or guests will not wait long.

1 pound penne, fusilli or small rigatoni
1½ cups fresh ricotta cheese
⅔ cup milk, warmed
3 tablespoons sugar
Several pinches ground cinnamon plus extra for garnish
¼ cup finely chopped chives

1. Bring a large pan of salted water (be liberal with the salt) to a rapid boil. Add the macaroni and cook according to package directions (usually about 10 minutes), until tender.

2. While the pasta is cooking, combine the ricotta, warm milk, sugar and cinnamon in a bowl large enough to receive the cooked macaroni and whip together until smooth.

3. Drain the macaroni and add it to the bowl with the ricotta mixture. Toss to coat the macaroni. Divide among six plates. Add another dash of cinnamon and top each serving with a sprinkle of chives. Serve right away.

Notabene:
If you cannot get really fresh ricotta, use the store-bought variety but instead of using milk in the recipe, use half-and-half.

ROMAN SOUR CHERRY TART

Crostata di visciole
MAKES 6 TO 8 SERVINGS

Traditional pastry-making in Rome dictates that fruit tarts are made almost invariably with jam from sour cherries called *visciole*. There are two main types of cultivated cherries: sweet and sour. In the United States, sweet cherries are cultivated in far greater numbers than sour cherries. The best-known sour variety is called Montmorency, and most of those grown are usually canned or frozen for use as pie fillings or sauces. (Bing cherries, by the way, are sweet cherries.) Sour cherries come from mostly Eastern and Midwestern states, and during the summer you may find local harvests at farmers' markets and local roadside stands, if you want to make your own sour cherry jam. To make this tart on a year-round basis, it's far simpler to buy a good brand of sour cherry jam, such as Crosse & Blackwell or Smucker's.

As a rule, most people in Italy do not make their own pastries as their custom is not to end a meal with a sweet dessert. Instead, they will purchase elegantly made pastries at a local *pasticceria* and eat them either in the afternoon with a *caffe* or perhaps on very special holidays. Italians generally want fresh fruit and cheese for dessert. The American sweet tooth dictates something sweet at the end of a meal.

2 cups all-purpose unbleached flour
½ cup sugar
Pinch salt
8 tablespoons butter, softened
2 eggs
1 teaspoon vanilla extract
½ teaspoon grated lemon zest
1½ cups sour or black cherry jam
1 egg, lightly beaten
1 tablespoon confectioners' sugar

1. Sift the flour, sugar and a pinch of salt together and put on a work surface. Make a well in the center. Put the butter, eggs, vanilla and lemon zest in the well and incorporate these ingredients with your hands. Do not add any water. Knead lightly just until smooth. Shape into a ball, wrap in waxed paper and chill for 30 minutes. Cut the dough into 2 pieces, one a little larger than the second (about two-thirds and one-third).

2. Preheat the oven to 375F. On a floured board, roll the larger piece (it helps to do this between 2 pieces of waxed paper) to fit a shallow 9-inch tart pan with a removable bottom. Trim neatly. Roll out the smaller piece into a 10-inch circle and cut it into strips about ½ inch wide.

3. Spread the jam over the dough in the tart pan. Arrange dough strips in a lattice pattern, trimming the edges neatly at the rim of the tart pan but sealing the dough to the bottom crust. Brush the lattice strips with the beaten egg and bake about 40 minutes or until the pastry is golden.

4. When the tart has cooled a bit, put the confectioners' sugar is a small strainer, and with the help of your finger swirling around in the strainer, dust the tart lightly.

Notabene:

1. If you wish to make the pastry in a food processor, the butter must be cold and cut into bits, use 1 egg only, and add 2 tablespoons dry white wine. Process flour and butter together until crumbly. Then add the egg, sugar, a pinch of salt and the wine. *Important:* When processing, bring the dough just to the point where it begins to form a ball. Remove from the processor bowl, bring together with your hands quickly, cut the dough into one-third and two-thirds, wrap each piece separately and chill for 30 minutes.

2. This crostata can be made with a prepared pastry pie crust, such as Pillsbury, treating the pastry as in the above recipe. But you must make two adjustments: Use only 1 cup of cherry jam, and reduce baking time to 15 minutes.

A DELICIOUS MEAL FOR 4 AT HOME IN MONTEPORZIO, JUST OUTSIDE ROME

MENU

Emilia Mastracci's Roman Minestrone
Minestrone all' Emilia

Agata and Romeo's Sole Fillets Wrapped in Leeks with Brussels Sprouts
Filetti di spigola in sfloglie di porro

Orange Panna Cotta with Blueberry Sauce
Panna cotta di arancia con salsa di mirtilli

A friend, Clotilde Treves, lives in Princeton, New Jersey, and Monteporzio, Italy. I know for a fact that her heart is in Monteporzio, where she has a fine manor house called Casale Sonino, and it has been in her family for many years. It is surrounded by vineyards and olive trees. Homemade wine and olive oil are an integral part of this home, as both are made there. The approach to the house through a long road with vineyards on either side is spectacular. From the second-floor terrace, the view of Rome in the distance, especially at night, is breathtaking. Clo, as friends call her, has a warm, friendly, talented housekeeper and cook; the minestrone below is hers. Do not be alarmed at the number of ingredients (minestrone is an exception to the rule of not too many ingredients); this is an easy and delicious soup, and it tastes as good or better when the leftovers are reheated the next day.

Wine Selection

There are several verdicchios from nearby Rome, such as those from Castelli di jesi, Podium and San Sisto being two of them from the le Marche region that would suit both the minestrone and the fish dishes. Or be Roman—try a special Roman wine, Virtu Romane, a DOC Montecompatri Superiore.

Preparation Advice

1. Make the minestrone 2 or 3 days ahead and refrigerate. It usually gains flavor and will be easy to reheat.

2. The fish packets can be prepared the morning of the meal, covered and refrigerated and brought to room temperature (15 to 30 minutes) before cooking.

3. The dessert molds and sauce may be made 2 days ahead, refrigerated separately and brought together just before serving.

EMILIA MASTRACCI'S ROMAN MINESTRONE

Minestrone all' Emilia
MAKES 8 SERVINGS

Each region, each city, each village, each person has an unique version of this famous, classic soup. For example, in Milan, you'll find potatoes, zucchini, cabbage, peas, rice and red kidney beans. In Emilia-Romagna, the beans are white and fresh green beans are added, and the rice is left out. In Piedmont and other northern areas, the inclusion of rice is traditional, but you'll find that Umbrians and Tuscans are wedded to beans, and plenty of them, rather than rice. The minestrone made in the south of Italy are flavored with oil, garlic and tomatoes and more so than not, pasta is added. Fresh herbs predominate in these soups in the Italian Riviera. The Roman preparation is based on beef broth, cooked beef, (especially if any is left over), red beans, red wine and pastina, a tiny pasta we used to call baby food.

> ¼ cup (about 1 ounce) finely chopped pancetta or bacon
> 2 medium onions, cut into ½-inch dice
> 2 large cloves garlic, minced
> 1 (15-ounce) can red kidney beans, drained and rinsed under fresh water
> 8 cups beef broth
> ¼ cup extra-virgin olive oil
> 2 large carrots, peeled and thinly sliced
> 3 medium potatoes, peeled and cut into ½-inch cubes
> 1 small zucchini, scrubbed and cut into ¼-inch-thick slices
> 1 rib celery with leaves, thinly sliced
> 1½ cups thinly sliced cabbage
> 1 cup dry red wine
> 1 (14½-ounce) can plum tomatoes with juice, seeded and chopped
> 2 tablespoons finely chopped basil or 1 teaspoon dried
> ⅓ cup pastina
> 1½ cups chopped cooked beef (4 ounces rare roast beef)
> Sea salt and freshly ground pepper
> ¾ cup freshly grated pecorino cheese, such as Romana

1. Sauté the pancetta and the onions in a large soup pot over medium-high heat until most of the fat is rendered, about 5 minutes. Add the garlic and cook until lightly browned, about 2 minutes.

2. Add the beans and beef broth. Bring to a boil, then reduce the heat to a very slow but steady simmer and cook, covered, for 10 minutes.

3. Heat the oil in a large skillet over medium-high heat. Add the carrots, potatoes, zucchini, celery, and cabbage and sauté, stirring several times, until the vegetables brown a bit, about 10 minutes. Transfer the vegetables to the soup pot. Add the wine, tomatoes and basil and cook, uncovered, to cook off some of the wine, about 30 minutes.

4. Stir in the pastina and beef. Season with salt and pepper and cook, partially covered, until the pastina is softened, 10 minutes. Serve with the pecorino.

AGATA AND ROMEO'S SOLE FILLETS WRAPPED IN LEEKS WITH BRUSSELS SPROUTS

Filetti di spigola in sfloglie di porro
MAKES 4 SERVINGS

This dish is inspired by one created by one of Rome's top women chefs, Agata Parisella Caraccio. She and her husband, Romeo Caracci, married some thirty years ago, share their passion for updated Italian cuisine and showcase it at their restaurant on via Carlo Alberto. The restaurant was founded 80 years ago as a neighborhood *osteria* by Agata's grandmother. Today, it is an elegant restaurant and a Roman institution.

> 4 (½-inch-thick) fillets fresh sole (1 to 1½ pounds), or any fresh filleted snapper of same thickness
> 2 leeks
> Sea salt
> 1 pound Brussels sprouts
> Freshly ground pepper
> 4 tablespoons extra-virgin olive oil

2 shallots, peeled and minced
½ cup Fish Broth (page 9) or bottled clam juice
1 teaspoon chopped fresh thyme
2 tablespoons butter, cut into 4 pieces
4 radicchio leaves from center of head

1.   Rinse the fillets and pat dry with paper towels. Cut each fillet into 3 or 4 pieces, depending on the size of the fillet. Set aside.

2.   Trim the leeks by cutting off the stem end; separate the leaves, cutting off the deep, dark green ends. Rinse well. Bring 2 cups water to boil in a large skillet, add some salt, and cook the leeks over medium heat to soften them, 3 or 4 minutes. Remove with a slotted spoon, reserving the juices in the skillet. Dry the cooked leaves and set aside.

3.   Trim the stem ends of the Brussels sprouts and remove outer leaves as necessary. Cut a cross, ¼ inch deep with a sharp paring knife, in the stem end of each sprout. Add these to the skillet and cook over medium-high heat until tender, about 10 minutes, stirring several times. Remove them with a slotted spoon.

4.   Season sole with salt and pepper and wrap each piece with a leek leaf and tie with a piece of kitchen string.

5.   In a smaller skillet, heat 1 tablespoon oil and sauté the Brussels sprouts for 3 minutes, seasoning to taste. Keep warm.

6.   Heat 2 tablespoons oil in a large skillet with a cover, add the shallots and sauté for 2 or 3 minutes. Carefully add the sole bundles, the fish broth, thyme, salt and pepper to taste. Bring the juices to a boil, reduce the heat, cover the pan, and simmer for 6 minutes. Divide the sole packets among 4 plates. Boil the juices, about 3 minutes, to reduce. Add a piece of butter and stir to dissolve. Repeat until all the butter is melded into the sauce.

7.   Toss the radicchio leaves with the remaining tablespoon of oil, adding salt and pepper to taste. Arrange 1 leaf per plate, and add several Brussels sprouts to the side. Spoon the reduced sauce over the fish and serve immediately.

ORANGE PANNA COTTA WITH BLUEBERRY SAUCE

Panna cotta di arancia con salsa di mirtilli
MAKES 6 SERVINGS

Panna cotta is a pudding and very Italian, with its origins in Piedmont. It has a light, subtle flavor and these days, Italians serve them everywhere with all sorts of fruit sauces, or just plain, sliced fruit. This tasty version uses an orange flavor in the pudding with a blueberry sauce. They can be made a day ahead and unmolded as you need them.

2 tablespoons orange liqueur
2 tablespoons water
1 envelope unflavored gelatin
6 ounces cream cheese or mascarpone cheese, softened
6 ounces sour cream
½ cup sugar
1 teaspoon vanilla extract
¾ cup heavy cream

FOR THE SAUCE
1 cup fresh blueberries, stemmed, rinsed and drained (reserve 12 berries for garnish)
½ cup freshly squeezed orange juice
2 tablespoons orange liqueur
⅓ cup sugar
2 teaspoons finely grated orange zest

1.   Combine the orange liqueur, water and gelatin in a small saucepan and let sit for 5 minutes. Place over low heat and simmer slowly, stirring constantly, until the gelatin is dissolved, 1 to 2 minutes.

2. In the bowl of an electric mixer, beat the cream cheese until it is light and fluffy, about 3 minutes. With the mixer on low speed, add the sour cream, sugar, vanilla and the gelatin mixture and combine well. Slowly add the heavy cream and mix until well combined. Divide the mixture among 6 (½-cup) molds that have been lightly sprayed with nonstick cooking spray. Cover with plastic wrap and refrigerate for several hours, until firm. The panne cotta can be made up to two days ahead. (This menu is for 4, but 6 desserts are made in case there is difficulty in turning 1 out or running into another difficulty. If there are any extra, they are good the next day, so save a little of the sauce.)

3. *To make the sauce:* Put the berries in a saucepan and add the orange juice, orange liqueur and sugar. Bring to a boil, lower the heat and simmer 5 minutes, stirring most of the time. The sugar should dissolve. Remove from the heat, and let reach room temperature.

4. To serve, dip the mold very quickly into hot water or wrap a warm cloth around the mold to loosen it from its edges. Turn each mold out onto individual dessert plates and add the sauce, covering one side of the mold and letting it run into the plate. Add 2 fresh blueberries to the top of each and serve.

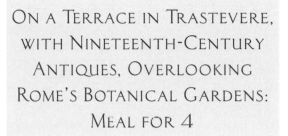

ON A TERRACE IN TRASTEVERE, WITH NINETEENTH-CENTURY ANTIQUES, OVERLOOKING ROME'S BOTANICAL GARDENS: MEAL FOR 4

MENU

Foie Gras with Hazelnuts
Fegato d'oca con nocciole

Gnocchi, Roman Style
Gnocchi alla Romana

Fig and Pine Nut Tart
Crostata di fichi e pinoli

Rome is a city of surprises, gardens and terraces hidden behind high walls, and paneled rooms in a worn-out fourth floor walk-up, but by far, the most interesting surprises are those that reflect the personalities and quirks of the people Rome attracts, transplanted foreigners who bring a piece of home with them and fit it into Rome's ancient setting. My friend, who lived in Sharon, Connecticut, had a terrace in Rome with scented climbing roses that perfumed the air and provided a sense of privacy. She placed banquettes, with pillows and cushions, which stretched invitingly, under one of her garden's sky-high coconut palms. She had a way with antique birdhouses, perching them where least expected. Her apartment reflected the ancient Roman garden it overlooked. Rome's climate enabled her to treat this terrace as her living and dining room six months of the year. She always welcomed me to the terrace for a meal, where her tiny kitchen, delineated by fragrant jasmine, and rugosa roses, focused on the elegant dome of the nearby church. Imagine this setting, as you enjoy this meal.

Wine Selection

Montepulciano d'Abruzzo DOC by Valentini, a beautiful wine that glows with purple and ruby colors (especially when held to a light). The flavors and aromas are of berries and spices and are well-paired with the foie gras in this menu. Let it linger into the pasta course. Because you are serving an expensive first course, you should serve a good wine.

Preparation Advice

1. The dessert tart may be made one day ahead or in the morning on the day the meal is to be served.

2. The gnocchi may be made early the same day or the day before and reheated.

3. The goose liver takes only a few minutes in a skillet so the first course should be done at the last minute, although the lettuce and dressing may be made ahead, but not combined until mealtime.

●FOIE GRAS WITH
●HAZELNUTS

Fegato d'oca con nocciole
MAKES 4 SERVINGS

Although we think of foie gras as strictly French, foie gras was an invention of the ancient Romans, and it is a popular dish in Rome today. Customarily, the foie gras is sautéed in butter, then put on top of bread also fried in butter and topped with a sauce that includes pine nuts and raisins. The appetizer below is lightened somewhat by serving it with a simple arugula salad and optional slices of Italian bread, not fried. If you'd rather not deal with a fresh lobe of foie gras, use slices of chilled foie gras terrine or mousse, which is offered in most delicatessens; these, of course are not to be sautéed.

> ¼ cup hazelnuts, skins removed
> 3 tablespoons extra-virgin olive oil
> 1 tablespoon red wine vinegar
> Sea salt and freshly ground pepper
> 4 tablespoons finely chopped chives
> 1 bunch arugula, trimmed, rinsed and dried
> 4 cherry tomatoes, halved
> 2 tablespoons butter
> ½ pound fresh foie gras, sliced into 4 pieces
>   (see Notabene, below)
> 4 to 8 thin slices Italian bread (optional)

1. Preheat oven to 400F. Bake the hazelnuts in a pie dish until lightly browned, 4 to 6 minutes. Remove, cool and chop coarsely.

2. Combine the oil and vinegar with some salt and pepper in a bowl. Add the chives, arugula, tomatoes and hazelnuts. Toss lightly but well. Distribute among 4 plates.

3. Heat the butter in a skillet and when it bubbles, add the foie gras slices and sauté for 2 to 3 minutes each side.

4. Lay a slice of sautéed foie gras on each of the plates, slightly overlapping some of the salad leaves and serve with thin slices of Italian bread (if using).

Notabene:

Some companies sell foie gras in convenient 2-ounce packages, an ideal amount for an individual serving. See Sources, page 269.

GNOCCHI, ROMAN STYLE

Gnocchi alla Romana
MAKES 4 SERVINGS

Gnocchi are usually eaten as a first course *(primo piatto)* but here, for the American table, they are the main course. They are usually made of flour or potatoes, or both, and sometimes may be combined with other foods such as spinach. The shapes vary from cook to cook, region to region. What makes these gnocchi Roman, is that they are made with semolina flour (cooked in milk), with eggs added to make a rich spread of "dough" that is cut into rounds (the squares are creative license), layered with some overlap and sauced with butter and Parmesan cheese and baked. Some gnocchi are called *strangolopreti* (priest-stranglers), others may be shaped small and added to broths or soups, casseroles and stews. In Italian dialect, *gnocco* (the singular term for *gnocchi*) means "dumb-head", as one would use "pudding-head" in England or *tete de lard*, lard-head, in France. These have been made in Italy as early as Renaissance times but they were made with crustless bread. They are made with bread in the very north of Italy (Trentino-Alto Adige) even today and they are called *canderli*. But let's have them the Roman way today.

> 4 cups milk
> 6 tablespoons butter
> Sea salt and freshly ground white pepper
> Pinch freshly grated nutmeg
> 1 cup semolina flour or white cornmeal
> 4 eggs, beaten
> 1 cup freshly grated Parmesan cheese

1. Butter 2 baking sheets and set aside.

2. In a saucepan, combine the milk, 2 tablespoons butter, some salt and freshly ground white pepper and the nutmeg. Bring to a boil over medium heat. Slowly add the semolina (the Italians say *a pioggia*, like soft rain drops), stirring all the time to prevent lumps from forming. Reduce the heat to low and cook until very thick—thick enough for a wooden spoon to stand in it. Remove from the heat.

3. Add the eggs and $1/2$ cup of the Parmesan and mix well. Spread the mixture on one of the buttered baking sheets, smoothing it off with a wet spatula, making a rectangle $1/2$ inch thick. Place in the refrigerator to firm.

4. Preheat the oven to 350F. Cut semolina mixture into rounds, $1 1/2$ to 2 inches wide, or in squares, if you wish. Arrange them in a row in the other buttered cookie tray (or large ovenproof platter), slightly overlapping each other. Make a second row until all of them are so arranged. Melt the remaining butter and drizzle over the gnocchi. Sprinkle with the remaining Parmesan cheese.

5. Bake for 15 to 20 minutes, until golden and the butter is bubbling. Remove from the oven and let rest 5 minutes before serving.

FIG AND PINE NUT TART

Crostata di fichi e pinoli
MAKES 8 SERVINGS

The food shops all over Italy inspire most people to want to cook, even if you may not want to cook on vacation. If you are in an Italian home, cooking will happen. In fact, this is an easy way to learn something about Italian food. We bought some fig preserves (they are always so beautifully made and packaged) and decided to create this tart. Once home in the United States, we recreated it with a prepared pastry crust and enjoyed it also. In Italy, this is usually made with a heavier crust, called *pasta frolla*. The recipe for that crust is added below if you choose to make your own.

½ cup butter, at room temperature
½ cup plus 2 tablespoons confectioners' sugar
3 egg yolks
1 cup plus 2 tablespoons ground almonds
1 egg white
1 cup plus 2 tablespoons pine nuts
1 prepared pie crust, preferably Pillsbury
½ cup fig preserves or jam
1 cup whipped cream (optional)

1. Preheat the oven to 325F. With an electric mixer, cream the butter and the sugar until fluffy and the color has paled. Beat in the yolks, one at a time, with some of the ground almonds until all is incorporated. Add the egg white and mix until thoroughly blended.

2. Toast the pine nuts in a small skillet over medium heat until slightly golden, 3 to 4 minutes, stirring most of the time. Keep your eye on this to avoid burning them. Fold the pine nuts into the egg mixture with the help of a rubber spatula.

2. Fit the pastry according to the manufacturer's directions into a 9-inch tart pan with a removable bottom. Carefully spread the fig preserves on the bottom of the pastry.

3. Spoon the nut mixture over the fig preserves. Bake for about 30 minutes, until a wooden skewer inserted into the center of the pie comes out clean.

4. Allow to cool for 10 to 15 minutes. Remove the side of the tart pan by pushing up from below, but leave the tart on the bottom base. Serve with whipped cream, if desired.

ITALIAN PASTRY

Pasta frolla
MAKES 2 ROUNDS FOR 8-, 9-, OR 10-INCH TART PAN

2 cups all-purpose unbleached flour
2 tablespoons sugar
Pinch salt
½ cup plus 1 tablespoon butter, cut into tiny squares, kept cold
1 egg
1 egg yolk
1 teaspoon vanilla extract
2 to 3 tablespoons cold white wine

1. Place the flour, sugar and salt in the bowl of a food processor fitted with the steel blade. Pulse two or three times. Sprinkle the butter pieces over the flour and pulse five times, until the mixture resembles coarse meal.

2. In a small bowl, combine the egg, egg yolk, vanilla and 2 tablespoons wine. Pour this mixture into the feed tube with the motor on; stop as soon as the dough gathers on top of the blade. If it appears too dry, add the remaining 1 tablespoon wine. Do not let it form a ball or the pastry will toughen.

3. Transfer the pastry to a lightly floured work surface and knead only slightly, just to bring the dough together and to overcome the stickiness. Cut the dough in half.

4. Pat one half into a buttered tart pan, cover with plastic, and chill until it is ready to be filled as in the above recipe. The pastry should chill about 1 hour, and not more than overnight. Wrap the remaining dough in plastic or waxed paper and refrigerate, but bring to room temperature at least 30 to 40 minutes before using. Roll

it out to fit another tart or to make strips for a lattice top.

Notabene:

If you want to make this by hand, the butter has to be at room temperature. Follow the steps as above except bring the ingredients together on a work surface. Mix the flour, sugar and salt, create a well, pour in the liquids and bring together to form a dough and knead at little as possible. Pat one half into pan and chill and wrap remaining pastry for later use.

Lunch for 4 under the Cinzano Umbrella at Grottaferrata

MENU

**Roasted Beet Salad with Red Onions
and Dried Fennel**
Insalata di barbabietole arrostite

Spaghetti with a Lemon Sauce
Spaghetti al limone

**Canteloupe Melon Balls in
Honeydew Puree**
Misto di due meloni

One goes to Grottaferrata, just a few miles outside Rome, to visit the important monastery Abbazia di Grottaferrata. If you didn't know it was there, you would notice something important because of its surrounding massive walls and bastions. It is very old and was started by a Greek abbot who lived and died in Italy. Still today, there are about twenty-six Basilian monks who live there; they are Roman Catholics who celebrate according to the Byzantine Greek rite. It is quite private; you ring a bell and a monk comes to greet you and guide you through its many museum-quality rooms. The entrance is underneath a magnificent portico with Corinthian columns beneath which are archaeological fragments. But I remember Grottaferrata as much for the discovery of good places to eat; the via Anagina has some attractive places. We went to one unannounced, Al Fico-La Locanda dei Ciocca; waiters were busy setting up outside tables with pale yellow tablecloths, and opening up umbrellas after a May sprinkle of rain. We were encouraged to sit under the Cinzano umbrella for this delightful lunch.

Wine Selection

Select Fontina Candida's Vigneto Santa Teresa, one of the wines made by the Gruppo Italiano Vini, winemakers who have created this wine that has become the model for the revival of Frascati wines. It reaches its peak between one and two years.

Preparation Advice

1. The beets and the fruit dessert may be made early on the day you are serving them.

2. The pasta is simple enough to be prepared at the last minute.

ROASTED BEET SALAD WITH RED ONIONS AND DRIED FENNEL

Insalata di barbabietole arrostite
MAKES 4 SERVINGS

The leaves of small to medium beets can be used in several ways to keep up with the Italian parsimonious way with vegetables and some other foods. Most Americans discard them. An Italian will trim and sort them, rinse carefully and dry them, and add them to fresh green salads; or he will cook them as he does spinach. See page 202.

8 medium beets, washed, left whole and
   untrimmed
6 tablespoons extra-virgin olive oil
Sea salt and freshly ground pepper
1/2 teaspoon dried fennel seeds
1 red onion, thinly sliced
2 tablespoons balsamic vinegar
1 teaspoon sugar
4 radicchio leaves

1. Preheat the oven to 375F. Dry the beets and put them in a bowl. Add 1 tablespoon of the olive oil and toss to coat them. Place each one in a foil square, large enough to envelop it. Add salt, pepper and several dried fennel seeds. Wrap and place them directly on a rack in the middle of the oven.

2. Bake about 1 hour, until the beets are tender. Test for doneness by opening one package and inserting a wooden skewer into the beet. If it meets no resistance, the beet is cooked. Remove them from the oven, unwrap them and discard the foil. When cool enough to handle, peel each beet and thinly slice into a bowl. Add the remain-

ing oil, remaining fennel seeds, onion, balsamic vinegar and sugar, and toss lightly but well.

3. Leave at room temperature until ready to serve, for up to three or four hours. If longer than that (they may be made ahead by two or three days), refrigerate and bring to room temperature thirty minutes before serving.

4. To serve, place a radicchio leaf on each of four plates and arrange beet slices and onions over the leaf. Spoon whatever liquid may have accumulated in the bottom of the bowl over the beets. Adjust seasoning and add more salt and freshly ground pepper, if needed.

SPAGHETTI WITH A LEMON SAUCE

Spaghetti al limone
MAKES 4 SERVINGS

This is an unusually creative way to prepare spaghetti; it is one of my favorites. The lemon intoxicates the cooked cream, which envelops the pasta strands, and every forkful is delicious.

2 cloves garlic, minced
2 tablespoons butter
1 cup half-and-half
1 teaspoon finely minced lemon zest
Sea salt and freshly ground pepper
1/2 pound spaghetti
1 tablespoon fresh lemon juice

1. In a skillet large enough to hold the pasta when cooked, sauté the garlic in the butter until it just begins to turn color, 2 or 3 minutes.

2. Add the half-and-half and lemon zest and cook over medium heat, uncovered, 3 or 4 min-

utes, stirring most of the time with a rubber spatula; the half-and-half should thicken a little. Add salt and pepper and set aside.

3. Cook the pasta, drain it and add it to the sauce. Add ½ tablespoon of the lemon juice, toss the pasta lightly but well, and cook it 1 to 2 minutes over low heat. Taste for lemon flavor, and add more lemon juice if you feel it needs it.

CANTALOUPE MELON BALLS IN HONEYDEW PUREE

Misto di due meloni
MAKES 4 SERVINGS

In the sixteenth century, interest in cooking in Italy was growing, and the clergy were among the forefront in participating, even the popes themselves exerted keen interest. It has been reported that because of this, the tiny melon used by the ancient Romans became the one we know today as cantaloupe. It is claimed that it was developed on papal property near Rome called Cantelupo. Here is the perfect follow-up to a bowl of freshly cooked pasta.

1 cantaloupe
Pinch salt
Juice of ½ lemon
½ honeydew melon
4 tablespoons honey
8 raspberries or strawberries

1. Cut the cantaloupe in half. Discard the seeds. With a melon baller, cut melon balls out of both halves and put them into a bowl. Add the lemon juice and salt. Toss to coat the balls.

2. Cut the honeydew melon into slices and remove the outer skin, cutting far enough into the melon slices to avoid any unripe parts. Coarsely chop the slices and puree them in a food processor. If the melon is too watery, spoon some of the liquid away and discard. Fold in the honey.

3. To serve, spoon some of the honeydew puree into oversized red wine goblets. Add some cantaloupe balls and 2 raspberries to the top and serve.

AL FRESCO MEAL FOR 6 IN ROME

MENU

Grilled Eggplant with Capers and Anchovies
Melanzane ai capperi

Roasted Chicken Salad in Round Loaf of Italian Bread
Insalata di pollo arrosto in pane

Fava Beans, Country Style
Fave alla campagnola

Fresh Seasonal Fruit and Italian Cheeses
Frutta di stagione e formaggi

If you've ever been to Italy, you know that Italians love to eat outdoors; so do Americans. They will picnic alongside a river, under the shade of a pergola. As we do, they include collapsible chairs with table and tablecloth, and often they carry an umbrella for shade. Beverages, of course, are iced. The outdoor meals are not dainty; they are full-fledged meals as they might enjoy in their homes or at restaurants on Sundays, at least as far as quantity is concerned. Think of yourself on the outskirts of Rome, with a blue Botticelli sky, gnarled olive trees and a faraway hill, as you prepare and enjoy this meal, to be enjoyed outdoors.

Wine Selection

One of the better-known Castelli wines is Frascati. It is a fragrant, dry, semisweet wine with a delightfully clear, golden color. Italians in Frascati say they know their wine to be Frascati just by looking at it. It is very easy to drink. At our house in Monteporzio, we enjoyed chilled carafe after carafe. The wine is from the lovely town with the same name Frascati, a town so near to Rome yet with so much character of its own, with enchanting villas and beautiful gardens, fabulous food shops and sweeping views of the majestic countryside. Frascati wines are protected; genuine bottles of it are labeled.

A Second Wine for the Pecorino Romano

If you fly in or out of Rome from the Leonardo da Vinci airport at Fiumicino, you may have noticed the vineyards below. The reds are from the Cesanese (and other) grapes and are light and dry. It would be better to go for the fuller and stronger variety of Castel San Giorgio. Or a second choice would be to go for a stronger red from south of Rome, in Campania (Naples). Look for Aglianico or Taurasi in U.S. wine shops.

GRILLED EGGPLANT WITH CAPERS AND ANCHOVIES

Melanzane ai capperi
MAKES 6 SERVINGS

I have had eggplant prepared this way since I was a child and have found it or something similar on almost every antipasto table in Italy. My friend Al Panariello said he had it in Capri, and I'm sure he did. What I like about this dish, besides its flavor, is that it can be made one, two or three days ahead. I often serve it with drinks by putting pieces of it on crostini (dried pieces of bread), dotting them with some cheese and heating them in the oven.

FOR THE EGGPLANT
2 small eggplants (about 3/4 pound each)
8 tablespoons extra-virgin olive oil

FOR THE SAUCE
6 tablespoons extra-virgin olive oil
3 tablespoons red wine vinegar
1 anchovy fillet
2 cloves garlic, minced
4 tablespoons finely chopped Italian parsley
2 tablespoons finely chopped shallots
2 tablespoons capers, drained
Freshly ground pepper

1.   *To prepare the eggplant:* Cut the ends off each eggplant, but leave it unpeeled. Stand each eggplant on end, and cut it lengthwise into the thinnest possible slices. Salt each slice lightly, lay the slices flat in a colander and allow them to drain for 30 minutes. Dry each slice with a paper or cloth towel.

2.   In a large skillet, heat 2 tablespoons of the oil and sauté the first batch of slices slowly on both sides, until they are cooked through. Test doneness with the tines of a fork; if they go through the eggplant, it is done, but don't allow the slices to blacken (as they will be difficult to roll later). Eggplant absorbs lots of oil; don't add more oil until ready to sauté the next batch. As you remove each slice, roll it and set it aside to cool.

3.   *To prepare the sauce:* Combine the oil and vinegar and mash the anchovy in it. Add the garlic, parsley, shallots, capers and pepper.

4.   Place the eggplant rolls in a plastic or glass container with a tight-fitting cover. Pour the oil and vinegar mixture over the eggplant. Cover the container and marinate for several hours or overnight. To serve, remove it from the refrigerator 1 hour before serving and serve at room temperature.

ROASTED CHICKEN SALAD IN ROUND LOAF OF ITALIAN BREAD

Insalata di pollo arrosto in pane
MAKES 6 SERVINGS

As a boy of eight in New York City, I had a weekly chore: carrying my grandmother's white-enameled basin, filled with fresh yeasty dough, to the local Italian bakery. There, my grandmother, along with a dozen or so other ladies, all clad in black, would turn out their doughs and shape several loaves of Italian bread, a week's supply. They paid the baker a penny a loaf for placing the loaves into the wood-burning oven with a wooden peel and for retrieving them. The smell of that bread has lived with me for many years, and the experience of that "chore" instilled in me the deep desire for a good loaf of Italian bread. Here's a loaf filled with tasty roasted chicken salad.

> Boned chicken pieces, cut into chunks, from a roasted 3-pound chicken (see page 30)
> 3 inner celery ribs with leaves, thinly sliced
> 3 scallions, thinly sliced
> 1 cup cubed Pecorino cheese
> ½ cup chopped prosciutto or mortadella
> 2 bunches fresh arugula, washed, dried and cut into 2-inch pieces
> ½ cup extra-virgin olive oil
> 3 tablespoons herbed white wine vinegar
> Pinch red pepper flakes
> Salt
> 1 (8- to 10-inch) round loaf Italian bread
> 2 hard-cooked eggs, cut into wedges

1.   Combine the chicken pieces in a large bowl with the celery, scallions, cheese, prosciutto and arugula. In a smaller bowl, combine the oil, vinegar, red pepper flakes and some salt. Pour over the chicken mixture.

2.   Slice the top off of the bread, reserving it, and remove the soft inner part of the bread. Reserve for another use or discard.

3.   Spoon about ½ of the chicken mixture into the bread container, garnish with the egg wedges and put back the top of the bread that was cut off. This can keep at room temperature for up to 2 hours. Just before serving, remove the top of the bread and lean it against the loaf to show the salad. Have ready additional oil and vinegar if someone wants more. After the bread with chicken is cut in slices, add spoonfuls of the remaining chicken salad to the plate alongside of the bread.

ROASTED CHICKEN

1 (3-pound) chicken, readied for roasting
3 tablespoons extra-virgin olive oil
1 cup dry white wine
2 tablespoons finely chopped rosemary
2 cloves garlic, peeled and halved

1. Preheat the oven to 425F. Rub the chicken all over with the oil. Liberally salt and pepper the bird, inside and out. Add some rosemary and half the garlic to the cavity. Put the chicken in a roasting pan just large enough to hold the chicken.

2. Pour the wine into the pan, add the remaining garlic and rosemary and bake for 1 hour, until nicely browned. Baste frequently with the juices in the pan. To test for doneness, put a fork in the top of the thigh near the body and if the juices run clear, the chicken is done.

FAVA BEANS, COUNTRY STYLE

Fave alla campagnola
MAKES 6 SERVINGS

Fava beans, sometimes called broad beans, look like large lima beans. Their texture is mealy and granular with an assertive flavor. Favas are very popular in Italy; they are eaten raw with Parmigiano or Pecorino cheese. Their thick skins have to be peeled before eating. At certain times of the year, it is difficult to find fresh favas in the United States, so use canned beans. They must be drained and rinsed several times before adding the other ingredients. This is a simple preparation with a great flavor.

2 (15- to 16-ounce) cans fava or lima beans,
    drained and rinsed several times
1/2 cup extra-virgin olive oil
1 tablespoon finely chopped fresh oregano or
    1 teaspoon dried
1/3 cup finely chopped chives
Sea salt and freshly ground pepper

1. Pat beans dry with paper towels as best you can. Set aside.

2. In a medium saucepan or large skillet, heat the oil over medium heat. Add the beans, stir and cook until the beans are heated through. Add the oregano and chives, stir well and cook for 2 minutes longer. Add salt and pepper. Remove from the heat. These may be served hot or at room temperature, and will keep unrefrigerated for up to 2 hours; or, refrigerate for 1 or 2 days and reheat.

Notabene:
Hungry Sultan is the brand of canned fava beans used in this preparation, but other brands may be used.

FRESH SEASONAL FRUIT AND ITALIAN CHEESES

Frutta di stagione e formaggi

Our markets sell small, dark-purple plums sometimes labeled Italian plums; Romans love this kind of plum and irreverently call them "nun's thighs." Add some ripe pears, which are ideal with most cheeses, and be sure to serve some watermelon. In Rome, across the Tiber in the district known as

Trastevere, when the weather is warm, there are stands filled with watermelon on ice.

As for cheese, serve the two cheeses most often associated with Rome: Pecorino Romano (see below) and fresh ricotta. The fresh ricotta can be sprinkled with sugar, espresso granules and cinnamon, as it is in Rome, or eaten as is.

Pecorino Romano

Pecorino is a name given to all Italian cheeses made from sheep's milk. The best known, and the oldest, is pecorino Romano, so called because it was first made near Rome. It is hard grana cheese made in round shapes up to ten inches in diameter. This type of cheese can be aged for up to one year; at that time they become brittle, hard-textured and yellow-white in color. It has a sharp, piquant, pronounced aroma and taste. It is used as a grating cheese, sometimes in place of Parmigiano. *Pepato* is a pecorino spiced with peppercorns, making the flavor of the cheese more sharp. For a dessert cheese, it is better to use a younger pecorino Romano, as it is softer, more moist and a little less assertive. It is delicious with a full bodied red wine.

EASTER DINNER FOR 8 IN ROME WHERE THE DOME OF ST. PETER'S RISES IN THE DISTANCE

MENU

Asparagus and Leek Soup with Crushed Amaretti and Crisped Leeks
Crema di asparagi e porri

Lasagna Squares with Braised Broccoli Rabe
Quadrati di lasagna con broccoletti

Rosemary-Scented, Butterflied and Grilled Leg of Lamb
Coscia di agnello grigliata al rosmarino

Slow-Cooked Roasted Plum Tomatoes
Pomodori al forno

Spring Greens with Oil, Vinegar and Mint
Insalata di stagione con vinaigrette alla menta

Maria Michele's Special Cheesecake
Torta di formaggio alla Maria Michele

The first time I saw Rome was at Eastertime, some years ago. The Spanish Steps were filled with azaleas—off-white, pink, deeper pink and magenta—a sweep of color that seemed to reach the sky at the top of the steps, at the church, the Trinita dei Monti. Whenever I think of Rome, that scene comes to mind, automatically. But I also remember the shops and their oversized Fabergé-style chocolate eggs and their windows madly decorated with ribbons. The smell of young lamb roasting with rosemary filled the air. Restaurants, open for this special holiday, were primped with their pink and orange linens on tables, inside and out. Every time I return to Rome, I feel the young, festive spirit alive in this old, eternal city and the contrast intrigues me. "There is in Rome," writes Doris Muscatine in *A Cook's Tour of Rome*," . . . a zest, an earthiness, a *vivicita,* that surround, excite the Anglo-Saxon temperament. The Roman citizen breathes deep and attacks life with gusto. When he cooks, serves and eats, it is with the same capacity to enjoy that marks his other activities." There is no better time to witness this than at Easter, in Rome. *Abbacchio,* a milk-fed baby lamb, which has never tasted grass, is necessarily, and by tradition, an Easter dish. This is the time of year when baby lambs are plentiful. For it to be cooked Roman style, rosemary is an essential ingredient; don't be alarmed at the amount of it in the lamb recipe below. Romans want lamb when it is between thirty and sixty days old, when most of the baby fat is gone but the meat has not toughened.

There are two thoughts about the derivation of the word *abbacchio: abbacchiare* means to beat down, but it also means to sell at bargain sale prices. Because baby lambs are so abundant in spring, they were brought to market for sale; some say "dumped" on the market, and this brought down the prices. Eating the lambs around Easter made sense because they were cheap and available. Times have changed; however, as upscale marketing strategies now focus on higher prices for the lamb because it is Easter food, although it has been for over two thousand years.

Many Romans will roast not only the saddle of the lamb, but also its head, as it is considered by some to be the best part of the animal. I've seen Americans shy away from this, and therefore, I am not offering it here. In fact, I'm suggesting an alternate lamb dish for those who would rather not have the baby lamb. Artichokes, which are a favorite of Romans, are offered in other menus, but the one recipe on page 15 may be substituted in this menu for either the soup or salad course.

Wine Suggestion

Use a dry Castelli white, as they are fresh wines with plenty of body, quite enough, for instance, for them to be drunk with, and not overwhelmed by the savoury baby lamb or pasta dishes of Rome. They are produced in an area of about fifty square miles, in the Alban hills, southeast of Rome. They are known as *vini dei Castelli Romani.* They are easy to find in U.S. wine shops. Frascati is probably the best known among these wines.

A red is definitely in order here also. I'd go for a Taurasi DOCG by Feudi di San Gregorio, from Campania, just south of Rome. The estate is owned by the Ercolino and Capaldo families, who typify the new wine enthusiasts in this region. Their new winery at Sorbo Serpico (in the hills near Avellino) is thought by the experts to produce one of the most impressive groups of estate wines in Italy today. This particular wine is ruby-rich, and its bouquet is of plums, berries, spices and vanilla.

Preparation Advice

1. The soup can be made up to two days ahead, except for the final touches.

2. The pasta squares can be made ahead and frozen or refrigerated, well packed in plastic, for two days. The broccoli can be prepared several hours ahead and kept at room temperature until ready to use.

3. The lamb should be cooked the day of the meal but all the prep work can be done the day before.

4. The tomatoes cook slowly, so they have to be started three or four hours before mealtime.

5. The salad should be made at mealtime, although lettuces can be rinsed, dried and stored

in plastic bags and refrigerated. The dressing can be made ahead and left at room temperature.

6. The cheesecake can be made the day before and left at room temperature. You may lightly reheat it before serving, if you wish.

ASPARAGUS AND LEEK SOUP WITH CRUSHED AMARETTI AND CRISPED LEEKS

Crema di asparagi e porri
MAKES 8 SERVINGS

This is delicious. Make it ahead by two days but add the amaretti and crisped leeks just before serving. This makes an excellent lunch dish if you add a salad with some sliced beets, cooked broccoli or other vegetable.

> 2 cups thinly sliced leeks (about 4; see notabene below)
> 4 tablespoons butter
> 2 cups peeled, diced boiling potatoes (3 or 4)
> 2 cups 1-inch-long asparagus pieces, tender parts only
> 1½ quarts chicken broth
> Sea salt and freshly ground pepper
> 1 to 2 cups half-and-half
> Oil for deep-frying leeks, for garnish
> 4 amaretti cookies, crumbed

1. Reserve about ¼ cup of the leeks for garnish.

2. In a large saucepan, melt the butter, and sauté the leeks very lightly. Dry the potato cubes and add them to the saucepan, toss them with the leek pieces and sauté them for 4 minutes. Add the asparagus pieces, broth and a little salt pepper. Bring to a boil, reduce the heat, and sim-

mer for 30 to 40 minutes, until the vegetables are tender.

3. Put the mixture through a food mill, or press it through a fine sieve. Return the pureed mixture to the saucepan and add the half-and-half to achieve the desired thickness. Simmer until the mixture is warmed.

4. To serve, heat some oil in a small saucepan and fry the ¼ cup leeks until crisp. Remove with a slotted spoon to a paper towel. Ladle the soup into individual warmed bowls, sprinkle a bit of the crumbed amaretti in the center and top with a bit of the crisped leeks. Serve right away.

Notabene:

Cut the leeks in half lengthwise and wash them well, separating the leaves with your fingers as you rinse them under cool running water, to remove any sand. Drain the leeks, and cut them crosswise into thin slices.

LASAGNA SQUARES WITH BRAISED BROCCOLI RABE

Quadrati di lasagna con broccoletti
MAKES 8 SERVINGS

Without question, this is a favorite dish of mine. I make it also by substituting the broccoli rabe with fresh ricotta, spiked with 1 to 2 tablespoons freshly grated Parmesan cheese, and adding besciamella and pesto sauces over each serving.

> 2 bunches fresh broccoli rabe
> Sea salt
> 3 tablespoons extra-virgin olive oil
> 2 large cloves garlic, minced
> Pinch red pepper flakes

24 fresh pasta squares, each about 4-inches
    square (see page 34)
2 tablespoons butter, melted
1 to 1½ cups fresh ricotta cheese
Ground nutmeg

1. To prepare broccoli rabe, wash it well and trim the ends. Remove the strings on the larger stalks as on large celery. Cut the larger leaves in half and let them stand in cool water until ready to cook them. Heat 2 or 3 cups water in a large saucepan. Add 1 teaspoon salt and bring the water to a rapid boil. Add the broccoli rabe and cook until just tender; depending on size and freshness of stalks, this may take 5 to 10 minutes. Drain well.

2. Heat the oil in a large skillet. Add the minced garlic and cook for 1 minute. Add the broccoli rabe and move it around in the oil and garlic. Add the pepper flakes and cook for 2 or 3 minutes. Remove from heat. Keep warm.

3. Bring a large saucepan of water. Add 1 table-spoon salt just before boiling. Cook the pasta squares until al dente, 6 at a time. After a few minutes, they will rise to the top, indicating they are cooked. Using a slotted spoon, remove the pasta, drain well and place in a large bowl. Add the butter to the bowl and stir the pasta to coat it. Repeat this until all the pasta is cooked.

4. To serve, set out 8 plates (shallow bowls with rims are best) and put a buttered square of pasta in each plate. Add a heaping tablespoon of the ricotta to each square and cover each with another square. Put 1 tablespoon of the broccoli rabe over each and cover again with a pasta square. Add a bit more of butter to the top and a sprinkling of nutmeg. Serve hot.

ROSEMARY-SCENTED, BUTTERFLIED AND GRILLED LEG OF LAMB

Coscia di agnello grigliata al rosemarino
MAKES 8 SERVINGS

Serving a leg of lamb has a distinct advantage: Because of the uneven thickness of the meat, some of it will be well-cooked and some of it will be less done. This feature can please most diners for some will want it more cooked, some want it less cooked.

1 (6- to 8-pound) leg of lamb
1 cup extra-virgin olive oil
4 large cloves garlic, minced
¼ cup balsamic vinegar
6 tablespoons freshly minced rosemary leaves or
    3 teaspoons dried
2 teaspoons freshly ground pepper

1. Ask your butcher to butterfly the leg of lamb and to remove as much fat as he can, including the thin silvery membrane that envelops the leg. At home, wipe the leg with damp paper towels and remove any additional fat.

2. Combine all remaining ingredients in the bowl of a food processor and blend until the herbs and garlic are minced. Place the lamb in a nonaluminum roasting pan and pour the marinade over. Turn to coat all sides. Cover with plastic wrap and refrigerate overnight, turning occasionally. Remove from the refrigerator 1 hour before cooking.

3. This may be either grilled or broiled. If broiling, preheat the broiler and set the rack 5 to 6 inches below the heat source. Broil for about 15 minutes per side, basting frequently with the marinade. If grilling, the coals should be gray;

grill the lamb on an oiled grid about 5 inches over the coals for 12 to 14 minutes per side, basting frequently. If you prefer your lamb well done, add several minutes to each time given. Most important, let the lamb stand for 10 minutes, then cut across the grain into thin slices to serve. Because of the various thicknesses of the butterflied lamb, it will be possible to offer some meat well done and some less done.

SLOW-COOKED ROASTED PLUM TOMATOES

Pomodori al forno
MAKES 8 SERVINGS

At times, it is incredible to think that the tomato is a native South American plant that was brought to Europe in the sixteenth century, and that it wasn't until the nineteenth century that is was accepted as a food. In Italy, they say the best tomatoes are grown in San Marzano, an area of exceedingly rich soil, south of Rome toward Naples. Plum tomatoes, known as Italian or Roma are meatier and less juicy than slicing tomatoes, so they are ideal for making sauces. Here they are slow-cooked and used as a condiment for the lamb. There are many canned plum tomatoes to choose from: Progresso, Pastene and Vitelli; read the labels to be sure the tomatoes come from San Marzano, Italy.

> 8 tablespoons extra-virgin olive oil
> 1 small onion, finely chopped
> 2 cloves garlic, minced
> 1 tablespoon finely chopped fresh rosemary leaves
> 1/4 cup finely chopped fresh Italian parsley
> 2 (28-ounce) cans plum tomatoes, drained
> 2 tablespoons sugar
> Sea salt and freshly ground pepper

1. Preheat the oven to 275F. Pour 4 tablespoons of the oil into a ceramic or glass baking dish. Add the onion, garlic, rosemary and parsley. Toss well and spread on the bottom of the baking pan.

2. Snip off any visible stem ends and gently squeeze each tomato in the palm of your hand to release the seeds and excess juices. (It helps to puncture the tomato with a paring knife to create the opening for the seeds and juice to escape.) Fit the tomatoes, side by side, in a single layer in the baking pan. When all the tomatoes are in, sprinkle the remaining oil over all. Sprinkle the sugar over the tomatoes and season with salt and pepper.

3. Bake for 3 to 3½ hours. Serve warm.

SPRING GREENS WITH OIL, VINEGAR AND MINT

Insalata di stagione con vinaigrette alla menta
MAKES 8 SERVINGS

A *misticanza* salad in Italy is determined by the farmer, who sows a variety of seeds together and harvests the small plants together. At times, this could mean as many as fifteen, more or less, varieties of greens and herbs sold together. Each farmer and therefore each vendor at the markets has his or her own specialty mixture. Customers usually get to know one or two vendors and trust their combination. This kind of salad greens is difficult to find in our supermarkets, but a close relative would be mesclun mixtures and it would be wonderful if you were located near an open green market that sells fresh farm produce of this sort. A popular salad green, especially at Eastertime in Rome and elsewhere, is a dandelion known as *puntarelle*. I've been in restaurants in and around Rome on Sundays and families can't seem to get enough of it. It is made with oil and vinegar and a touch of anchovy.

> 8 cups fresh greens such as baby dandelion or hearts of chicory, washed, dried and torn into bite-size pieces
> 2 tablespoons finely chopped fresh mint
> ½ cup extra-virgin olive oil
> 2 tablespoons garlic-flavored red wine vinegar
> 1 anchovy

1. Place the greens and the mint in a large bowl.

2. In a smaller bowl, combine the oil and vinegar and mash the anchovy in it. Season to taste by adding more salt, if needed, and freshly ground pepper. Blend well and pour over the greens. Toss lightly but well, and serve.

MARIA MICHELE'S SPECIAL CHEESECAKE

Torta di formaggio alla Maria Michele
MAKES 8 SERVINGS

Maria loves this cake and makes it several ways. She will add the slightest bit of candied lemon or orange peel, or a piece of vanilla bean, or a spoonful of a liqueur to alter the taste of the cake to fit her mood.

> 2½ pounds fresh ricotta
> 5 eggs (see notabene, page 48, concerning raw eggs)
> 1½ cups sugar
> 1 teaspoon finely chopped candied lemon or orange zest, ½ finely grated fresh vanilla bean or 1 tablespoon fruit brandy

1. Preheat the oven to 400F. Process the ricotta in a food processor until it is smooth.

2. Beat the eggs, sugar and one of the flavors until well blended. Beat this into the ricotta, 1 tablespoon at a time.

3. Butter a springform pan and line the bottom of it with parchment paper. Pour the filling into it and place it in the oven. Immediately turn the oven down to 350F. Bake for 30 minutes. The cake will still be soft in the middle. Turn off the oven and leave the cake in the oven for 15 minutes. Open the door and let the cake sit in the opened oven for 15 minutes longer. This should be served warm.

ONE-DISH MEALS

BRAISED OXTAIL STEW

Coda alla vaccinara
MAKES 8 SERVINGS

This dish is unchallenged as a native Roman creation. It is a "stew" of oxtail, cut into chunks, and simmered for a long time in beef broth, wine and vegetables, especially celery. *Alla vaccinara* means cowboy style. A fresh cucumber salad would make a sensible accompaniment for this rather rich Roman dish.

In my mind this was probably a dish enjoyed by the young British noblemen who traveled to Italy on the Grand Tour that reached its culmination in the eighteenth century. The goal of the Grand Tour was to reach Italy, the touchstone of the classical past, where personal, intellectual and civic identity could be forged. The Grand Tourists commissioned portraits of themselves in their traveling costumes or besides famous antiquities (the Colosseum or Mount Vesuvius, for example). One painter, Pompeo Batoni, executed more than two hundred portraits of British tourists. These tourists bought landscapes that captured their perceptions of the Italian countryside and they collected antique sculpture, vases and gems and refashioned the interiors of their homes into elaborate backdrops for the display of these objects. Grand Tourists stimulated the development of a full-scale tourist industry that still exists today, with its illustrated guidebooks, maps, travel diaries, postcards and souvenirs. Think then, of enjoying this one-dish meal, with a view of Rome from Monte Mario, as did many of the Grand Tourists.

6 pounds oxtails, disjointed
Olive oil
Sea salt and freshly ground pepper
2 tablespoons all-purpose flour
½ pound pancetta or lean bacon, cut in small
    pieces
2 ounces prosciutto, finely chopped
2 bay leaves
2 carrots, sliced
4 cups sliced celery ribs
2 medium onions, chopped
2 cloves garlic, minced
2 cups dry white wine
2 cups tomato puree from plum tomatoes (put
    through a food mill)
1 tablespoon finely chopped rosemary
2 to 3 cups beef broth
¼ teaspoon ground cinnamon

1.   Soak the oxtail pieces in cool water for 2 or 3 hours. Drain and discard water. Pat dry with paper towels.

2.   Preheat the broiler. Lightly brush the oxtail pieces with olive oil and put them in a shallow baking pan. Salt and pepper them and broil 6 inches below the heating element to brown, about 5 minutes per side. Sprinkle some flour over the meat, and set aside.

3.   In a large saucepan or casserole, sauté the pancetta and prosciutto until some fat is rendered. Add the bay leaves, carrots, ½ cup of the celery, and the onions, and cook over medium heat, uncovered, 6 minutes. Add the garlic and cook until the onions are golden.

4.   Add the oxtail pieces and the wine and simmer, uncovered, until the wine evaporates. Add the tomatoes and the rosemary. Bring to a boil, reduce the heat, cover, and simmer 2½ to 3 hours. Add ½ cup beef broth every ½ hour or so until a sauce evolves.

5.   Cook the remaining celery in boiling, salted water 10 minutes. Drain the celery pieces and add to the saucepan 30 minutes before the end of the cooking time in Step 4. Add the cinnamon and check for salt and seasoning. Liberally add freshly ground pepper before serving.

SPAGHETTI WITH PECORINO CHEESE AND BLACK PEPPER

Spaghetti al pepe e pecorino
MAKES 4 TO 6 SERVINGS

This dish can be enjoyed in the many excellent trattorias in Rome and in most Roman homes. Like most other pastas, it makes an easy, yet wonderful one-dish meal if a hearty salad, probably one with some vegetables (steamed broccoli, green peas, steamed zucchini, or sliced red ripe tomatoes and basil dressed with oil, vinegar and some salt) and some good crusty bread is served.

Pecorino Romano is probably the best pecorino available and therefore it is used widely in and around Rome. It is found all over Italy and in the United States (every supermarket I have been into in this country has had block or grated pecorino cheese). I have made this dish with the Sardinian pecorino pepato, peppered pecorino cheese, and it works well also.

1 pound spaghetti
1 cup freshly grated pecorino cheese
Freshly ground pepper

1. Bring 4 quarts of water to boil and cook the pasta until al dente, 8 to 10 minutes. (It is a good idea to check the boxed instructions offered by the manufacturer of the pasta you have chosen to use.) Drain the pasta but reserve 1 cup of the cooking water. Transfer the pasta to a large, decorative bowl and add 1/4 cup of the cooking liquid.

2. Add the cheese and a very liberal amount of black pepper and toss well. If too dry, add more cooking liquid by tablespoons but this pasta should be fairly dry. Serve immediately.

BAKED PASTA WITH ZUCCHINI AND HERBS

Pasta al forno con zucchine e erbe aromatiche
MAKES 6 SERVINGS

Wine bars in Rome have proliferated and one of the early initiators was the wine merchant's shop Bleve, which now offers, in addition to wine, an exciting array of appetizers, pastas and desserts. Although Rome is known for its *cucina povera* (poor man's cuisine), the simple trattorie offering these simple dishes are disappearing, and fancier establishments, using more costly ingredients appear to be taking over. Yet, even in these more chic restaurants, there are offerings of simple pasta dishes such as the one presented here. Imagine yourself at the glamorous restaurant Ar Galletto, in the Piazza Farnese, surely one of Rome's most beautiful squares, eating this baked pasta dish while looking at a movie star who has driven up in a silver Mercedes convertible.

Serve with a crisp salad of mixed lettuces dressed with oil and vinegar.

5 (1 inch wide, 6 inches long) zucchini
1 medium onion, chopped
2 scallions, thinly sliced
1 celery heart, thinly sliced
1/4 cup finely chopped fresh basil
Sea salt and freshly ground pepper
1/4 cup all-purpose flour
2 ripe plum tomatoes, cored, finely chopped
6 tablespoons extra-virgin olive oil
1 pound small rigatoni or penne, cooked until al dente
Good pinch red pepper flakes
1 cup freshly grated pecorino cheese

1. Rinse and dry the zucchini. Cut off the ends and cut in halves to make 1 × 3-inch pieces. Slice each piece lengthwise into 1/4-inch sticks.

2. Preheat the oven to 425F. Combine the zucchini, onion, scallions, celery and basil in a bowl. Add salt and pepper, and sprinkle with the flour. Toss well. Add the tomatoes and toss again.

3. Use 1 tablespoon of the oil to coat a 9 × 13-inch baking pan. Transfer vegetable mixture to the pan. Drizzle with 2 tablespoons olive oil. Bake for 10 minutes, stirring twice.

4. Remove pan from the oven (keep the heat on), add the cooked pasta and the red pepper flakes, and toss well. Drizzle with the remaining 3 tablespoons oil and sprinkle with the cheese. Add more salt and a liberal amount of pepper.

5. Return to the oven and bake for 15 minutes. Remove from the oven and allow to rest for 5 minutes.

II

JEWELS OF TUSCANY

FLORENCE, LUCCA AND SIENA

This part of Italy has everything: art and architecture, rolling countryside and soft pastures, *fettuccine con salmone, cavolo nero con crostini, gallina stufata,* olive trees and cypresses, bread and oil, beans and "bistecca," fennel and *fette.*

Located in the valley of the Arno River, which flows under its magnificent bridges and between the lovely palaces looking onto its banks, Florence is universally recognized as one of the most beautiful cities in the world, the seat of masterpieces of every kind. In spite of many fratricide battles described by Dante, the arts florished in the thirteenth and fourteenth centuries and this city became the cradle for artists too numerous to mention: Dante, Ciambue, Giotto, Petrarca, Boccaccio, Brunellesachi, Botticelli, Donatello, da Vinci and Michaelangelo, to mention a few. These artists left traces that today make Tuscany a well-known center of culture and the destination of elite tourism, but they come also for the food. Purity is the keynote of Tuscan cooking. Whereas they say cooking elsewhere in Italy is a passion, here it is an art, as that of the great masters. The Tuscan seeks good raw materials for cooking. The *bistecca alla fiorentina* (page 46) must be the right cut, the right thickness, the salt must go on at a certain time, as does the last rite of oil brushing. Tuscans take special care in preparing vegetables, especially their classic White Beans with Mushrooms (page 69). The term *girarrosto* seen all over Tuscany is the name for restaurants where cooking revolves around the hearth, grill or spit, where just about every kind of meat and fowl revolves around a heat source. For a Tuscan grilled chicken, see page 59.

These three examples of Tuscan dishes clearly show that the Tuscan cook cannot depend on elaborate sauces or fancy gravies to disguise the flavor of his food. When the Tuscan cooks a classically simple dish, he basically counts on the quality of the raw ingredients and on his skill to pull it off. Perhaps the one exception to this classic simplicity occurs along Tuscany's coast, the Tyrrhenian Sea, home to Piobino, Cecina and the well-known Livorno (Leghorn), and farther north near Lucca, the seaside city of Viareggio; all these coastal towns and cities are famous for their seafood preparations. Perhaps the most famous is the *cacciucco*. I hesitate to call it a soup because they don't think of it as soup but more like a dish of seafood in which many kinds of fish appear; it must contain rockfish, tomatoes, onion, garlic, parsley and wine. Often it is white wine, but it could be red. They also like to cook red mullet and dried cod.

The Tuscan love affair with the bean may not exclude other vegetables (they love Swiss chard, zucchini and artichokes, too), but it is the bean that is everywhere, in antipasti, in soups, cooked in flasks, cooked with rice or fish or with lentils. There is a reason the Tuscans are called *mangiafagioli,* bean-eaters.

A MEAL FOR 4 WITH THE ORSINIS IN RADDA-IN-CHIANTI

MENU

A Country Spinach Pie
Torta di ricotta e spinaci

Fettuccine with Smoked Salmon all' Orsini
Fettuccine con salmone affumicato all' Orsini

Fresh, Sugared Red and White Grapes, Vin Santo and Almond Biscotti from Prato
Confetti di uva fresca con vin Santo e biscottini di Prato

Radda-in-Chianti is one of the prettiest villages in the Chianti area of Tuscany. Nestled snuggly in the intensely cultivated lands around it, the famous Chianti vineyards stretch all around. The town's medieval streets radiate from the central piazza and sipping a caffe there is the place to soak up the slow and peaceful pace of Italian village life.

In Tuscany, *all'inzimino* means something (fish, meat, poultry, dairy, whatever) cooked with leaf vegetables, usually spinach or Swiss chard. They also enjoy using these leaf vegetables in tarts. Here is a crustless version enjoyed in Georgianna and Armando Orsini's home.

Wine Selection

Serve an important dry white wine, such as Vernaccia di San Gimignano. It is made from the Vernaccia grape and its production is protected and labeled by the association that looks after the Chianti of the Colli Senesi, and the Vin Nobile di Montepulciano. San Gimignano is the picturesque hill town of many towers near Siena.

Preparation Advice

1. The spinach pie can be made a few hours ahead and reheated before adding the important garnish.

2. In preparing the fettuccine, have ready all the ingredients ahead of time, but the dish should be brought together at the last moment.

3. The grapes can be sugared ahead by several hours and the biscotti can be made several days ahead.

A COUNTRY SPINACH PIE

Torta di spinaci e ricotta
MAKES 6 TO 8 SERVINGS AS A FIRST COURSE OR 4 SERVINGS AS A MAIN COURSE

This is a crustless tart, simply a blend of spinach, ricotta, onion, basil and eggs, that is baked until it sets. To achieve a creamy tart, the ricotta should be drained as explained below.

1 pound ricotta cheese
12 ounces fresh spinach, stems removed
2 tablespoons butter
1/2 cup finely chopped onion
1/2 cup freshly grated Parmesan cheese
2 tablespoons freshly minced basil
1/4 teaspoon freshly grated nutmeg
2 eggs, beaten
1 egg white, beaten
Sea salt and freshly ground pepper

GARNISH
4 to 6 large fresh spinach leaves, shredded, or 8 thinly sliced fresh mushrooms
1/4 fresh red or orange bell pepper, trimmed and sliced thinly
1 tablespoon extra-virgin olive oil
1 teaspoon fresh lemon juice

1. Wrap ricotta tightly in fine cheesecloth, place in a colander over a bowl and let it drain, refrigerate for a minimum of 3 hours, or overnight.

2. Prepare the spinach by thoroughly rinsing, draining and spinning dry. Chop roughly and set aside.

3. Heat the butter in a small skillet and sauté the onion until opaque, 4 or 5 minutes.

4. Heat the oven to 350F. Lightly oil a 9-inch glass pie dish.

5. Combine the ricotta, spinach, sautéed onion, Parmesan cheese, basil, nutmeg, salt and freshly ground pepper in the bowl of a food processor. Process until smooth. Add the eggs and egg white and blend a few seconds longer. Pour the mixture into the prepared dish and bake for about 40 minutes, until set. To serve, let the pie rest about 5 minutes, loosen the edges with a knife and cut into wedges.

6. Combine all the garnish ingredients in a bowl and toss well. Add salt and pepper. Put some of the dressed spinach on each serving, placing it next to the spinach tart wedge, slightly overlapping.

1. Bring 4 quarts of water to a rolling boil. Add 1 tablespoon salt. Add the pasta and cook until al dente.

2. While the pasta is cooking, heat the butter in a large skillet. Add the smoked salmon and cook 1 to 2 minutes. Add the cognac and stir well. Add the half-and-half and bring to a boil.

3. Drain the pasta well and add it to the skillet. Taste for salt. Add pepper and the cheese. Toss quickly over heat and serve while very hot.

FETTUCCINE WITH SMOKED SALMON ALL' ORSINI

Fettuccine con salmone affumicato all' Orsini
MAKES 4 SERVINGS

Almost all the smoked salmon eaten in Italy is imported, and therefore expensive, as it also is in this country. The amount of salmon needed in this recipe is minimal and therefore affordable. The first time I enjoyed this dish was at the Tuscan home of Armando and Georgianna Orsini. They owned the Orsini restaurant in New York, famous for many years and frequented by Hollywood, political, television and publishing people. This particular dish is not basically regional in character, for as far as can be discerned, it appeared on Italian menus a short while ago. It can be found in better restaurants in major cities all over Italy, and may be considered an international or national-type dish that has cut across the regions.

In cooking this dish, be sure all ingredients are ready to be used: the salmon is cut into pieces, the cheese is grated, and so on. The dish must be prepared quickly and served almost at once.

Sea salt
½ pound fettuccine, fresh or dried
4 tablespoons butter
¼ pound thinly sliced smoked salmon, cut into 1-inch squares
2 tablespoons cognac
½ cup half-and-half or heavy cream
Freshly ground pepper
⅓ cup freshly grated Parmesan cheese

FRESH, SUGARED RED AND WHITE GRAPES

Confetti di uva fresca
MAKES 4 SERVINGS

These sugared grapes may be made a day ahead and refrigerated until needed.

8 small clusters of grapes (4 red, 4 white)
2 egg whites, beaten until frothy
½ cup sugar

1. Dip grape clusters into egg whites, coating completely. Pour the sugar into a wide saucer and press the grapes lightly into it.

2. To serve, put one of each color grape cluster on a plate and serve with a glass of vin Santo and pass some biscotti.

ALMOND BISCOTTI
FROM PRATO

Biscottini di Prato o Cantuccini
MAKES ABOUT 25 BISCOTTI

Prato is only seventeen kilometers from Florence, and because it is heavily industrialized, it is sometimes looked down at by the Florentine. But everyone in Florence, and elsewhere, will agree that the biscotti produced in Prato have earned a place in the hall of gastronomy. I recall buying some in Prato at the pastry shop called Forno Mattei; they were totally delicious. These biscotti are perfectly paired with the vin Santo Toscana, and everyone there thinks this is the only way to end a meal. The vin Santo is amber-colored and aromatic. The story is that it was given its name in 1440 by Cardinale Bessarione, who was so impressed that he said "Questo e Xanto," meaning this is holy. The wine is made from semi-dried Malvasia or Trebbiano grapes that are hung from beams or dried on straw mats and pressed and put into small barrels for three years, usually stored in attics, winter and summer. Quite a lot of this wine is made throughout Tuscany, and in fact, elsewhere in Italy, such as the Trentino–Alto Aldige. The quality varies widely; the best are said to come from the *zona classica* of Chianti, from the Val di Pesa, just south of Florence and from the Casentino Hills to the east, along the curve of the Arno.

There are several variations to this biscotti, such as toasting the almonds before incorporating them, or adding another nut such as pine nuts, or also adding saffron to make the biscotti a stronger yellow in appearance. There are many commercial versions of this cookie. They are exported all over the world, but nothing tastes as good as the ones made at home, or made in the local Italian pastry shops.

The local bakers will tell you that the following recipe is the most traditional and perhaps the best.

2 scant cups all-purpose unbleached flour
1 cup sugar
1 teaspoon baking powder
2 eggs
2 egg yolks
1/2 teaspoon vanilla extract
Pinch salt
3/4 cup almonds, coarsely chopped
1 tablespoon milk

1. Preheat the oven to 350F. Butter and flour a baking sheet and set aside.

2. Put the flour, sugar and baking powder into a mixing bowl. In a small bowl, combine the eggs, one yolk, the vanilla and salt. Add it to the flour mixture, and with a wooden spoon, stir until a soft dough is formed. Add the almonds and stir again to distribute the almonds throughout the dough. Turn out onto a lightly floured work surface, and knead the dough for 4 or 5 minutes.

3. With lightly floured hands, divide the dough into 2 equal parts, and roll each into a sausage shape, about 12 inches long, 1 inch thick and 2 to 3 inches wide. Combine the remaining egg yolk with the milk, and lightly brush over the tops of each sausage shape. Transfer them carefully to the prepared baking sheet and bake for about 30 minutes, until they turn golden.

4. Remove the baking sheet from the oven and diagonally slice each into 1/2-inch pieces, separating the slices from one another as you do this. When all the slices are cut and separated, lay them on their sides. Return the baking sheet to the oven and bake for 7 minutes; turn them over and bake for 7 minutes. Remove from the oven. Cool them first before storing in an airtight container.

PORTERHOUSE STEAK DINNER FOR 6, OLIVIERO'S STYLE IN FLORENCE

MENU

Kale Soup in the Tuscan Style
Zuppa di cavolo nero con crostini

Grilled Porterhouse Steak
Bistecca alla fiorentina

Chicory and Smoked Mozzarella on the Grill
Cicoria e mozzarella affumicata alla griglia

Tina's Praline Mousse Cake
Dolce di praline alla Tina

Oliviero's is a refined and sophisticated restaurant in Florence and has been in business a long time. Its tables are elegantly set with fine linens and stemware. The lighting is low, and many Hollywood stars have been there, not for its glitz, but for its food. It is considered innovative with restraint, showing classic flavors at their best. It has a reputation for serving one of the best Florentine steaks in Tuscany, the memory of which one carries back home.

Steak may not seem sufficiently exceptional to qualify as a regional specialty, but this one is unusual because you cannot get a Florentine steak anywhere else. Basically, they cut a T-bone steak, which is a rarity in Europe. I think of it more as our porterhouse, and in Florence it is cooked rare indeed.

Wine Selection

Serve a big Italian red, Brunello di Montalcino, one of the great red wines of Italy. It is aged in casks for five to six years before bottling, and then stays in the bottle for two more years before being sold. Most experts think this wine should be decanted as much as twenty-four hours before drinking. This wine is made from the Brunello grape only, a variety of the noble Sangiovese grape that goes into Chianti, but without the other Chianti grapes. The wine is expensive, but so is the steak.

Preparation Advice

1. The soup and the dessert may be made ahead by one or two days.

2. This leaves considerable time for the steak and vegetable dish to be prepared just before mealtime.

KALE SOUP IN THE TUSCAN STYLE

Zuppa di cavolo nero con crostini
MAKES 6 SERVINGS

Peasant-style cooking continues to predominate in Tuscany and it is usually described as "pillars of tradition," plain, simple and wholesome, just like this soup. Kale is another green leaf vegetable liked by the Tuscans and they have told me that the tenderest, tastiest kale leaves are those that have been zapped by frost and cold weather. What is really strange about this soup is that there are no beans in it, but it is made with other essentials and every ingredient counts. Its flavor depends on the fresh kale, Tuscany's extra-virgin olive oil and a generous sprinkling of Parmesan cheese.

1½ pounds fresh kale, thick stems removed
3 cups each beef and chicken broth, or 6 cups mixed broth (page 8)
12 (1½-inch-thick) slices whole-wheat Italian bread
3 large cloves garlic, halved
About 8 tablespoons Tuscan extra-virgin olive oil
Sea salt and freshly ground pepper
½ cup freshly grated Parmesan cheese

1. Rinse, drain and thinly slice the kale. Put it in a large saucepan and add the broth. Bring to a boil over medium-high heat. Reduce the heat to a slow, steady simmer and cook, partially covered, until the kale is tender, about 30 minutes.

2. Preheat the broiler. While the kale is cooking, place the slices of bread in a single layer on a broiler pan and place 5 inches below the heat source. Toast both sides, about 2 minutes per side. Rub both sides of the toasted bread with the garlic halves.

3. Drain the kale, reserving the broth. Carefully dip each toast slice into the hot liquid and quickly put 2 slices into one of six rimmed soup bowls. Repeat until all toast slices have been dipped and placed in the bowls. Drizzle 1 teaspoon of the olive oil over each toast slice. Add salt and a liberal amount of pepper.

4. Spoon some kale over each slice and add a few more drops of olive oil over the kale, adding more salt and pepper. Ladle some of the broth into each bowl and serve. Pass the grated cheese.

GRILLED PORTERHOUSE STEAK

Bistecca alla fiorentina
MAKES 6 SERVINGS

Rib-eye or shell steaks may be cooked in the same manner; they should be at least 1 inch thick or thicker. It is important not to add salt before the meat cooks; add it during the grilling process as described below. Be sure the meat is at room temperature before grilling it. This is surely one time you should seek the best meat possible. The simplicity of this dish is all the more reason to enjoy it. For the American table, this is a treat.

1 beef porterhouse steak, about 3 pounds, trimmed, at room temperature
4 tablespoons extra-virgin olive oil
4 cloves garlic, cut in half lengthwise
Sea salt and freshly ground pepper
6 wedges fresh lemon, seeded

1. Build a charcoal fire and allow it to reach the gray ash stage. Gently tap the coals to shake off the ash. Move the coals slightly so they are about ½ inch apart to moderate the heat.

2. Using less than 1 tablespoon of the oil, brush the steak lightly on both sides. Put the remaining oil and the garlic in a small saucepan or skillet and heat until the garlic turns light brown. Do not let the garlic get darker. Remove from the heat, discard the pieces of garlic and set the oil aside.

3. When the fire is ready, place the steak on the grill as close as possible to the heat source. Sear for 2 minutes, on one side only to seal in the juices. Raise the grill about 4 inches from the coals and continue grilling until tiny bubbles of juice appear on top of the steak, 3 to 5 minutes, depending on the thickness of the steak.

4. Turn over the steak with tongs and liberally add salt and pepper. Repeat grilling procedure for the second side, 2 minutes close to the heat source and raising the grill rack and grilling the steak about 2 minutes more to achieve a rare steak. A Florentine steak is never overcooked.

5. If you wish you to use a gas-fired grill, heat it and follow the same procedure for oiling, salting and peppering the steak as above. Grill for 5 to 7 minutes per side depending on the thickness.

6. To serve, let the steak rest for a few minutes before slicing. Reheat the flavored oil. Slice the meat against the grain, put some slices onto each plate, and spoon some of the garlic-flavored oil over the meat. Add a lemon wedge to each serving; the lemon is to be squeezed over the meat as a final touch.

CHICORY AND SMOKED MOZZARELLA ON THE GRILL

Cicoria e mozzarella affumicata alla griglia
MAKES 6 SERVINGS

Lavagna is the Italian word for slate, and this black stone from Liguria, when heated, is often used in Italy instead of grilling something on a gas-fired flattop. I was surprised to see it in use in New York City at the restaurant Il Cantinori on East 10th Street. The slate is first oiled, then heated in a broiler until almost red-hot. Then it is put on a heatproof countertop, and there, vegetables, of almost any description can be grilled. The *lavagna* stays hot for about thirty minutes. Chicory is used in this recipe, but the method works also for radicchio, sliced fennel, turnips, leeks, sliced eggplant or zucchini.

As interesting as *lavagna* cooking may be, use your gas-fired flattop grill if you have one; otherwise, use a large skillet on the stove.

6 small heads green chicory
6 tablespoons extra-virgin olive oil
Sea salt and freshly ground pepper
6 thin slices smoked mozzarella

1. Remove the green leaves from each head of chicory so only the hearts are left. Trim each head, and if necessary, wash them and drain well.

2. Heat a gas-fired flattop grill until very hot. Place the chicory hearts on the grill and sprinkle each with 1 tablespoon of the oil. With a spatula, press down on each head and cook until lightly browned, 1 to 2 minutes. Quickly turn them over and press down with a spatula again. Add salt and pepper.

3.   Just before removing, cover each head with a mozzarella slice. When the cheese melts, remove them to a serving plate. (If using a skillet, heat a little oil in it, add the chicory, pour more oil over the chicory and follow the remaining steps above.)

TINA'S PRALINE MOUSSE CAKE

Dolce di praline alla Tina
MAKES ABOUT 10 SERVINGS

The cake must be made one day ahead and refrigerated overnight.

½ pound butter or margarine, at room
     temperature
½ pound sugar
6 eggs, separated (see Notabene below,
     concerning raw eggs)
½ pound ground almonds
½ pound bittersweet chocolate
2 tablespoons coffee
2 tablespoons cognac

1.   Preheat the oven to 350F. Liberally butter a 10-inch springform pan. Cream the butter and sugar with an electric mixer on medium speed. Add 1 yolk at a time, beating until all are incorporated. Fold in the ground almonds.

2.   Melt the chocolate with the coffee in the top of a double boiler. Cool slightly and then fold into the almond mixture. Fold in the cognac.

3.   In a clean bowl with clean beaters, beat the egg whites until stiff. Fold them into the chocolate mixture until well blended.

4.   Put half of the chocolate mixture into the prepared pan and bake for 30 minutes. Let cool.

5.   Spoon the remaining half of the chocolate mixture over the cooled, cooked cake. Cover with plastic or foil and refrigerate overnight (this half of the chocolate is not baked). Remove side of the springform pan before serving.

Notabene:

Uncooked eggs should not be eaten by young children, the elderly or anyone with a compromised immune system, because they may contain salmonella bacteria that can cause serious illness. Pasteurized eggs are available in many markets and are safe to eat raw in sauces or desserts that are not cooked.

BEYOND THE
LEANING TOWER OF PISA:
A MEAL FOR 6
DEDICATED TO THE
YOUNG WINE-CONSCIOUS
RESTAURATEURS IN PISA

MENU

**The Yellow Pepper Soup of
Cibreos in Florence**
Passato di peperoni gialli alla Cibreo (Firenze)

**Cornish Hens with Ricotta and Tarragon
under the Skin**
Gallina stufata al dragoncello

**Green Beans with Pancetta and Savory as
Eaten by the Benedictine Monks**
Fagiolini con pancetta e santoreggio
alla maniera dei Monaci Benedettini

Tiramisu with Amaretto from Caffe Poliziano in Montepulciano
Tiramisu con amaretto Caffe Poliziano a Montepulciano

Baby eels, *le cieche,* or in dialect called *le cee,* cooked in oil with salt and pepper, are considered Pisa's contribution to Tuscan cuisine; otherwise, its cooking is all basically Tuscan. Its restaurants, however, and their dedicated young chef/owners bring a special culinary touch, so evident in this fabulous city. Sergio's prepares mussels with saffron, tagliatelle with squid and vegetable sauces and ravioli filled with all sorts of fish. The *zuppa di pesce* at Al Risatoro dei Vecchi Macelli is simply delicious, as are the gnocchi prepared with shrimp. Da Bruno stuffs calamari and makes the special tomato and bread soup called *ribollita.* La Mescita, a charming trattoria with vaulted brick ceilings, makes delicious vegetable molds and salt cod with chickpeas. Here is a menu inspired from this area with something special from Florence to help keep peace between the two rival cities.

Wine Selection
Serve a young Chianti wine, such as Chianti Colli Senesi, which comes from the area directly south of the *zona classica* for Chianti. The Association's neck label shows Romulus and Remus and the she-wolf, the badge of Siena, as well as Rome. If you prefer a white, consider the fancy-named wine Lacrima d'Arno, given to the white wines from the upper Arno region, very much like Arbia.

Preparation Advice
1. The Yellow Pepper Soup and the tiramisu may be made one day ahead.

2. The Cornish hens may be prepared several hours ahead, refrigerated and brought to room temperature before broiling. The beans may be cooked, wrapped in pancetta and held for several hours at room temperature before broiling.

THE YELLOW PEPPER SOUP OF CIBREOS IN FLORENCE

Passato di peperoni gialli alla Cibreo (Firenze)
MAKES 6 TO 8 SERVINGS

This soup is an almost indescribably warm and inviting yellow. It was created by Fabio Picchi, a superstar chef and owner, with his wife, Benedetta Vitali, of the famous restaurant Cibreo in Florence. As one of his signature dishes, Fabio adds milk to smooth out the acidity of the peppers and to give them a more even consistency. In the raw, the peppers should be brightly colored, without wrinkles and shiny. They should be firm to the touch and feel heavy for their size when you heft one in the palm of your hand. There is a huge outdoor market next to Cibreo, and when you see ripe yellow peppers (the color you see on some palazzi walls), with no streaks of green whatever, you are looking at the peppers used in this soup. The unique garnish of crushed amaretti cookies and grated Parmesan cheese should be sprinkled on top of the soup for an intriguing and eye-catching presentation, a superb visual tasty treat.

> 2 tablespoons extra-virgin olive oil
> 1 medium red onion, cut into ½-inch dice
> 2 medium carrots, peeled, cut lengthwise in half and thinly sliced crosswise
> 1 medium celery rib, thinly sliced
> 8 large yellow peppers, stemmed, seeded, ribs removed and cut into 1-inch pieces
> 2 pounds potatoes, peeled and cut into ½-inch dice

3 cups canned low-sodium beef broth, or more if
     needed
1 cup water, or more if needed
Salt
½ cup milk
2 bay leaves
2 to 3 tablespoons crushed amaretti cookies
2 to 3 tablespoons freshly grated Parmesan
     cheese

1.   Heat the oil in a large soup pot over medium heat. Add the onion, carrots and celery, and sauté until the onion turns golden, about 5 minutes, stirring often.

2.   Add the bell peppers and potatoes, and sauté until lightly softened, about 5 minutes, stirring often. Add the beef broth and water and don't be alarmed if they don't cover the vegetables. Add a pinch of salt and bring to a boil. Reduce the heat to a slow and steady simmer. Cook, partially covered, for 20 minutes, until the vegetables are tender. Remove from the heat.

3.   Puree the soup in batches, using a food mill. For a smoother soup, put the puree through the food mill again. (Do not use a food processor as it will pulverize the pepper skins.) Return the puree to the pot.

4.   Add the milk and the bay leaves and reheat the soup without boiling or it will lose some of its bright yellow color. Remove the bay leaves and add more salt if you wish. The soup should be thick but you may thin it with more broth and/or water, but only ½ cup at a time. In Florence, this is a thick soup.

5.   Ladle the soup into warmed bowls and top each with a scant teaspoon crushed amaretti cookies to one side and a scant teaspoon Parmesan cheese to the opposite side.

CORNISH HENS WITH RICOTTA AND TARRAGON UNDER THE SKIN

Gallina stufata al dragoncello
MAKES 6 SERVINGS

It is best to prepare the hens with the ricotta mixture under the skins several hours ahead to allow flavors to develop. Keep the hens refrigerated, but take them out and leave at room temperature about one-half hour before broiling them. These hens may also be grilled following the same procedure as for broiling, but be sure the coals are gray to prevent flare-ups. Boneless chicken breasts with skins may be substituted for the hens.

1 cup fresh ricotta cheese
3 tablespoons freshly grated Parmesan cheese
1½ tablespoons butter, at room temperature
1 tablespoon finely chopped fresh tarragon or
     1 teaspoon dried, crushed
2 medium cloves garlic, minced
Freshly ground pepper
3 (about 1-pound) Cornish hens, trimmed, split in
     halves, lengthwise, rinsed and dried
1 tablespoon extra-virgin olive oil

1.   Combine the ricotta and Parmesan cheeses with the butter, tarragon, garlic and pepper in a bowl.

2.   Lay each hen half on a flat surface and carefully separate the skin from the flesh with your fingers, enough to allow you to put some of the ricotta mixture under the skin. Do this with each of the remaining halves. Brush oil over both sides of each hen.

3. Preheat the broiler and line a broiler pan or a flat pan (such as a baking sheet with a rim) with foil. Arrange the halves, skin side down, 4 to 6 inches below the heat source, and broil for 12 to 15 minutes, until browned. Carefully turn over the halves with the skin side up and broil until brown, 10 to 12 minutes.

GREEN BEANS WITH PANCETTA AND SAVORY AS EATEN BY THE BENEDICTINE MONKS

Fagiolini con pancetta e santoreggio alla maniera dei Monaci Benedettini
MAKES 6 SERVINGS

Savory is a rather bitter herb vaguely like thyme, used in sausages, stuffings and as a flavoring for beans and peas. A Mediterranean herb, it was valued for its affinity for green beans and its medicinal use. It was known by the Romans but enjoyed a rediscovery by the Benedictine monks who, as far back as the ninth century, cultivated it in the monastery gardens. This dish is updated in fancier Italian restaurants by wrapping the beans in pancetta slices and broiling them, a delicious idea.

> 1 pound fresh green beans, trimmed
> ¼ cup butter
> 2 sprigs fresh savory or 1 pinch dried
> 6 thin slices pancetta, about ⅓ pound

1. Cook the beans in salted, boiling water until tender, about 10 minutes. Drain and dry them with paper towels.

2. In a large skillet, melt the butter, add the savory and beans and sauté. Remove from the heat and cool somewhat, just enough to be able to handle them by arranging them into 6 bundles. Trim the edges to make uniform packets.

3. Place a pancetta slice on top and slightly around each bundle, fitting it as if it were a wide belt.

4. Arrange the packets of beans with their belts of pancetta on a broiler pan. Broil 5 or 6 inches under the heat source to brown and sizzle the pancetta, about 4 minutes.

TIRAMISU WITH AMARETTO FROM CAFFE POLIZIANO IN MONTEPULCIANO

Tiramisu con amaretto Caffe Poliziano a Montepulciano
MAKES 6 TO 10 SERVINGS

Tiramisu has been claimed by the Venetians, but the dish is so popular all over Italy and in the United States, so much so that it is no longer claimed to be regional. Everywhere in Italy, each cook puts his or her own imprint on the dish. I recall one version quite clearly. After a delightful meal at the restaurant Diva e Maceo, in the center of Montepulciano, we decided on a dessert, after having refused it at the restaurant (the only reason being we were too full of food). Our stroll led us to a nearby coffeehouse and restaurant called Caffe Poliziano (people from Montepulciano are called *poliziani*). The view of the hillside was fantastic from the caffe, as was the tiramisu (which means "lift me up"). This is a no-fail recipe and a delicious one. I find it is good the next day, if any is left over. Some shops sell "Savoie" biscuits in the shape of ladyfingers. If you find these, use them instead of other ladyfingers as they are already dried out.

>   16 to 20 ladyfingers
>
>   3 eggs, separated (see notabene, page 48, concerning raw eggs)
>
>   ½ cup sugar
>
>   1 tablespoon espresso or strong black coffee
>
>   ¼ cup amaretto liqueur
>
>   8 ounces mascarpone cheese
>
>   2 cups strong black coffee
>
>   ¼ to ⅓ cup unsweetened cocoa powder

1.   Dry the ladyfingers in a 250F oven for about 30 minutes. Combine the egg yolks, sugar, espresso and amaretto and beat for 2 to 3 minutes. Add the mascarpone and whip until the mixture is smooth.

2.   Beat the egg whites until nearly stiff and fold into the yolk mixture.

3.   Moisten half of the ladyfingers with coffee, and arrange them in a glass or ceramic dish or bowl. Do this by quickly dunking half of each ladyfinger into the coffee and quickly laying it in the bowl. If you don't move quickly and carefully, the ladyfinger will disintegrate.

4.   Carefully spread half of the mascarpone mixture over the layer of ladyfingers. Sprinkle with half of the cocoa powder.

5.   Repeat with the remaining ladyfingers, mascarpone mixture and cocoa. Cover and refrigerate for a minimum of 3 hours or overnight. Serve by first sprinkling some cocoa (through a small sieve) onto individual dessert plates, and then spooning some of the tiramisu over it.

TO THE SOUND OF PUCCINI AT TORRE DEL LAGO: A MENU FOR 4 FROM LUCCA

MENU

The Resident Cook's Penne Pasta in Timbale, Lucca Style
Timballo di penne con il sugo alla Lucchese

Veal Scallops with Ham and Sage
Involtini di vitello con prosciutto e salvia in umido

The Owner's Roasted Broccoli and Cauliflower
Broccoli e cavolfiore arrostiti alla maniera del padrone

Peach "Cobbler" from the Countess d'Orbicciano
Dolce di pesche al forno alla Contessa d'Orbicciano

Purple Plum Ice Cream
Gelato di prugne

Giacomo Puccini was born in Lucca but composed *Tosca, La Bohème* and *Madame Butterfly* in Torre del Lago, outside Lucca, where he lived while doing this work. The location is perfect, for it has Lake Massaciuccoli on one side and the sea on the other. When he was in Lucca, he loved and frequented Caffe di Sima, an antique tearoom still popular for quick panini and long coffees. Lucca, one of the most pleasant towns in Tuscany, is famous for its olive oil and can boast a finer cuisine than tea sandwiches. I believe I have eaten in most of Lucca's restaurants and have enjoyed them immensely. They often served as inspiration for cooking at the home of American friends Jim and Warrie Price, whose Le Tre Casa lies in the suburb of Orbicciano. Cinzia Ricci was and is the resident cook. I can still see and smell the flour in her hair and on her cheeks as she dug in to make homemade pasta with Lucca olive oil. She was not silent as she flattened veal pieces with a wooden hammer with a very large head. She wouldn't hesitate a minute to run out the kitchen door in the rain to pick fresh sage and rosemary growing furiously along the stone wall outside the house to add to food already cooking on the stove.

Wine Selection

According to an old Italian saying, Tuscany was baptized in wine. Siena is the official wine capital of the country. The Italian Academy of Wine and Grapes and the Italian Wine Institute have their headquarters there. An annual wine fair in held in Siena. The one wine everyone knows is Tuscan Chianti. This wine is the best-known Italian wine outside Italy and it's easy to understand why. It is grown in a big zone, so there is a lot of wine, of the same kind, of the same name. Because most of the vineyards belong to large estate owners, they could afford the costs of modernization. Chianti gained in popularity because of its wicker-covered *fiasco*, although this method of bottling is giving way to plastic and other types of bottling; in fact, the better Chiantis are put up in claret bottles. Nonetheless, Chianti has become the archetype of Italian wines. Consider one produced by Querciabella, either the Chianti Classico or a five-year-old Toscana IGT Camartina.

Preparation Advice

1. The pasta in timbale can be made several hours ahead and reheated. However, the tomato sauce and the pastry can be made well ahead, by as much as two days; and the same applies to the besciamella sauce.

2. The veal scallops can be rolled and refrigerated four or five hours ahead and brought to room temperature before cooking.

3. The cauliflower may be prepped ahead and even cooked, but save the adding of the bread crumbs until just before serving.

4. The ice cream may be made ahead by a week or so and kept frozen.

THE RESIDENT COOK'S PENNE PASTA IN TIMBALE, LUCCA STYLE

Timballo di penne con il sugo alla Lucchese
MAKES 6 TO 8 SERVINGS

This is a typical dish from Lucca that is country-style, a good hearty dish that is served as a first course, or it can be a main dish. It will serve more than four persons, but it is a good left over and will reheat, or it can be eaten at room temperature.

FOR THE PASTRY
2 cups sifted all-purpose unbleached flour
1/2 cup sugar
Pinch salt
8 tablespoons butter, at room temperature
2 eggs, beaten
1/2 teaspoon grated lemon zest

FOR THE TOMATO SAUCE (2 TO 3 CUPS)
1 (28-ounce) can plum tomatoes, chopped
    coarsely, with juice
2 teaspoons tomato paste
1 teaspoon sugar
1 large onion, chopped
2 celery ribs, chopped coarsely
Sea salt and freshly ground pepper
4 tablespoons extra-virgin olive oil

¾ pound ground beef
¼ cup good-quality red wine
1 tablespoon butter

FOR THE BESCIAMELLA SAUCE
3 tablespoons butter
3 tablespoons all-purpose unbleached flour
1 cup half-and-half
Sea salt and freshly ground pepper
Pinch nutmeg

½ pound penne pasta, or other short pasta such
    as fusilli, cooked al dente and cooled
½ cup freshly grated Parmigiano cheese
1 egg, beaten

1. *To make the pastry:* Sift the flour, sugar and salt together and put on a work surface. Make a well in the center. Put the butter, eggs and lemon zest in the well and incorporate these ingredients with your hands. (Do not add any water.) When smooth, shape into a ball, wrap in waxed paper and chill for at least 30 minutes.

2. *To make the tomato sauce:* Combine the plum tomatoes, tomato paste, sugar, onion, celery, salt, pepper and 2 tablespoons of the olive oil in a saucepan. Cook over medium heat for 15 minutes. Process the tomato mixture through a food mill. Leave the saucepan as is.

3. In a large skillet, heat the remaining 2 tablespoons olive oil and add the ground meat. Break up the meat with a wooden spoon and cook over medium heat until the meat has changed color and looks half-cooked, about 6 minutes. Transfer to the reserved saucepan, adding the strained tomato mixture and the wine. Bring to a boil, reduce the heat and simmer, partially covered, for 40 minutes. Add the butter and check for seasoning.

4. *To make the besciamella sauce:* In a small saucepan, melt the butter over medium heat, add

the flour and stir well. Add the half-and-half and beat with a whisk to dissolve the flour. Bring to a boil, reduce the heat and simmer for 3 minutes, stirring frequently, until thick and smooth. Taste to see if the taste of raw flour is gone. If it isn't, cook for 1 to 2 minutes. Season with salt, pepper and nutmeg. Remove from the heat.

5. *To assemble the pie:* Preheat the oven to 400F. Cut the pie dough into two pieces, two-thirds and one-third of the dough. Roll out the larger piece and fit into a 1½-inch-deep, 9-inch baking pan.

6. Add the cooled pasta to the 2 cups of the tomato mixture, stir well and transfer to the pastry shell. Then pour the besciamella sauce over the pasta and sprinkle with the cheese.

7. Roll out the smaller piece of dough and fit in over the filling, bringing the upper and lower pastry together by uniting them with the tines of a fork. (If you have leftover dough, make a leaf, star or other cut-outs and add to the center of the top crust.) Brush the top pastry with the beaten egg and bake for 30 minutes, until the pastry is brown.

8. Allow to rest for 4 or 5 minutes before cutting into wedges.

VEAL SCALLOPS WITH HAM AND SAGE

Involtini di vitello con prosciutto e salvia in umido
MAKES 4 SERVINGS

It is best to ask your butcher to pound the veal thinly for you. The prepackaged veal scallops offered in most supermarkets will not do here. If your supermarket has a special meat counter with a butcher, explain what you want.

> 1½ pounds veal scallopine, pounded thin
> 4 thin slices good-quality ham
> 4 fresh whole sage leaves
> 3 tablespoons extra-virgin olive oil
> 1 onion, finely chopped
> 2 carrots, finely chopped
> 1 celery rib, finely chopped
> Sea salt and freshly ground pepper
> 1 cup dry white wine
> 1½ cups chopped fresh or canned tomatoes

1.   Place the veal slices on a flat surface and add a ham slice and then a sage leaf to each. Roll them up and secure with string or with a toothpick. If the slice is wide, use 2 toothpicks.

2.   In a large skillet, heat the oil and sauté the onion, carrots and celery until they are browned at the edges, about 10 minutes. Add salt and pepper.

3.   Place the veal rolls in the skillet and sauté until browned on all sides, 10 to 15 minutes. Add the wine and cook for 4 minutes. Add the tomatoes and bring to a boil. (Cinzia, the resident cook described above, said most Italians would add half a bouillon cube, either chicken or vegetable,

at this point). Reduce the heat and simmer until the veal is cooked and the sauce has thickened, about 30 minutes. If you want a thinner sauce, add chicken broth by tablespoons.

THE OWNER'S ROASTED BROCCOLI AND CAULIFLOWER

Broccoli e cavolfiore arrostiti alla maniera del padrone
MAKES 4 TO 6 SERVINGS

The discussion of the simplicity of Italian food may seem overdone, and it is not my aim to persist in it; however, here is another classic example. For me, the deliciousness of this simple preparation cannot be surpassed. It is without question one of my favorite dishes in this book, and it is perfect on any American table.

> 1 bunch broccoli
> 3 cups cauliflower florets (1 small to medium head)
> ½ cup extra-virgin olive oil
> Sea salt and freshly ground pepper
> ¼ to ½ cup freshly made bread crumbs (page 7)

1.   Separate the broccoli florets. Take some of the heavy stems and cut away the bottom half of each and discard. Pare the remaining stems, using a small sharp knife, and cut in ½-inch slices. Use about 1 cup of the stems plus 3 cups of the broccoli florets to make 4 cups.

2.   Put the broccoli and cauliflower pieces in a large bowl and pour the olive oil over them. Toss well to be sure to coat all the vegetable pieces, as this helps seal in their moisture.

3. Preheat the oven to 425F. Arrange the vegetables in one layer in a baking pan. Bake for 8 minutes, turn over the vegetables and bake 8 minutes, until a wooden skewer can be inserted easily into the vegetables.

4. Remove the vegetables from the oven and season with salt and liberal amounts of pepper. Drizzle 1 or 2 tablespoons olive oil over the vegetables. If ready to serve now, sprinkle with bread crumbs. If serving later, add the bread crumbs when ready to serve. The dish may be served lukewarm.

PEACH "COBBLER" FROM THE COUNTESS D'ORBICCIANO

Dolce di pesche al forno alla Contessa d'Orbicciano
MAKES 4 TO 6 SERVINGS

Warrie Price, my friend who has a house just outside Lucca, was born in Texas instead of Italy. To compensate, she is an Italianophile of high order and is more Italian than Italians. Her home is filled with Italian antiques and artifacts down to the silverware and linens. Her plantings of rosemary and sage alongside her home seem larger than others in Italy and the Italian umbrella on the other side of her house seems larger than most and it is Italian. Her kitchen, though modern in every way, has the appearance that it has been there for hundreds of years. For example, she has a special place to cut fresh Lucca bread on a worn bread board, and below, a gathered skirt of a fine Italian print fabric to cover several utility shelves. She concocted this fabulous dessert in Italy because she says the peaches there taste better.

2 to 3 cups sliced, peeled fresh peaches
2 cups sugar
½ cup (1 stick) butter, melted
2 teaspoons baking powder
¼ teaspoon sea salt
¾ cup all-purpose flour
¾ cup milk
Purple Plum Ice Cream (page 57), to serve

1. Combine the peaches and 1 cup of the sugar in a bowl; toss and set aside.

2. Put the butter into an 8-inch-wide, 3-inch-deep soufflé or other baking dish. Preheat the oven to 350F.

3. Combine the remaining 1 cup sugar with the baking powder, salt, flour and milk in a bowl and stir well. Pour the batter into the soufflé dish with the butter; do not stir. Carefully spoon the peaches and their juices over the batter and again, do not stir.

4. Place the filled soufflé dish on a baking sheet with a rim and bake for 1 hour. (The cooked dough will have risen to the top of the dish and it will seem like a cobbler.) Remove from the oven, let rest a few minutes and serve with the ice cream.

PURPLE PLUM ICE CREAM

Gelato di prugne
MAKES 4 TO 6 SERVINGS

Purple plums make a wonderful ice cream that is sold all over Italy. These plums flood our supermarkets in summer and you can cook the plum pulp and freeze and save it for making ice cream anytime you wish.

3 cups, diced, pitted, peeled purple plums
    (6 to 8 plums)
¾ cup sugar
2½ cups milk
½ cup heavy cream, whipped
8 edible nasturtiums

1. In a medium saucepan, combine the plums and sugar and cook over medium heat until the sugar is dissolved and the plums are soft, 6 or 7 minutes. Transfer the plum mixture to the bowl of a food processor and pulse to a count of 10, until it is smooth. Strain this mixture, discarding the solids, and measure 2¼ cups puree; reserve remaining puree. Cover and refrigerate to chill completely.

2. Put the milk and 1½ cups of the chilled plum puree in an ice cream machine and freeze according to the manufacturer's instructions. When the ice cream is formed, transfer it to a freezer container with a lid and freeze for at least 1 hour.

3. If serving the ice cream on its own without the peach dish included in this menu, fold the remaining plum puree into the whipped cream; do not over combine, keep it streaked. Serve the ice cream with the plum cream and a nasturtium to the side of each serving.

A PICNIC FOR 6 IN PIENZA WITH THE CARDINAL GHOSTS OF THE POPE

MENU

Bacon Frittata with Parsley
Frittata con gli zoccoli

Fresh Beans with Tuna
Fagioli freschi al tonno

Herbed Chicken on the Grill
Pollo al mattone

Baked Mushrooms with Hazelnuts
Funghi con nocciole al forno

**Marinated Swiss Chard Stalks in
Poor Boy Wraps**
Coste di bietole nel sacco del mendicante

Famous Cookies from Siena
Ricciarelli di Siena

Italians love to eat outdoors, as do Americans, and this is a happy menu. The idea of a picnic in Italy isn't finger food on a checkered tablecloth; it is more like a four- to five-course Sunday lunch, eaten outdoors, under an umbrella or at wooden benches and tables with a grill nearby. Italian and American tastes come together here for these foods, many familiar to Americans, are comfortable and pleasurable.

Pienza is a tiny Renaissance gem of a town. It is essentially one street, now the Corso Rossellino, with a magnificent square, the Piazza Pio II, at its center. This square's main attraction is the Palazzo Piccolomini with its colonnaded courtyard the inner elegant courtyard is open to the sky, with a three-story arcade at the sides. It overlooks the hanging gardens at the back of the palace, a truly magnificent view of dome-shaped trees and clipped hedges. This town is the birthplace of Aeneas Silvius Piccolomini, born in 1405, and who became pope in 1458 as Pope Pius II. Next to the palazzo is the Duomo, a fine cathedral with lots of light; its interior contains worthy Sienese altarpieces. The picturesque well between these two major buildings makes it look like a stage set. The Corso is an avenue of food shops, and one of the most unique is the Club delle Fattorie, a mail-order food and wine business. On the spot, and through mail order, they sell dried porcini mushrooms, extra-virgin olive oils, balsamic vinegars, candied fruit, capers, pasta, marmalades, chocolates, candies and more. They will ship everything to the United States except alcohol. See Sources, page 269. The palace is oriented toward the volcanic cone of Monte Amiata, and in the summertime, the pope convened his cardinals under the shade of the chestnut trees. Let us find a chestnut tree, for this is the setting of this picnic.

Wine Selection

Two wines, a white and a red, are suitable. For the white, serve Terre di tufi, Bianco di Toscana IGT, produced by Teruzzi and Puthod. This is a bright straw-yellow colored wine with fresh fruit flavors of peach and apricot. For the red, serve Poggio Rosso Chianti Classico Riserva DOCG, produced by San Felice near Siena. It is ruby-rich with bouquets of berries and plums; it should be at least five years old.

Preparation Advice

1. All this food can be made the day ahead; it would be best to make the frittata in the morning of the day for the picnic and leave it at room temperature.

2. The cookies can be made days ahead, if stored properly or frozen.

BACON FRITTADA WITH PARSLEY

Frittata con gli zoccoli
MAKES 6 SERVINGS

Frittate are cooked until set on both sides (unlike the French who fold them over) in a skillet, and they are always filled with a variety of foods, especially vegetables, herbs, meats and cheese. They are served often at room temperature or cold, so they are ideal for picnics. They are served flat and cut into wedges or slices.

6 ounces unsmoked bacon (pancetta), cut into
    very small cubes
4 tablespoons extra-virgin olive oil
6 eggs, at room temperature
Sea salt and freshly ground pepper
3 tablespoons finely chopped fresh Italian parsley
¼ cup freshly grated Parmesan cheese

1. Sauté the bacon in 2 tablespoons of the olive oil in a large nonstick skillet over medium heat until it begins to crisp, stirring frequently, about 5 minutes. Drain and set aside. Leave the skillet as is, to receive the egg mixture below.

2. In a large bowl, whisk the eggs and add salt and pepper. Add the parsley, cheese and cooked bacon.

3. Add the remaining 2 tablespoons oil to the skillet the bacon was cooked in, heat it and pour the egg mixture into it. Cook over medium heat until the bottom of the frittata is lightly browned and the top begins to set, 6 to 8 minutes. Place a large plate over the skillet and turn it onto the plate. Slide the frittata back into the skillet and cook for several minutes, until set. Slide it onto a plate and serve at room temperature.

Notabene:

If you feel unsure about turning over a frittada and returning it to the skillet, turn on the broiler and set the skillet under it to finish cooking. Do not overcook.

FRESH BEANS WITH TUNA

Fagioli freschi al tonno
MAKES 6 SERVINGS

Classically simple, and Italian cooking at its best, this combination of foods should be made ahead and allowed to marinate for several hours. If using canned beans, put them in a colander, and run cool water over them for several washings to rid them of salt.

- 2 pounds fresh cranberry beans, shelled and rinsed, or 2 (16-ounce) cans cannellini beans, drained
- Salt
- 2 (6-ounce) cans Italian tuna packed in oil, such as Pastene or Genova
- 1/3 cup extra-virgin olive oil
- 1 tablespoon red wine vinegar
- 2 cloves garlic, minced
- 1/3 cup finely chopped red onion
- 1 tablespoon finely chopped fresh Italian parsley
- Pinch nutmeg
- Freshly ground pepper

1. Put the fresh beans in a large saucepan and cover them with cold water. Add some salt. Bring

to boil over medium-high heat, cover and cook until al dente, about 20 minutes.

2. Drain the cooked beans and let cool to room temperature. Combine the beans with all remaining ingredients. Toss lightly but well. Serve at room temperature.

HERBED CHICKEN ON THE GRILL

Pollo al mattone
MAKES 6 SERVINGS

This is a special way to prepare chicken in Tuscany. Although an entire half chicken is grilled, and here it is suggested that each grilled half then be cut in two, it can be sliced in even smaller portions, almost small enough to be eaten by hand at a picnic.

- 2 (about 3-pound) chickens, halved
- 2 tablespoons each finely chopped rosemary, thyme, basil and mint
- 4 tablespoons finely chopped fresh Italian parsley
- 4 medium cloves garlic, minced
- 1/2 cup plus extra-virgin olive oil
- Sea salt and freshly ground pepper

FOR BASTING
- 1/3 cup fresh lemon juice
- 1/3 cup extra-virgin olive oil

1. Taking care not to tear the skin, partially bone the chicken halves as follows: Cut off the wing tips, remove the drumstick bones and breastbones. Leave the wing bones, thigh bones and ribs in place to retain the shape. Wipe the chicken halves clean with a damp cloth. (If you choose not to bone the chickens in this manner, ask your butcher to do it for you.)

2. Combine the herbs, parsley, garlic, oil, salt and pepper to make a spreadable paste. (Add more oil if you think it should be thinner.) Coat the chicken halves with the paste, inside and out. Marinate, covered, overnight in the refrigerator. Bring the chicken to room temperature before grilling.

3. If you have a flattop grill, wipe it clean and preheat it to 325 to 350F and lightly oil it. If you don't have a flattop, prepare your fire for the grill and let it come to the gray ash stage. Be careful not to disturb the herb coating when placing the chicken on the grill. Top each piece with a heavy flat weight, such as a brick wrapped in foil.

4. Combine the basting ingredients, adding some salt and freshly ground pepper. After the chicken has cooked 5 minutes, drizzle 1 teaspoon of the basting mixture, using a spoon, not a brush, to avoid breaking the herb crust. Baste again in the same way after another 5 minutes, and carefully turn over the pieces. Carefully replace the weights. Baste again after 5 minutes and again after 10 minutes, at which time the chicken should be done. Cool and cut each chicken half in two or more pieces. This is very tasty at room temperature.

BAKED MUSHROOMS WITH HAZELNUTS

Funghi con nocciole al forno
MAKES 6 SERVINGS

It is amazing to discover the extent to which one ingredient can alter, or even glorify, the nature of a dish. In this case it is actually two ingredients, the hazelnuts and the bread crumbs (hopefully home-made), that glorify the mushrooms.

> 12 large mushrooms
> 2 tablespoons fresh lemon juice
> Sea salt and freshly ground pepper
> 4 tablespoons butter
> ½ cup finely chopped hazelnuts
> ¼ cup fresh bread crumbs (page 7)

1. Carefully remove the stem from each mushroom. If part of the stem is still attached to the cap, cut it away with a small paring knife. Reserve stems for another use or discard. Wipe each mushroom with a damp towel; do not wash. Lay the mushrooms on a baking sheet and sprinkle with lemon juice, salt and pepper.

2. Preheat the oven to 375F. Melt the butter in a skillet over medium-high heat, add the hazelnuts and sauté for 1 minute, stirring all the time. Remove from the heat.

3. Fill each mushroom cap with the hazelnuts. Sprinkle with the bread crumbs. Bake for 15 minutes, until golden brown, watching carefully for the last few minutes of baking; the mushroom caps should stay firm and not fall apart. Serve at room temperature.

MARINATED SWISS CHARD STALKS IN POOR BOY WRAPS

Coste di bietola nel sacco di mendicante
MAKES 12 PACKETS

Swiss chard looks like oversized spinach with very long white or red stems. Italians love this vegetable and prepare it in many ways. When buying it, go for a deep green color with crinkly and crisp leaves. Many Americans discard the long white or red stems; Italians do otherwise, and use them these ways: fried, steamed, baked, with marinades and salads and just sautéed with the green leaves, olive oil and garlic.

This picnic from Pienza, as most other alfresco meals, requires something special, a little out of the ordinary. Here, we take the stalks, cook and marinate them and put them in envelopes (some of which will be torn, thus the poor boy connotation) made with the dark green leaves. At first, this will seem labor-intensive, but if you read and reread the recipe, you will see it's quite a simple procedure, and best of all, they can be made ahead and travel well.

12 large fresh Swiss chard leaves, with red or
    white stalks
6 tablespoons extra-virgin olive oil
1 large potato, peeled and cut into ¼-inch dice
1 large or 2 small red onions, finely chopped
2 cloves garlic, minced
2 tablespoons red or white wine vinegar
1 tablespoon honey
2 tablespoons finely chopped fresh Italian parsley
Pinch red pepper flakes
Sea salt and freshly ground pepper

1. Wash and dry the leaves and cut out the stems with a scissors or a small sharp knife. If large, pare the stalks if they look stringy (as you would a celery stalk) and trim the rough edges and cut the stems into 1-inch lengths. Cook the stems in boiling, salted water until tender, 4 to 5 minutes. Drain well, dry with paper towels and put into a bowl. In the same boiling water, cook the whole leaves until tender, 2 to 3 minutes. Drain into cold water to keep them from cooking further and dry with paper towels. Set aside.

2. In a small skillet, heat 3 tablespoons of the oil and sauté the potatoes and onion until both are tender and take on some color, stirring constantly, 6 to 8 minutes. Add the garlic and cook 1 or 2 minutes. Transfer the potato mixture to the bowl with the stems in it. In a small bowl combine the remaining oil with the vinegar, honey, parsley, red pepper flakes, salt and pepper, and pour over the stem mixture. Mix lightly but well.

3. Carefully set 4 Swiss chard leaves on a flat work surface. In the center of each, put 1 tablespoon of stem mixture and fold the leaf into an envelope shape, first the flap closest to you, then fold in the two sides and then the top flap. Turn over and place it in an 11 × 7-inch glass dish. Continue making the envelopes and place them in the dish, making two rows of packets. If any of the stem mixture is left, spoon it down the center of the dish lengthwise, between the rows of packets. Do not cover the packets with this. Any liquid remaining in the bowl should be poured all over the packets. Cover and refrigerate if not ready to use, but be sure these come to room temperature before serving.

FAMOUS COOKIES FROM SIENA

Ricciarelli di Siena
MAKES 16 TO 20 COOKIES

When I was in Ilaria and Georgio Miani's sixteenth century house, which is situated in the soothing, undulating hills of the Val d'Orcia (an area recently made more famous by the filming of *The English Patient*), it was only a short drive to Siena where I could feast on fabulous cookies, called *ricciarelli*. One can buy them in many pastry shops, but the ones I liked best were made by San Domenico's on Via del Paradiso. I also found more in Pienza, Montalcino and Montepulciano, and other villages around Siena. They seem to be the regional cookie in these parts; eating one proves why. They are cookies one would expect to find in heaven. They are fairly easy to make and they were a treat in the afternoon with coffee, tea or an iced drink. While enjoying these in the pergola on a sunny afternoon, we were happy to look across the wheat fields, the clay hills and the landmark eleventh-century tower on the hill below and see the sky at sunset and the towns of Montalcino, Pienza, Montepulciano and Radiocafani perched on their hilltops and dream about this confection.

  2 egg whites, at room temperature
  7 ounces pure almond paste
  1 cup confectioners' sugar, plus extra for dusting
  1 teaspoon pure almond extract
  2 teaspoons minced orange zest

1. Preheat the oven to 275F. Line 2 baking sheets with parchment paper.

2. It is easiest to whip the egg whites in a mixer with a balloon whisk. Be sure the bowl is absolutely clean. Beat the egg whites until foamy and tripled to quadrupled in volume. (They will not be pure white as in meringue or form peaks. If they get to that stage, they have been whipped too much.) Set aside.

3. If the almond paste is in a block or formed like a sausage, it should be cut into $1/2$-inch cubes and then put in the bowl of a food processor and pulsed until softened. It should look like a smooth paste.

4. Add the 1 cup confectioners' sugar and the foamy egg whites to the food processor and mix until smooth. Blend in the almond extract and orange zest.

5. By teaspoonfuls, drop the mixture onto the parchment-lined baking sheets, spacing them at least 1 inch apart. Bake about 25 minutes, until the cookies are a very light tan or beige and firm to the touch.

6. The cookies should cool completely before removing them from the baking sheets; if they are not cool, some of the bottoms will stick to the parchment. Sprinkle with confectioners' sugar before serving. Store cooled cookies in an airtight container.

MEMORIES OF A TUSCAN GARDEN: LA FOCE: A MEAL FOR 8

MENU

Prosciutto with Cantaloupe
Prosciutto e melone

Chiara's Lasagnette with Meat Sauce
Lasagnetta di Chiara con ragu di manzo

Fresh Fennel Slices in Salad with Watercress
Insalata di finocchio e crescione

Orange Ring Cake, in a Modern Manner
Ciambellone all'arancia

In 1924, a property overlooking the Val d'Orcia in southern Tuscany, midway between Rome and Florence, was bought by Antonio and Iris Origo. They dedicated their lives to bringing prosperity and cultural and social changes to this once poverty-stricken land. When they bought the estate, they engaged the English architect Cecil Pinsent, who had previously done work on Bernard Berenson's villa, I Tatti, in Florence, to create a large garden and to restructure the main buildings. Today, there are formal Italian gardens surrounding the villa, divided in geometrical spaces by box hedges enclosing lemon trees in terra-cotta pots. Travertine steps lead to a rose garden, wisteria vines cover a pergola and there's an incredible lavender hedge. From this area, across the undulating hills, one can see the Renaissance towns of Pienza, Montalcino and Montepulciano. This scene and the food enjoyed there at lunch on several occasions is what memories are made of. If you haven't been there, no matter, just prepare this meal and envision the garden and the villa, which was originally built in the fifteenth century. Chiara is a young lady who cooks at La Foce. I have taken the liberty of interpreting this meal we enjoyed there.

Wine Selection

A lovely Tuscan wine, Vino Nobile di Montepulciano, is like a Chianti but it is made with more white grapes, and the method for making it is different from the Chianti because this wine is not intended to be drunk young from a *fiasco*. It comes from the pleasant town of Montepulcino, a small hill town near Siena. It may not live as long as Brunello, but it is certainly a fine red wine. It is protected by the Senese association of growers and carries the she-wolf label.

Preparation Advice

1. The main course and the dessert can be made the day before. Refrigerate the lasagnette but keep the cake, covered, at room temperature.

2. The fennel can be trimmed and sliced and may be stored with the watercress in a plastic bag in the refrigerator one day ahead.

PROSCIUTTO WITH CANTALOUPE

Prosciutto e melone
MAKES 8 SERVINGS

The reason Tuscan bread is not salted is because it is eaten most often with their salty ham preparations, such as Tuscan prosciutto. Because the ham is salty, it is a good match with the fresh lemony cantaloupe. It also works well with other melons such as Crenshaw and honeydew. If fresh figs are in season, purple or green, use them instead of the melon, another excellent combination. Some people like to peel the figs, but that is up to you.

> 2 ripe cantaloupes, peeled, seeded, and cut into
>   16 lengths
> 2 lemons, cut into 4 wedges each, trimmed of core
>   and seeds
> Freshly ground pepper
> 24 paper-thin slices of Tuscan prosciutto or Parma
>   ham

1. Arrange 2 melon slices on each individual plate and place a lemon wedge to the side. Liberally apply pepper over the melon.

2. Drape 3 prosciutto slices over each, being sure to expose at least one half of the melon. It is preferred that the prosciutto lays on part of the plate also. If the melon and prosciutto have been refrigerated, leave at room temperature for 15 minutes or so before serving.

CHIARA'S LASAGNETTE WITH MEAT SAUCE

Lasagnetta di Chiara con ragu di manzo
MAKES 8 SERVINGS WITH LEFTOVERS

Any leftovers will keep well, refrigerated up to a week, and may be reheated.

FOR THE PASTA
2 cups all-purpose unbleached flour
1½ cups semolina flour
Salt
4 large eggs
1 tablespoon extra-virgin olive oil, preferably Tuscan
2 tablespoons cold water

FOR THE MEAT SAUCE
¾ cup extra-virgin olive oil, preferably Tuscan
1 medium onion, minced
2 carrots, trimmed and minced
2 ribs celery, strings removed, and minced
¼ cup finely chopped basil
2 fresh sage leaves and 2 bay leaves
2 cloves garlic, minced
2 pounds lean ground beef
1 cup white wine
1 (35-ounce) can plum tomatoes, chopped with juice
Good pinch nutmeg
Sea salt and freshly ground pepper

FOR THE BESCIAMELLA SAUCE
3 cups milk, preferably whole
1 cup unbleached all-purpose flour
½ teaspoon freshly grated nutmeg
Sea salt and freshly ground pepper
1½ cups (3 sticks) butter, at room temperature

1 to 1½ cups freshly grated Parmesan cheese

1. *To make the pasta:* Sift both flours together with a good pinch of salt onto a flat work surface for kneading dough. Using your hands, make a well in the center.

2. In a small bowl, combine the eggs, oil and water. Whisk until combined and pour into the well. Start incorporating the flour into the well by using a fork in one hand and steadying the flour wall with the other. Keep doing this until all the flour has been mixed in. Then flour your hands and knead the dough for 8 to 10 minutes, until the dough is smooth. Divide the dough into six pieces.

3. Using a pasta machine (page 11), roll out first in the widest opening, lightly flour each strip and put aside until all six have been passed through the wide opening. Cut each in half, crosswise. Put them through the next to narrowest opening. Cut these lengths of dough into squares. These are called *lasagnette;* don't be too serious about all the squares being equal in size. If the pasta is 4 inches as it is cranked through the pasta machine, feel free to cut the pasta into 4 × 6 inches; if the pasta width is 5 inches, cut the "squares" into 5 × 5, or 5 × 6, or 5 × 7. Put these pasta pieces on lightly floured towels, cover with another cloth, and set aside until ready to cook them. If they sit more than 30 minutes, refrigerate until needed.

4. *To make the meat sauce:* Heat the oil in a large heavy saucepan and sauté the onion, carrots, celery, basil, sage leaves and bay leaves over medium

heat, uncovered, for 8 minutes, stirring frequently. Add the garlic and cook for 1 to 2 minutes.

5. Add the beef and break it up with a wooden spoon. Cook over medium heat, uncovered, until the meat loses its color, about 10 minutes, stirring frequently. Add the wine and cook about 5 minutes, to evaporate the wine.

6. Add the tomatoes and their juices, increase the heat and bring to a boil. Reduce the heat, cover the saucepan and simmer for 20 minutes, stirring once or twice. Add the nutmeg, salt and pepper.

7. *To make the besciamella sauce:* In a medium, heavy saucepan, bring the milk just to the boiling point. Whisking all the time, add the flour, nutmeg, salt and pepper. Cook over medium heat, stirring constantly, until the sauce thickens, about 10 minutes. If needed, reduce the heat.

8. Add the butter, a spoonful at a time, until all of it is incorporated.

9. *To assemble the lasagnette:* Preheat the oven to 350F. Bring a large pot of water to a boil. Add 1 teaspoon salt and the pasta. Bring back to a boil, cook 3 minutes and immediately drain the pasta and put it into cold water to stop the cooking. Drain the pasta, and place on cloth towels and pat dry with paper towels.

10. In a large (about 12 × 10-inch) baking dish, make layers as follows: Spoon some besciamella sauce first, then spoon some meat sauce, then layer with the pasta and some Parmesan cheese. Continue this layering until six layers of pasta have been used. (You may have a few pieces of pasta left; cover them, refrigerate and use later in soup or another dish.) Top the pasta with meat sauce, then besciamella sauce and finally some Parmesan cheese. Bake for 30 minutes. Remove from the oven, let sit for 5 to 10 minutes before serving.

FRESH FENNEL SLICES IN SALAD WITH WATERCRESS

Insalata di finocchio e crescione
MAKES 8 SERVINGS

Fresh fennel is a large white bulb with pale green, feathery leaves. The bulb should be snow white and firm when you buy it. A favorite in Italy long before it gained popularity in the United States, this anise-flavored vegetable is sometimes called sweet or Florentine (and sometimes Roman) fennel. Modern Italians fuss over it as much as did the ancient Romans.

> 3 large heads fresh fennel with some
>   leaves
> 2 bunches watercress
> 6 tablespoons extra-virgin olive oil, preferably
>   Tuscan
> 2 tablespoons herbed white wine vinegar
> 2 tablespoons capers, rinsed and dried
> 1/2 teaspoon sugar
> Sea salt and freshly ground pepper

1. Rinse and dry the fennel and trim, removing any blemished outer leaves. Cut each bulb in half, and slice each half as thinly as possible. Chop the very young pale green fronds to include in the salad. Put the fennel in a large bowl.

2. Rinse and pick over the watercress. Cut off tough stems but leave watercress as sprays. Dry as well as you can and add to the salad bowl.

3. In a smaller bowl, combine the oil, vinegar, capers, sugar, salt and a liberal amount of pepper, and mix well. Pour over the fennel and watercress. Toss lightly but well.

ORANGE RING CAKE, IN A MODERN MANNER

Ciambellone all'arancia
MAKES 8 TO 10 SERVINGS

Ciambellone is a Florentine orange-flavored cake that is usually served at teatime. It has been enjoyed by the Florentines for many years and one can still find it in some pastry shops, but I had difficulty finding it. Perhaps it is not as popular as it used to be. Here is an updated version, which is very tasty, served with a dollop of whipped cream. The secret of this cake lies in the syrup.

FOR THE CAKE
1 cup butter, at room temperature
1 cup sugar
4 eggs, separated, at room temperature
1 cup sour cream
2 tablespoons finely chopped orange zest
2 cups all-purpose flour
1 teaspoon baking powder
1 teaspoon baking soda

FOR THE SYRUP
Juice of 1 orange
Juice of 1 lemon
3/4 cup sugar
1/4 cup orange liqueur

TO ASSEMBLE AND SERVE
1 cup heavy cream, whipped
4 thin slices of orange, seeded, cut into halves

1. *To make the cake:* Preheat the oven to 325F. Oil and flour a 9-inch tube pan. Cream the butter and sugar until well blended. Add the egg yolks, sour cream and orange zest. Beat until light and fluffy and a ribbon is formed when the beaters are raised.

2. In a large bowl, sift together the flour, baking powder and soda. Fold the flour mixture into the butter mixture. Beat the egg whites until stiff, but not dry, and fold them into the mixture.

3. Pour the batter into prepared pan. Bake for 1 hour, until center of cake springs back when lightly pressed. Remove the cake and let it sit for 15 to 20 minutes. When the pan is cool enough to handle, very carefully loosen around the edge of the cake with a sharp knife, and invert the cake onto a cake platter.

4. While the cake bakes, combine the syrup ingredients in a small saucepan. Boil gently until the mixture turns into a syrup, about 5 minutes.

5. Spoon the syrup over the cake and let it soak in. Cut the cake into 1/2-inch slices and serve with whipped cream and orange slice half.

ONE-DISH MEALS

ROAST LOIN OF PORK WITH ROSEMARY

Arista di maiale
MAKES 6 SERVINGS

If you ask anyone what is the favorite meat dish in Florence, you undoubtedly will get as an answer: *bistecca*, beef steak. Or the answer might be *pollo alla diavolo*, chicken, split open, flattened and grilled, somewhat similar to the chicken preparation on page 59, except that this chicken dish is served with a ginger sauce. The third reply will surely be *arista alla fiorentina*, roast loin of pork. What makes the difference between roast pork in Florence and elsewhere is rosemary in its seasoning along with garlic and cloves. Another important difference is that it is basted with water and not oil. This is a very old preparation and has been cooked this way since the fifteenth century. I learned to cook it in this manner by an adopted niece of mine, Ivana Fabbrizzio in Contignano (a province of Siena), who emphasized again and again the importance of basting with water. It was wonderful to see her step outside the kitchen door and clip as much fresh rosemary as anyone would want or could use. Ivana always hung the day's laundry on a clothesline just outside the house, and I could catch a glimpse of her through the laundry pieces hung on the line, bending over to snip the rosemary. The road to Contignano winds uphill, affording views of an incomparable countryside. As you drive through acres of fields with wheat waving in the breeze as if to the beat of a metronome, and get closer to the village, you see luxuriant gardens, olive-clad slopes and lines of cypress trees. And there is always the ever-present clothesline of Ivana's laundry, soaking up the sun. Imagine this setting as you prepare this pork with rosemary.

1 (4-pound) loin of pork, center cut
2 pieces rosemary, each 4 or 5 inches long, plus
    2 teaspoons finely chopped
3 cloves garlic, minced
Sea salt and freshly ground pepper
6 whole cloves
12 small new potatoes, peeled
1 (15-ounce) can green peas or 1 (10-ounce)
    package frozen

1. Preheat the oven to 450F. Make 8 or 10 slits in the meat and insert some chopped rosemary and garlic in each slit. Transfer to a baking pan and liberally sprinkle salt and pepper all over the meat. Place 1 piece of rosemary on each side of the meat. Push the cloves into the meat. Pour 2 cups water around the meat.

2. Roast 1 hour and 45 minutes to 2 hours, basting every 15 minutes or so. As the roast cooks and its fat melts, it will combine with the water. Use this liquid to baste the meat. After 45 minutes of roasting, add the potatoes. Add more water, if needed; the baking pan should always have some water in it. Add canned or frozen peas 15 minutes before the pork is done.

3. Remove from the oven, let the roast stand 5 to 10 minutes. Slice and serve with potatoes and peas and a sliced beet salad.

CHICKEN, KALE AND CHICKPEA STEW

Pollo, cavolo nero e ceci in umido
MAKES 6 SERVINGS

Italians enjoy and use dried legumes *(legumi secchi)*; chickpeas, known as *ceci* are quite popular. In the United States, these dishes are easy to prepare because of the availability of canned legumes, which do not need to be soaked and cooked. In using these canned chickpeas or other beans, it is important to rinse the contents of the can under running water to flush away the large amount of salt they contain. Simply empty the contents of the can into a colander and run under cool water, tossing the legumes with your hands. Drain well and proceed with the recipe. This makes a good one-dish meal and it is better if served with a crisp fresh green salad with a simple oil-and-vinegar dressing. Consider hearts of curly endive with thin slices of celery hearts for the salad.

2 tablespoons extra-virgin olive oil
1 large onion, chopped
1 green bell pepper, chopped
2 cloves garlic, minced
3/4 pounds kale, chopped into 1-inch pieces
1 pound chicken breasts, cut into 1-inch pieces
1 (28-ounce) can plum tomatoes, undrained, chopped
2 (15-ounce) cans chickpeas, drained
2 cups Chicken Broth (page 8) or 1 (14 1/2-ounce) can low-sodium chicken broth
2 tablespoons tomato paste
1/2 teaspoon sugar
1/2 teaspoon each ground cumin, dried oregano, crushed red pepper flakes and dried thyme
1 bay leaf

TO SERVE
6 bruschetta (page 6, optional)
6 tablespoons freshly grated Parmesan cheese

1. In a heavy saucepan with a cover, heat the oil and sauté the onion and bell pepper for 6 to 8 minutes, stirring frequently. Add the garlic and sauté 1 minute.

2. Stir in the kale and all the other ingredients. Bring to a boil, reduce the heat to get a good, steady simmer. Partially cover the pot and simmer for 30 minutes, until the kale and chicken are cooked. Stir several times during cooking.

3. Serve over a piece of bruschetta if you wish. Top each serving with 1 tablespoon cheese.

RISOTTO WITH CHICKEN LIVERS, TUSCAN STYLE

Risotto coi fegatini di pollo
MAKES 6 SERVINGS

Any description of Tuscany that concentrates on its major cities would exclude the impact of the men and women and their families of the small towns and villages, whose inheritance is abundant. Quintessential Tuscany is expressed also in the many small, ancient, harmonious villages such as Artimino, Cetona, Saturnis or Pitigliano, not simply in the three or four largest cities. A dish may be called *alla fiorentina* or *alla Toscana*, and the large cities may claim ownership of these recipes, but village housewives created most of these dishes. This risotto with chicken livers may be known as *alla Toscana*, but it probably was created in one of the smaller towns, such as Radicofani, in southern Tuscany, where I enjoyed it at the Trattoria La Grotta. In Radicofani, the main square is dominated by the campanile of the thirteenth-century

Romanesque church of San Pietro, which houses important art works by the Della Robbia family. Everywhere in the countryside, there is the classic Tuscan landscape with a village perched up high. For miles, one sees Radicofani's hill crowned by the tower of San Pietro. In the village, the late Renaissance fountain in the Via Cassia bears the strong, unforgettable Medici coat of arms. Imagine a village cook concocting this dish in 1605.

1 pound chicken livers

Salt

4 tablespoons extra-virgin olive oil

1 large onion, finely chopped

1²/₃ cups Italian rice (Arborio, Vialone Nano or Carnaroli)

1 cup Buttery Tomato Sauce (page 164)

3 to 4 cups chicken or vegetable broth

6 tablespoons butter

Freshly ground pepper

¹/₂ cup freshly grated Parmesan cheese

2 tablespoons finely chopped fresh sage

1. Rinse the chicken livers and cut away fat and connecting tissues. Rinse again and pat dry. Salt liberally and chop each liver lobe into 2 or 3 pieces. Set aside in a bowl.

2. Heat the oil in a saucepan over medium heat and sauté the onion until translucent, about 5 minutes. Add the rice and stir well to combine the rice with the oil and onion.

3. Add the tomato sauce and ¹/₂ cup broth, bring to a boil, reduce the heat to achieve a steady simmer, and cook for 20 minutes, stirring almost constantly and adding additional broth, ¹/₂ cup at a time, until the rice is tender.

4. While the rice is cooking, melt 3 tablespoons of the butter in a skillet over medium heat and sauté the chicken livers until nicely browned, 6 to 8 minutes.

5. Add the livers to the rice, scraping the skillet with a rubber spatula. Simmer the rice for up to 10 minutes more. Taste for doneness and for seasoning. If more salt is needed, add it and a liberal amount of pepper. Fold in the remaining 3 tablespoons butter.

6. Combine the cheese and sage in a small bowl. Serve the rice and livers in a bowl, platter or individual plates with a good sprinkle of Parmesan and sage.

WHITE BEANS WITH MUSHROOMS

Fagioli ai funghi
MAKES 8 SERVINGS

Everyone knows of Tuscany and its Chianti wine and Fiorentina steak, but not everyone knows that the region's best-kept secret lies with its humblest ingredients: beans and bread. *Fagioli*, small white beans, are eaten in large quantities throughout the region, dressed up in many different ways at most meals. The Tuscans are known by their fellow countrymen as *mangiafagioli* (bean eaters), often said in a somewhat uncomplimentary fashion. As a rule, the beans are served simply. In one of the most dramatic Tuscan recipes, beans are cooked in a wine flask, *fagioli nel fiasco*; they are actually cooked in an empty Chianti wine flask because the narrow opening of the bottle keeps steam from escaping and the beans retain maximum flavor. They cool in the flask and are then served with olive oil, fresh lemon juice and seasonings. In the following upscale recipe, they are joined with mushrooms, onions, garlic, celery and wine to make a one-dish meal, served over the ubiquitous slice of bread, toasted and rubbed with garlic and oil. The unusual personal touch here is to reserve some of the beans and marinate them, to be added as an extra layer of taste. This is a nourishing dish on its own; however, enhance it by adding a salad of sliced fresh oranges, papaya or grapefruit with a splash of lemon juice and a sprinkle of freshly ground pepper.

6 tablespoons extra-virgin olive oil, preferably
    Tuscan
1 medium onion, finely chopped
2 cups thinly cut celery, including leaves
8 cloves garlic, minced
16 ounces dried white beans (2 cups), sorted,
    soaked overnight in water and drained
1 teaspoon salt
1 teaspoon plus ½ teaspoon freshly ground
    pepper
1 tablespoon white wine vinegar
1 teaspoon finely chopped fresh rosemary
2 pounds fresh mushrooms, wiped with moist
    paper towels, ends trimmed and thinly sliced
¼ cup dried mushrooms soaked in warm water 30
    minutes, drained and finely chopped
½ cup white wine
2 to 3 cups vegetable broth

TO SERVE
8 slices bruschetta (page 6)
1 cup freshly grated Parmesan cheese

1.   Heat 1 tablespoon of the olive oil in a large flameproof and ovenproof casserole over medium heat. Add the onion, celery and garlic and cook until the onion becomes translucent, about 5 minutes.

2.   Add the drained beans, salt and 1 teaspoon pepper. Add water to cover the beans by 1 inch. Bring to a boil, reduce the heat to get a steady simmer, cover the casserole and simmer for 1 hour, until the beans are tender. Remove 1 cup of the beans and put in a bowl with 3 tablespoons of the olive oil, the vinegar, rosemary and remaining pepper. Stir well and set aside.

3.   Heat the remaining 2 tablespoons of oil in a skillet and add the fresh and dried mushrooms. Cook over medium-high heat, stirring frequently, until the mushrooms are tender, about 15 minutes. Add the wine, toss lightly but well, increase the heat and cook until the wine is reduced by about half. Set the skillet aside.

4.   Puree the beans in the casserole (these are the ones not marinating) in a food processor and return to the casserole in which they originally cooked. Add the mushrooms and their liquid and 2 cups vegetable broth. Cook over medium heat for 15 minutes. If you think more liquid is needed add some or all of the remaining broth, but remember the mixture should be thick.

5.   To serve, put a bruschetta in each of 8 flat rimmed-bowls and spoon some of the bean mixture over the bread. Top with 1 tablespoon of the cold marinated beans. Sprinkle with some of the Parmesan and pass more of the cheese for those who want it.

THE ITALIAN RIVIERA

LIGURIA AND THE NORTHEAST CORNER OF ITALY, PIEMONTE AND VALLE D'AOSTA

P ut on the gastronomic map by the seafaring Ligurians whose cuisine is the color green, as in pesto, this area excels in fresh herbs, vegetables and sweet extra-virgin olive oil. Many of Italy's finest wines and food come from the Piedmont area of Italy.

The Italian region of Liguria—many call it the Italian Riviera—has always faced the sea because mountains lock in this northwest corner of the country. From the western border, curving around the Ligurian Sea (at Genoa), and going south to Tuscany, the Alps have forced the fishing villages into craggy coves and confined the city streets up the mountainside.

Pesto made this area famous and you will find it served on pasta called *trenette* (the local fettucine). See how a famous chef makes it on page 76. Fish and shellfish are emphasized in their cuisine, such as sea bass, *bronzino*, in white wine, tomatoes and garlic. See it as carpaccio on page 82. Portofino, perhaps its most fashionable resort, has dramatic sea views and a busy piazza on its tiny harbor where clams and mussels in various preparations appear on trattoria menus. For one of the best preparations, see page 79.

North of Liguria is Piedmont (Turin) and north of it is Val d'Aosta, both areas dominated by the Alps and their raw cliffs, evergreen forests and cradled pastures. Piedmont is known for Lago Maggiore and Lago d'Orta, its Barolo wine and the Fiats produced in Turin. Val d'Aosta is a land of skiers, mountain climbers and cold weather in which to enjoy the *fonduta,* the local cheese dish made with the world-famous Fontina cheese (page 89), and beef cooked in Barolo wine (page 87). The food in Piedmont is sophisticated and over hundreds of years, its fame has spread. Even in France, there are a number of dishes called *a la piemontese.*

Lunch for 6 at Home with the Ottolenghis in Genoa

MENU

Genovese Squid Salad with Vegetables for Ligurian Sailors
Insalata di calamari alla Genovese
con verdure

Focaccia with Marjoram and Olive Oil (page 5, substituting 2 tablespoons chopped fresh marjoram for the sage)
Focaccia col maggiorana, sale e olio

Chocolate Mocha Ricotta Cake
Torta di ricotta al cioccolato

The food here is wonderful but the story is sad. Renato Ottolenghi was an Italian, a Genovese, working in New York City. Our friendship was based on two important points: the first, we met frequently to go to Italian restaurants. Renato loved to eat. The second reason was that I could converse in Italian. I had not been to Genoa during these frequent meetings so he would fill the air with conversation about life in Genoa, much of which had to do with the food of the area, the *trenette* (pasta) with pesto sauce, the pizzas with the beautiful Ligurian olive oil, black olives and garlic, the eel and trout dishes from the River Nervia, the special salad called *condiglione* (page 76). He didn't talk much about his parents, both alive at the time, and I rarely questioned the subject. But when he heard I was planning a trip to Italy and would visit Genoa, he arranged for me to meet them and I did. The salon, or foyer, of their apartment was the size of most American apartments. It was huge and one entire wall was covered with etched glass doors, each door with a bullet hole; the holes were placed as if it had been planned. I knew something was wrong. I was taken to a small room with a potbellied stove and a table obviously set up for them to have meals, instead of using the large, heavily decorated dining room. They were gracious and welcoming. He was a pediatrician (I later found out he was considered one of the leading doctors in Italy); his wife was Jewish. At the time of World War II, the Nazis had burned the books in his library, shot at the antique glass doors and forced his wife into hiding. They were eventually reunited. I spent one evening with them in their home of broken glass. They offered me this salad, so typical of Genoese cooking. It was an evening I have never forgotten.

Wine Selection

The passing tourist in Liguria may notice many vineyards as he drives along the coastal road. Most of them are small pieces of land cultivated to provide a family with its own simple table wine; in other words, these wines are not for sale. Most of the wine production in this region is concentrated around Genoa, and near La Spezia. Not many Ligurian wines are found other than where they are grown. Perhaps the best known wine is Cinque Terre (five lands) and this is found in U.S. wine shops.

Preparation Advice

1. The bread and dessert can be made ahead; the cake by as much as a day. Make the focaccia the day of the meal.

2. The squid salad ingredients may be prepped in the morning but the salad should be brought together shortly before mealtime.

GENOVESE SQUID SALAD WITH VEGETABLES FOR LIGURIAN SAILORS

Insalata di calamari alla Genovese con verdure
MAKES 6 SERVINGS

Genoa, in the northern province of Liguria, is celebrated for its many fish preparations. This is easy to understand as the sea provides many of the raw materials of Genoese cooking. Two classic fish soups are *ciuppin*, a pureed soup similar to the French *bouillabaisse*, and *burrida*, a soup of vari-

ous fish difficult to get in the United States. They are featured in Genoa's restaurants. Fish salads are also among the dishes offered. A famous one in Genoa is *cappon magro* (a Christmas Eve tradition) and it is delicious, but it is rather difficult to make at home, as it requires a minimum of twenty-five ingredients. Here is a delicious fish salad from this part of the world that is considerably easier to make.

This squid salad was fashioned for Ligurian sailors who spent months away from home on the high seas transporting spices to be traded. During these sea journeys, they yearned for the fresh-tasting vegetables and herbs they sorely missed during their dangerous and long sea voyages. I first tasted this squid salad at the home of the Ottolenghis.

1½ pounds cleaned squid, cut into ¼-inch rings
4 cloves garlic, minced
2 cups Italian red wine
1½ pounds new potatoes
Sea salt
12 ounces fresh green beans, trimmed and cut into 2-inch lengths
4 sun-dried tomatoes packed in oil, drained and thinly sliced
Freshly ground pepper
7 tablespoons extra-virgin olive oil
3 tablespoons red wine vinegar
Good pinch of red pepper flakes
¼ cup thinly sliced fresh basil leaves or fresh marjoram

1. Preheat the oven to 350F. In a ceramic or glass baking dish, combine the squid, half of the garlic and the wine, and cook, covered, about 50 minutes, until the squid is tender.

2. Brush the potatoes clean and put them into a saucepan. Cover with water, add 1 teaspoon salt, cover and bring to a boil. Reduce the heat, and simmer for about 20 minutes, until tender. Remove

the potatoes but keep the water in the pan. Add the green beans to the water and cook for 5 minutes. Drain the beans.

3.   Slice the potatoes ¼ inch thick and put them into a large mixing bowl. Add the warm beans and the sun-dried tomatoes. Add salt and pepper.

4.   Combine the oil, vinegar, the remaining garlic and red pepper flakes and pour over the salad. Drain the squid, discarding the wine mixture, and fold it into the salad. Taste for salt and seasoning. Sprinkle basil or marjoram over the salad. This dish is usually served warm.

CHOCOLATE MOCHA RICOTTA CAKE

Torta di ricotta al cioccolato
MAKES 8 TO 10 SERVINGS

Ricotta is used in cooking all over Italy in both sweet and savory preparations. Ricotta means "recooked" because the remaining whey from hard cheeses and some fresh milk are heated to produce a white curd cheese with a wonderfully soft texture. When ricotta is freshly made, it is usually put into baskets to drain; the basket shape and markings are known as *cestelli*, meaning "little baskets." The Italians love ricotta so much, they eat it fresh with some honey and thyme (page 180). If at all possible, try to find a cheese shop near you that makes fresh ricotta; it is a different product than the one in plastic containers on supermarket shelves.

In Italy, cheesecake is made in every *pasticceria*, because the Italians love it.

15 ounces fresh whole ricotta
½ cup sugar plus 1 tablespoon sugar
¼ cup all-purpose flour

2 eggs
1 teaspoon vanilla extract
6 tablespoons unsweetened cocoa powder plus extra for dusting
1 tablespoon espresso granules
2 egg whites

1.   Put several thicknesses of cheesecloth into a colander and place the ricotta in it. Cover with more cheesecloth. Weight it lightly and let sit in a bowl in the refrigerator for 3 hours to drain. (This may sit overnight, but be sure the ricotta is covered).

2.   Preheat the oven to 350F. Add the drained ricotta, ¼ cup of the sugar, flour, eggs, vanilla, cocoa powder and espresso granules to the bowl of a food processor and process just until smooth. Transfer the ricotta mixture into a large bowl and set aside.

3.   Butter a 6-inch springform pan and sprinkle with 1 tablespoon sugar. Turn pan over slightly, tap it gently to remove any excess sugar. Set aside.

4.   Combine the egg whites and remaining ¼ cup sugar in a large bowl; place it over simmering water and whisk for several minutes, until the sugar is dissolved. Off the heat, beat with an electric hand mixer for about 10 minutes, until the whites form stiff peaks. Carefully fold the meringue into the ricotta in thirds. Transfer the mixture to the prepared pan.

5.   Bake for about 40 minutes, until the center is firm. Remove from the oven; set on a cooling rack for 15 or 20 minutes. Remove the side of the pan, dust the cheesecake with cocoa powder using a small strainer, and serve.

PASSING TIME IN PORTOFINO WITH CHEF GILBERTO PIZZI: MENU FOR 6

MENU

Spaghetti with Chef Gilberto Pizzi's Genuine Basil Pesto
Spaghetti al pesto di Gilberto Pizzi

Ligurian Vegetable Salad
Condiglione

Ice Cream with Sambuca and Espresso
Gelato con Sambuca ed espresso

The idyllic resort town of Portofino sits on a spectacularly beautiful harbor, just a short twenty or so miles from Genoa in the region called Liguria. It is one of my favorite places to visit in all of Italy and the location of one of my favorite spots, the Hotel Splendido. On my visits, I never miss an opportunity to climb the hill to the Splendido to sit on its terrace covered with 150-year-old wisteria vines. On one occasion, I had the opportunity to meet Chef Gilberto Pizzi, creator of this pesto recipe. As the sun sets on the Gulf of Rapallo, it is absolutely magical as the views unfold between the yew trees, sea pines and olive trees, their reflections shimmering in the gulf, and as the waning light of sunset washes over the terrace floor reflecting also the colors of the tranquil sky.

The history of this Ligurian province is essentially the history of its main port, Genoa, which along with Pisa and Venice, were the great seafaring city states of the Middle Ages. Christopher Columbus and Andrea Doria were from Genoa.

Genoa had a trading empire that reached from Sardinia into North Africa on to Syria, its riches beyond belief. In 1293, its customs duties were seven times the entire revenue of the King of France. These days, the region is better known for its small beach resort towns and its pesto than for its history. Portofino is considered one of the most picturesque of these coastal towns and the Hotel Splendido its most stunning hotel. All over Liguria, basil is everywhere, on windowsills, doorsteps, balconies, rooftops, terraces, alleyways and in window boxes where the herb flourishes in saucepans, vases, empty tins, new and old flowerpots, each tended with loving care. Products of this warm Mediterranean climate include fresh herbs, tasty early-ripening vegetables and the delicately perfumed olive oil, essential to the preparation of pesto, the crushed basil sauce that put Liguria on the food map.

Wine Selection

Make a choice between a white and red, or have a bottle of each. The DOC Riviera Ligure di Ponente produces a Vermentino that is a fresh, delicate, white wine. Or choose a Brolettino Lugana DOC produced by Ca'dei Fratu. A Pornassio Ormeasco is a spicy red wine.

Preparation Advice

1. The pesto can be made ahead by several hours and left at room temperature until needed, or made the day before and refrigerated and brought to room temperature one hour before needed.

2. The salad ingredients can be prepped and refrigerated until needed and then dressed.

3. The spaghetti should be cooked at the last minute.

SPAGHETTI WITH CHEF GILBERTO PIZZI'S GENUINE BASIL PESTO

Spaghetti al pesto di Gilberto Pizzi
MAKES 6 SERVINGS

Pesto purists will mash garlic and salt in a marble mortar with a wooden pestle adding a few basil leaves at a time; they work the pestle to pulverize the basil, adding pine nuts and mashing them. Then they add grated Parmesan and pecorino cheeses to form a thick paste. To finish off the pesto, extra-virgin olive oil is added to thin the paste. Of course, this is an excellent way to prepare it, but most people resort to blenders and food processors. I find a good compromise is to process the basil, nuts and garlic with a little oil and the cheeses, and then add the remaining oil slowly while the motor is running. I almost always have to thin the paste a little with some hot water. It is important to add some salt at the appropriate time.

> 80 small fresh basil leaves
> ¼ cup pine nuts
> 4 large cloves garlic, coarsely chopped
> ½ cup freshly grated Parmesan cheese
> ¼ cup freshly grated pecorino cheese, such as Romano
> 14 tablespoons extra-virgin olive oil, preferably from Liguria
> ¼ cup hot water
> Sea salt and freshly ground pepper
> 1 pound spaghetti

1. Combine the basil, pine nuts, garlic, cheeses and 7 tablespoons of the oil in a food processor. Turn on the processor, and as the ingredients become minced and combined with the oil (count to 15), pour the hot water and some salt and pepper in through the feed tube. Adding salt at this point is important for it will prevent discoloration of the pesto. Add just a little salt as the cheeses are salty. More salt can be added later if needed.

2. While the motor is running, add the remaining olive oil slowly through the feed tube until all is absorbed into the pesto (about a count of 10); the whole procedure should take less than 3 minutes. Transfer the pesto to a large bowl or platter, large enough to receive the pasta.

3. Cook the spaghetti in salted water according to the package directions, drain well, setting aside 1 cup of the hot salted water. Put the cooked pasta into the bowl or platter with the pesto and toss lightly and well. If it seems dry, add some of the pasta water, by tablespoons, until you achieve the desired sauce consistency. Serve right away.

LIGURIAN VEGETABLE SALAD

Condiglione
MAKES 6 SERVINGS

The Ligurians have a penchant for fresh green herbs and fresh vegetables and here is a famous salad of the region. The desire for fresh herbs and vegetables dates to the region's history of seafaring—sailors on long voyages, subsisting on salt meat and dried beans, wanted and were given the freshest foods as part of the celebration of their homecoming.

> 1 (6-ounce) can tuna in oil
> 6 ripe medium tomatoes, peeled, cut into wedges

1 small cucumber, peeled and thinly
    sliced
2 shallots, peeled and thinly sliced
1 red, yellow or orange bell pepper, seeded, ribs
    removed and thinly sliced
10 black olives, pitted and chopped
2 hard-cooked eggs, cut into wedges
1 teaspoon finely chopped anchovies
1 teaspoon dried oregano, crushed
¼ cup finely chopped fresh basil
1 clove garlic, minced
¾ cup extra-virgin olive oil
Sea salt and freshly ground pepper

1. Add the ingredients from the tuna to the eggs
to a large salad bowl or large platter.

2. In a small bowl, combine the remaining
ingredients. Pour the dressing over the salad and
toss lightly but well. Let the salad stand at room
temperature for about an hour. Toss again lightly
and serve.

ICE CREAM WITH SAMBUCA AND ESPRESSO

Gelato con Sambuca ed espresso
MAKES 6 SERVINGS

Simple and elegant, this is a dessert you can use
again and again. Add a little more Sambuca and
espresso granules if you wish.

1 quart vanilla ice cream
6 tablespoons Sambuca
⅓ cup instant espresso granules

1. Place 2 small balls of ice cream in each of six
individual dishes.

2. Pour 1 tablespoon Sambuca over each serving
and dust with instant espresso.

AT SEA LEVEL WITH LUIGI MIROLI: MENU FOR 6

MENU

Prosciutto with Roasted Peppers
Prosciutto con peperoni arrostiti

Fresh Clams with Wine in Portofino
Vongole in salsa di vino bianco alla Portofino

Green Peas, Grandmother's Way
Piselli della nonna

Lemony Apple Cake
Torta di mele al limone

The thousands of miles of Italy's coastline that
rim the eastern, southern and western shores of
the boot, and the hundreds of miles of coast
around its many islands, teem with seafood. Italians love seafood. Is it any wonder? In Venice, the
pescheria that is part of the colorful outdoor market at the famous Rialto Bridge, overlooking the
Grand Canal, is one of the most extraordinary
sights in all of Italy. In the early morning as the
barges come in, the variety of people and fish is
astounding. The Adriatic coast, the major fishing
areas of Ancona, Porto Recanati, San Benedetto
del Tronto and Vasto, are famous for their fish
stews or soups, made with mullet, cod or dogfish,
and so it is with the other vast Italian coastlines.
    One of my favortie spots to eat is Ristorante da

Puny, above which owner Luigi "Puny" Miroli conveniently lives. On my visits, I never miss an opportunity to take a stroll toward the water, and to Puny's. If I time it perfectly, I can arrive at the restaurant and settle down at one of the green tables for a plate of fresh clams with wine just as the waning light of sunset washes over the sea of yellow tablecloths and the gray slate terrace floor that reflects the colors of the tranquil sea just a few feet away. Only Puny's livewire energy interrupts the quietude, as he sets the plate of fresh clams before me.

Wine Selection

A DOC Cinque Terre dry white wine, made with the Albrola, Bosco and Vermentina grapes, goes well with seafood.

Preparation Advice

1.   Make the lemon cake a day before, cover and keep at room temperature.

2.   The peppers can be also roasted by several days ahead, refrigerated and combined with the prosciutto just before serving.

3.   The clams can be readied ahead by several hours, but it is best to cook them just before mealtime, doing the peas at the same time.

PROSCIUTTO WITH ROASTED PEPPERS

Prosciutto con peperoni arrostiti
MAKES 6 TO 8 SERVINGS

Italy was traditionally an agricultural country, so almost every rural family kept a pig and cured every part of it, from snout to tail, to provide food for the family throughout the year. In any Italian larder, a range of home-cured hams, sausages and bacon would be found hanging from the ceiling. In many places, they still do. Not long ago, I met with Claudio Bonzagni, proprietor with his wife, Evelina, of the famous small, luxurious hotel in Ferrara, the Hotel Isabella Duchessa. In his private *salumeria* he offers friends tastings of homemade salami, prosciuttos and *culatellos* (very special small hams) accompanied by thick slices of yellow and red bell peppers in vinegar, which he urges you to try with a sprinkling of sea salt and extra-virgin olive oil. Cured ham and vinegar peppers are a classic food combination.

Nowadays, hundreds of different types of hams, cured meats and sausages are commercially produced, many still using the old artisanal methods. Wherever you travel in Italy, you will find regional variations on the same theme. Slices of cured meats make excellent antipastos. The *affettati* antipasto of sliced hams and *salame* is a famous Tuscan dish, and it is often served with pickled vegetables, which are designed to whet the appetite. Although the variety of these delicacies is infinitely greater in Italy, many are now available in the United States, especially in shops concentrating on imported foods. See Sources, page 269.

4 roasted red or yellow bell peppers, cut into
    strips
2 tablespoons extra-virgin olive oil
1/2 teaspoon balsamic vinegar
1 clove garlic, halved
Salt and freshly ground black pepper
8 thin slices white bread
2 tablespoons butter, at room temperature
8 thin slices prosciutto

1.   Combine the bell pepper strips, olive oil, vinegar, garlic, salt and pepper in a medium bowl. Allow the mixture to stand for 1 hour. Discard the garlic.

2.   Butter each slice of bread and lay the slices on a flat surface. Arrange 1 prosciutto slice on each piece of bread so that as little of the meat as

possible hangs over the edge. Then arrange the pepper strips to cover the prosciutto, again with as little overhanging as possible. Trim the crusts on all four sides, cutting through the prosciutto and peppers to make clean edges. Cut each slice in thirds.

3. Serve as an hors d'oeuvre or as a first course. If made ahead, cover with plastic wrap to keep the bread from drying out.

FRESH CLAMS WITH WINE IN PORTOFINO

Vongole in salsa di vino bianco alla Portofino
MAKES 6 TO 8 SERVINGS

One evening, Puny and I discussed the matter of clams, and he knows all about them. Always purchase clams in the shell from a reliable source. Most clams keep their shells tightly closed when out of the water, so if you notice a shell is open, just tap on it. If there is a live clam inside, it will respond by swiftly snapping the shell shut. Discard any that are either unusually heavy (these are usually sealed with mud) or light—they are probably dead.

Many people place clams in a pot of cold water for several hours, sometimes along with a spoonful of cornmeal, in the hope that this will release the sand inside the shells. Puny believes the clams, unfortunately, lose most of their flavorful juice in this process. If you do this, he recommends that you strain the water through a sieve lined with a double layer of dampened cheesecloth or a coffee filter, to get rid of the sand, and pour the strained water into the dish you are preparing. Puny and I clean clams in about the same way. Put the clams in the sink and cover them with cool water, then scrub the clams all over with a stiff wire brush. Drain the water from the sink, making sure you rinse away any sand at the bottom, and refill with cool water. Let the clams soak for about five minutes. Repeat the soaking and scrubbing procedure three times; the last sink of water should be clear. Drain the clams and set aside until ready to use.

The creative culinary Italian hand is evident by the addition of anchovies and capers (and hopefully, you'll add the red chili pepper, too) to what otherwise would be just another good clam dish. It's difficult to improve on steamed clams and white wine, but in this preparation, my friend Puny shows how it can be done.

3/4 cup extra-virgin olive oil
3 large cloves garlic, minced
5 anchovies packed in oil, drained and patted dry
1 tablespoon capers, drained
3 pounds small clams, such as littlenecks, in their shells, cleaned (see headnote, above)
1 1/2 cups dry white wine
6 ripe medium tomatoes, peeled, seeded and cut into 1/2-inch dice
1/4 cup finely chopped fresh Italian parsley
1/2 beef or vegetable bouillon cube
1 dried red chili pepper (optional)

1. Heat the oil in a large, nonreactive pot over medium-high heat. Add the garlic, anchovies and capers and sauté until the garlic just begins to take on a little color, about 2 minutes; do not let the garlic brown. Add the clams and the white wine and cook, uncovered, until some of the wine cooks off, about 5 minutes.

2. Add the tomatoes, parsley, bouillon cube and the chili pepper, if using. Stir well, then cover tightly and cook until all the clams have opened, about 5 minutes. Discard any clams that have not opened.

3. To serve, bring the pot to the table if at all possible. Spoon the clams into warm bowls, dividing evenly, but avoid any at the very bottom of the pot, because you might pick up any additional sand that has sunk there. Provide extra plates for the discarded clams shells.

●GREEN PEAS, ●GRANDMOTHER'S WAY

Piselli della nonna
MAKES 6 SERVINGS

When the early spring peas come into the markets, people rush out to buy them as quickly as they can, and they are often prepared homestyle *(casalinga)* or in mother's way or grandmother's style. Here is a recipe given to me by a vendor who happens to be a grandmother.

4 tablespoons butter
6 thin slices prosciutto, cut crosswise into thin strips
1/2 cup finely chopped onion
1 teaspoon all-purpose flour
1/2 cup white wine or 1 cup chicken broth
2 pounds fresh peas, shelled, or 1 1/2 (10-ounce) packages frozen peas, preferably tiny green peas
1 small packet fresh herbs (basil, rosemary and marjoram) or a pinch of each, dried

1. Heat the butter in a large skillet over low heat sauté the prosciutto and onion until the prosciutto crisps, for up to 10 minutes. Remove the prosciutto and onion, leaving whatever juices may be in the pan. Stir in the flour.

2. Add the wine and bring to a boil. Add the peas and herbs and cook for 10 minutes if the peas are fresh; if frozen and thawed, cook for 3 or 4 minutes.

3. Add the cooked prosciutto and onion, and cook a few minutes more, stirring. Remove the herb packet if there is one and serve.

●LEMONY APPLE CAKE

Torta di mele al limone
MAKES 6 TO 8 SERVINGS

This cake is from Liguria, and it is best served warm. It calls for a dollop of whipped cream, and you should whip the cream with some lemon zest to get the true Ligurian taste of freshness.

9 tablespoons butter, melted
1 1/2 pounds apples (Golden Delicious, Cortland or Rome Beauty), peeled, cored and sliced
Zest and juice from 1 lemon
1/4 teaspoon lemon extract
4 eggs
3/4 cup confectioners' sugar plus 1 teaspoon for sprinkling
1 1/4 cups all-purpose flour
1 teaspoon baking powder
Salt
1/2 cup heavy cream, whipped

1. Preheat the oven to 350F. Use 1 tablespoon of the butter to grease a 9-inch, 10-inch or 11-inch springform pan. Put the apple slices in a bowl and pour the lemon juice over the apples. Add the lemon extract. Toss well.

2. Put the eggs, sugar and lemon zest (reserve a pinch for the whipped cream) in a bowl and whisk until the mixture becomes thick and mousselike, up to 5 minutes. (The whisk should leave a trail in the mixture.)

3. Combine half of the flour, the baking powder and some salt and sift it over the egg mixture.

Pour the remaining 8 tablespoons butter to the sides of the bowl, and fold in with a rubber spatula. Sift the remaining flour over the mixture and fold in. Add the apples and lemon juice and fold in carefully. Pour the apple mixture into the prepared pan.

4. Bake for about 60 minutes, until a wooden skewer comes out clean. (Check after 50 minutes, if using the larger pan.) Remove from the oven and let rest for 10 minutes. Remove the side of the springform pan. Sprinkle with the confectioners' sugar, using a small strainer. Serve the cake warm with whipped cream to which has been added some lemon zest.

ALONG THE COAST NORTH OF LA SPEZIA AND ITS CHAIN OF FIVE VILLAGES: MENU FOR 4

MENU

Carpaccio of Sea Bass with Herbs
Carpaccio di branzino alle erbe aromatiche

Veal Scaloppine with Pepper Grains
Scaloppine di vitello con pepe in grani

Vegetable Matchsticks in Bundles, with Italian Green Sauce
Bastoncini di vegetali con salsa verde all'italiana

Sweet Slices of Tomatoes with Chives
Pomodori con cipolline

Almond Cheese Tart
Torta di formaggio alle mandorle

Cinque Terre is at the eastern end of the crescent-shaped coastal strip called Liguria. Actually, Genoa cuts the strip in half, into the Riviera Levante (of the rising sun) to the east, and the Riviera di Ponente (of the setting sun) to the west. All together, this coast is about two hundred miles long between France and Tuscany. It is a prosperous and lively area, filled with tourists. The landscape in summer is alive with fiery reds and purples and the air is perfumed by the almond and lemon trees. The olive trees in winter shade the flower beds and these trees produce what some experts call the best olive oil made in Italy

The five towns host a bevy of overpriced seafood restaurants, but the seafood is fresh and a good place to have a fish carpaccio followed by a light, peppery veal dish. Although the villages are the least developed on the Riviera, there are busloads of Italian students and Germans with knapsacks who come here to hike and to take the train from one town to another. One of the five towns, Monterosso, is fairly pedestrian, although it has more facilities than the others, and the local color is its laundry, dangling on windowsills, its crowded smoke-filled espresso bars and its parade of tens of perambulators crowding the byways. Yet the drama of hiking across vineyards, lemon and olive groves and the beautiful fields of wildflowers is the reason people rave about Cinque Terre, and have vivid memories that last year after year.

Not easy to reach, the rugged coast here, with its vineyards and fishing villages, is a hospitable region. Of the five villages, perhaps Vernazza is the most attractive, with its churches and colorful houses, clustering at the beginning of a protected cove. What a beautiful sight to imagine as preparing and enjoying this menu.

Wine Selection

Consider a white wine from Emilia, a region bordering Liguria. Try an Albana di Romagna. It comes dry and semisweet, and sometimes sparkling. It is made from the Albana grape. The dry white would be perfect with the fish carpaccio and holds up to the veal. The semisweet would be a great partner with the cheese tart, or continue with Liguria's DOC Cinque Terre.

Preparation Advice

1. The almond cheese tart may be made a day ahead, and so can the vegetable bundles, but do not sauce them until ready to serve.

2. The remainder of this special menu can be prepared an hour or so before mealtime except for the veal, which should be cooked just before eating.

CARPACCIO OF SEA BASS WITH HERBS

Carpaccio di branzino alle erbe aromatiche
MAKES 4 SERVINGS

Harry's Bar in Venice is usually credited with the creation of *carpaccio*, a dish featuring thinly sliced raw meat. Since its creation the term and procedure for *carpaccio* has extended itself to fish of all kinds. Here it is made with fresh sea bass. The very fresh sea bass is "cooked" with lemon juice, spiced with fennel and served with a cream sauce.

1¼ pounds fresh sea bass fillet in 1 piece
4 tablespoons extra-virgin olive oil
5 tablespoons fresh lemon juice
Salt and freshly ground pepper
1 cup half-and-half
Pinch red pepper flakes
¼ teaspoon fennel seeds, crushed
1 small fresh fennel bulb with feathery leaves

1. Slice the fish fillet into 4 pieces and then again into 8. Lay them flat on a dish or small plat-

ter and sprinkle them with the oil and 3 tablespoons of the lemon juice. Season liberally with salt and pepper. Cover with plastic wrap and refrigerate for 4 to 5 hours.

2. Pour the half-and-half into a bowl and fold in the remaining 2 tablespoons lemon juice, pepper flakes, crushed fennel seeds, salt and freshly ground pepper.

3. About 30 minutes before serving, drain the fish well and transfer it to a fresh plate or platter and pour the cream mixture over the fish.

4. Trim the fennel and slice into very thin julienne strips, including the light green feathery leaves. Arrange some thin fennel slivers over the fish and serve.

VEAL SCALOPPINE WITH PEPPER GRAINS

Scaloppine di vitello con pepe in grani
MAKES 4 SERVINGS

Wherever Italian food is served, there are enticing food combinations of veal scaloppine. Veal of this cut marries beautifully with lemon, orange, marsala, vermouth, capers, tomatoes, cured meats, cheeses and a wide array of herbs and spices. Cooking veal scaloppine that have been properly cut is one of the simplest things one can do in the kitchen, and one of the fastest. It is easy in the United States to buy this meat, plastic-wrapped, in the refrigerated meat sections in supermarkets, but they are not properly cut. It is best to ask your butcher to cut the scaloppine from the top round, from the upper part of the hind leg, and to cut across the muscle's grain. Once cut in this way, they can be pounded properly. The reason for cutting across the grain is to keep the meat flat while it is sautéeing. Here is a simple, elegant way to prepare them *all' italiana*.

> 1½ pounds veal scallops, pounded to ¼-inch thickness
> Salt
> 1 teaspoon coarsely ground black pepper
> ½ cup all-purpose flour
> 5 tablespoons butter
> 1 tablespoon extra-virgin olive oil
> ⅓ cup dry vermouth
> 2 tablespoons fresh lemon juice
> 2 teaspoons finely grated lemon zest

1.   Just before sautéeing the scallops, dust them with salt and the coarsely ground pepper. Dip them into the flour and remove any excess. It is best to have as thin a coating of flour as possible.

2.   Heat 3 tablespoons of the butter and the oil in a large skillet over high heat. Brown as many pieces of veal at a time as you can for 2 or 3 minutes on each side, using tongs to turn them. They should brown without burning. Remove the scallops to a serving dish, arranging them in one layer.

3.   Quickly deglaze the pan with the vermouth and remaining butter, scraping up all the bits of brown particles clinging to the skillet. If the vermouth cooks off too quickly, add another 1 or 2 tablespoons. Pour this quickly over the scallops. Sprinkle all with some lemon juice and zest and serve right away.

VEGETABLE MATCH-STICKS IN BUNDLES, WITH ITALIAN GREEN SAUCE

Bastoncini di vegetali con salsa verde all'italiana
MAKES 4 SERVINGS

Bastone in Italian means a stick, staff, cane or baton, and *bastoncini* means little sticks; this play on words is part of the Italian spirit in their kitchens. These are fun to make, are tasty with the sauce and add a touch of Italian chicness in presentation.

> 8 snow peas, trimmed
> 2 celery ribs, trimmed and strings removed
> 2 small zucchini, scrubbed and ends trimmed
> 12 green beans, trimmed
> 1 large green bell pepper, stemmed, ribs removed, seeded and cut into ¼ × 2½-inch lengths
> 2 scallions
>
> **FOR THE GREEN SAUCE (SALSA VERDE)**
> ¼ cup extra-virgin olive oil
> 1 large clove garlic, minced
> 2 anchovy fillets, minced
> 1 tablespoon finely chopped gherkins
> 1 tablespoon capers
> 1 tablespoon finely chopped Italian parsley

1.   Cut the snow peas, celery, zucchini and green beans the same size as the bell pepper. If the zucchini has a seedy, limp center, cut it away and discard. Keep in mind that the vegetables are being cut to form bundles that will be tied with a scallion length.

2. Steam each vegetable, except the scallions, to the crisp-tender stage. When all the vegetables are done, pat them dry with paper towels.

3. Trim the scallions and carefully separate the leaves, keeping them as long as possible. Drop the raw scallion leaves into a skillet of boiling water. Immediately turn off the heat and remove the scallion lengths to a towel to dry. Preheat the oven to 325F.

4. Place one scallion length on a work surface. Over it, arrange a variety of vegetables to make a bundle about 1 inch in diameter. Wrap the bundle with the scallion, tying it gently. Repeat with remaining vegetables and scallion leaves. Arrange the bundles in a shallow baking dish.

5. *To make the sauce:* Combine all the ingredients in a small bowl.

6. Spoon the green sauce over each bundle and warm in the oven for 10 to 15 minutes before serving.

SWEET SLICES OF TOMATOES WITH CHIVES

Pomodoro con cipolline
MAKES 4 SERVINGS

The tomatoes must be ripe and the skins must be removed. The taste of sweet/sour of this simple preparation is perfect between the veal and the almond cheese tart. Leave the tomatoes at room temperature for several hours and serve on separate small plates.

> 4 medium to large ripe tomatoes
> 2 tablespoons extra-virgin olive oil
> 2 teaspoons red wine vinegar
> Sea salt and freshly ground pepper

1 tablespoon sugar
⅓ cup finely chopped fresh chives

1. Core the tomatoes and blanch them in boiling water just long enough to loosen the skins, 30 seconds to 2 minutes, depending on ripeness. Drain tomatoes, run under cold water and remove the skins. Slice as thinly as you can and arrange slices on a plate with a little overlap.

2. Combine the oil, vinegar, salt and pepper. Spoon the dressing over the tomatoes. Carefully sprinkle the sugar and chives on the tomatoes and allow to marinate at room temperature for 20 to 30 minutes. To serve, arrange slices of tomatoes on 4 individual plates, overlapping them in a pattern with the sugar-and-chive side up.

ALMOND CHEESE TART

Torta di formaggio alle mandorle
MAKES 6 TO 8 SERVINGS

This cheese tart should be made a day ahead so the flavors have time to blend. It will serve more than four people, but the tart keeps well for several days.

FOR THE CRUST
1½ cups unbleached all-purpose flour
⅓ cup confectioners' sugar
¼ teaspoon baking powder
Pinch of salt
8 tablespoons butter, chilled and cut into small dice
1 egg yolk

FOR THE FILLING
1 (8-ounce) package cream cheese, at room temperature

4 ounces mascarpone cheese, at room
    temperature
1/3 cup plus 2 tablespoons sugar
2 small eggs, beaten
1/2 tablespoon vanilla extract
1 teaspoon grated lemon zest
1/4 teaspoon almond extract
1/2 cup almond slivers, toasted
1/4 cup sour cream

1. *To prepare the crust:* Preheat the oven to 350F. Sift the flour with the sugar, baking powder and salt onto a work surface. Make a well in the center and add the diced butter into it. Add the egg yolk. Using your fingertips, or a pastry blender, bring the ingredients together to form a dough.

2. Fashion the dough together and press it into a deep 9-inch fluted tart pan with a removable bottom. Bake for 12 minutes. Cool before adding the filling.

3. *To prepare the filling:* Preheat the oven to 350F. Combine the cream cheese, mascarpone cheese and sugar in a large bowl. Beat until smooth. Beat in the eggs, vanilla, lemon zest and the almond extract until combined.

4. Spread 1/4 cup of the almonds in the bottom of the baked crust. Carefully spread the filling into the crust. Bake for about 40 minutes, until the cheesecake is puffed and the center is firm to the touch.

5. Remove the cheesecake from the oven and spread the sour cream evenly over the top. Sprinkle with the remaining 1/4 cup of toasted almonds. Cool on a rack for 1 hour. May be refrigerated overnight.

VAL D'AOSTA AND FONTINA CHEESE: THE HALLMARK OF LA CUCINA VALDOSTANA: MENU FOR 4

MENU

Val d'Aosta's Fontina Fondue with Steamed Vegetables
Fonduta con verdure

Beef Braised with Red Wine and Spices
Brasato di bue al barolo

Wedges of Savoy Cabbage with Fresh Lemon
Verza al limone

Chestnut Puree with Sweet Whipped Cream and Candied Orange Strips
Purea di castagne con arance caramellizzate e panna montata

Inside its ancient Roman walls, Aosta is frozen in medieval time. It is traffic-free and the main street, Via Sant'Anselmo, connects with the Arco di Augustus (built in 25 B.C.) with the original main gate of Porta Pretoria. From the center of town, an easy town in which to stroll, the history is visible with its cloisters, churches, museums and ruins.

Meat and dairy products are the main features of cooking in this mountainous area of valleys and rivers. Pasta is not seen anywhere although rice, polenta and gnocchi are served as first courses along with the many soups (and black bread) that make up a diet to keep one warm.

Many dishes contain butter and cheese, primarily Fontina cheese, which is the hallmark of their cuisine. One of their best-known dishes (along with fonduta) is beef stewed with red wine, and both are included in this menu.

Wine Selection

The Val d'Aosta is Italy's smallest region and it is also the smallest producer of Italian wines. They make Chambave Rouge, a full, dry red made from the Petit Riouge grape blended with other grapes. They also make a Pinot Noir of the same grape, but these will be difficult to find in U.S. shops. Choose a full-bodied red from Piedmont. Because Barola is used in the meat preparation, consider another bottle to drink. If that is too expensive, consider a Barbera d'Alba or a Barbera d'Asti, both excellent wines.

Preparation Advice

1. Most of this menu may be made as far ahead as the day before. Vegetables may be steamed and held, the beef braised in red wine. The chestnuts can be mashed ahead of time. This leaves the cabbage dish to be done at the last minute.

•VAL D'AOSTA'S FONTINA
•FONDUE WITH STEAMED
•VEGETABLES

Fonduta con verdure
MAKES 4 SERVINGS

This is one of the most delicious Italian cheeses. There are American imitations of this great Italian cheese, but they do not measure up to the original. The real fontina comes from the Piedmont's Valle d'Aosta, a mountainous area south of Switzerland. Fontina looks like Swiss gruyère; it has a rather light brown crust and comes in large wheels like Swiss cheese, but it doesn't have the network of holes.

Fontina is made from cow's milk and has a fat content of 45 to 50 percent; the flavor is delicate, somewhat fruity and nutty and is excellent with the light, fruity wines of Piedmont. It is frequently used in vegetable and pasta dishes, especially those that require cheese for stuffing and baking. When fully cured, it is hard and used for grating. Italians bake it with Savoy cabbage and bread because it melts easily and it is a simple, tasty, comforting way to use and enjoy it.

2 cups 1½-inch broccoli florets
2 cups 1½-inch cauliflower florets
8 baby carrots, 2 to 3 inches long
1¼ cups milk, warmed
¾ pound thinly sliced fontina cheese
Salt and white pepper
Freshly grated nutmeg

4 egg yolks
4 tablespoons butter, at room temperature
8 small white mushrooms, trimmed,
    cut in half

1. Steam the broccoli, cauliflower and carrots separately for 5 to 10 minutes, depending on thickness of stems. Set aside all vegetables.

2. Pour 1 cup of the milk into the top of a double boiler set over simmering water. Add the fontina, salt, white pepper and a pinch of nutmeg and stir constantly with a wooden spoon until the cheese has melted and the mixture is smooth.

3. Combine the remaining ¼ cup milk with the egg yolks, stir until combined and add to the cheese mixture. Add the butter, 1 tablespoon at a time, stirring until the mixture is creamy and smooth. Remove the top pan to stop the cooking.

4. *To serve:* Transfer the fonduta into a small bowl and center it on a large platter. Arrange the mushrooms, broccoli, cauliflower and carrots in an attractive fashion surrounding the bowl and serve. Or, you can put the fonduta into 4 small bowls, centered on smaller plates, adding some of each vegetable to each plate and serve individually.

BEEF BRAISED WITH RED WINE AND SPICES

Brasato di bue al barolo
MAKES 4 SERVINGS

The grape vine has been established in Piedmont since Roman times and its soil, tradition and climate have been responsible, and still are, for producing some of Italy's best wines. One of these is Barolo, made of the Nebbiola grape; it is deep red in color, full and fragrant. It spends at least three years in casks before bottling, and ages as well and as long in the bottles as a good claret (longer than Burgundy). They are expensive wines and you may cringe at the price of a bottle in the United States, but using it in this dish will be special. If you decide to use it, you should also serve a bottle to drink with the beef. There are other good Italian reds that could be used that cost less. Your wine merchant will tell you what else he has available.

2 onions, sliced
2 carrots, trimmed and sliced
2 inner ribs celery, trimmed and sliced
2 cloves garlic, sliced
1 bay leaf and 1 rosemary sprig
4 whole cloves
1 (3-inch) cinnamon stick
2 pounds beef top round in one piece, ready for
  cooking
1 bottle Barolo or other red wine
4 tablespoons extra-virgin olive oil
2 tablespoons tomato paste
¼ cup beef broth
Sea salt and freshly ground pepper

¼ cup brandy or cognac
4 rosemary sprigs, for garnish

1.　Place the onions, carrots and celery in a large bowl. Add the garlic, bay leaf, rosemary, cloves and cinnamon.

2.　Place the meat in the bowl and pour in the wine. Cover tightly and marinate overnight in the refrigerator. Remove from the refrigerator 1 hour before cooking. Drain the meat and reserve the marinade with the vegetables and spices.

3.　Heat the oil in a large stove-top casserole and brown the meat on all sides over high heat, uncovered, turning as needed.

4.　Add the reserved marinade of wine, vegetables, spices and herbs. Cook for 20 minutes, uncovered, over medium heat.

5.　Combine the tomato paste with the beef broth and add to the casserole. Add salt and pepper. Cover the casserole, reduce the heat and simmer until the meat is tender, about 2 hours.

6.　To serve, remove the meat to a slicing board. Add the mixture in the casserole to a food processor and puree it. Strain the puree through a sieve. Return the puree to the casserole, add the brandy and reheat, cooking off some of the brandy, 4 or 5 minutes. Slice the meat for individual servings and spoon some of the brandied wine sauce over half of the meat on the plate. Add a rosemary sprig to the side of each serving.

WEDGES OF SAVOY CABBAGE WITH FRESH LEMON

Verza al limone
MAKES 4 SERVINGS

Cabbage has been domesticated for over twenty-five hundred years. The Greeks and Romans loved it. Cabbage did not grow in compact heads as we know it today. It was during the Middle Ages that farmers in northern Europe developed compact-headed varieties. These cabbages are capable of thriving in cold climates. Savoy cabbage has crinkled, ruffled, yellow-green leaves that form a less compact head than other types. It is very popular in Italy and Italians advise not to pick a head of Savoy until it has been hit by the frost, for only then will it have reached full flavor.

> 1 small head of Savoy cabbage
> Juice of 2 lemons
> 4 tablespoons butter
> Sea salt and freshly ground pepper
> Freshly grated nutmeg

1. Core the cabbage and remove the outer green leaves. Cut the cabbage into 4 wedges and put in cold, salted water for a minimum of 30 minutes.

2. After draining, place the cabbage in the top part of a steamer set over boiling water. Cover the cabbage with one of the outer green leaves, which has been rinsed and dried; this will help keep in the steam. Cook until tender, 10 to 15 minutes.

3. Add the lemon juice and butter to a large skillet. Heat until the butter melts. Add salt, pepper and a sprinkle of nutmeg. Add the cabbage

wedges to the sauce. Spoon the sauce over the cabbage and heat just long enough to immerse the cabbage in the lemon sauce.

CHESTNUT PUREE WITH SWEET WHIPPED CREAM AND CARAMELIZED ORANGE STRIPS

Purea di castagne con arance caramellizzate e panna montata
MAKES 4 SERVINGS

Italians would normally boil fresh chestnuts to puree them, but whole canned cooked chestnuts are easier to handle and are available in most specialty food shops. If the puree is too thin, it will not pass through the food mill properly. The chestnuts may be cooked one or two days ahead, but do not put them through the food mill until just before serving. The caramelized orange strips make this a delightful dessert.

> ½ cup milk
> 2 tablespoons unsweetened cocoa
>   powder
> ½ cup sugar
> 15 ounces canned or jarred cooked whole
>   chestnuts
> ¼ cup dark rum
> ½ cup heavy cream
> ¼ cup confectioners' sugar
> Caramelized Orange Strips (page 210)

1. Heat the milk in a saucepan over low heat and stir in the cocoa and sugar.

2. Add the chestnuts and cook over medium heat to heat them thoroughly, 6 to 8 minutes. Remove from the heat.

3. Add the rum and mash thoroughly. Pass the mixture through a food mill to fall on a plate.

4. Whip the cream with confectioners' sugar, and dollop it on the top of the chestnut puree. Carefully place about 1 tablespoon of candied orange strips over the cream.

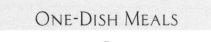

ONE-DISH MEALS

POLENTA AND FONTINA CHEESE WITH TOMATOES AND ROASTED RED PEPPERS

Polenta con formaggio Fontina e peperoni
MAKES 6 SERVINGS

In this recipe, fontina cheese is strewn over polenta, cooked with tomatoes and roasted red peppers and topped with fresh basil, a combination of foods made in heaven. Just add a fresh green salad dressed with extra-virgin olive oil and fresh lemon juice.

FOR THE POLENTA
2 quarts water
1½ teaspoons salt
1 pound polenta
2 tablespoons butter

3 large red bell peppers
1 tablespoon olive oil
1 (15-ounce) can chopped tomatoes

1½ cups (6 ounces) shredded fontina cheese
½ cup finely chopped fresh basil

1. *To make the polenta:* Bring the water to boil. Add the salt. Add the polenta a little at a time, stirring constantly with a wooden spoon to prevent lumping. Cook for 20 to 30 minutes, until the polenta thickens. Mix in the butter and let stand several minutes. Pour into a flat dish or pan with a 1-inch rim to cool and solidify. Cut into 3-inch squares.

2. Broil the bell peppers on all sides until blackened. Put them into a paper bag, close the bag and let rest for 10 minutes. Peel, core and seed the peppers. patting them dry with paper towels. Cut them into thin strips and set aside.

3. Heat the oil in a large nonstick skillet over medium heat. Add the tomatoes and their juices and cook for 3 minutes. Add the pepper strips and cook for 5 minutes over low heat. Set aside.

4. Preheat the oven to 350F.

5. Put one-fourth of the tomato/pepper sauce into a 12 × 9 inch ovenproof dish. Arrange the polenta squares over the sauce. Spoon the remaining sauce over the polenta. Sprinkle with the cheese and bake for 20 to 30 minutes, until the sauce is bubbling and the polenta is heated through. Sprinkle basil over the top and serve hot.

ANGELA'S SUNDAY-BEST STUFFED BREAST OF VEAL

Petto di vitello facito all'Angela
MAKES 8 SERVINGS

My mother loved making this dish and our family enjoyed eating it. It was always served on a Sunday, the time of the major meal in our home. No excuses—everyone had to be seated at the table. It is an adaptation of the Ligurian veal dish known as *cima alla genovese*. A breast of veal is filled with a stuffing of offal, vegetables and nuts. There are a variety of ways to cook this dish, as you may imagine, and here, it is filled with ground veal and pork, nuts and cheeses; in other words, without the variety meats, which did not appeal to us as children.

You will need a large veal breast from an animal over one year old. Ask your butcher if he can accommodate you. He should bone it for you and create a pocket so it can receive a filling. Ask for the bones, as you can make a veal broth to use in this recipe.

1 (1-pound) loaf Italian bread, one or two days old
1 cup milk
6 large eggs
1¼ pounds (total) ground veal and pork
1 pound fresh ricotta cheese
1 cup freshly grated Parmesan cheese
½ cup finely chopped fresh Italian parsley
3 large cloves garlic, minced
⅓ cup golden raisins
⅓ cup pine nuts, toasted
Sea salt and freshly ground pepper
1 (8-pound) breast of veal (see headnote above)
1 cup veal or chicken broth
1 cup dry white wine
1 cup diced canned tomatoes
1 large onion, thinly sliced

1. Preheat the oven to 450F.

2. Break the bread into chunks and put them and their crumbs into a large bowl. Add the milk, toss to moisten the bread and let stand for 20 to 30 minutes. Squeeze the bread dry and set aside.

3. Whisk the eggs in a large bowl. Add the ground meat, ricotta and Parmesan cheeses, parsley, garlic, raisins, pine nuts, salt and pepper. Add the bread and mix with splayed fingers. Combine these ingredients well but don't overdo. Do not mix in a food processor or other mechanical device.

4. Fill the pocket of the veal breast. Do not overstuff, as the filling will expand while it bakes. Secure the opening all the way by sewing with needle and thread.

5. Put the filled veal breast on a roasting rack in a large roasting pan and roast for 30 minutes, until the meat is browned. Remove from the oven and reduce the heat to 300F.

6. Add the broth, wine, tomatoes and onion to the roasting pan. Cover with foil and roast for 3½ to 4 hours. Remove the pan from the oven and let the veal rest, covered, for 20 minutes or so. To serve, cut into ½-inch-thick slices and serve with a fresh, lightly dressed arugula salad.

BAKED BEANS FROM PIEDMONT

Tofeja (Fagioli di grasso)
MAKES 6 TO 8 SERVINGS

This is a dish of baked beans with pork and herbs. In some parts of Italy, this dish is still made in a *tofeja*, a low terra-cotta cooking pot with four handles, but an ovenproof casserole will suffice. It is a rich, fragrant, marvelously thick preparation laden with velvety beans and meltingly tender pork, a treat for the senses in every respect. The dish is traditionally served at Carnevale, and its richness is appreciated because this celebration is the last opportunity to eat meat before the beginning of Lent. Years ago, the dish was flavored with pig's feet and rolls of pork fat filled with herbs (especially rosemary) and spices, which was how my father made it. To keep up with current cooking trends in Italy and America, small chunks of lean pork shoulder are now substituted for the pig's feet and the amount of pork fat is substantially cut back to reduce the fat, but not the flavor.

Forget American pork and beans; there is no comparison to this Italian bean dish. To accompany this dish, cook up any vegetables you like, and mix them with oil, vinegar, salt, freshly ground pepper and some finely chopped fresh herbs. Or cook asparagus and combine it with a salad dressing, and serve with the beans.

1 pound dried Great Northern beans
2 large cloves garlic, minced
2 teaspoons rubbed sage
1 teaspoon finely chopped rosemary
½ teaspoon freshly grated nutmeg
¼ teaspoon red pepper flakes
Sea salt and freshly ground pepper
4 ounces fresh pork fat
2 tablespoons extra-virgin olive oil
1 pound lean pork shoulder, cut into ½-inch pieces, or 2 pig's feet cut into 2-inch pieces
1 large onion, cut into ½-inch dice
4 bay leaves
2 medium carrots, peeled and thinly sliced
1 medium rib celery, thinly sliced
7 cups chicken broth
½ cup freshly grated pecorino cheese, such as Romano
¼ cup finely minced fresh chives

1. Pick over the beans, discarding any stones. Soak them overnight in cool water to cover by 2 inches. Drain and set aside.

2. Combine the garlic, sage, rosemary, nutmeg, red pepper flakes, salt and pepper in a small bowl. Set aside.

3. Thinly slice the pork fat to make 4 pieces, each about 3 × 2½ inches in size. Sprinkle about ½ of the garlic mixture over the slices of fat, dividing evenly. Roll up each slice and tie with string in two places. Set aside.

4. Preheat the oven to 350F.

5. Heat the oil in a flameproof casserole over medium heat. Add the pork rolls and sauté until they lose color and become somewhat translucent and lightly browned, about 15 minutes. Fat splatters when very hot; use a splatter guard if you have one. Remove the pork rolls and set them aside on a plate or paper towels. Add the pork shoulder to the drippings in the casserole, turning the pieces to brown on all sides, about 10 minutes. Add the onion and the remaining garlic mixture. Sauté, stirring, until the onion softens, 3 to 4 minutes.

6. Add the beans, bay leaves, carrots, celery, reserved pork rolls, and broth to the casserole.

Remove from the heat, cover tightly and place in the oven. Bake for 1 hour without removing the cover. Reduce the heat to 300F and cook until the beans are very tender and the mixture is very thick, about 2 hours more. Remove and discard the pork fat and bay leaves.

7.   Combine the grated cheese and chives in a small bowl. Serve the beans with 1 teaspoonful of the cheese mixture on top of each serving. Serve the remaining cheese mixture alongside.

PASTA WITH CABBAGE, CHEESE AND POTATOES

Pasta con verza, formaggio e patate (pizzocheri)

MAKES 6 SERVINGS

This is a gutsy, earthy dish from the north that has traveled to many parts of Italy. I first learned of it at home, as it was a dish my father enjoyed making. For whatever reason, he loved cooking Savoy cabbage, which was always available in Italian markets in New York. These days, it is in every greengrocer section of most supermarkets. The cabbage adds a lot to the taste of this dish, but it is as tasty as it is because of the pecorino cheese, a cheese strong in taste, which seems to marry well to these other ingredients.

It is an adaption of the Ligurian dish called *pizzocheri*, which is made with buckwheat *(grana saracena)* pasta served with cabbage, potatoes, cheese, butter and sage.

Sea salt
3 medium potatoes, peeled and cut into ½-inch dice to make about 3 cups
1 (about 1-pound) head Savoy cabbage, trimmed, cored and sliced thinly as for slaw
1 pound fresh fettucine
1½ sticks (10 ounces) butter, sliced into thin pats
4 large cloves garlic, halved
8 sage leaves
1½ cups freshly grated pecorino cheese
Freshly ground black pepper

1.   Bring 4 quarts water to a boil, add some salt, the potatoes and cabbage and cook for 12 minutes, stirring frequently. Add the pasta and cook until the pasta is al dente, for up to 5 minutes. Drain well and transfer to a large serving platter. Add one-third of the butter and toss with the pasta, cabbage and potatoes.

2.   Melt the remaining butter in a skillet and sauté the garlic with the sage leaves until garlic is lightly browned, about 4 minutes. Remove the garlic, discard it and spoon the flavored butter and sage over the pasta. Top with the pecorino cheese and dust liberally with the pepper. Serve now or hold as in step 3.

3.   To hold, place the cooked ingredients into a baking dish and keep warm in a 250F oven, or if prepared ahead and refrigerated, place in a baking dish and reheat in a 350F oven until heated through, about 15 minutes. Serve with a freshly made arugula or curly endive and sliced tomato salad, or sliced cucumbers and finely chopped Italian parsley dressed lightly with oil and vinegar.

· I V ·

LOMBARDY AND THE LAKES

MILAN, BERGAMO, COMO AND THE
FERTILE PLAINS OF THE PO RIVER

Lombardy is a land of contrast. There is the fertile basin of the Po River, flat as far as one can see, fogged all winter long, yet in summer, one views the flowing patterns of the river and the poplars. Then there are Como, Garda and Maggiore, the glacier-formed lakes contrasted to the majestic Alps, both strongly admired by the Romans. Lombardy was invaded almost as many times as Sicily. Milan itself was captured forty times and razed to the ground twice. The region was part of the Roman Empire, robbed by barbarian tribes, united under the Longobards (thus the name Lombard), ruled by the Franks, fought over again and again by the strong families of Visconti, Sforza, Gonzaga, Scaligeri, taken over by Venice, France, the Spanish Hapsburgs, given to Austria, absorbed by Napoleon and then again by Austria.

With all this going on, *a cucina di Lombardia* seemed to be undisturbed. Butter, cream and cheese come from the mountain pastures, and rice and polenta from the alluvial plains. *Risotto alla milanese* and polenta are two famous dishes from the region and are included here (pages 101 and 110). Pasta is freshly made, especially in the form of tagliarini and ravioli. Pork and veal, especially veal shanks, are important meats and are prepared in special ways. Cheeses figure strongly in their eating habits. As Italy's greatest producer of milk, the cuisine is rich in butter, cream and cheese; Gorgonzola, Bel Paese, stracchino, grana padana and mascarpone are some examples.

Its invaders, especially the German and Austrians, are responsible for the heavy and rich foods, unlike the more Mediterranean-oriented areas of Italy. In Lombardy, they like meat to be stewed, *stufato,* such as the braised veal shank (page 99). Instead of grilled beefsteak, as in Florence, they prefer veal sautéed as *costoletta* (page 96). There are peaches from the Po valley, walnuts and mushrooms from the north and trout from the lakes. The vineyards produce the famous wines Sassella and Grumello, the Lugano whites, the Franciacorta's reds, and chardonnays and spumante from Brescia.

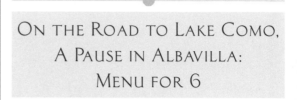

On the Road to Lake Como, a Pause in Albavilla: Menu for 6

MENU

Poached Eggs and Parmigiano in Broth
Zuppa alla Pavese

Veal Cutlet in the Milan Manner
Costoletta alla milanese

Arugula and Tomato Salad with Lemon Dressing
Insalata di rucula al limone

Apples and Pears with Ginger in a Milan Charlotte
Mele e pere allo zenzero in charlotte alla milanese

A day's outing to Lake Como from either Milan or Bergamo is easy to accomplish and worth the trip. Not long ago, on such a trip, I stopped at a renovated farmhouse in Albavilla to "take a look." The logs in the fireplace were crackling and I wished I could have stayed but friends were waiting in Como. I've often dreamed of this serene setting, at this place called "Il Cantuccio" and here's a dream meal I've envisioned from there.

Wine Selection

Choose a wine known as Valtelline, such as the Sassella and Grumello mentioned above. There is another good one called Inferno. These are all red and some compare these to the greater Piedmontese Nebbiolo wines, Barolo and Gattinara. Many will dispute this statement. However, if you can find one of these from a good grower, with five or six years of bottle-age, it should be good. Also look for a red wine made close to Pavia, known as the Oltrepo wines, produced by Ca'Longa, LaFracee and Maga Lino.

Preparation Advice

1. The dessert can be made ahead, preferably the morning of the day it is to be served, but bake it at mealtime.

2. The salad can be prepped ahead and, undressed, stored in plastic bags. The soup may be prepped ahead but brought together before mealtime, as can the veal dish.

POACHED EGGS AND PARMIGIANO IN BROTH

Zuppa alla Pavese
MAKES 6 SERVINGS

This is a famous Italian soup created in Pavia, a city in Lombardy, in 1525, for a king who was ruling the region at the time.

Some people poach the eggs before adding them to the soup so that they can be sure the eggs are cooked. Others place the eggs raw into the bowl; if the broth is boiling hot, the eggs will cook in it, as long as the broth is gently poured over the eggs to avoid breaking the yolks. I think you will find it easier to poach the eggs first. Remember, butter takes over for oil in Lombardy, so the soup is enriched by butter, and butter is also used to brown the bread.

4 tablespoons (½ stick) butter, melted
12 slices Italian bread, each 1 inch thick
4 cups each beef and chicken broth, or 8 cups
    mixed broth (page 8)
1 teaspoon distilled vinegar
6 eggs

6 tablespoons freshly grated Parmesan cheese
Sea salt and freshly ground pepper, to taste

1. Preheat the oven to 350F. Butter all the bread slices on both sides and place them on a baking sheet. Toast the bread in the oven, turning once, until golden on both sides, about 10 minutes total.

2. Bring the two broths to boil in a medium-size saucepan over medium heat. Cover the pan, reduce the heat, and simmer.

3. In a nonreactive skillet, add water to fill three-fourths full. Add the vinegar and bring to a boil. Reduce the heat to a simmer. Break an egg into a saucer and slip it into the skillet. Add 2 more eggs. Poach 5 minutes or until the whites are set and the yolks semi-soft. Carefully remove the eggs with a slotted spoon to 3 layers of paper towels. Repeat this for the other 3 eggs. Then trim off the ragged egg white, leaving ½ to 1 inch of white around each egg.

4. Place 2 slices of the toasted bread into 6 warmed wide bowls, arranging the slices side by side. Place a poached egg over the bread slices and sprinkle with 1 tablespoon grated cheese. Carefully ladle the hot broth into the soup bowls. Add salt and pepper.

VEAL CUTLET IN THE MILAN MANNER

Costoletta alla milanese

MAKES 6 SERVINGS

The true Milanese chop is the one with the bone, and the chop should be nicked with a knife on the outer edge so that during cooking it doesn't curl up. According to the Milanese, pounding the veal helps the crumbs adhere better. If the meat browns too quickly, the heat is too high.

> 6 veal chops with bone
> Milk to cover the chops
> 2 large eggs
> 1 cup plain bread crumbs
> ½ cup butter
> 2 tablespoons vegetable oil
> 6 large lemon wedges, seeds removed
> Sea salt and freshly ground pepper, to taste

1. Trim any fat from the chops and be sure to nick them at the outer edge to prevent curling. Flatten each chop with a heavy knife or meat pounder to the thickness of a finger as they do in Milan. Put the chops in a deep nonreactive bowl or casserole and pour milk over them. Let stand for 1 hour to soften and tenderize the meat. Remove the chops, discard the milk, and pat the chops dry with paper towels.

2. Beat the eggs in a flat-type bowl. Put the bread crumbs on a flat plate. Dip the chops into the egg and then into the bread crumbs. Press the crumbs into the chops with the palms of your hands.

3. Heat half of the butter and a tablespoon of oil in a large, heavy skillet, large enough to hold 3 chops. When the butter is bubbly, add the chops and cook over medium-high heat until both sides are browned, 2 to 3 minutes per side. Reduce the heat and cook about 5 minutes longer, to cook the insides. Remove the veal to a platter. Clean the skillet with paper towels, and cook the other 3 chops in the same way.

4. Serve with a lemon wedge after salting and peppering the chop.

ARUGULA AND TOMATO SALAD WITH LEMON DRESSING

Insalata di rucula al limone

MAKES 6 SERVINGS

Arugula, usually sold in small bunches, consists of small flat leaves on long stems. It is often taken for dandelions. In Italy, its roots are almost always attached. Its mustard-like taste is distinctive and the more mature, the stronger the taste. It is fun to grow because the leaves can be snipped at the base of the plant and in a few days there will be new growth. One can find it in most supermarkets these days, although it wasn't around some years ago until the popularity of Italian ingredients took hold in this country.

> ⅓ cup extra-virgin olive oil
> 3 tablespoons fresh lemon juice
> ½ teaspoon freshly grated lemon zest
> 1 teaspoon sugar
> 1 clove garlic, minced
> Sea salt and freshly ground pepper,
>   to taste
> 8 cups arugula leaves, washed and dried
> 2 ripe medium tomatoes, trimmed, sliced into
>   thin wedges

1.   Whisk together the oil, lemon juice and zest, sugar, garlic, salt and pepper until blended. Let rest for 2 or 3 minutes to let the sugar dissolve.

2.   Whisk the dressing again. Add the arugula and toss well. Add the tomatoes and toss lightly. Serve right away.

APPLES AND PEARS WITH GINGER IN A MILAN CHARLOTTE

Mele e pere allo zenzero in charlotte alla milanese

MAKES 6 SERVINGS

There is an old dessert in Milan that is made in a ring mold by placing buttered and sugared pieces of French bread in the bottom of the mold, layering the bread with apples, raisins and pine nuts and again more sugared and buttered bread on top. When it is cooked, some rum is added and set aflame. I have updated this dessert by lining small timbales with thin bread pieces, filling it with apples and pears, baking them and turning them out. They are as pretty as a picture and delicious. Lining the timbales with the bread is quite simple. Think it through before attempting it, and you'll see how easy it is. No rum, no flambé. That is too French for my Italian taste.

FOR THE FILLING
3 Fuji apples, peeled, cored and sliced fine
3 pears, peeled, cored and sliced fine
4 tablespoons butter
1 cup sugar
4 tablespoons finely chopped candied ginger
4 tablespoons fresh lemon juice

FOR THE MOLDS
12 slices Pepperidge Farm thin-sliced white bread, crusts removed
1 stick butter (½ cup), at room temperature

TO SERVE
½ cup heavy cream, whipped
2 tablespoons softened Gorgonzola cheese
2 tablespoons finely chopped candied ginger

1.   *To make the filling:* Combine all the ingredients in a large skillet or saucepan and cook over low heat, stirring frequently, until the fruit is tender, about 20 minutes.

2.   *To make the molds:* Preheat oven to 350F. The timbales (mold) should hold 5 ounces. (I use ones that are 2¼ inches deep with a top diameter of 2⅝ inches and the bottom has a diameter of 2 inches.) Butter 6 slices of bread, and cut each in 4 equal pieces. Cover with plastic and set aside.

3.   Lay the remaining 6 slices on a flat work surface. Using appropriate-size round cutters, cut 2 rounds, one for the bottom and top of each timbale. If you don't have the right size cutters, improvise. Glasses that are 2 inches wide at the mouth and 1-ounce bar (jigger) glasses can be used to cut the bread into rounds. Liberally butter the inside of each timbale and liberally butter the 6 smaller and 6 larger rounds of bread.

4.   Place a small round of bread in each of the 6 timbales, buttered side down. Then take 4 buttered squares and place them inside the mold, buttered side against the mold, to fit around the inside. Simply lay one next to the other, and they will fit. Spoon in some of the apple and pear mixture, almost to the top of the mold. Place a larger bread round, buttered side up, in the top of each timbale, covering the apple and pear filling.

5.   Set the 6 timbales in a small baking dish and bake for about 45 minutes, until the bread is

golden. Remove from the oven and let rest for 5 minutes or so.

6. *To serve:* With a sharp paring knife, insert it into the timbale between the bread and the outer rim and go around the mold to help loosen the mold. With the help of a cloth napkin, turn out each mold onto the center of a dessert plate. Combine the whipped cream and the Gorgonzola by swirling the cheese into the whipped cream. Do not try to combine them completely. Spoon some of this sauce to the side of each mold. Sprinkle some of the ginger over each of the plates, and serve.

MILAN'S DIVINE RISOTTO AT AURORA'S: MENU FOR 6

MENU

Broccoli, Baked with Prosciutto
Broccoli con prosciutto al forno

Veal Shanks, the Milan Way
Fetta di stinco di vitello brasato alla Milanese

Risotto, the Milan Way
Risotto alla Milanese

Baby Spinach Salad with Oil and Lemon Dressing
Spinaci in insalata con olio e limone

Fresh Orange Slices with Slivers of Orange Zest
Arance con scorza

The most famous of all Italian rice dishes is risotto, which originated in Milan in the sixteenth century, when rice began to be cultivated on a large scale in the Po Valley in Piedmont. More rice, and a greater variety of it, is produced in Italy than anywhere else in Europe. Rice, along with beans and polenta, are almost as important in Italian cooking as pasta. All these dishes are served as *primi piatti* (first courses) in many forms. Italians, as others in agricultural nations, relied on these protein-rich ingredients in place of meat, and consequently, many wonderful, healthy and tasty recipes were developed over the years.

To make risotto properly, one needs superfine rice such as Arborio, Carnaroli or Vialone Nano. Italians classify their rice by size: the shortest, called *ordinario,* is used for puddings; *semifino* for soups and salads; *fino* for more soups and salads; and the *superfino,* which is the longest grain. *Superfino,* able to grow to three times its size in cooking and enabling it to absorb all the broth and flavors of other foods while keeping its shape, is the ideal rice for risotto. Most restaurants in Italy, as in many homes, especially in the north, feature risotto, but one divine risotto I remember was at a restaurant called Aurora's, on Via Savona, in Milan. I ran into it quite by accident. As anyone who has traveled in Italy knows, not all restaurants stay open on Sundays and in some locations, it may be difficult to dine out on this day, even in a big city such as Milan; Aurora's was open. Here is a place where Piedmontese cooking triumphs. Special Piedmontese cheese, wines, mushrooms and truffles are literally poured into the cooking of this restaurant. The decor and feeling of the place is a 1900s look, and weather permitting, it is still possible to play bocce ball and dine outdoors.

Wine Selection

Select either a Sassella, Grumella or Inferno. These are considered the great reds of Lombardy, made mostly of the Nebbiolo grape as in Piedmont. They sometimes seem to have a more brillant color and a prettier nose than the Piedmontese wines, to make up for their shortcomings elsewhere.

Preparation Advice

1. The veal shanks can be cooked ahead and reheated. The dessert can be made ahead and refrigerated. Prep the lettuces and store in plastic bags; make the salad dressing and leave at room temperature.

2. Make the broccoli and the risotto shortly before mealtime.

BROCCOLI, BAKED WITH PROSCIUTTO

Broccoli con prosciutto al forno
MAKES 6 SERVINGS

I have never seen this dish served outside Italy, yet it is an ideal preparation for the American table. It is the way to serve broccoli to someone who may not be fond of it. Remember, this is a cooked broccoli dish, not one in which broccoli has been dipped in hot water and pulled out almost immediately. The prosciutto slice should crisp, allowing its juices and flavor to permeate the broccoli.

> 2 bunches fresh broccoli
> 2 tablespoons fresh lemon juice
> 4 strips lemon zest
> 1/4 cup chicken broth
> 6 tablespoons butter
> Sea salt and freshly ground pepper
> Freshly grated nutmeg
> 6 tablespoons freshly grated Parmesan
>   cheese
> 6 thin slices prosciutto

1. Trim the broccoli spears by removing all the leaves, keeping the florets in as large bunches as is possible. Pare the stalks and cut off the bottom parts of the stems. Keep removing pieces of stems until you reach the tender portion. (Most Italians prefer the tender stems as much as the florets.) Rinse the trimmed broccoli and stems and drain.

2. Preheat the oven to 400F. Bring a large pot of water to a boil. Add the broccoli, lemon juice and zest, and cook until tender, uncovered, over high heat, for about 5 minutes. Drain.

3. Add the broth and butter to a large ceramic or glass baking dish. Bake until the butter melts. Arrange the broccoli in 6 "bundles," and spoon the melted butter and broth over each. Add salt and pepper. Sprinkle the nutmeg and cheese over each portion. Place a slice of prosciutto over each bundle and bake for 8 to 10 minutes. When serving, spoon some of the buttery juices remaining in the baking pan over each portion.

VEAL SHANKS, THE MILAN WAY

Fetta di stinco di vitello brasato alla Milanese
MAKES 6 SERVINGS

When all is said and done, it is again the Italians that use lemon peel most creatively. One of their Milanese dishes; osso buco, composed of thick pieces of veal shank braised in wine, vegetables and tomatoes, is garnished, when it is served, with a colorful combination of finely chopped lemon peel, garlic and parsley. This inspired mixture, called *gremolata*, transforms the osso buco, an essentially lusty dish, into a masterpiece. Imaginative cooks also use this garnish on other braised and sautéed veal dishes, and may even, on occasion, sprinkle it over broiled or sautéed fish. Osso buco means the "bone with a hole." To complete the experience of eating this dish, one must pick the marrow out of the bone and serve the osso buco with risotto, cooked the Milan way.

2 celery ribs, trimmed
1 leek, white part and some tender green part
2 large cloves garlic, peeled
1 onion
1 large carrot, trimmed
3 tablespoons butter
1½ cups pureed canned plum tomatoes (after putting through a food mill)
1 tablespoon finely chopped fresh basil or 1 teaspoon dried, crushed
½ cup all-purpose flour
Sea salt and freshly ground pepper
6 (about 3-inch-long) veal shanks (4 to 5 pounds total), each tied with a string to hold the meat in place
4 tablespoons plus extra-virgin olive oil
1 cup dry white wine
1 cup beef broth
Bouquet garni composed of 6 parsley sprigs, 2 bay leaves and 2 (2 × ½-inch) pieces lemon zest, tied together in a small bundle

FOR THE GREMOLATA
¼ cup finely chopped fresh Italian parsley
1 tablespoon finely chopped lemon zest
1 tablespoon finely minced garlic

1. Pare the strings off the celery and wash thoroughly; also carefully wash the leek to be sure you rid it of its sand. Chop the celery, leek, garlic, onion and carrot as finely as you can. Together, if chopped finely and firmly packed, it should make about a full cup. If there is a little more, do not be concerned. The Italians call this mixture *soffrito*.

2. Melt the butter in a heavy, deep casserole, large enough to hold the 6 shanks snugly, and add the chopped vegetables. Cook over low heat,

uncovered, stirring occasionally, until soft, 7 or 8 minutes. Do not brown.

3. Add the tomatoes and basil, increase the heat to high and cook for several minutes to cook off most of the tomato juices and to thicken the mixture. Set the casserole aside.

4. Put the flour in a flat plate and add a liberal amount of salt and pepper. Mix well. Put a shank into the flour mixture and coat evenly, shaking off the excess flour. Repeat with the other 5 shanks. In a large skillet, heat the oil (not quite to the smoking point) over medium-high heat and sauté 3 of the shanks on all sides to brown them. As each piece turns golden, remove from the skillet and put it in the casserole. Continue until all shanks are browned. If more oil is needed during the sautéeing, add it 1 tablespoon at a time. Pour off any oil in the skillet, but return the skillet unwashed to the heat.

5. Add the wine and bring it to a boil, scraping the bottom of the pan. Boil for about 5 minutes to evaporate the wine; add the broth and bring just to a boil. Pour the broth mixture over the shanks and vegetables in the casserole. Add the bundle of herbs and lemon zest. Cover tightly, bring to a boil, reduce the heat and simmer for 1 hour, until the meat is tender and appears as if it will fall off the bone. If the casserole becomes dry, add more broth as needed.

6. *To make the gremolata:* Combine all the ingredients, making sure the zest is as thinly peeled from the lemon as is possible. If this is made before the shanks are ready to be served, put in a small bowl and cover tightly with plastic wrap.

7. To serve, transfer the meat from the casserole to individual plates or to a large platter. Be sure the marrow does not fall out of the bone. Italians consider the marrow the essential reason for cooking veal shanks in this way. Taste the sauce and if it satisfies your taste, spoon some over the shanks and add the gremolata. (If the sauce needs more cooking, continue to cook, uncovered over medium heat.)

RISOTTO, THE MILAN WAY

Risotto alla Milanese
MAKES 6 SERVINGS

Americans love risotto but many of them fear cooking it. There is no mystery to cooking this if one follows the cardinal rule that the liquid should be added to the pan in small amounts and it should be absorbed by the rice, before adding more liquid.

- ¼ cup dried mushrooms
- ½ pound (2 sticks) butter
- 1 small onion, finely diced
- White pepper
- 2 tablespoons dry white wine
- 1 pound Arborio, Carnaroli or Vialaone Nero rice
- 5 cups chicken broth
- ¼ teaspoon saffron threads, soaked in ¼ cup chicken broth
- ¾ cup freshly grated Parmesan cheese

1. Put the mushrooms in a large strainer and run under cool water to rid them of any dirt that may be there. Rinse several times until they are thoroughly clean. Then put them in a small bowl with about ½ cup warm water to soak, preferably for 2 hours, but minimally for 1. (Do not soak mushrooms beyond several hours.) Drain and have ready for use.

2. Melt the butter in a large saucepan and sauté the onion until golden, about 5 minutes. Add some white pepper. Add the wine and cook over high heat, uncovered, until the wine evaporates, 2 to 3 minutes.

3. Add the rice, stir well to coat the rice and cook for 5 minutes. Stir in the drained mushrooms.

4. Add the broth, ½ cup at a time, stirring all the time. When the broth is absorbed, add another ½ cup. Keep doing this until the broth is used up, about 20 minutes. When the rice is al dente, add the saffron and its liquid. The saffron will make the rice a wonderful yellow color. Stir in ½ cup of the cheese.

5. To serve, put all the rice in a shallow bowl, or put some on each of six plates alongside the veal shanks, and top with the remaining cheese.

BABY SPINACH SALAD WITH OIL AND LEMON DRESSING

Spinaci in insalata con olio e limone
MAKES 6 SERVINGS

Olive oil and fresh lemon juice with freshly ground pepper and sea salt dresses Italian salads more than any other dressing. This is a heavenly salad if the spinach is young and tender and the dressing kept as simple as it is stated here. Trimmed, washed and dried spinach may be prepared hours ahead and refrigerated in a plastic bag; remove from the refrigerator 15 minutes prior to using and add the dressing just before serving.

- 1½ pounds young, fresh spinach
- 1 small celery heart with leaves, thinly sliced
- ¼ cup finely diced red onion
- ¼ cup extra-virgin olive oil
- 2 tablespoons fresh lemon juice
- Sea salt and freshly ground pepper

1.   Trim the spinach and remove outer leaves if they are large and blemished. Cut off stem ends and any stems that appear too large. Wash the spinach several times in cool water to rid the leaves of sand. When they are clean, spin the spinach dry. Put it in a large bowl with the celery and onion.

2.   In a small bowl, combine the oil and lemon juice. Add some salt and a liberal amount of pepper. Pour over the greens and toss lightly but well. Serve right away.

FRESH ORANGE SLICES WITH SLIVERS OF ORANGE ZEST

Arance con scorza
MAKES 6 SERVINGS

The Vin Santo wine used here is an Italian term used for strong, sweet, white wines. Actually, this sweet dessert wine is made all over Italy, but wine experts prefer those from Umbria, Tuscany, Trentino (near Venice) and Urbino (in the province of Marche). The grapes (varying from one region to the next) are dried on straw after the vintage and not pressed until as late as the following Easter. Since it is made during Holy Week, it is called Vino Santo. It is then aged in cask for four to six years and produces a scented, luscious, delicate amber-colored dessert wine. This dish can be made ahead by as much as six or eight hours before serving. Refrigerate it, and remove from the refrigerator one half hour before serving.

6 large oranges or 8 smaller ones with good, clear skins
⅔ cup sugar
½ cup Vin Santo
½ cup fresh orange juice

1 cup fresh raspberries or 1 (10-ounce) package frozen, thawed

1.   With a vegetable peeler, remove the orange zest from 3 of the oranges, taking as little pith as possible. Peel all the oranges. Cut the zest into the thinnest strips you can and set aside. Discard the other peels or save for another use.

2.   Slice the peeled oranges crosswise, remove any seeds and overlap the slices on a large platter.

3.   Over low heat and without stirring, cook the sugar in a saucepan until it turns dark brown around the edges. Remove from the heat and add the wine, orange juice and zest. If the sauce appears too thin, cook a while longer. Then remove from the heat to cool, and pour over the fresh orange slices. This may be made ahead by 6 or 8 hours and refrigerated. Remove the oranges from the refrigerator about 30 minutes before serving, and add some raspberries, fresh or frozen atop the oranges.

A SPECIAL FAMILY EVENT OUTSIDE MILAN AT COMO: MENU FOR 4

MENU

Octopus with Oil, Garlic and Lemon
Polipo con olio, aglio e limone

Regional Lentil Soup
Zuppa di lenticchie

Fresh Trout on the Grill
Trota alla griglia

Fried Zucchini with Caper and Chive Sauce
Zucchine piccanti

Cream with Lemon and Brandy
Crema al limone

Rome, Florence and Venice are loved, but on occasion, the Roman strikes, the Florentine motorcycles and the Venetian crowds turn my head in the direction of quieter, easier-to-visit towns and villages in the inimitable Italian countryside where home cooking is passed on from one generation to the next. Getting out of Milan or Venice can be a living nightmare, but the countryside between the two is meant to be enjoyed, mile by mile. Como is an antique city that had a place in the Roman Empire, and continued as an important center during the Middle Ages. In the 1500s, it was a center for silk, and though raw fiber is no longer produced there, Como still produces about two-thirds of Italy's finished silk (and one-third of the world's). I remember the Duomo and the *broletto* (town hall) and the shops filled with thousands of silk ties for sale, but I remember most the meal I had at a charming restaurant, Navedano, on Via Pannilani, not easy to find. "*La strada e brutta*, the street is ugly, but people come here to eat and they don't mind the ugly road," said Lella Casartelli, who with her husband, Giuliano, are the chefs/owners. His family has had this restaurant for over 120 years.

The art of eating is evident at Navedano. There are no printed menus, people sit for hours at lovely tablecloths of vivid yellow under vases of red and pink roses and enjoy the food suggested by a family member, including Giuliano's 80-year-old mother. They eat the cooked octopus in garlicky flavors with great ease. With tranquillity, and no rush whatsoever, they move to a delicious regional lentil soup. No small talk over the tagliarini with fresh watercress, lightly sauced with cream, pine nuts and fresh basil. No fanfare, no back-slapping, just the gentle swish of long, thin pasta, easily twirled around a fork, making its way into the bodies of young and old. Was it an event to be served trout, just fresh out of Lake Garda, in cartaccio? No, everyone seem to take it for granted. Good food is expected; everyone seems comfortable, satisfied and happy, *a tavolo*. It is like having a wonderful meal at home. Here is a smaller meal from Navedano for your American table.

Wine Selection

Select a Lugana, probably the best white wine of the Garda district, and one of the best in all of Lombardy. It is made from the Trebbiano grape and is aged in casks for as many as four years before bottling—unusual for a white wine. While it ages in wood, it gains a beautiful pale golden color. It is a good wine to drink with fish. Or, select a Frecciarossa with the brand name La Vigne Blanche—a clear dry white wine with a slightly bitter finish. It is made of equal quantities of Pinot Nero and Reisling Renano with the Pinot being more noticeable to the nose and palate. The vineyards are in the village of Frecciarossa, near Casteggio, and belong to the Odero family.

Preparation Advice

1. Make the lentil soup ahead by one or two days.

2. The octopus dish may be prepared one day ahead and refrigerated, saving the presentation of radicchio until just before serving. The zucchini may be made ahead.

3. The fish should be grilled just before mealtime.

4. The dessert may be made early in the day of the meal.

OCTOPUS WITH OIL, GARLIC, AND LEMON

Polipo con olio, aglio e limone
MAKES 4 SERVINGS

Octopi, small and large, are appreciated by Italians all over the boot. It is an ingredient in the well-known fish soup, *zuppa di pesce alla gigliese*, meaning in the style of Giglio, an island off the Tuscan coast where ancient Romans once built vacation villas. In Grossetto, also in Tuscany, it is combined with mussels and cooked in oil. Rome distinguishes its fish chowder by adding octopus, and in Emilia-Romagna they are given local dialect names according to size from the very large to the smallest, which they call *polipetti* or *fragoline di mare*, meaning sea strawberries because of their rosy color. In the south, they cook *polipi alla Lucania* a long time in a sauce of oil, parsley and hot red pepper. In Lombardy, they are cooked for salads and antipasti, and I've added some shrimp here more for American tastes (quite frankly, to help bring those Americans who shy away from octopus closer to eating it). In Como and elsewhere, it would be served alone or with squid or cuttlefish.

1 large onion, chopped
1 large carrot, trimmed and cut into small dice
2 ribs celery, trimmed and strings removed, cut into small dice
Sea salt
4 lemons
1 small octopus, about 1 pound, no larger, cleaned by fishmonger, or see Notabene, below
1 pound shrimp, shelled and deveined
Freshly ground pepper
1/3 cup plus 2 tablespoons extra-virgin olive oil
1/4 cup finely chopped fresh Italian parsley
4 radicchio leaves, rinsed and dried

1. Bring a large saucepan of water (about 3 quarts) to a boil, adding about one-third of the onion, one-third of the carrot and one-third of the celery, a good dash of salt and 2 of the lemons, cut in 4 pieces each. When it has reached the boil again, add the octopus and the shrimp. Remove the shrimp with a slotted spoon as soon as they have turned pink, 3 or 4 minutes. Do not overcook the shrimp or they will toughen. Set aside to cool.

2. Continue to cook the octopus and the vegetables until tender, for 45 minutes to over 1 hour. When the octopus is tender, remove it carefully and allow to cool. Discard the liquid and its contents.

3. While the octopus is cooking, heat 2 tablespoons oil in a medium skillet. Add the remaining onion, carrot and celery and sauté until tender, about 10 minutes. Transfer to a bowl. Add salt and pepper. Add the shrimp. Cut the octopus into small bite-size pieces, 1/2 to 3/4 inches, and add to the bowl.

4. Squeeze the juice from the remaining lemons and add to the bowl with 1/3 cup olive oil. Toss lightly. Add the parsley and toss until well mixed. Check for salt and pepper seasoning, and adjust the lemon and oil flavoring to your liking.

5. If individual servings are to be made, spoon some of the antipasto on a radicchio leaf, or put the radicchio leaves on a platter and spoon antipasto into them.

Notabene:

To prepare octopus for cooking: Most fish shops sell octopus precleaned. If it isn't, ask your fishmonger to do it for you. If the answer is no, then invert the octopus by turning it inside out as you would a swimsuit. Remove the beak and the viscera from the mouth and also the ink sac. Rinse it very well under cool, running water. Luigi Miroli, in Portofino, told me that there is a little trick to tenderizing octopus; after cleaning it, put it into boiling water, holding it by its mantle. Count to 12 and remove it. Do this two more times before adding it to the saucepan as in Step 2 above.

REGIONAL LENTIL SOUP

Zuppa di lenticchie
MAKES 4 SERVINGS

The lentils will absorb the flavor of the onions, carrots and celery, and of the oil and butter, to make a delicious-tasting soup. This soup seems to taste better after it sits in the refrigerator for a day or two.

1 tablespoon extra-virgin olive oil
3 tablespoons butter
½ cup finely chopped onion, carrot and celery (about 3 tablespoons of each)
2 tablespoons finely chopped prosciutto or pancetta
1 large clove garlic, minced
1 cup canned Italian plum tomatoes with juices, seeded and chopped
1 cup lentils, picked over
3 to 4 cups combined beef and chicken broth
Freshly ground pepper
6 tablespoons or more freshly grated Parmesan cheese

1.   Heat the oil and 1 tablespoon of the butter in a medium saucepan over medium heat. Sauté the onion, carrot and celery, stirring often, until the onion begins to turn golden, about 5 minutes.

2.   Add the prosciutto and sauté until lightly browned, 2 minutes. Add the garlic and cook 1 minute. Add the tomatoes and cook for 10 minutes.

3.   Add the lentils and 3 cups of broth. Liberally sprinkle with pepper. Bring to a boil and reduce the heat to a slow, steady simmer. Cover the saucepan and simmer until the lentils are tender, 35 to 40 minutes. If the soup appears too thick, add some or all of the remaining broth. Remove from the heat and stir in the remaining butter and 3 tablespoons of the cheese. Pass remaining cheese.

FRESH TROUT ON THE GRILL

Trota alla griglia
MAKES 4 SERVINGS

For centuries, Italians and other Mediterranean natives have cooked fish in simple ways, which are better and healthier than other preparations. A few drops of good olive oil will make all the difference, and it seems now that Americans are getting the know-how of the way Italians cook. This simple, effective dish goes well with the zucchini dish whose recipe follows.

If you caught your own fish, see the Notabene below for how to clean it.

4 fresh trout, slightly under 1 pound each, dressed, washed and dried (head and tails removed if you choose)
¼ cup finely chopped fresh Italian parsley
1 clove garlic and 1 tablespoon finely chopped scallions, minced together
6 tablespoons extra-virgin olive oil
Sea salt and freshly ground pepper
8 thin slices of lemon, seeds removed
2 tablespoons fresh lemon juice
4 full sprigs fresh Italian parsley, for garnish

1.   Preheat the broiler or grill. With a sharp paring knife, cut 3 slashes in the skin of each fish.

2.   Combine the parsley, garlic mixture, 2 tablespoons of the oil, salt and pepper. Work the parsley mixture into the slashes. Put the trout on an oiled baking pan and sprinkle 2 tablespoons of the oil over the trout.

3.   Broil or grill the trout about 5 inches from the heat source. If using a grill with charcoal, be sure the coals are at the ashen stage (gray with the coals somewhat separated). Either broil or grill for 3 or 4 minutes per side. To check for doneness, spear one trout with a wooden skewer. If the skewer penetrates the trout easily, it is done; if it meets resistance, it is not. When done, the inside of the trout should be opaque.

4.   When the trout are done, transfer to individual plates and add a lemon slice at the head and tail ends. Sprinkle with remaining olive oil and lemon juice. Garnish with parsley sprigs.

Notabene: How to Clean a Whole Fish

1.   Cut off the pelvic, pectoral and anal fins (all on the sides) with scissors; then snip off the dorsal (on the underbelly) fins.

2.   Hold the fish by the tail with one hand, and scale the fish from the tail to the head, using a scaling knife.

3.   Using a small sharp knife, make a small incision from the vent (just forward of the anal fin, along to the gill (just under the mouth), being careful not to cut into the entrails. Remove all the entrails and scrape away any remaining tissue.

4.   Cut out the reddish gills by lifting the gill cover with one hand with scissors in the other. The reddish gill is underneath the gill. Do the same on the other side of the fish. Rinse the whole fish thoroughly under cool running water and dry with paper towels.

●FRIED ZUCCHINI ●WITH CAPER AND ●CHIVE SAUCE

Zucchine piccanti
MAKES 4 SERVINGS

The secret to this dish is thoroughly drying the zucchini pieces before adding them to the skillet. If you would rather not use anchovies (I can't imagine why not but some Americans are still squeamish about them), be sure to salt adequately. These must be served with fresh bread crumbs and they should be added at the last moment.

4 zucchini, about 1 × 6-inches each
5 tablespoons extra-virgin olive oil
2 anchovy fillets, drained and dried
1 tablespoon each chopped fresh Italian parsley, capers (drained and chopped) and chopped fresh chives
2 tablespoons white wine vinegar
Sea salt and freshly ground pepper
1/4 cup fresh bread crumbs, toasted (page 7)

1.   Rinse the zucchini and cut both ends off of each. Cut each in half across the middle to make two smaller zucchini. Then cut these in half lengthwise. There should be 4 pieces from each zucchini. Dry with paper towels and set aside.

2.   Heat 2 tablespoons of the oil in a large skillet and sauté the zucchini pieces on both sides until they are tender and lightly browned, 3 to 4 minutes per side. Leave in the skillet.

3.   In a small bowl, combine the remaining oil and the anchovies, and with a fork, mash the anchovies so they blend into the oil. Add the herbs and the vinegar. Taste for salt and add

some, if needed. Liberally add pepper. Mix well and pour over the zucchini. Toss lightly but well. Transfer to a small platter and sprinkle with the bread crumbs.

CREAM WITH LEMON AND BRANDY

Crema al limone
MAKES 4 SERVINGS

This simple dessert is an example of the fine Italian hand and its use of lemon. The zest and the lemon juice must be fresh.

    1 pint heavy cream
    1 tablespoon finely minced lemon zest
    ½ cup confectioners' sugar
    1½ tablespoons fresh lemon juice
    2 tablespoons brandy
    8 chocolate curls, for garnish

1. Whip the cream until it forms peaks. Fold in the lemon zest with the help of a rubber spatula.

2. Fold in the sugar, 2 tablespoons at a time. Add the lemon juice and again fold gently. If it should need additional whipping, do so with a wire whisk. Fold in the brandy.

3. Fill 4 stem glasses with the cream mixture and refrigerate for a minimum of 2 hours to allow the flavors to blend. Before serving, add 1 or 2 chocolate curls to the top.

LOVING ITALY WITH FRIENDS IN BERGAMO: OL GIOPI E LA MARGI: MENU FOR 4

MENU

Ravioli, Bergamo Style
Casansei alla Bergamasca

Roasted Rabbit in Red Wine
Coniglio arrosto al vino rosso

Polenta in Bergamo
Polenta Taragna

Cheese with Mixed Salad
Formaggio con insalata mista

Sambuca-Flavored Cocoa Roll
Torta di cioccolato con Sambuca

Signs are everywhere in Bergamo, a city twenty miles or so outside Milan, that tell you there are two towns: Bergamo Bassa, the modern city several hundred feet below Bergamo Alta, the historic hill town. They are connected by a road and a *funicolare* and one should try both. The Bassa town is a hub of activity and architecturally reminiscent of the Mussolini era, although much of it was built at the turn of the century. In the Bassa part of Bergamo, there is a magical restaurant, Ol Giopi e la Margi (two fictional characters). There, Ivar Foglieni, as president of the *Associazione Cuochi Bergamaschi,* reigns supreme as a regional food authority. He tells a tale of his youth. He started work as a young intern at one of Bergamo's fine restaurants. On the day he was hired, he asked the chef/owner what time should he be at work the following morning. He was told 9 A.M. Young Ivar arrived promptly at 9 A.M. and to his surprise, noted that everything was cooked. Ivar explained that the chef didn't want to reveal his cooking secrets to him, the new apprentice.

Today, Ivar has no phobia about sharing his knowledge and experience in the Italian food world; so much so, that he wants to bring a crew of fourteen culinary experts to the United States to promote and share the cooking of Bergamo with Americans. "Rice is Milanese," he said one evening, "but in Bergamo, it's pasta. And here, the three most important pastas are ravioli, tagliatelle and gnocchi, and in that order," he added. He described the most important pasta sauces and listed them in this order of importance: butter and sage, cream and mushrooms and tomatoes with herbs. "Rosemary, sage, and basil dominate in our cooking, and polenta is one of the most popular foods in this area." He mentioned a typical Sunday meal, when entire families come to the restaurant. They eat polenta, not bread. Ravioli with a butter and sage sauce is the first course, then polenta with roasted rabbit for the second. Cheeses follow: taleggio, formagele del valcavallina, branzi, stracchino and a very rich one called colature.

Wine Selection

One of Italy's finest sparking wines is Spumante, white or rosé. It is made from the Pinot Bianco, Nero or Grigio and Chardonnay. Ca'del Bosco is considered Italy's finest sparkling winemaker, but there are many others. See which Spumante is offered by your local wine shop. Serve it throughout this meal.

Preparation Advice

1. Make the dessert one day ahead, cover well and refrigerate. Bring to room temperature before serving the next day. The ravioli may be made ahead, also covered and refrigerated. Cook and sauce them just before serving.

2. Salad ingredients can be prepared and refrigerated in a plastic bag, one day ahead. Dressing may be made ahead, but the salad should be combined just before eating.

3. The rabbit and polenta should be made shortly before mealtime.

RAVIOLI, BERGAMO STYLE

Casansei alla Bergamasca
MAKES 40 TO 50 RAVIOLI

These ravioli are made basically the same as most others, except for the filling, which combines pork, chicken and salami. It is difficult to find this particular type of ravioli in food shops, even Italian specialty stores in the United States, so they have to be homemade. Because the filling is somewhat complex in taste and texture, they are dressed simply in melted butter and sage with the delightful crisped crumbs.

FOR THE PASTA
1½ to 2 cups unbleached all-purpose flour
2 eggs, lightly beaten
1 tablespoon extra-virgin olive oil

FOR THE FILLING
4 tablespoons extra-virgin olive oil
¼ pound ground pork and chicken (equal amounts)
2 tablespoons finely chopped salami
2 tablespoons each finely chopped carrot, shallot and celery
2 tablespoons freshly grated Parmesan cheese
3 tablespoons fresh bread crumbs (page 7)
1 large egg, lightly beaten
1 tablespoon finely chopped Italian parsley
Sea salt and freshly ground pepper

FOR THE SAUCE
8 tablespoons butter
10 fresh sage leaves
Freshly grated Parmesan cheese
3 tablespoons fresh bread crumbs (page 7)

1. *To make the pasta:* Put 1½ cups flour into a bowl or on a flat work surface. Make a well in it and add the eggs, oil and some salt. Mix with a fork, holding the outer rim of the flour to keep its shape while mixing in the center. Keep doing this until most of the flour has been absorbed. If too moist, add a little more flour. Knead the dough, pushing down with the palms of your hands to make a smooth, satiny dough. Knead for 4 or 5 minutes; let rest for 1 or 2 minutes, then knead some more. Cover with a damp cloth and let rest for 30 minutes.

2. *To make the filling:* Heat 2 tablespoons of the oil in a saucepan over medium heat and sauté the pork, chicken and salami until they are browned, about 6 minutes. Add the carrot, shallot and celery and sauté for 10 minutes, stirring every few minutes.

3. Remove the saucepan from the heat, allow to cool for 5 minutes, and then add the cheese, bread crumbs, egg, parsley and the remaining olive oil. Mix lightly but well. Add salt and pepper. Set aside.

4. *To make the ravioli:* Cut the dough into four pieces and roll through a pasta machine working up to the next to last setting. The strips should be at least 4 to 5 inches wide. Lay a strip of pasta on a flat work surface and spoon a scant teaspoon of filling onto the pasta, making 2 rows at least 2 inches apart down the middle, and between each filling, the length of the strip. Dip a very small brush in warm water and brush around each mound of filling. Cover with another sheet of pasta. Press down with your fingers, going around each mound of filling, to secure the two pastas together. Use a ravioli cutter and cut into individual ravioli. Set aside on very lightly floured cloth towels if ready to cook them within 30 minutes. If not, put them on a plate and cover with damp towels and set in the refrigerator for several hours or overnight.

5. Cook the ravioli in rapidly boiling salted water until they come to the top, 4 or 5 minutes.

6. While the ravioli are cooking, make the sauce: In a large skillet, melt the butter over low heat and add the sage leaves. Brown the butter slightly to cook the sage. Drain the ravioli well, and add to the skillet. Stir carefully to coat the ravioli. Transfer to a large platter and sprinkle with the cheese and bread crumbs. Serve right away.

ROASTED RABBIT IN RED WINE

Coniglio arrosto al vino rosso
MAKES 4 SERVINGS

This recipe is for farmed rabbit; if you should use wild rabbit, marinate the pieces in a cup of red wine overnight before proceeding with the recipe. Discard the marinade.

2 tablespoons extra-virgin olive oil
1 medium onion, finely chopped
1 clove garlic, minced
1 small sausage link, casing removed
1 (2½-pound) rabbit, cleaned and readied for
    roasting, cut into 8 pieces
2 tablespoons finely chopped fresh
    rosemary
Sea salt and freshly ground pepper
1 cup red wine
½ cup vegetable broth

1. Preheat the oven to 350F. In an ovenproof casserole or baking pan, add the olive oil, onion, garlic, and sausage and bake until the onion begins to brown, about 10 minutes, stirring 2 or 3 times.

2. Add the rabbit pieces, rosemary and some salt and pepper. Turn the rabbit pieces over to coat them with the oil and sausage. Bake for 15 minutes.

3. Add the wine and bake, uncovered, about 40 minutes, until most of the wine has evaporated. As the wine cooks off, add some vegetable broth, a few tablespoons at a time and baste the rabbit several times. The total baking time should be 1 to 1½ hours. Cover with foil after the liquid has evaporated. Serve with the polenta offered in this menu.

POLENTA IN BERGAMO

Polenta Taragna
MAKES 4 SERVINGS

It is best and easiest to use Arrowhead Mills's yellow corn grits, organically produced, to make this polenta. It is available in most supermarkets. Also use the buckwheat flour made by Arrowhead Mills. The original recipe calls for the local Italian cheese called *formaggio di monte grassi*, which is difficult to find in most cheese shops, so I have found it easy to use taleggio or fontina as a satisfactory substitute.

    6 cups water
    Sea salt
    1¼ cups yellow corn grits
    ¼ cup buckwheat flour
    ½ cup taleggio or fontina cheese, cut in small
        pieces

    4 tablespoons butter
    6 fresh sage leaves; 4 chopped finely, 2 cut in
        halves, lengthwise

1. In a medium saucepan, bring the water to a boil. Add some salt.

2. Slowly stir in the grits and the buckwheat flour. Bring to a boil, reduce the heat and simmer, uncovered, for 5 minutes, stirring often.

3. Remove the pan from the heat. Add the cheese, butter and finely chopped sage leaves. Stir to melt the cheese and butter. Transfer to a flat-type bowl. Arrange 4 half sage leaves to resemble a flower with 4 petals in the center on top of the polenta. Serve or keep warm in a 250F oven for up to 30 minutes or so.

CHEESE WITH MIXED SALAD

Formaggio con insalata mista
MAKES 4 SERVINGS

Taleggio cheese, a stracchino type, is semisoft, but supple and springy feeling to the touch. It is mild but rich in flavor, full and creamy. It is made from cow's milk and is ripened for about two months. The interior color varies from creamy white to light yellow. It is similar to Bel Paese and comes from the Taleggio Valley in Lombardy.

    1 large bunch arugula leaves, rinsed and dried
    ½ head radicchio, rinsed, dried and shredded like
        cole slaw
    2 heads Belgian endive, trimmed and each cut
        into 4 lengths
    2 shallots, peeled and minced
    4 tablespoons extra-virgin olive oil
    2 tablespoons fresh lemon juice

1 teaspoon finely chopped orange zest
1 teaspoon minced fresh thyme
½ pound taleggio cheese

1.   Put everything, except the cheese, in a large bowl and toss lightly but well.

2.   Serve the salad with the cheese.

SAMBUCA-FLAVORED COCOA ROLL

Torta di cioccolato con Sambuca
MAKES 4 SERVINGS

This will serve more than four people but it will keep in the refrigerator for up to three days. It may also be frozen up to one month.

6 eggs, separated
1 cup sugar
6 ounces dark sweet chocolate
4 tablespoons Sambuca
3 tablespoons unsweetened cocoa powder
1 cup heavy cream

1.   Whip the egg yolks with ¾ cup of the sugar until they form a ribbon when the beaters are raised. Preheat the oven to 350F.

2.   Slowly melt the chocolate in the top of a double boiler pan over simmering water just until it is smooth. Add 3 tablespoons of the Sambuca, stir to combine and allow to cool until it is lukewarm. Blend into the yolk mixture.

3.   Beat the egg whites until they hold firm peaks and fold them into chocolate mixture.

4.   Butter a baking sheet, about 10 × 13 inches. Cover the bottom with waxed paper and butter the waxed paper. Spread the batter over the paper, smoothing it with a rubber spatula. Bake for 10 minutes, reduce the heat to 300F and bake for 5 minutes. Check for doneness by inserting a toothpick into the cake; if it comes out dry, the cake is done. Do not overcook the cake. Remove from the oven and cover with a damp towel.

5.   When the cake is cool, remove the towel and loosen the cake from the baking sheet. Dust the cake with 1½ tablespoons of the cocoa powder, using a small sieve. Turn the cake out onto another piece of waxed paper, and carefully peel off the buttered waxed paper from the bottom (which is now on top); be careful not to tear the cake.

6.   Whip the heavy cream with the remaining 1½ tablespoons cocoa powder, ¼ cup sugar and 1 tablespoon Sambuca. Spread this over the cake evenly and roll up jelly-roll style. Sprinkle with more cocoa powder before slicing and serving.

ONE-DISH MEALS

•BAKED MEAT-STUFFED •TURKEY ROLL

Petto di tacchino ripieno al forno
MAKES ABOUT 8 SERVINGS

Turkey was brought to Europe from America by the Spaniards in the early sixteenth century. The Italians took to it quickly. It may be the most popular form of poultry in Italy today. Milan, in Lombardy, features a roast turkey at Christmastime, but turkey preparations appear all over the boot any time of the year. This stuffed and rolled turkey breast is an adaptation of Milan's roast turkey with its complex, yet delicious filling. This can be made ahead and served cold with a salad. Or serve it warm with a sauce, as in the following recipe.

- 2 pounds turkey breast, boned and skinned
- 3 tablespoons butter
- 2 tablespoons extra-virgin olive oil
- 1 pound Italian sausage, removed from casing
- 1 carrot, finely chopped
- ½ onion, finely chopped
- 1 tablespoon each finely chopped rosemary and sage
- Sea salt and freshly ground pepper
- 6 ounces canned or jarred cooked chestnuts, coarsely chopped
- 12 walnut halves, coarsely chopped
- 4 tablespoons freshly grated Parmesan cheese

- 2 eggs, beaten
- 1 to 1½ cups white wine

1. With a sharp knife, cut part of the way through the turkey breast and open out the 2 halves, leaving them still attached. Pound the turkey with a mallet to get one large piece of meat. Your butcher should be willing to do this for you, if you ask.

2. In a large skillet, heat 2 tablespoons of the butter and 1 tablespoon of the olive oil over medium heat. Add the sausage, carrot, onion, rosemary and sage, and sauté until the meat begins to brown, about 10 minutes. Add some salt and pepper. Transfer this mixture to a large bowl to cool. Keep the skillet, as is, for a later step. Drain the sausage mixture into the skillet.

3. Add the chestnuts, walnuts, Parmesan cheese and eggs to the bowl with the sausage mixture and toss well. The stuffing should be slightly moist but not liquidy.

4. Spread the mixture over the turkey, leaving a ½-inch border all around. Roll up the turkey and tie it in four or five places across the roll, and once down the length, with kitchen string. Preheat the oven to 375F.

5. Reheat the skillet that sautéed the sausage, adding the remaining butter and oil. When bubbly, add the turkey roll and brown over medium-high heat, rotating to brown all sides, 12 to 14 minutes. Transfer to an ovenproof casserole with a cover.

6. Deglaze the skillet with ½ cup of the wine and pour over the turkey roll in the casserole. Add another ½ cup wine. Cover and bake for 20 minutes. Remove the cover, add the remaining wine, and cook, uncovered, for 25 minutes, basting every 10 minutes.

7. Remove from the oven and let the roast sit for about 10 minutes before slicing. Continue to cook the sauce to reduce it to your liking (thin or thicker). Remove the string and cut the turkey into thin slices. Serve the turkey with a little sauce to the edge of the slice. As a salad, use fresh or frozen green peas, thawed and cooked, with finely cut onions tossed with an oil-and-vinegar dressing.

Notabene:

If your butcher doesn't have a turkey breast of this size, use 3 smaller ones, each weighing about ¾ pound. Slice each almost through so you have 2 pieces of breast attached at one side. Open up, and flatten. Flattening is important because it increases the size of the roll; try to get an even thickness of about ⅓ inch. Repeat with the other two breasts. Lay the three pieces of turkey slightly overlapping one another with the shorter widths facing you. (the longer lengths will go from your left to right) Join each overlap with a long wooden skewer (you will need 2 of them, and they can be removed easily after the roll has baked and is to be served). Arrange the filling over all and start to roll up beginning with the side just before you. Tie in five places across the roll and once across the length.

COLD VEAL IN TUNA SAUCE

Vitello tonnato
MAKES ABOUT 8 SERVINGS

There is a popular Milanese saying (in dialect), *"Mai scoeud via l'acqua del coverc,"* meaning "Never shake off the water on the cover." This simple expression just about describes the cooking of Milan and the rest of Lombardy: slow cooking, covered, for a long time. The only exception to this is veal scaloppine, which is quick-fried. Osso bucco (veal shanks), one of the most popular Lombardian preparations, is perhaps the best example of slow cooking. Another, is one of my favorites, *vitello tonnato*, veal with tuna sauce; the veal is cooked about two hours in this typical Milanese style of cooking. Place yourself in the glass-roofed Galleria, a Milan landmark, just off the Cathedral Square, studded with cafes, restaurants and ice cream parlors where women exchange fashion notes, men read the *Corriere delle Sera* newspaper and others feast on this exquisite veal dish.

One of the reasons this is a favorite, is that it may be made well ahead and refrigerated. I have had leftover veal prepared this way in the refrigerator for a week, still very delicious. There are many recipes available to make this dish. Some call for lots of wine; I would not use more than suggested here. Do not cook the veal in salted water and use just enough water to cover the veal in the saucepan. Some recipes require globs of mayonnaise, and as good as homemade mayonnaise may be, there can be too much of it. My solution is to puree the vegetables in which the veal cooked, adding some of the broth and adding the puree to the mayonnaise-type sauce. At no time should you use commercial mayonnaise to make this dish.

1 medium carrot, chopped
1 rib celery, chopped
1 medium onion, chopped
4 parsley stems
1 cup dry white wine
1 tablespoon plus 1 cup extra-virgin olive oil
2½ pounds top round of veal
2 (6-ounce) cans tuna packed in oil, drained
4 anchovy fillets, drained and dried
1 tablespoon plus 1 teaspoon capers, drained
1 egg yolk or hard-cooked egg yolk
Juice of 1 lemon
Half-and-half (optional)
Sea salt
2 tablespoons finely chopped fresh tarragon

1. In a large saucepan (large enough to hold the veal, vegetables and liquid comfortably), add the carrot, celery, onion, parsley stems, wine, 1 tablespoon of the olive oil and enough water to fill the pan about half. Bring to a boil over medium-high heat, reduce the heat and simmer 15 minutes.

2. Carefully add the veal to the simmering water, making sure the water just covers the veal, bring again to a boil, reduce the heat and simmer for 1½ hours. Let the veal cool in the broth.

3. Remove the veal to a cutting board. Strain the broth, and place the vegetables, minus the parsley stems, into the bowl of a food processor. Add 2 cups of the broth and puree. Set aside the remaining broth.

4. Add the drained tuna to the processor bowl with the anchovies, the 1 tablespoon capers, egg yolk and lemon juice. Puree until smooth. With the motor running, add the remaining cup of the olive oil to the processor in a slow, steady stream, to incorporate it into the tuna sauce. Taste for salt seasoning, adding some if needed. If the sauce is too thick, thin with more of the reserved broth or add some light cream. The sauce should be like heavy cream in consistency.

5. Slice the veal into ⅛-inch slices. Put some of the sauce on the bottom of an oval ceramic or glass dish, approximately 9 × 14 × 2½ inches. Arrange a single layer of the veal on top of the sauce. Spoon more sauce over the veal and repeat in this way until all veal slices are layered and sauced. If sauce remains, put in a small bowl and refrigerate it for later use as additional sauce for the veal. Cover the oval dish with plastic wrap and refrigerate, overnight. Remove from the refrigerator at least 30 minutes before serving. Add the tarragon to the top, sprinkled with a teaspoon of capers. A salad of watercress, arugula and curly endive, dressed simply with oil, vinegar, salt and pepper and crisped pancetta bits is appropriate.

Notabene:

Uncooked eggs should not be eaten by young children, the elderly or anyone with a compromised immune system, because they may contain salmonella bacteria that can cause serious illness. Pasteurized eggs are available in many markets and are safe to eat raw in sauces or desserts that are not cooked.

FRESH CODFISH, POTATOES AND ONIONS

Merluzzo con patate e cipolle
MAKES 6 SERVINGS

Merluzzo e patate, dried salted cod and potatoes, is a dish offered in Milan; in fact, salted cod (*baccala*) appears in the cuisine of many of the other regions, each one having its special way to prepare it. The trouble with this dish, in my view, is the overnight soaking of the cod and the changing of the water in which it soaks three and four times. Even after overnight soaking, salted cod has a fairly strong taste. For the American table, fresh cod is used in this recipe; the taste is milder, yet the dish has all the components of the original Italian way of preparing it. Add a fresh green salad with a sliced ripe tomato and the meal is complete.

> ¾ cup extra-virgin olive oil
> 4 medium onions, sliced ¼ inch thick
> 2 cloves garlic, minced
> 1 bay leaf
> 6 tiny dried red chili peppers or ½ teaspoon red pepper flakes
> 1 teaspoon finely chopped fresh thyme or ½ teaspoon dried, crushed
> Sea salt and freshly ground pepper

2 pounds fresh codfish, rinsed, dried and cut into
   2-inch pieces
4 large potatoes, boiled, peeled and sliced
   $\frac{1}{2}$ inch thick
$1\frac{1}{2}$ cups dry white wine
$\frac{1}{2}$ cup water
$\frac{1}{3}$ cup finely chopped fresh Italian parsley

1. Heat the oil in a large skillet over medium heat. Add the onions and cook until they begin to turn color, about 5 minutes. Add the garlic, bay leaf, chili peppers and thyme. Stir and cook for 2 minutes.

2. Salt and pepper the cod pieces and add them to the skillet with the potato slices, wine and $\frac{1}{2}$ cup water. Cover the skillet. Bring to boil, reduce the heat, and simmer until the fish flakes and the potatoes are thoroughly heated, 8 to 10 minutes. Sprinkle with parsley and serve with a salad on the side.

A NOTED CHEF'S VEGETABLE SOUP FROM THE RIVIERA

Zuppa con verdura alla Genovese
MAKES 6 SERVINGS

Chef Gilberto Pizzi, who created this recipe, uses fresh beans, and it is best to do so, but if this is not possible, use frozen. The Lombards vacation frequently on the Riviera and for a simple meal, there or at home, they will opt for this delicious soup, if a crusty loaf of Italian bread is served with it.

4 ounces fresh or frozen lima beans
10 cups water

7 tablespoons extra-virgin olive oil from Liguria,
   plus 3 teaspoons for serving
Sea salt
4 medium potatoes, peeled and cut into
   $\frac{1}{4}$-inch dice
3 small zucchini, scrubbed and cut into
   $\frac{1}{4}$-inch dice
2 medium carrots, peeled and cut into
   $\frac{1}{4}$-inch dice
2 medium celery ribs with leaves, thinly
   sliced
2 large fresh, ripe tomatoes, peeled, seeded
   and cut into $\frac{1}{4}$-inch pieces
$\frac{1}{2}$ medium onion
4 ounces fresh green beans, trimmed and cut
   into $\frac{1}{2}$-inch pieces
$\frac{1}{2}$ cup fresh or frozen green peas
1 large leek, white part only, cut in half
   lengthwise, well rinsed and thinly sliced
   crosswise
12 small leaves fresh basil, chopped

1. If using frozen limas, thaw and set aside. Bring the water, 7 tablespoons olive oil and a pinch of salt to a boil in a large pot over medium-high heat. Add the potatoes, zucchini, carrots, celery, tomatoes, onion, green beans, peas, leek and the lima beans. Return the liquid to a boil.

2. Reduce the heat to a lively simmer and cook, covered, until the vegetables are almost tender, about 25 minutes. Let the soup rest off the heat for 15 minutes or so to gain flavor.

3. To serve, ladle into warmed soup bowls. Lightly drizzle some olive oil in the shape of your initial over each serving, then top with a sprinkle of the chopped basil.

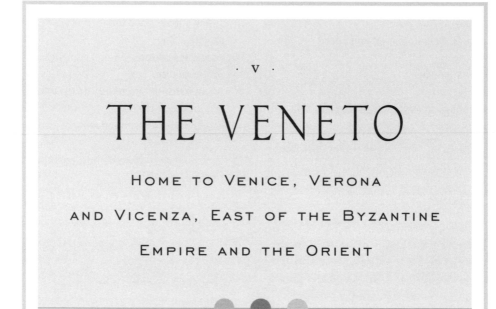

· V ·

THE VENETO

HOME TO VENICE, VERONA
AND VICENZA, EAST OF THE BYZANTINE
EMPIRE AND THE ORIENT

The *Reppublica Veneziana* ruled for over four hundred years and its history is because of its location, the Adriatic Coast, flooded by marshes and nibbled away by lagoons. Its countryside is embroidered with Palladian villas and Bernini altarpieces. On its tables are corn and rice for polenta and risotto with the seafood of the Adriatic dominating. Scampi, tiny clams, crabs and sole are brought together in salads, put over pasta, cooked into risotto or simply grilled and fried. The kinds of fish are without limit. And then there is radicchio.

Venice has been called the most beautiful city in the world and it well may be. For me, a particular fascination of the city is that it always seems to be a stage setting for an opera. Its buildings appear as facades and reflect in the water; after all, it is a city set in water.

It was not important in Roman times and for hundreds of years it was independent of the pope, the emperor and any ruling family. It was, at one point, the world's greatest maritime power and had control of the Adriatic and secured the route to the Holy Land. In the 1200s, the Venetian gold ducat was accepted everywhere. In the 1400s, she traded with Turkey, Egypt and Asia Minor and ruled many Greek islands including Cyprus and Crete. Venice reigned supreme in supplying spices, which her ships brought from the East, pepper being one of the most important. These spices preserved food. Saffron was welcomed for it rekindled the culinary practice of adding it to *brodetti,* the fish chowders made popular by the Greeks in their Italian cities along the Adriatic. There was also tarragon, nutmeg, mace, shallots, cinnamon, cloves and ginger, all carried and traded by many travelers, most notably Marco Polo. These spices shipped all across Europe impacted food preparations wherever they were used and to the present day are kitchen staples.

Most Italians think Venice's most famous dish is *risi e bisi*—rice and peas, and in the springtime when peas are at their best, the dish is a real delight. People still argue over its soup or vegetable status. It is listed as a *primi (minestre),* not a *contorni* (vegetable) but it is served with a fork. Some say this dish can only be made in Venice, but actually it can be made elsewhere if the recipe on page 118 is followed carefully. Rice is used in a variety of ways in Venice, especially with vegetables and fish.

The other most famous Venetian foods are scampi, liver with onions, codfish *mantecato* (sort of mashed) and *pasta e fagioli,* pasta and beans. Prepared *alla veneziana,* scampi are cooked, cooled and marinated in olive oil, lemon, salt and pepper. Liver prepared *alla veneziana* must be made by slow-cooking the onions and fast-cooking the liver, which is always cut in thin strips. *Mantecato* is when dried cod is creamed with milk, oil and garlic and ends up looking like creamy, mashed potatoes. An important fish dish is *sfogi in saor,* fried sole in a sweet and sour sauce. Its recipe is on page 119.

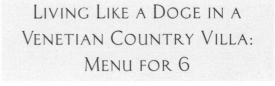

Living Like a Doge in a Venetian Country Villa: Menu for 6

MENU

The Doge's Rice and Pea "Soup"
Risi e bisi

Fried Marinated Sole in Sweet and Sour Sauce
Sogliole In sapore

Stewed Sweet Peppers
Papriche stufate

A Rich Venetian Nut Cake
Strangolapreti

This menu concentrates the varied flavors of Venice and begins with the simple, famous dish of peas and rice, *risi e bisi.* Fish and polenta are as well known in Venice as rice and peas. Since polenta is included elsewhere, fish is included here in the cuisine of a city whose history has been built on its seas. A fish dish reflecting the food history of Venice lies in the fried, marinated fish in a sweet and sour sauce. The required fillet of sole is available in the U.S. fish markets. Another good reason for its selection: make it ahead, marinate it, and serve it later. The stewed peppers add a different taste of sweet and tart and partners well with the fish. The *strangulapreti* cake (priest stranglers) is a nutty concoction, and ready for *Carnevale,* if you plan this dinner at that time.

Wine Selection

Choose a Soave, one of the best known and, deservedly, one of the most highly regarded of the white wines of Italy. It is made largely from Garganega grapes with about 20 percent Trebbiano. Soave is a pretty town at the southern edge of the hill country between Verona and Vicenza. It is widely available in the United States. Look for these winemakers: Anselmi, Masi and Capitel Foscarino-Guerrieri-Rizzardi.

Preparation Advice

This menu, a really delicious one, may be prepared almost entirely ahead. The fish dish must be made ahead by two days and refrigerated. The stewed peppers and the rice and pea "soup" may be made one day ahead. In all honesty, it would be best to make the "soup" before mealtime, especially to preserve the freshness of the peas. The cake may be made a day ahead.

THE DOGE'S RICE AND PEA "SOUP"

Risi e Bisi
MAKES 6 SERVINGS

A good Venetian friend, with whom I shared many meals in Venice, was Hedy Giusti. This is her recipe. I saw a lot of Venice through Hedy's eyes and heard even more via her tongue. She was fierce in her opinion, if it had anything to do with Venice. I dare not alter the recipe. This is probably the most famous of all Venetian rice dishes. It was served by the doges, the city's rulers, on April 25 each year at a banquet held to celebrate the feast day of Saint Mark, the patron saint of Venice. The spring banquet was held just as the first sweet, tender young peas, this dish's main ingredient, were harvested. Hedy only made this when fresh peas were in season. It may be cooked out of season by using frozen baby peas.

> 8 tablespoons (1 stick) butter
> 1 medium onion, cut into ½-inch dice
> 2 slices prosciutto, finely chopped
> 3 pounds (in the shell) fresh peas, shelled, or 1 (16-ounce) package frozen small peas
> Sea salt
> 4 cups each chicken and beef broth
> 2 cups Arborio, Vialone Nero or Carnaroli rice
> 2 tablespoons finely chopped Italian parsley
> 1 cup freshly grated Parmesan cheese

1. Melt the butter in a large saucepan over medium heat. Add the onion and prosciutto and sauté until the prosciutto crisps, about 5 minutes.

2. Add the fresh peas, and some salt if you wish, and cook for 2 minutes, stirring all the time. Add the broth and bring to a boil; reduce the heat to simmer and cook, uncovered, for 10 minutes. (At this point, if using frozen peas, add them when the liquid reaches the boil; add the rice and parsley and continue with the rest of this step.) Add the rice and parsley; reduce the heat to a slow and steady simmer. Cover and cook until the rice is tender but still firm to the bite, about 15 minutes.

3. Remove the saucepan from the heat and stir in the cheese. Taste and adjust the seasoning, adding salt if needed, and ladle into warmed bowls.

●FRIED MARINATED SOLE ●IN SWEET AND SOUR ●SAUCE

Sogliole in sapore
MAKES 6 SERVINGS

The Venetian name for this dish is *sfogi in saor*. It is traditionally eaten for the great Venetian holiday, the Feast of the Redeemer, the third Sunday in July, with fireworks late in the evening after dinner. Simply put, this dish is made by flouring sole fillets, cooking them in olive oil and covering them with lightly sautéed onion, carrot, celery, bay leaves, vinegar and white wine. Pine nuts, raisins and a couple of spices are also added. The dish marinates in the mixture for two days and is served cold.

> 6 fillets of sole (about 2 pounds)
> ½ cup all-purpose flour
> ⅓ cup extra-virgin olive oil
> Sea salt
> 1 onion, finely sliced
> 1 carrot, trimmed and cut into ¼-inch dice
> 1 rib celery, trimmed and cut into ¼-inch dice
> 1 cup white wine vinegar
> 1 cup dry white wine

> 2 bay leaves
> ¼ cup golden raisins
> ¼ cup pine nuts
> Pinch each ground cinnamon, clove and black pepper

1. Rinse and dry the fish fillets. Put the flour in a flat dish and lightly dredge the fillets in the flour, shaking off any excess. Set aside.

2. In a large skillet, heat the oil and sauté the fillets until lightly browned on each side, about 3 minutes per side over medium-high heat. Remove to drain on paper towels. Sprinkle with salt to taste.

3. Using the same oil in the skillet, sauté the onion, carrot and celery for 5 minutes, stirring frequently. Add the vinegar and wine, bring to a boil, reduce the heat and simmer for 5 minutes.

4. Arrange the fillets in a large, flat earthenware container and pour the wine mixture over the fish. Add the bay leaves, raisins, pine nuts and spices. Cover tightly and refrigerate for 2 days. This is to be served cold, but remove from refrigerator about ½ hour before ready to serve.

● ●STEWED SWEET ●PEPPERS

Papriche stufate
MAKES 6 SERVINGS

The market gardens of the Veneto coast are well known and it's a joy to see the luscious peas, red ripe tomatoes, shiny yellow peppers, pale green curly-leafed cabbages and especially the grand-looking, multicolored "baroque squashes" for sale. One can buy roasted slices, scalding hot from the booths in the market of Venice. This is one of the most popular vegetable dishes called, in dialect, *papriche stufato*, stewed sweet peppers, which is easy to cook.

> 4 yellow bell peppers
> 2 large cloves garlic, peeled and halved lengthwise
> ½ cup extra-virgin olive oil
> 2 pounds fresh plum tomatoes, peeled, seeded and chopped, or 1 (28-ounce) can whole plum tomatoes, drained, seeded and coarsely chopped
> Sea salt and freshly ground pepper
> ¼ cup finely chopped fresh Italian parsley

1. Rinse the bell peppers well, drain and dry and cut them lengthwise into quarters. Remove the stem ends, ribs and seeds. Slice the bell peppers in thin strips not wider than ¼ inch. Set aside.

2. Put the garlic in a skillet with the oil. Over medium-high heat, sauté the garlic until it turns light brown. Discard the garlic. Add the pepper strips and cook them, stirring frequently, uncovered, for 15 minutes.

3. Spoon the tomatoes over the peppers, add salt and pepper. Simmer, uncovered, until the tomatoes thicken, about 30 minutes. Sprinkle with parsley and serve hot, or let it stand and serve at room temperature.

A RICH VENETIAN NUT CAKE

Strangolapreti
MAKES 6 SERVINGS

It is a common practice in Italy to devise amusing nicknames for food, often poking fun at the clergy. *Strangolapreti* means literally, "priest stranglers." According to most Italian men, the explanation for this is simple: Priests love to eat and they eat a lot. This term is also applied to pasta preparations of many kinds, all over Italy. Legend has it that a priest who loved a certain spinach dumpling gobbled them down so fast he choked to death. Let's hope this is not the case with this rich nut cake.

> ½ cup golden raisins
> ½ cup rum
> 1 sponge cake (page 121)
> ½ cup diced candied orange or lemon peel
> ½ cup each walnut pieces, chopped almonds and pine nuts
> 1 cup sugar
> ½ cup water
> 2 tablespoons butter for baking pan
> 1 cup heavy cream, whipped

1. Put the raisins and rum in a small bowl and macerate for 30 minutes. Preheat the oven to 350F. Crumb the sponge cake by cutting it into 1-inch pieces and processing briefly in a food processor to make large crumbs.

2. In a large bowl, add the crumbed sponge cake, candied peel, nuts, soaked raisins and any rum in the small bowl. Mix lightly with your splayed fingers.

3. Combine the sugar and water and over medium heat, bring to a boil. Stir frequently until the sugar is dissolved. Pour some syrup over the sponge cake mixture and mix. Add the remaining syrup and mix to bring the mixture together.

4. Liberally butter an 8- or 9-inch springform pan. Spread the cake mixture in the prepared pan. Use a rubber spatula or your hands to press and smooth out the mixture. Bake for 30 minutes. Cool, slice and serve with whipped cream.

SPONGE CAKE

Genoese
MAKES 1 (9-INCH) CAKE

This cake is called by the French word *genoise*, but in actuality, it is a cake from Genoa, and that name should be *genoese*; in other words, Italians think the French named the cake after the Genoese, for that is where the cake came from. Many people simply call it sponge cake.

> 4 eggs
> ⅔ cup sugar
> 1 cup sifted all-purpose flour
> ½ cup (8 tablespoons) butter, melted and cooled

1. Preheat the oven to 350F. Put the eggs and sugar in a bowl and beat with an electric mixer. Place the bowl over simmering water, without touching the water, and continue to beat until the mixture is warmed and doubled in volume, about 5 minutes. Remove from the simmering water and beat until the mixture has cooled.

2. Fold in the flour and butter with a rubber spatula. Do not overwork the mixture; the goal is simply to incorporate the flour and butter. Trans-

fer, with the help of a spatula, to a well-buttered 9-inch cake pan, and bake until the center feels firm, about 40 minutes. Invert and turn out onto a flat dish.

LIVING IT UP IN VENICE, A CITY BETWEEN SEA AND SKY, LIKE VENUS RISING FROM THE WAVES: MENU FOR 4

MENU

Thin Spaghetti with Clams, Cherry Tomatoes and Basil
Vermicelli con vongole, pomodoro e basilico

Quail with Herbs and Truffle Oil
Quaglie al forno alle erbe, con olio di tartufo

Marinated and Sautéed Radicchio
Radicchio marinato soltato in padella

Zabaglione from Bassano del Grappa
Zabaglione da Bassone del Grappa

Venice and Rome are two entirely different cities but they have one common denominator: vanished greatness. With all its beauty, the charm of its canals, the pellucid light on its rooftops and in its squares, let alone its waters, there is a feeling of a continuous threat to its very existence. One September evening, at almost midnight, we were having a nightcap in the lower bar of the Gritti. I was shaken when tens of waiters pulled the Oriental carpets from under our feet, rolled them hurriedly and put them away. The water was surely coming in. The sea breezes are cool and the masterpieces in her galleries prove the intellectual, and emotional pleasures derived from this great city, yet there is a sense of tragedy, because of the rising level of the surrounding waters. Living it up in Venice is to take the *vaporetta,* the little steamer that provides omnibus service along the Grand Canal, or splurge and take a gondola. Venice may have 400 bridges, 117 islands and 150 canals, but the hub of activity is in Piazza San Marco. It seems as if the whole world sits there in the famous Florian and Quadri cafes, as Goethe, Byron, Wagner and George Sand did before them. As you prepare and enjoy this meal, dream and see the mosaics of St. Marks glow under the rays of the setting sun. Listen to the music of the square.

Wine Selection

San Leonardo, a Trentino wine of Cabernet Sauvignon, Cabernet Franc and some Merlot is similar to a fine Bordeaux. If you can get a bottle after four or five years of aging, you will have a fruity wine with a strong bouquet, somewhat peppery and chocolatelike.

Preparation Advice

1. Most of the food can be prepped ahead but the spaghetti should be combined with the sauce just before dining.

2. While the quail or Cornish hens are in the oven, the radicchio can be prepared.

3. It is best to make the zabaglione after the birds have been served and eaten. The warmth and freshness of the zabaglione is important with the fresh berries.

●THIN SPAGHETTI WITH ●CLAMS, CHERRY ●TOMATOES AND BASIL

Vermicelli con vongole, pomodoro e basilico
MAKES 4 SERVINGS

Cherry tomatoes do not have to be peeled or put through a food mill and therefore, make this sauce quite easy to prepare. They are not cooked very long, so they keep their shape. You can cook the sauce as you cook the pasta and this dish can be made in less than fifteen minutes.

4 tablespoons extra-virgin olive oil
4 cloves garlic, minced
1 pound cherry tomatoes, washed, trimmed and
    cut in half
3 (6-ounce) cans chopped clams, drained and
    liquid reserved
½ cup finely sliced fresh basil leaves
12 ounces thin spaghetti or vermicelli pasta,
    cooked until al dente
1 cup freshly grated Parmesan cheese
3 to 4 tablespoons fresh lemon juice (1 lemon)
Sea salt and freshly ground pepper

1. Heat the oil in a large skillet over medium heat. Add the garlic and sauté until the garlic just begins to turn color, 2 minutes, stirring constantly. Add the tomatoes and cook for 5 minutes.

2. Add the clams and basil, stir well and cook for 2 minutes. Set aside.

3. Cook the pasta according to package instructions, drain well and return to the pot in which it cooked. Add the clam sauce from the skillet, the cheese and lemon juice. Toss lightly but well over medium heat until heated through. Add the reserved clam liquid a little at a time. Season with salt and pepper and cook, tossing all the time, for 2 or 3 minutes, to marry the sauce with the pasta.

QUAIL WITH HERBS AND TRUFFLE OIL

Quaglie al forno alle erbe, con olio di tartufo
MAKES 4 SERVINGS

When I was a boy, I used to hear all the time about shooting *quaglie*, quail, in Italy. My grandfather used to say that they were easy targets. These days I hear that most quail in Italy are farm-raised, as they are in this country. They are very small birds and have a subtle, delicate, gamey flavor; they are small enough that one needs to serve two per person.

Quail are not always in the markets, and sometimes there isn't enough time to get them through mail order. Using Cornish game hens is a satisfactory substitute; one game hen can serve two people.

8 quail, ready for roasting
¼ cup finely chopped fresh chives
¼ cup finely chopped fresh basil
¼ cup finely chopped fresh tarragon
½ cup finely chopped shallots
½ cup extra-virgin olive oil
1 tablespoon finely chopped fresh
    rosemary
8 juniper berries (optional)
2 bay leaves
4 tablespoons butter
8 paper-thin slices pancetta
1 tablespoon truffle oil

1. Ready the quail for cooking by rinsing and drying thoroughly. Set aside.

2. Combine the chives through the bay leaves and rub some of the mixture inside and outside the birds. Put the birds in a large plastic bag, pour in the remaining herb-olive oil mixture, seal the bag tightly and refrigerate overnight. Remove from the refrigerator 1 hour before cooking to bring them to room temperature.

3. Preheat the oven to 425F. Melt the butter in a very large skillet and sauté the birds over medium heat until lightly browned on all sides, 10 to 15 minutes. Transfer them to a baking pan, cover each bird with a slice of pancetta and bake until juices run clear when pierced with a knife in thickest part, about 15 minutes. Baste after 5 and 10 minutes, spooning some of the marinade over them. Remove from the oven and sprinkle the truffle oil over the birds. Serve them with the Marinated and Sautéed Radicchio (page 124).

Variation

Cornish Game Hens: Substitute 2 Cornish game hens, quartered, for the quail.

1. Marinate overnight as above, and bring to room temperature before baking. Sautéing them in a skillet, as for quail, is not necessary.

2. Preheat the oven to 450F. Place the hen pieces in a baking dish and bake for 45 minutes, until tender, following the procedure as in Step 3 above.

MARINATED AND SAUTÉED RADICCHIO

Radicchio marinato soltato in padella
MAKES 4 SERVINGS

There are two kinds of radicchio: the radicchio from Treviso, which is long, purplish-red and with definite cream-colored veins; the radicchio from Verona is rounded. Both have a slightly bitter taste and can be cooked or used in salads.

> ½ cup balsamic vinegar
> ¼ cup extra-virgin olive oil
> Sea salt and freshly ground pepper
> 2 heads radicchio
> 1 cup beef broth
> ¼ cup finely chopped shallots
> 2 teaspoons grated lemon zest
> 1 teaspoon truffle oil

1. In a small bowl, combine the balsamic vinegar and olive oil. Add sea salt and freshly ground pepper and mix well.

2. Cut each head of radicchio into 4 wedges. Place them in a large skillet and pour ½ cup of the vinegar-oil mixture over the radicchio, reserving ¼ cup. Marinate the radicchio for 3 or 4 hours.

3. In a small saucepan, combine the broth, shallots and the reserved ¼ cup vinegar-oil mixture and cook over medium heat for 5 to 8 minutes, to reduce the mixture to ½ cup. Add the lemon zest and the truffle oil and allow to cool. Season with salt and pepper.

4. Put the skillet with the radicchio wedges over high heat and sauté until lightly browned. The radicchio will lose some of its color. Cook about 4 minutes per side. To serve, put two cooked wedges on each plate and pour over the sauce made in Step 3. This should be served in the center of a dinner plate, with a quail on either side.

ZABAGLIONE FROM BASSANO DEL GRAPPA

Zabaglione da Bassone del Grappa
MAKES 4 SERVINGS

The Ponte degli Alpini is a Palladio-designed bridge that crosses from the ceramics-thriving city of Bassano del Grappa into the old town. At the town edge of the bridge is the famous Nardini grappa distillery. The distillery is now moved, but there remains a shop for tasting. It has been in operation since the eighteenth century, for grappa was invented here. The alcoholic content of grappa, a brandy, is about 40 percent. It is distilled from the pressed skins and seeds of grapes left after making wine. It can taste like raw alcohol when new, but as it ages, its taste is more refined, and its cost also goes up.

The more expensive grappas come in beautifully designed hand-blown bottles. It is rarely used in Italian cooking, but it can be used for flambéeing and for preserving berries. Many Italians preserve berries this way; later, they eat the berries and then have a small glass of the flavored grappa as a *digestivo*. In this recipe, grappa is used to flavor the egg and wine mixture to make a zabaglione and, of course, it is served over a variety of fresh berries.

> 1½ pints of fresh berries (raspberries, strawberries, blueberries or a combination)
> 4 egg yolks
> ¼ cup sugar
> ½ cup dry white wine
> ¼ cup grappa

1. If the berries have been refrigerated, bring them to room temperature. Put 8 berries aside for garnish. Arrange the berries on 4 plates. Set aside to receive the warm zabaglione when it is made.

2. Combine the egg yolks and sugar in the top pan of a double boiler over boiling water. With the top pan off the heat, beat the eggs and sugar until the mixture is thick and lemony in color. Reduce the boiling water in the bottom pan to a simmer.

3. Put the top pan over the bottom pan, and cook, whisking constantly, until the mixture thickens and foams, about 10 minutes. Add the wine and grappa, a little at a time, whisking constantly to increase the volume of the egg mixture. The zabaglione should be thick enough to coat a spoon. Spoon the zabaglione immediately over the berries; top each dessert with 2 berries and serve.

LUNCH FOR 4 TO 6 WITH JULIET IN VERONA

MENU

Roasted Pepper and Eggplant Puree Appetizer
Purea di melanzane e peperoni

Pasta Bows with Fresh Spinach, Mushrooms and Cream
Farfalle con spinaci e panna

Fruit Compote with Citrus Sauce
Composta di frutta con salsa agli agrumi

Verona is a city blessed by nature because of its majestic river, the Adige, which winds through the city because of its pleasant hills. It is a city also blessed by man who built its buildings and created its art. These combined forces—nature and man—are so beautifully combined to make this city graceful and harmonious. Verona, a city of diverse styles, succeeds with having a Gothic church next to a Romanesque house, a neo-classical building next to a medieval tower. The slow passage of time, over centuries, is responsible for the patina of the city whose stones have the same pale coloring capable of changing color at different times of the day, also when mountain winds sweep down to bring a change of weather, and color.

To experience the sense of magic and romance of this city, one must walk through it, lose himself or herself in narrow, ancient streets, pass his or her hand over its stones, wet with dampness of the ages, find the hidden gardens, open creaking iron gates, enter its old, old churches and disturb its silent cloisters. And yes, feel the presence of Romeo and Juliet (Giulietta), Shakespeare's symbols of a perfect and immortal love on the richly, evocative Verona stage.

One of the most picturesque squares in all of Italy is the Piazza Erbe (Square of the Herbs, so called because only green vegetables were sold there at one time). The stalls in the piazza are sheltered by a panoply of white umbrellas and now sell everything. Fresh figs were so deliciously displayed the last time I was there, I purchased a pound and ate them all. The square is irregular in form and around it are buildings of different styles and colors. There are a number of cafes and *trattorie* at which you can sit and enjoy food prepared *all Veronese*. One food specialty of Verona is *pandoro*, golden bread, a rich dome-shaped vanilla cake, dusted with confectioners' sugar. The Veronese love gnocchi, made from potatoes, which everyone eats on Good Friday.

I'm always amused by the fact that they call this day *venerdi gnoccolaro,* Gnocchi Friday. Only a few steps from the Piazza Erbe is the building on Via Cappello, No 27, once owned by the Dal Cappello, or Capulet family. According to legend, this is where the most beautiful Giulietta lived. It has been dated back to the thirteenth century and has a brick facade with large trilobate windows. A small marble balcony records the most famous verses of Shakespeare's tragedy, in which Romeo declares his love for Juliet as she stands on the balcony.

Wine Selection

Serve a 100 percent Chardonnay from the Ronc di Juri in the Colli Orientali del Friuli Zona DOC. It has a bright straw-yellow color with spicy aromas of vanilla and peaches. This wine is usually drunk when it is between three and five years old.

Preparation Advice

1. The eggplant and pepper appetizer may be made a day ahead and refrigerated, and brought to room temperature one hour before serving.

2. The pasta ingredients may be prepped in advance but the cooking and saucing should be done just before eating.

3. The fruit can be prepared ahead but do not add the citrus sauce until about one hour before serving.

ROASTED PEPPER AND EGGPLANT PUREE APPETIZER

Purea di melanzane e peperoni
MAKES 4 TO 6 SERVINGS

This delicious puree may be served in two ways: first, some of it may be put in an attractive bowl, surrounded by cucumber slices and served as a dip. Or it may be served as a first course. On individual plates, put about one tablespoon finely sliced spinach leaves on individual plates. Add four cucumber slices to each and top each slice with ½ teaspoon of the puree. Add salt and pepper.

1 medium eggplant
2 cloves garlic, halved lengthwise
2 red bell peppers
¼ teaspoon fennel seeds, toasted and crushed
About 4 tablespoons extra-virgin olive oil
2 tablespoons fresh lemon juice
12 to 16 thin slices of cucumber
4 tablespoons thinly sliced fresh spinach, for
  garnish

1. Preheat the oven to 425F. Make 4 knife slits into the eggplant, and tuck in the garlic deeply. Grease a baking sheet and place the eggplant on it. Bake until the eggplant is soft, about 25 minutes.

2. Place the peppers directly on the grill or under a broiler and broil, turning, until the skins are blackened all over and the peppers are soft and cooked. Rinse them under running warm water to remove the charred skins. Remove the cores and seeds. Pat dry with paper towels.

3. Toast the fennel seeds in a dry skillet until fragrant. Crush them in a mortar with a pestle, or put them on a counter and run a rolling pin over them.

4. Peel the eggplant and put the flesh in a food processor. Add the bell peppers, crushed fennel seeds, salt and pepper. Process until pureed. While the motor is running, trickle in the 4 tablespoons olive oil, which will be absorbed as in making mayonnaise. Add more oil, by tablespoon, if needed. Add the lemon juice, process briefly and turn the puree into a bowl. Serve warm or cold on thin slices of cucumber; garnish with the spinach.

PASTA BOWS WITH FRESH SPINACH, MUSHROOMS AND CREAM

Farfalle con spinaci e panna
MAKES 4 TO 6 SERVINGS

Primaverile means springlike, and it would be wonderful if this dish can be made when spinach is as fresh from the garden as it can be. However, this dish can be made any time of the year, as spinach is almost always available in the markets. Purchase young, fresh spinach or if packaged, baby spinach. I believe Giulietta would have preferred this dish to potato gnocchi. When I was staying at Giorgio and Ilaria Miani's home in Contignano, south of Sienna, I cooked this dish, because it's easy, and easy to double for a large group. I had invited eleven nieces and nephews to join me. Ivana Fabbrizzi, the Miani's treasured cook and housekeeper, liked the idea of this dish and its springlike nature. She saw the pasta bows as things little girls put in their hair, only as Italians can imagine, and asked if she could be the twelfth niece.

1 pound cremini or button mushrooms
¼ cup fresh lemon juice
6 tablespoons butter
2 cloves garlic, minced
¼ cup Marsala wine
1½ cups heavy cream
Sea salt and freshly ground pepper
1 pound pasta bows
4 cups finely shredded fresh spinach leaves
½ cup freshly grated Parmesan cheese

1. Wipe the mushrooms with damp kitchen towels, cut off and discard the tough stem ends and slice the mushrooms thinly. Put in a bowl with the lemon juice and toss well.

2. Melt the butter in a large skillet and add the garlic and Marsala. Cook for about 3 minutes and add the mushrooms. Stir well and cook 8 minutes longer. Add the cream and bring the mixture to a boil. Season with salt and pepper. Keep this sauce at a simmer for about 5 minutes and then remove from the heat.

3. Cook the pasta until al dente according to directions on the package. Drain and return the pasta to the pan in which it cooked. Add the spinach, reserving about ⅓ cup, and the cream sauce. Toss lightly but well. To serve, apportion the pasta and add a heaping tablespoon of Parmesan over the top of each serving. Arrange the reserved spinach over the cheese. Serve right away.

FRUIT COMPOTE WITH CITRUS SAUCE

Composta di frutta con salsa agli agrumi
MAKES 4 TO 6 SERVINGS

The citrus sauce in this recipe makes the dish. The first citrus fruit to be introduced in Italy was the citron in the third century; the lemon appeared in the seventh, the bitter orange in the tenth, and the real orange in the fourteenth. No Italian kitchen is complete without a bowl of lemons and oranges.

FOR THE COMPOTE
8 fresh strawberries, hulled and sliced
1 ripe pear, peeled, seeded and cut into ½-inch pieces
1 small banana, peeled and thinly sliced on the bias
½ cup fresh blueberries, stemmed, rinsed and dried
1 cup diced fresh pineapple

FOR THE CITRUS SAUCE
1 cup fresh orange juice
¼ cup fresh lemon juice
1½ cups sugar
1 tablespoon Marsala wine

1. *To make the compote:* Combine all the fruit, toss well, and distribute among 4 large red wine goblets.

2. *To make the sauce:* Combine all the ingredients. Pour it over the fruit in the glasses. Refrigerate until ready to use. Remove from the refrigerator 20 to 30 minutes before needed.

A BACHELOR PARTY WITH ROMEO AT THE BOTTEGA DEL VINO: MENU FOR 4

MENU

Shrimp and Smoked Salmon in a Sweet and Sour Sauce
Involtini di gamberi e salmone in salsa agrodolce con dadolada di legumi

Fried Soft-Shell Crabs in the Veneto
Moleche alla Veneziana

Asparagus with Oil, Vinegar and Hard-Cooked Eggs on Radicchio
Asparagi alla bassanese

Sweet Semolina Diamonds with Grana and Honey
Gialetti "zaleti" con grana e miele

There is actually a splendid fourteenth-century dwelling in Verona in the Via delle Arche Scaliegere that is claimed to be the home of the Montecchis, or Montagues, the family to which Romeo belonged. When I saw it, it was not in good repair but it is one of the oldest buildings in the city. It has a brick facade and many of the original battlements. The setting for this meal is at a very popular wine bar, the Bottego del Vino, in Verona. Elia Rizzo used to cook there but he now is the owner of the elegant Il Desco restaurant. I learned to make several dishes from Barzan Severino, who owns several restaurants, the Bottega del Vino being one. It is located just a few steps from

Juliet's balcony. Everywhere one looks in the restaurant, an old proverb is there to greet you. *Amico e vino dogliono esser vecchi* (Friends and wine should be old), and *Il vino e l'anima della poesia* (Wine is the soul of poetry), are two examples. Signor Severino enjoys dispensing folklore and when I was with him he said, "There are five doors by which to enter Verona and the groups of people who live near each of these doors have minds of their own, especially about food. Take pasta. One 'door' prefers *dialetti* (like the small pasta called ditallini). Another 'door' wants *bigoli* (like a large spaghetti). The third insists on *tagliatelle di seta* (literally meaning pasta strands of silk) and others want *maltagliati*," which he described as the borders of pasta left over from cutting other pasta.

Wine Selection

Fontego, a Soave Superiore DOC from La Cappuccina is mostly garganega grape with a little Chardonnay; it is a bright yellow with a few gilded highlights that has a citrus scent.

Preparation Advice

1. The shrimp and salmon dish may be made the morning of the day the meal is to be served.

2. The dessert may be made the day before.

3. The asparagus and crab dishes may be prepped early in the day but they should be brought together a short time before serving.

SHRIMP AND SMOKED SALMON IN A SWEET AND SOUR SAUCE

Involtini di gamberi e salmone in salsa agrodolce con dadolada di legumi
MAKES 4 SERVINGS

Fresh lemon juice must be used. The shrimp can be cooked ahead by a day, dried carefully, and refrigerated. Sweet and sour sauces are particularly prevalent in this region of Italy; the sauce may be made ahead but do not add it to the dish until it is ready to be served.

> Sea salt and freshly ground pepper
> 1 pound large shrimp (16 to 20 count)
> 2 tablespoons fresh lemon juice
> 4 thin slices smoked salmon, each large
>   enough to make a cornet
> 1 clove garlic, coarsely chopped
> 1/3 cup white onion, coarsely chopped
> 1 teaspoon prepared Dijon mustard
> 3 tablespoons herbed vinegar
> 1 cup extra-virgin olive oil
> 1 teaspoon sugar
> 1 tablespoon cooked small green peas
> 1 tablespoon cooked corn kernels
> 2 tablespoons finely chopped fresh
>   chives

1. Bring 4 cups water to boil in a medium saucepan, add some salt and the shrimp. Let the water come back to a boil, and cook until the shrimp turn pink, 2 to 4 minutes after the water returns to a boil. Remove from the heat and add some cold water to stop the cooking. Drain the shrimp, peel, devein, place in a small bowl and toss with the lemon juice.

2. On individual plates, arrange a piece of salmon around 2 cooked shrimp, wrapping the salmon around in cornet-fashion (like a small ice cream cone). Add more shrimp as if coming out of the cone.

3. Put the garlic, onion, mustard, vinegar, 2 tablespoons of the oil and the sugar in the food processor and pulse to a count of 8. Pour remaining oil through the food tube, while the motor is running. Add salt and pepper. Stir in the peas and the corn. Do not refrigerate the sauce if using the same day.

4. Spoon some of the sauce on the shrimp in a flowing effect and dot with a sprinkle of chives.

FRIED SOFT-SHELL CRABS IN THE VENETO

Moleche alla Veneziana
MAKES 4 SERVINGS

Soft-shell crabs appear in Venice at the end of April and the beginning of May. At this time of the year the crabs are changing their shells, and they are so light that they float to the surface and are caught in the shoals. Thousands of these *moleche*, as they are called in the Veneto, are caught, battered and fried. They are dull green in color and about two inches wide. The whole crab is eaten but properly clean them before using, as described below. In the Veneto, they are usually deep-fried; an adjustment is made here to sauté them.

> 8 soft-shell crabs
> 2 eggs, well beaten
> 1 cup all-purpose flour
> Sea salt and freshly ground pepper
> 4 tablespoons olive or vegetable oil
> Juice from 2 lemons
> 4 tablespoons butter
> 2 tablespoons finely chopped fresh Italian parsley

1. Clean the crabs, one at a time, as follows: Place the crab, top side up, on a flat work surface. Cut off the protruding eyes. Turn the crab over, on its back, and remove the triangular-shaped apron. Lift the flaps on each side and remove the spongy gill tissue underneath. Rinse the crab in cool water and pat dry with paper towels.

2. Dip the crab in the beaten eggs and then dredge in the flour, seasoned with some salt and pepper.

3. Heat 2 tablespoons of the oil in a large skillet and add 4 of the crabs. Cook over medium heat for 3 minutes, until the crabs are golden. Turn and cook until golden on the other sides. The total time should be about 6 minutes, or longer if the crabs are especially thick. Transfer the crabs to a platter. Heat the remaining 2 tablespoons of oil in the same skillet and repeat the process with the other 4 crabs. When all 8 crabs have been cooked, sprinkle them with the lemon juice.

4. Pour off any fat in the skillet and wipe it clean with a paper towel. Heat the butter in the skillet and let it brown. Pour this over the crabs. Sprinkle with the parsley.

ASPARAGUS WITH OIL, VINEGAR AND HARD-COOKED EGGS ON RADICCHIO

Asparagi alla bassanese
MAKES 4 SERVINGS

Bassano del Grappa is a town in the Veneto known for its fat asparagus and for its grappa distillery. The eggs here are boiled and worked into the sauce and this is why it is called *alla bassanese*, Bassano style. It is quite popular in Italy to fry eggs and lay them atop cooked asparagus with a little butter and cheese; this can make a good lunch.

1 bunch fresh asparagus
2 hard-cooked eggs, chopped
3 tablespoons white wine vinegar
1/2 cup extra-virgin olive oil
Sea salt and freshly ground pepper
1 head radicchio, preferably the long Treviso style
2 tablespoons finely chopped white onion

1.   Break each asparagus stalk at the tender point and discard the tougher ends. If needed, pare the tender stalk and put into cool water to keep them fresh if not using immediately. Steam them standing up in an asparagus cooker until slightly crisp-tender, 10 to 12 minutes. Drain right away. If you don't have an asparagus cooker, improvise by using a coffeepot with the inside parts removed. Dry the asparagus with paper towels, being careful not to break off the tips. Set aside.

2.   Put the eggs into a bowl and add the vinegar. Mash with a fork. Add a little oil and mash more. Add salt and pepper. Slowly continue adding the oil and incorporating it until all the oil is used. Set the sauce aside.

3.   Trim the long head of radicchio by removing any worn or tattered leaves. Cut off the stem end and separate the leaves. Rinse and dry them. (If using the rounded head, trim it in the same way. Cut it in half and slice each half into slivers.)

4.   *To assemble:* Lay one or two long leaves on a plate, or a sprinkle of radicchio slivers. Arrange 5 or 6 asparagus spears on top of the radicchio, with the spears facing in the same direction, and spoon the sauce over the center portion of the asparagus. Sprinkle with the onion. Add more salt and pepper, if you wish.

SWEET SEMOLINA DIAMONDS WITH GRANA AND HONEY

Gialetti "zaleti" con grana e miele
MAKES ABOUT 36 COOKIES

Semolina flour, made from durum wheat, is the basis of many pastas. Here, it is combined with sugar and all-purpose flour to produce a slightly sweet, crunchy rum-raisin cookie that is beautifully served with cheese and honey.

1 cup light rum
1 cup seedless golden raisins
4 egg yolks, at room temperature
1 cup sugar
2 cups all-purpose flour
1 1/2 cups semolina flour
1 cup (2 sticks) butter, melted and cooled
1 teaspoon vanilla extract
Grated zest from 1 lemon
Sea salt
1/2 cup pine nuts
2 tablespoons confectioners' sugar
8 to 12 thin shavings grana cheese
4 tablespoons acacia honey

1.   Combine the rum and raisins in a small bowl and set aside for several hours (or overnight, if you wish) to plump. Drain the raisins, reserving the liquid. Pat the raisins dry.

2.   Preheat the oven to 375F. Generously butter 2 baking sheets. Beat eggs and sugar in the bowl of an electric mixer until a slowly dissolving ribbon forms when beaters are lifted, 6 or 7 minutes.

3.   Combine the flours and gradually mix into the egg mixture. Blend in the butter, vanilla, lemon zest, the reserved raisin liquid and some salt. Turn dough out onto a floured surface. Knead until smooth, about 5 minutes (or do this in a mixer with a dough hook). Sprinkle the raisins and pine nuts over dough and continue kneading just until incorporated.

4.   Lightly flour the work surface again and roll the dough out to a thickness of 1/3 inch. Using a very sharp knife, cut the dough diagonally into 2-inch-wide strips, then cut diagonally in opposite directions to form diamonds.

5.   Transfer diamonds to baking sheets, spacing evenly. Bake until cookies are lightly colored, about 20 minutes. Cool and store in an airtight container.

6.   Sprinkle with confectioners' sugar before serving. To serve, arrange 2 or 3 cookies on a plate. Add 2 pieces of cheese and put 1 tablespoon of the honey next to the cheese.

At a Trattoria Near Vicenza with Pietro Tecchio: Menu for 6

MENU

Pietro Tecchio's Fresh Asparagus Soup
Zuppa di asparagi alla Vicentina

Ricotta Gnocchi with Light Picante Tomato Shrimp Sauce
Gnocchi alla ricotta in salsa di gamberi e pomodoro "piccante"

Cubes of Butternut Squash with Cinnamon
Zucca alla cannella

Fresh Figs with Kirsch
Fichi alla Veneziana

The Veneto is often called the California of Italy, because this region in northeast Italy is a thriving agricultural center and the basket of some of Italy's most colorful and abundant outdoor markets. The varied terrain here produces some of the greatest variety of fruits and vegetables in Italy. The key cities of the Veneto, Verona, Vicenza, Treviso and Padua reflect this rich tradition. I was with Pietro Tecchio, in the kitchen of his Trattoria Leoncino in Altavilla Vicentina, a tiny village on the outskirts of Vicenza, when he made fresh asparagus soup. It is easy to make and is so satisfying.

While preparing this soup, Pietro had many words of advice, after he explained the use of asparagus by the ancient Romans, who not only loved the taste, they also valued it for medicinal purposes, using it, among other things, as a toothache remedy. Pietro said Italians really love white asparagus, which is slightly more tender and bitter tasting than the green. He made a sketch showing how it is grown under mounds of soil, which shut out chlorophyll-producing daylight. He added that the white spears are harvested at the first sign that the tip is ready to push up through the soil. Because it takes more effort to grow and harvest, it is scarcer and more expensive than the green. Pietro cautioned me about buying asparagus with bent or unfurled tips, a sure sign of age. Italians cook their asparagus with only the stalks in water; the tips are cooked by the trapped steam. Pietro dramatically took an asparagus stalk in his hands, stalk end in one, tip end in the other and he bent the stalk carefully until it broke. He said to use the part of the stalk with the tip. He wrote across a large white paper placemat, *celerius quam asparagi cocuntur,* meaning as fast as the cooking of an asparagus. It is an old Roman phrase predicated on the fact that asparagus cooks quickly.

Wine Selection

Choose a Muller-Thurgau Trentino DOC made from only Muller-Thurgau grapes. It is produced by Pojer and Sandri, a very reasonably priced wine, that is bright yellow with fruit scents and will be delicious with the ricotta gnocchi.

Preparation Advice

1. The soup may be made the day before as may the gnocchi, which should be covered and refrigerated until cooking time.

2. The squash may be prepared ahead by a day and reheated. The figs are really a last-minute task for just before serving.

PIETRO TECCHIO'S FRESH ASPARAGUS SOUP

Zuppa di asparagi alla Vicentina
MAKES 6 SERVINGS

This is a lovely soup and can be made with green asparagus only. I like it best served warm with garlic bread, but since it can be made ahead by several days and refrigerated, you might like to try it served cold, or at room temperature.

2½ pounds fresh asparagus, half green, half white
4 cups chicken broth and 4 cups beef broth or 8 cups Mixed Broth (page 8)
2½ tablespoons semolina flour
Sea salt and freshly ground pepper
½ cup freshly grated Parmesan cheese
12 thin slices bruschetta (page 6)

1. Carefully bend each stalk of asparagus and break off and discard the tough end. Using a vegetable peeler, pare the skin on the lower end of the tender stalk and rinse. Cut off the tips and reserve. Repeat with all the stalks. Thinly slice the tender stalks without tips.

2. Bring the broths to boil in a large saucepan over medium-high heat. Slowly sprinkle the semolina into the broth, while stirring all the time with a wooden spoon. Cook until lightly thickened, about 10 minutes.

3. Add the sliced asparagus pieces, and bring to a boil. Reduce the heat and simmer until tender, about 20 minutes. Add the asparagus tips and cook, uncovered, 5 minutes. Add salt and pepper.

4. Sprinkle with the cheese and accompany each serving with 2 slices of the bruschetta.

RICOTTA GNOCCHI WITH LIGHT PICANTE TOMATO SHRIMP SAUCE

Gnocchi alla ricotta in salsa di gamberi e pomodoro "piccante"
MAKES 6 SERVINGS

These lovely gnocchi are some of the easiest and lightest ones to make. Follow these steps carefully and you will be surprised at the simplicity and ease of the dish.

The butternut squash (page 135) can be mixed with the gnocchi for serving if desired.

FOR THE GNOCCHI
2 cups fresh ricotta cheese
1½ cups freshly grated pecorino cheese
1 egg, beaten
1½ cups all-purpose flour

FOR THE SAUCE
3 tablespoons butter
¼ cup finely chopped onion
1 clove garlic, minced
1 cup heavy cream
½ cube fish bouillon
½ cup fish or clam broth
1 teaspoon tomato paste
Pinch red pepper flakes
Sea salt and freshly ground pepper
1 cup finely chopped cooked shrimp, preferably fresh

1. *To make the gnocchi:* Combine the ricotta and the pecorino cheese in a large mixing bowl with the help of a rubber spatula. Blend in the egg to make a smooth mixture. (Do not add salt as the cheese is salty enough.)

2. Before measuring the flour, put 1½ cups of flour into a large bowl and aerate it by tossing lightly with a fork. Then spoon and measure the flour, always topping off the measuring cup with a straight-edged knife. Put the flour on a flat work surface, as in making dough. With your fingers, make a well in the center of the flour. Add the ricotta mixture to the well. Work in the flour a little at a time to make a dough, with your fingers or a fork. This will only take 1 or 2 minutes and a light dough will be formed.

3. To test the dough before cooking, cut off a tiny piece and form a little ball, about the size of a small marble. Add it to boiling water and if it keeps its shape, the dough is fine. If it breaks up, a little more flour should be added to the dough; this shouldn't happen, but if it does, this is how to correct it.

4. Form a large disk of the dough, flattening it out to about 2 inches thick. Cut the disk into ½-inch slices and then cut the slices lengthwise into ½-inch-wide strips. On a lightly floured surface, roll the strips with splayed fingers to form a ½-inch-thick rope. Cut the rope into 1-inch lengths and put them on a lightly floured cloth that has been placed in a baking sheet or pizza pan. Repeat until all the ropes are rolled and cut. If not using right away, cover them with another cloth and let rest for 30 minutes, or longer in the refrigerator.

5. *To make the sauce:* Heat the butter in a large skillet and sauté the onion until limp, 4 or 5 minutes. Add the garlic and cook for 1 minute. Add the cream. Dissolve the bouillon in the fish broth, and add it to the cream mixture. Bring the broth mixture to a boil. Reduce the heat immediately, and simmer until the sauce is thickened a little more than heavy cream, about 10 minutes. Stir all the time, especially around the edges; a rubber spatula is helpful here.

6. Stir in the tomato paste and combine it well. Add the pepper flakes, salt, pepper and the shrimp. Cook until the shrimp are thoroughly heated.

7. *To bring the sauce and pasta together:* Cook the gnocchi in boiling water and as they rise to the top remove them with a slotted spoon. Drain them well and add them immediately to the skillet with the sauce. Toss lightly but well. Serve right away. If serving on individual plates, arrange 3 or 4 pieces of the cooked butternut squash (see below) among the gnocchi. If serving on a platter, arrange the pieces of squash among the gnocchi, or you may wish to serve the squash separately as a vegetable.

CUBES OF BUTTERNUT SQUASH WITH CINNAMON

Zucca alla cannella
MAKES 6 SERVINGS

This is a popular vegetable dish in northern Italy, especially in this region. Pumpkin and other winter squashes can be cooked the same way. Don't overcook the squash; it should keep its shape. I test it with a wooden skewer, or a toothpick will do; just put it into the piece of squash and you will discover its state of tenderness.

1 butternut squash, about 1½ pounds
4 tablespoons butter
Dashes ground cinnamon
Sea salt and freshly ground pepper

1. Peel the squash after removing the stem and bottom ends. Cut it in half crosswise and then half lengthwise. Remove the seeds and cut all four sections into 1-inch pieces.

2. Steam the squash until tender, for up to 20 minutes. Drain and put the pieces into a shallow bowl.

3. Melt the butter in a small skillet over low heat, browning it a little. Add salt and pepper and pour this over the squash. Use a rubber spatula to get all the butter transferred from the skillet to the squash. Sprinkle with cinnamon overall and serve with Ricotta Gnocchi (page 134) or as a separate vegetable.

FRESH FIGS WITH KIRSCH

Fichi alla Veneziana
MAKES 6 SERVINGS

This simple way to serve figs is the way they are served in the famous hotel Hotel Gritti in Venice. They elegantly peel the figs, after trimming the ends, cut them in halves and pour the kirsch over them. I like not to peel them.

18 fresh ripe figs
6 tablespoons kirsch

1. Ready the figs for serving by running under cool water and drying with paper or cloth towels. Trim the ends and cut each fig in half.

2. Arrange the fig halves, cut side up, in a bowl and carefully spoon the kirsch over them. Let them stand for about 10 minutes before serving. These must be at room temperature.

3. Serve 6 fig halves per person.

ONE-DISH MEALS

LAYERED, BAKED POLENTA, VENETIAN STYLE

Polenta Pasticciata alla Veneziana
MAKES ABOUT 6 SERVINGS

Venice in winter is the home of the grandiose *Carnevale*; in summer it boasts the historic regatta on the Grand Canal. But the best times in Venice can be spring and autumn, when some feeling of tranquillity may be possible. Walk slowly through the shopping streets (called the *Mercerie*) leading to the Rialto Bridge; along the way, see the greengrocer and fishmonger shops that receive their goods by boat. Think of the trattorie along the beach and recall Thomas Mann's *Death in Venice*. Feast on squid, eels, mussels, clams and calf's liver, roasted quail with butter and herbs, and yes, on layered, baked polenta, Venetian style.

Northern Italians love polenta, but no more is it loved than in the Veneto. It can be cooked in hundreds of ways as it blends so easily with meats, poultry, fish, all kinds of vegetables; it can be sauced, but it doesn't have to be, it can be fried, baked, grilled or served plain, hot from the saucepan in which it cooked. It is amazing to think that a food that came from America could take hold this way in the northern regions of Italy. The great ships of the Venetian Republic came from Turkey and its empire by sea, and from the day it brought its first sack of maize to the Rialto Market in Venice, maize was called *granoturco*—Turkish corn—thinking it came from Turkey, not America.

FOR THE POLENTA
6 cups water
1 teaspoon sea salt
2 cups Arrowhead Mills' yellow corn grits

FOR THE SAUCE
¼ pound salt pork, finely chopped
1 medium onion, finely chopped
1 medium carrot, finely diced
1 rib celery, trimmed and finely diced
1½ cups imported dried mushrooms, soaked
　　30 minutes in warm water, water reserved
1 (14½-ounce) can diced tomatoes
Freshly ground pepper
Sea salt
8 tablespoons butter
8 tablespoons freshly grated Parmesan cheese

1. *To make the polenta:* Bring the water and salt to boil in a large saucepan. Pour in the cornmeal with one hand while stirring constantly with the other, using a wooden spoon. The cornmeal should be added slowly. Cook, stirring constantly, for 20 to 25 minutes, until a spoon stands up by itself.

2. Pour into 2 oiled 5 × 9-inch loaf pans and cool in the refrigerator for 2 hours. Unmold and slice, and proceed as described below.

3. *To make the sauce:* Sauté the salt pork in a saucepan over medium heat and when it has rendered some fat, add the onion, carrot and celery and sauté until the vegetables take on some color, about 8 minutes.

4. Drain the mushrooms and finely chop them. Add to the vegetables and cook for 2 or 3 minutes, stirring most of the time. Add the tomatoes and some pepper. Taste for salt seasoning and add some if needed (remember that the salt pork is quite salty). Add ½ cup of the mushroom soaking water and cook for 15 minutes. Set the sauce aside.

5. *To complete the dish:* Preheat the oven to 375F. Butter a 15 × 10-inch baking dish, deep enough to hold 3 layers of polenta.

6. Arrange a layer of polenta in the bottom of the baking dish. Spoon half of the sauce over it. Dot with 2 tablespoons of the butter and sprinkle with 3 tablespoons of the Parmesan cheese.

7. Make another polenta layer, add the remaining sauce, 2 tablespoons of the butter and 3 tablespoons of the Parmesan cheese. Add a third layer of polenta and just dot with the remaining butter and sprinkle with the remaining Parmesan cheese.

8. Bake until the top is golden, about 40 minutes. If the top isn't browned enough, place under the broiler. Remove from the oven, let sit for several minutes, and serve with any one of the green salads in this book.

SHRIMP AND BASS RISOTTO WITH SAFFRON

Risotto con gamberi e bronzino allo zafferano
MAKES 6 SERVINGS

Giuseppe Mazzoti, the Italian gastronomic writer, said there's not much difference between a risotto and rice soup, and that the people of Venice like risotto *all'onda*, wavelike risotto (it seems natural that a city of navigators would prefer it this way). What this really means is that Venetian risotto, unlike that of Milan, should not only be creamy, it should be almost liquid, or as they say, *ondoso*, meaning wavy. There are an infinite variety of rice and fish dishes in the Veneto; almost every imag-inable fish out of water, if fresh, can be added to rice.

When I prepare this dish, I see gondolas in the canals or moored to the tall barber shop–like posts called *briccole* near the Paglia Bridge, home for the gondolier's Madonna. There are gondolas for every purpose, even funeral ones with black pompoms. I see the sailor jumpers and straw hats with gay ribbons. I hear the soft hums of the songs they sing, and smell the risotto that they and I will eat a bit later.

4 cups Fish Broth (page 9), heated to the boiling point
1 pound fresh shrimp (16 to 20 count), shelled (reserve shells for broth) and deveined
2 small zucchini, 1 × 6 inches
1 stick (8 tablespoons) butter
½ cup finely chopped shallots
2 cups Italian rice, preferably Vialone Nero
1 cup dry white wine
½ teaspoon saffron threads
4 tablespoons freshly grated Parmesan cheese, plus extra for serving
½ pound fresh sea bass fillets (or similar white fish fillets), rinsed, dried and cut into 1- to 2-inch squares
Sea salt and freshly ground pepper

1. Make the Fish Broth, using the reserved shrimp shells; keep at the boiling point.

2. Rinse the shrimp and pat dry with paper towels. Set aside.

3. Rinse the zucchini. Cut off ends and slice each zucchini in half lengthwise. Cut each half again lengthwise. With a small sharp knife, cut away and discard seedy pulp. Cut the strips crosswise in ¼-inch pieces. Set aside.

4. In a large saucepan, melt 4 tablespoons of the butter over medium heat. Add the shallots, and cook, stirring frequently, until they begin to take on some color, about 4 minutes. Add the rice and stir to coat it, 1 to 2 minutes.

5. Add the wine, zucchini and shrimp. Cook until the wine evaporates, about 5 minutes. Add some hot fish broth, ½ cup at a time, waiting for the rice to absorb the liquid before adding the next ½ cup of broth, stirring almost constantly to prevent sticking.

6. When the rice has cooked for 10 to 12 minutes, add the saffron and 2 tablespoons of the Parmesan cheese. Cook, stirring and adding more broth as it is absorbed by the rice. Add the pieces of bass or other fish and stir gently.

7. The rice should be cooked properly in 25 to 30 minutes. The rice should not appear dry and be firm to the bite (al dente). The whole dish should appear "wavy," so add a little more broth to make this as they do in Venice. If more salt is needed, add it now.

8. Remove from the heat. Stir in the remaining 4 tablespoons butter and 2 tablespoons Parmesan cheese, and let rest for several minutes before serving. Transfer to a serving dish and top with a liberal grinding of pepper, and more Parmesan cheese.

CHICKEN RISOTTO WITH VEGETABLES, VENETIAN STYLE

Risotto alla sbiraglia (Veneziana)
MAKES 6 SERVINGS

In northern Italy, rice is served as a first course, but this dish lends itself to serving as a main course. All it takes is the addition of a salad and a loaf of good Italian bread. Adding the butter and Parmesan at the end of its cooking time is an important finishing step. When I am asked if I reheat risotto, I sheepishly admit that I do so in a microwave for a minute or two, depending on quantity, after adding a few drops of water over the rice and covering it with plastic wrap.

4 tablespoons extra-virgin olive oil
1 onion, finely chopped
1 carrot, finely chopped
1 rib celery, finely chopped
1 pound skinless, boneless chicken breasts,
    cut into ½-inch dice
½ cup dry white wine
1 cup tomato puree (do not use tomato
    paste)
Sea salt and freshly ground pepper
2¼ cups Italian rice
4 to 6 cups Chicken Broth (page 8), heated
6 tablespoons butter, at room temperature
1 cup freshly grated Parmesan cheese

1. Heat the oil in a large saucepan and sauté the onion, carrot and celery for 5 to 6 minutes, stirring frequently until they take on some color.

2. Add the chicken pieces and cook for 5 minutes, stirring constantly. Add the wine, let it boil and cook off, about 5 minutes.

3. Add the tomato puree, salt and pepper. Bring to a boil, reduce the heat to achieve a slow, steady simmer, partially cover the pan and simmer for 15 minutes. During this period, check to see if the mixture is too dry; if so, add ½ cup of the hot broth.

4. Add the rice and stir thoroughly. Adding ½ cup of the hot broth at a time, add the broth to the rice, stirring carefully so that the rice absorbs the broth. Continue doing this for 20 to 25 minutes, adding more broth when the rice has absorbed it. When the rice is tender (it is always best to taste a little of it to test for doneness), add a little more hot broth to make the risotto "wavy," as the Venetians like it.

5. Remove the pan from the heat and fold in the butter and ½ cup of the Parmesan cheese. This should be served right away, passing the remaining Parmesan cheese. Add a fresh baby spinach salad to complete this one-dish meal.

TURKEY BREAST BAKED WITH PROSCIUTTO AND CHEESE TO RESEMBLE A CARDINAL'S HAT

Petti di tacchino al forno alla cardinale
MAKES 6 SERVINGS

Here is a very good one-dish meal, because it is easy to make and also because boned turkey breasts can be found in most food markets. In fact, often they are sold sliced. Again, here is an Italian touch that may seem too cute for words, but it makes an attractive luncheon or light supper one-dish meal if accompanied by a beet salad or two or three slices of red ripe tomatoes that are dressed simply with oil, salt, pepper and a couple of drops of balsamic vinegar. Either the beets or the sliced tomatoes will enrich the color of the cardinal's hat.

Prosciutto di Parma is considered the best by many people but there are others who give that accolade to the San Daniele ham. The San Daniele hams come from the Fruili area in the northeast of Italy where their pigs for this particular ham are kept outdoors and fed a diet of acorns, which results in the prosciutto's distinctive flavor. It imparts this flavor to the turkey, which is somewhat bland to begin with, therefore making a good food combination.

> 6 (about ¾-inch-thick) slices uncooked turkey breast (about 1½ pounds)
> 1 cup milk
> 6 tablespoons butter
> Sea salt and freshly ground pepper
> 3 or 4 teaspoons tomato paste
> 1 lemon wedge, seeded
> 12 thin slices buffalo mozzarella
> 6 thin slices prosciutto di San Daniele or di Parma
> ¼ cup finely chopped fresh chives

1. Put the slices of turkey in a flat glass dish, large enough to hold the pieces in one layer. Pour the milk over the slices and let them rest for 30 or 40 minutes, at room temperature. Drain the turkey slices, pat them dry with paper towels and put each slice between 2 sheets of waxed paper and pound them with a meat pounder to flatten them somewhat.

2. Melt 3 tablespoons of the butter in a large skillet over medium heat and sauté 3 of the slices until they turn golden on both sides, a few minutes per side. Remove them to an ovenproof pan (such as a baking sheet with a rim) and repeat this procedure for the remaining 3 turkey slices, using the remaining 3 tablespoons butter. Add one teaspoon of the cooked melted butter to the tomato paste with 3 or 4 drops of lemon juice and stir well. Put the tomato paste mixture aside until needed. When all the slices are cooked, arrange them on the ovenproof pan, season with salt and pepper and put 1 slice of mozzarella on each turkey slice; there should be a visible edge of turkey meat around the cheese.

3. Preheat the broiler. Wrap a slice of prosciutto around each cheese-topped turkey slice and then put another smaller slice of cheese over the prosciutto wrapping. Broil just long enough to melt the mozzarella, 2 to 3 minutes. Remove the pan from the broiler; spread $1/2$ teaspoon of the tomato paste mixture on the top of each piece. Return to the broiler to reheat but be careful not to burn the tomato paste. Arrange the cooked turkey pieces on a platter and sprinkle with the chopped chives, or put on individual plates, sprinkling each with some chives.

EMILIA-ROMAGNA'S STAR CITIES

BOLOGNA, PARMA AND MODENA, AND OTHERS ALONG THE 125-MILE ROMAN ROAD, THE VIA EMILIA

The Roman Road, Via Emilia, built in 187 B.C., stretches about 125 miles on the Po, from Piacenza to Rimini on the Adriatic. Its soil, intensely cultivated, is among the best in Italy with its mulberries and vines, maples and elms. Many towns are strung along this pearl neck lace, the Via Emilia, and the most important are Parma, Modena, Bologna and Ravenna, with Ferrara a little farther north. This area today is called Emilia-Romagna.

Until recently, the region was not unified; instead, these cities were ruled by powerful families such as the Bentivoglio of Bologna, the Este of Ferrara and the Malatesta of Rimini, no one family strong enough to rule the others. Known as the breadbasket of Italy because of its wheat production, the region's glory rests on Parmigiano-Reggiano cheese, prosciutto and homemade pasta in many forms. The cuisine benefits from the richness of the Po Valley; the durum wheat grown there makes its pasta so flavorful, outstandingly high-quality livestock yield the rich butter, cheese, veal, pork and ham so essential for the cooking. In the delta region of the Po, near Ferrara, vegetables prosper and orchards grow vigorously. Around Modena are the most beautiful sweet cherries, pears and peaches. The earthy flavor of balsamic vinegar is there, too. It seems everyone can cook in this area.

Today, Emilia-Romagna is also a center of modern technology, applied to the processing and export of food. Bologna is the heart of this regional trade. In addition to Parmigiano and prosciutto, tagliatelle (noodles made with eggs), tortelli (stuffed pasta), tortelloni (larger stuffed pasta) and spinach lasagna began in Bologna. Noticeably absent are olive trees, but in their places grow vines.

Traditional cooking is firmly entrenched in the heart of Emilia-Romagna and it stretches outward. It seems as if *la cucina nuova* was a whistle stop on a fast train through this part of Italy where *la cucina regionale* reigns supreme. Irma and Roberto Molossi, who own the trattoria Il Cortile (the courtyard) in Bologna, prepare traditional dishes with passion. Roberto's mother makes pasta daily as his father generally polices the kitchen. Between two small dining rooms and a bar area, there is a long enclosed portico with outdoor gardens on each side. The last time I was there, the sun was setting and the colors of the nearby buildings seen from inside the trattoria reflected in the window panes and on the soft terra-cotta floor's charismatic ochres, umbres and reds. I thought this is why they call the city Bologna, the Red. Actually, it is because of the red tile roofs. Roberto described some traditional preparations such as *minestra del paradiso,* pieces of egg custard in a mixed beef and poultry broth (*brodo misto*) in which he does not add tomatoes, as others do. The poultry must be a *gallina,* a hen. No oil is added, and the water added to make the broth must be cold to properly cook the hen. He explained further that a *cappone,* a castrated chicken, is used for *brodo di Natale,* broth for Christmas, and simmers for three hours, uncovered. With passion he described the 250-member culinary group that meets every year to honor the *salame* of the Bologna area. They eat at long tables under wisteria vines enjoying *piadina,* the flat bread of the region (see page 158), stuffed with salami, drinking Lambrusco wine. The Malossi are only one of many other restaurateur families who study the history of foods and take pride in recreating them, adding a new touch here and there, but being true to the basic core of the recipes.

Delicious food is the epitome of Bologna and her sister towns. The rich cooking has earned Bologna the name *la grassa,* the fat one. However, it is also known as the town of *la dotta,* the learned one, because her university is almost 1,600 years old. It is a great, human city to enjoy and from which to visit its equally enticing environs.

A TART FROM THE TAMBURINI SPECIALTY FOOD SHOP IN BOLOGNA: MENU FOR 6

MENU

Parmesan Custard Tart
Crostata di parmigiano

Sliced Cucumbers with Mint
Centrioli con la menta

Baked Stuffed Peaches with Amaretti and Almonds
Pesche ripiene

This shop in Bologna is unbelievable; it is no ordinary delicatessen. The shop has a wood-burning fireplace with a large spit turning over meats and poultry of all kinds. Filled with local products, the number of *salumi* alone are breath-taking. There are tens of different *prosciutti di Parma,* culatella, coppa, salamis, zampone and sausages. You will think the mortadella is the largest you've ever seen. The take-out department is just as varied, and you will not be able to resist any of it. This shop is a tribute to the kitchen of Bologna.

Wine Selection

Serve Cinque Terre Bianco, quite the most famous of all the wines of Liguria, full-flavored, yet dry. It is usually drunk early, a year after the vintage.

Preparation Advice

1. The pastry can be made ahead, set in the tart pan and refrigerated until it is ready to be filled and baked.

2. The cucumbers can be made several hours ahead and refrigerated. If the ice cubes have melted, pour off some of the liquid and add a few fresh cubes before serving.

3. The peaches can be prepared for filling ahead of time, filled, and kept at room temperature for about 30 minutes before baking.

PARMESAN CUSTARD TART

Crostata di parmigiano
MAKES 6 SERVINGS

The eggs and cream are the perfect foil in this tart for the sharp, nutty, flavorful cheese. Its smooth-ness is only interrupted by the occasional bite of crisped pancetta or bacon. The flaky pastry adds to the richness and mouthwatering quality of the tart.

FOR THE PASTRY
6 tablespoons chilled butter, cut into ¼-inch pieces
2 tablespoons chilled vegetable shortening
1½ cups all-purpose flour
Sea salt
1¼ tablespoons ice water

FOR THE FILLING
2½ tablespoons butter
¼ cup small pieces (¼ inch) pancetta or bacon
2 eggs
2 egg yolks
1¼ cups heavy cream

3/4 cup freshly grated Parmesan cheese
Pinch white pepper

1. *To make the pastry:* Combine the butter, shortening, flour and some salt in a bowl. Blend until the mixture looks like coarse meal. Add the water, toss quickly and form a ball. If the dough is too crumbly, add another 1 tablespoon water. If too moist, sprinkle with a dash of flour. Dust with flour and wrap in plastic wrap. Refrigerate for several hours until the dough is firm.

2. Preheat the oven to 400F. Remove the dough from the refrigerator several minutes before rolling it. Press by hand into a circle about 1 inch thick. Lightly dust both sides with flour and roll out into a 12-inch circle.

3. Butter the sides and bottom of a 9-inch tart pan with a removable bottom. Carefully arrange the pastry in it. Roll the rolling pin over the edge to remove any extra pastry. Prick all over the bottom and press a sheet of buttered foil over the dough in the tart pan to help keep the shape of the tart. Bake 10 minutes. Remove the foil, and cook 2 or 3 minutes longer to brown the pastry. Remove the pan from the oven and reduce the heat to 350F.

4. *To make the filling:* Heat 1/2 tablespoon of the butter in a skillet and sauté the pancetta until crisp. Remove to paper towels. Discard the fat in the skillet or save for another use.

5. Beat the eggs, egg yolks and cream in a medium bowl. Stir in the cheese and pepper.

6. Dot the bottom of the cooked tart shell with the pancetta and carefully pour in the cheese mixture. Fill up to 1/4 inch of the top of the tart pan; do not overfill. Cut the remaining butter into small bits and sprinkle over the filling. Bake for about 30 minutes, until the custard has firmed and browned. Remove from the oven. After resting for several minutes, remove the

cooked tart from the tart pan. Cut into wedges and serve hot.

SLICED CUCUMBERS WITH MINT

Centrioli con la menta
MAKES 6 SERVINGS

This is one time you don't have to drain and dry a vegetable. Cucumbers are stacked high in the Italian markets and are used mostly in salads with oil, vinegar and herbs. In our household, they were a staple, although my grandfather disliked them as much as zucchini. "They're nothing but water," he would say as my mother and grandmother continued to fill their antipasti plates and salad bowls with fresh, succulent cucumbers.

You'll find three basic types of cucumbers in the markets. The slicing cucumber is the most commonly seen in supermarkets. These are field grown, six to eight inches long, with dark green, glossy skins, usually waxed after harvesting for shelf life (be sure to remove all the waxed peel before using). The Kirby cucumber, a second variety, used for commercial dill pickles, is also sold fresh. The size is smaller, squatter with lighter green skins. As a cucumber lover, I like these for their crispness, freshness, tiny seeds and thin skins. The third type, greenhouse or European type cucumbers are now widely available. You can't help noticing them in the markets, as they are sometimes almost two feet long (and usually covered in plastic). These are not only more expensive but somewhat bland. For this recipe, use the Kirby variety or small slicing regular cucumbers to avoid seeds—if your cucumber has large seeds, simply cut them away.

6 nicely shaped small Kirby cucumbers
1 tablespoon sea salt

6 large mint sprigs—3 whole, 3 finely chopped

2 cups ice cubes

1. Slice off ends of the cucumbers and remove almost all of the skin with a vegetable peeler. Run the tines of a fork up and down the full length of the cucumbers; this makes a nice design and some say it makes the cucumbers less bitter. Cut in eighths, lengthwise.

2. In a serving dish wide enough to hold the cucumber wedges, combine them with the salt, chopped mint and the ice cubes. Refrigerate for 1 hour or longer to crisp and scent the cucumbers.

3. Serve just as they are but add the 3 remaining mint sprigs for garnish.

BAKED STUFFED PEACHES WITH AMARETTI AND ALMONDS

Pesche ripiene

MAKES 6 SERVINGS

Italians love peaches, fresh, peeled, sliced and served in wine, or combined with wine and baked. I have made these with good-quality canned peaches and found that they work, perhaps not as well as fresh peaches, but they still make a fine ending to a lunch or other meal. Here's a favorite recipe of mine. If you can't find Italian amaretti, use American made macaroons but reduce the number of cookies to eight.

6 ripe peaches, halved and pitted

6 blanched almonds, finely chopped

12 amaretti cookies, crushed

1/2 cup sugar

1/3 cup unsweetened cocoa powder

10 tablespoons dry white wine

12 teaspoons mascarpone cheese

1. Preheat the oven to 325F. With a melon baller, remove a bit of the flesh from the inside of each peach half. Put the flesh in a bowl with the almonds, amaretti, 1/4 cup of the sugar, cocoa powder and 2 tablespoons of the wine. Mix well.

2. Fill the cavities of each peach half. Carefully place 1 teaspoon of the mascarpone on top of each filling and place the peach halves in a buttered baking pan. Add the remaining wine to the pan and sprinkle with the remaining sugar.

3. Bake for 30 minutes, until the peaches are tender. To test for doneness, spear the peach with a wooden skewer. If the skewer penetrates easily, the peach is cooked. Serve warm.

CHRISTMAS DAY DINNER FOR 10 TO 12 IN EMILIA-ROMAGNA

MENU

Homemade Tortellini in Broth
Tortellini in brodo alla casalinga

Christmas Capon with Condiment from Cremona
Cappone Natalizio con Mostarda di Cremona

A Special Stuffing
Il ripieno, speciale

Fennel Mold with Herbs
Sformata di finocchio e besciamella

Steamed Green Beans with Onion Sauce
Fagiolini con salsa di cipolle

Brandied Hazelnut Tart
Crostata di nocciole al cognac

Strawberries in Balsamic Vinegar with Fresh Mint and Whipped Cream
Fragole con balsamico, menta e panna montata

All over Italy, by mid-December, you can smell Christmas in the chilled air, in the intoxicating aromas coming from the *trattorias* and the *pasticcerias,* and in the chestnuts roasting in the blackened pans at street corners. You notice the smell of orange peelings roasting to oblivion on the logs burning in the fireplaces where Italian families will meet to prove their saying *Natale con i tuoi* (Christmas with your family).

In the cities, towns and villages, you see shopping streets and rich window displays; tiny white lights strewn to catch your eye; *crèches,* antique and some modern, most of them looking like whole villages. By Christmas Eve, the shops close, the streets become empty and quiet (and traversable) and families are really coming together. Homes are filled with *panettone, pangiallo, panpetato* or other holiday bread, and there are truffles from Umbria, buttery cheeses from Apulia, *bottarga* from Sicily and all kinds of nuts, candies, chocolates, fruits and cheeses. Christmas dinners (early in the day) start with stuffed pasta in broth.

Christmas dinners all over Italy are never fail feasts. One could enjoy this time of year in Rome, Milan, Venice, Naples or anyplace in Italy. Here we are in Bologna and, as elsewhere in Emilia-Romagna, one eats extremely well. Christmas dinner in Bologna traditionally starts with tortellini; without tortellini, there can be no Christmas in Bologna.

HOMEMADE TORTELLINI IN BROTH

Tortellini in brodo alla casalinga
MAKES 8 TO 12 SERVINGS

Tortellini are hat-shaped, meat-filled little pasta that are usually served floating in broth. It is one of the most famous dishes of the Emilia region, especially in Bologna at Christmastime. Fillings vary greatly, even in Bologna. Some preparations add ground veal to the pork, some use capon instead of chicken or turkey, others prefer prosciutto to Parma ham. They are all delicious but I like this one, which combines pork, chicken or turkey and Bologna's most famous sausage, mortadella, which is available in the United States.

> 6 tablespoons butter
> 2 ounces pork loin, minced
> 2 ounces chicken or turkey meat, minced
> 2 very thin slices prosciutto, minced
> 4 very thin slices mortadella, minced
> 1¼ cups freshly grated Parmesan cheese
> 2 large eggs, lightly beaten
> Sea salt and freshly ground pepper
> Pinch freshly grated nutmeg
> Fresh Pasta (page 10)
> 4 cups each beef and chicken broths

1. Melt the butter in a medium skillet over medium heat. Add the pork and chicken and sauté, breaking up any meat clumps, until the mixture turns golden, about 5 minutes. Transfer the mixture to a food processor.

2. Add the prosciutto and mortadella to the food processor and pulse until the mixture resembles medium bread crumbs. Transfer the mixture to a large bowl. Stir in ¾ cup of the cheese and the eggs. Add a little salt, pepper and the nutmeg.

3. Prepare the pasta. Roll out, then cut the dough into rounds with a 2-inch cutter (you should get about 80 rounds) and keep covered, to keep the pasta from drying out.

4. Mound ½ teaspoon of the filling in the center of each pasta round. Fold over to form half moons. Press the edges of the half moons with the tines of a fork to secure the filling. Bend each half moon around your index finger and press one end over the other. Set aside.

5. Bring the broths to boil in a large soup pot over medium heat. Add the tortellini, stirring gently to prevent them sticking to each other, and cook until the pasta rises to the top, 2 to 4 minutes. Ladle into warm bowls, dividing the tortellini evenly, and serve with the remaining ½ cup cheese.

CHRISTMAS CAPON WITH CONDIMENT FROM CREMONA

Cappone Natalizio con Mostarda di Cremona
MAKES 8 TO 12 SERVINGS

This condiment, quite famous in Italy and becoming more popular elsewhere, is crystallized fruit of many kinds, in a sauce flavored with mustard. It has been made in Cremona for well over a hundred years. It is usually served with sausages or roasted beef and pork. I think it is excellent with roasted capon, chicken or turkey.

2 (6-pound) capons
2 lemons
Sea salt and freshly ground pepper
1 end piece of prosciutto, 2 or 3 ounces

2 small onions, finely chopped
2 medium carrots, trimmed and cut into ½-inch slices
4 celery ribs with leaves, trimmed and cut into ½-inch slices
2 cloves garlic, peeled, mashed with 2 teaspoons fresh sage
4 tablespoons butter, at room temperature
1½ cups chicken broth
1½ cups white wine
1 (560-gram) jar (about 2½ cups) *mostarda di frutta* (available in specialty food shops: see Sources, pages 269 to 270)

1. One day prior to serving, remove the giblets, necks and livers from inside the capons. Save the livers for another use. Cut away all excess fat and discard. Put the birds on a platter with the giblets and necks next to it. Cut one of the lemons in half and rub as much of the cavities with lemon and its juice as is possible. Cut the other lemon in half to rub outside the birds, squeezing the juice all over. Liberally salt and pepper the birds, inside and out. Chop the prosciutto coarsely and put inside the cavities with the onions, carrots and celery, garlic and sage. Cover with plastic wrap and refrigerate overnight. Remove from the refrigerator the next day 1 hour before putting them in the oven.

2. Preheat the oven to 400F. Rub the butter all over the outside of the birds after moving them from the platter to a baking pan, remembering to add the necks and giblets to the pan. Cover with foil and bake for 1 hour. Remove the foil and bake for 1 hour. Combine the broth and wine. Spoon the broth mixture over the birds every 30 minutes during the roasting period until the liquid is gone. Baste with juices in the bottom of the pan until ready to remove from the oven.

3. The capons are cooked when a fork inserted in the thigh near the body releases clear juice. If you want to use an instant thermometer, look for a reading of 170F.

4. To serve, run a knife down each side of the breast bone following the bone until you have cut out 2 breast halves. Remove the legs by cutting at the leg-thigh joints. Slice the breast and thigh meat. Serve with the *mostarda di frutta*.

Notabene:

Some Bolognese cooks will bone the bird and use the stuffing, as below, to stuff the deboned capon. It is then wrapped in cloth towels and tied with string, put in a large pot with cold water, onions, carrots, celery and salt and simmered for 2 to 2½ hours, before cooling and slicing. Or it may be baked as a stuffed, deboned capon. The point in cooking it in water is to provide the broth for the tortellini, which is the first course. If you decide on either one of these alternatives, and decide to stuff the deboned bird, you must decrease the amount of bread in the stuffing recipe by 3 cups.

A SPECIAL STUFFING

Il ripieno, speciale
MAKES 8 TO 12 SERVINGS

Italian stuffings use less bread than called for here but almost always include cured meats, ground fresh meats, nuts, cheese, parsley and eggs. I like the stuffing to cook separately, as it is a neater way to do it from all points of view, and you can cook more of it in a bowl than inside the bird. It is a great leftover dish, either cold or reheated.

  2 tablespoons butter
  ½ pound ground veal
  ½ pound ground pork
  4 hard-cooked eggs, chopped coarsely

½ cup freshly grated Parmesan cheese
½ pound cooked ham, finely chopped
⅓ pound mortadella, finely chopped
¼ cup shelled pistachios
2 tablespoons each finely chopped fresh basil and
  Italian parsley
Good pinch of freshly grated nutmeg
4 cups prepared bread stuffing, such as
  Pepperidge Farm
2 eggs, beaten lightly
½ cup Marsala wine
1½ cups chicken broth

1. Preheat the oven to 350F. Melt the butter in a large skillet over medium heat. When it bubbles, add the veal and pork, breaking it up with a wooden spoon. Sauté for 6 to 8 minutes, stirring often. Transfer to a large mixing bowl.

2. Add the remaining ingredients. Toss with splayed fingers, lightly but well.

3. Liberally butter a large soufflé or other baking dish (about 9 inches in diameter and 3 inches deep). Transfer the stuffing mixture to the pan and bake for 1 hour.

FENNEL MOLD WITH HERBS

Sformata di finocchio e besciamella
MAKES 8 TO 12 SERVINGS

This is one of my favorites and will impress your family and friends. It is simply a white sauce (*besciamella*) joined with a puree of fresh fennel and combined with cheese and eggs. It is cooked in a water bath and will keep in the bath for up to an hour before serving.

1-pound fennel bulb with fronds, trimmed
2 cloves garlic, minced
2 tablespoons extra-virgin olive oil
1 teaspoon each finely minced sage, rosemary and
    Italian parsley
Butter and bread crumbs for pan
1/2 cup butter
1 cup all-purpose flour
3 1/2 cups milk, warmed
1/2 teaspoon dried fennel seeds, toasted, crushed
1 1/2 cups freshly grated Parmesan cheese
6 eggs, separated
2 tablespoons anisette, optional

1. Use the fennel bulb only and some of the soft green fronds. Chop these coarsely and put in salted boiling water with the garlic and oil and cook until the fennel is tender, about 15 minutes. Drain and dry; it is important to drain well. Transfer to a strainer and press down with the back of a wooden spoon to release excess liquid, or arrange in a cloth towel and slowly wring. Put in a food processor with the herbs and pulse to make a puree. Transfer to a bowl and set aside.

2. Preheat the oven to 400F. Butter and sprinkle bread crumbs in an oval 15 × 10 × 2 1/2-inch glass or ceramic baking dish. Melt the butter in a heavy saucepan, add the flour and whisk until all lumps dissolve and the mixture is smooth, about 5 minutes. Reduce the heat and slowly add the warm milk, stirring until smooth and thick. Sample to be sure the taste of raw flour is gone, otherwise cook a bit longer. Transfer to a large bowl and cool slightly. Add the fennel puree and fold in the Parmesan cheese with the help of a rubber spatula. Check for salt and add some if needed. Allow to cool.

3. Add 1 egg yolk at a time, whisking fully after each addition. Beat the egg whites until they hold stiff peaks and fold in the anisette, if using, and fold the egg whites into the egg yolk mixture. Pour immediately into prepared dish.

4. Put the baking dish into a larger pan and fill the outer pan halfway with water. This creates a water bath. Bake for 1 hour and 10 minutes. As the top begins to brown, cover with a piece of foil to keep from browning too much. To test for doneness, insert a wooden skewer into the center; it should come out clean. Let rest for 15 minutes and serve.

STEAMED GREEN BEANS WITH ONION SAUCE

Fagiolini con salsa di cipolle
MAKES 8 TO 12 SERVINGS

Italians do not like green beans that are partially cooked, so cook them completely. The best way to cook these is to steam them so the green beans do not touch water.

1 1/2 pounds fresh green beans, trimmed, washed
    and left whole
1 clove garlic, coarsely chopped

⅓ cup chopped white onion
1 teaspoon prepared Dijon mustard
3 tablespoons herb-flavored vinegar
1 cup extra-virgin olive oil
Sea salt and freshly ground pepper
8 to 12 fresh radicchio leaves, rinsed and dried

1. Steam the beans over boiling water for about 15 minutes, until tender. Dry well and put them in a large bowl or platter.

2. Put the garlic, onion, mustard, vinegar and 2 tablespoons of the oil in a food processor and pulse to a count of eight. Pour the remaining oil through the food tube, while the motor is on. Add some salt and pepper.

3. Pour the sauce over the green beans. Toss lightly but well. Arrange some of the beans in radicchio leaves, on individual plates. Serve the beans warm or at room temperature; the sauce should always be served at room temperature.

BRANDIED HAZELNUT TART

Crostata di nocciole al cognac
MAKES 8 TO 12 SERVINGS

In Italy, hazelnuts are used in all sorts of confectionery. Probably best known is its use in *Baci* (kisses) from the chocolate manufacturer Perugina in Perugia. The "kiss" contains a whole hazelnut in the center of the chocolate piece. They are also used in the Italian nougat, *torrone*, and in a delicious fondant chocolate from Piedmont called *gianduiotti*. As children, we used to buy hazelnuts strung as necklaces at various celebrations. I wish I could tell you that this tart has a long Italian history and that it was made famous by an Emilian or other Italian baker, but I can't. It is something I've concocted in

my kitchen, which is Italian, heart and soul. I use it for special occasions, Christmas being one.

FOR THE PASTRY
1 cup hazelnuts, ground
2 tablespoons all-purpose flour
4 tablespoons sugar
3 tablespoons butter, melted
¼ teaspoon sea salt

FOR THE FILLING
4 egg yolks, at room temperature
½ cup sugar
1 tablespoon fresh lemon juice
3 tablespoons brandy
1 cup heavy cream, whipped, plus extra for
   decorating
Hazelnuts, for decorating

1. *To make the pastry:* Preheat the oven to 375F. Blend all the ingredients in a bowl. Press the dough into a 9-inch tart pan with a removeable bottom, covering the bottom and sides.

2. Bake for 10 to 15 minutes, until golden. Remove from the oven and set on a rack to cool. Remove the shell from the pan but keep it on the base.

3. *To make the filling:* In the top of a double boiler, combine the yolks and sugar, and cook over simmering water, stirring constantly with a wire whisk, until the mixture thickens to the consistency of mayonnaise, about 10 minutes. (This is important; if the yolks and sugar are undercooked the filling will not solidify.) Remove the top saucepan from the heat, add the lemon juice, and stir well. Add the brandy and stir again. Allow the yolk mixture to cool to room temperature.

4. Fold the whipped cream into the cooled yolk mixture. Pour the filling into the pastry

shell and refrigerate the tart until it is set, at least 2 hours.

5. This tart will keep nicely overnight. When you are ready to serve it, decorate with rosettes of whipped cream, topping each with a hazelnut.

STRAWBERRIES IN BALSAMIC VINEGAR WITH FRESH MINT AND WHIPPED CREAM

Fragole con balsamico, menta e panna montata
MAKES 8 TO 12 SERVINGS

At Christmastime, strawberries are especially colorful and in tune with the colors of the season. This preparation is best if it can be brought together one hour before needed and left at room temperature. Berries and balsamic vinegar may seem a strange combination, but you will find that the taste of the vinegar disappears when it gets overpowered by the taste of the berries, and the acidity brings out the taste and sweetness of the fruit.

> 2 pints ripe strawberries, rinsed, 4 left unhulled
> 2 tablespoons high-quality balsamic vinegar
> 1 tablespoon sugar
> ¼ cup finely chopped fresh mint

1. If any of the berries are extra large, cut them in half. Combine the strawberries, balsamic vinegar and sugar in a bowl. Toss lightly but well. Let stand at room temperature for 30 to 60 minutes; any longer will make the berries too soft.

2. To serve, pick out the ones with the stems and place them on top. Sprinkle the mint over the berries.

Notabene:

For Christmas especially, Italians will offer a bowl of beautiful oranges and other fresh fruit, a tray of roasted chestnuts, a hunk of Parmigiano-Reggiano cheese, and some home-baked holiday cookies or chocolates. You may wish to do the same.

LENTILS AND GOOD-LUCK DINNER FOR 8 TO 10, NEW YEAR'S DAY IN PARMA

MENU

Stewed Lentils with Duck
Lenticchie in umido con filetti di anatra

Tagliatelle in Parma Ham–Saffron Sauce
Tagliatelle con salsa al prosciutto e zafferano

Braised Pork Tenderloin with Marsala Sauce
Maiale arrosto con salsa al marsala

Individual Artichoke Mold with Taleggio Sauce and Sage
Budino di carciofi in salsa di taleggio

Muscat Sorbet
Sorbetto di moscato

Green Tomato Jam Tart with Zabaglione and Whipped Cream
Crostata di marmellata (pomodoro verdi) con zabaglione

The Flat Bread of Emilia-Romagna
Piadine

"You can be sure that no matter what else we eat on New Year's Eve or New Year's Day, there will be lentils and raisins," said an Italian friend as we were visiting the lobby of the old, handsome Corona d'Ora in Bologna. "Of course, Italians eat them because they resemble coins and this promises prosperity for the New Year." From this hotel, the city of Parma is a short distance. Let's celebrate New Year's there. Parma's patron saint is Sant'Illaria, who lost his shoe while crossing the river to Parma. On his feast day, *la cucina regionale* dictates the citizenry to bake cookies in the shape of the lost shoe. Parma is also the place where once a year almost two hundred people dine in the town hall to judge hundreds of the *culatello*, the heart of the prosciutto made from the center of the rump, a cured meat many people prefer to prosciutto. Prizes are awarded by two juries of experts dressed in ermine-velvet robes. The winners kneel and their heads are touched by swords and they promise to make an equally good or better *culatello* for the next competition. The best *culatello* I ever tasted was at a restaurant called La Greppia in Parma, and that experience serves as the basis for this menu. La Greppia is a long, narrow room with white stucco walls, beamed ceilings with some antique copper molds and hanging bouquets of dried herbs. At the far end of the room is a see-through kitchen window, displaying freshly made pasta on an enlarged windowsill, obviously designed for this showing. The owners, Maurizio and Paola Rossi, are young and knowledgeable. She is the chef. The cured meat was *culatello di Zibello,* indescribably delicious.

Budinis are puddings and in Italy they are made of vegetables or cheese. They are old-fashioned and traditional, and fit well into *la cucina regionale* cooking styles. The idea for the artichoke *budino,* below, comes from La Greppia. The Rossis grow their own herbs and they use them frequently but with care. "Rice as a course of food is not that important in Parma," said Mau-

rizio. He features only one rice dish to seven of pasta. For centuries, Parmigiano-Reggiano has been served as a separate course. A huge wheel of cheese is wheeled out on a serving table and pieces are cut with a special tool. It is eaten by hand after some of it is placed on individual plates. If one is there at the right time, one can participate in the celebration of Parmigiano-Reggiano, a once-a-year affair, where the cheese-making process is demonstrated using original, antique implements. Parmesan cheese has become so popular, it is now found in almost every supermarket in the United States.

Wine Selection

The people in this region will probably drink one of the Lambrusco wines with this holiday meal, so why shouldn't we? It is readily available in the United States. Although they are made in four DOC zones, try to find one of these: Lambrusco di Sorbara or Lambrusco Grasparossa di Castelvetro. These are dark red and sparkling and dry, produced by Manicardi, Moro, Villa Barbieri, Francesco Bellei and Cavicchioli.

For a white, try a dry wine from the Albana grape, produced by Fattoria Zerbina, Fattoria Paradiso and Fratelli Vallunga.

Preparation Advice

1. The tart can be made one day ahead and left at room temperature, covered. Zabaglione and cream should be made just before mealtime.

2. The soup can be made and refrigerated, one or two days ahead, but leave the crisping of the duck pieces for garnish until just before serving.

3. The pasta can be made ahead by as much as a week; dry it first and then store in a cardboard box with a lid until ready to use or up to one week. The sauce can easily be brought together a little before mealtime.

4. The pork tenderloins can be cooked ahead two hours (be sure to slightly undercook them); the sauce can be made before eating.

5. The mixture for the artichoke molds can be made ahead the morning of the meal and refrigerated. The cheese sauce can be made at the last minute.

STEWED LENTILS WITH DUCK

Lenticchie in umido con filetti di anatra
MAKES 8 TO 10 SERVINGS

In this recipe the lentils will absorb the flavor of the duck as they cook together. But an important part of the recipe requires crisping strips of duck to be added to the top of the dish. Look for the exquisite imported lentils from Umbria, small, medium or large brown ones. Italian lentils seem to keep their shape better than their American counterparts.

FOR THE LENTILS
1 pound lentils, picked over, rinsed and soaked for
   4 to 5 hours
¼ cup extra-virgin olive oil
1 medium onion, finely chopped
6 fresh sage leaves, cut into slivers and then
   minced
4 to 6 cups beef broth, warmed

FOR THE DUCK
2 (4- to 6-ounce) boneless duck breasts, with
   skin
2 tablespoons finely chopped prosciutto fat
   (see Notabene, below)
1 tablespoon butter
1 tablespoon extra-virgin olive oil
Sea salt and freshly ground pepper

2 tablespoons white wine vinegar
¼ cup finely chopped Italian parsley

1. *To prepare the lentils:* Drain the lentils well and set aside.

2. In a medium saucepan, heat the oil and cook the onion over medium heat until translucent, 4 to 5 minutes. Stir in the sage and cook for 1 minute, stirring. Add the lentils and stir to combine. Add enough broth just to cover the lentils. Bring to a boil, reduce the heat, cover and simmer for 30 minutes.

3. *Meanwhile, to prepare the duck:* Rinse the duck breasts and dry well.

4. In a medium skillet, cook the fat until it begins to crisp, 3 or 4 minutes over medium-high heat. Add the butter and oil and when the butter is melted and begins to bubble, add the duck breasts, skin side down. Sauté over medium-high heat for 4 minutes. Turn and sauté the other side. Remove the skillet from the heat and transfer the duck to a plate to cool. Keep the skillet with any liquid in it for a later step.

5. Cut the duck breasts carefully into very thin julienne strips, as thinly as possible. Take one half of the strips and cut them into fine dice. Set aside the remaining duck strips and cover with plastic. Add the diced duck and the vinegar to the pan with the lentils and continue cooking until the lentils are tender and the liquid has been absorbed, 30 minutes. The total cooking time for the lentils should be about 1 hour, but it is best to taste a few to test for doneness. Add some salt and pepper.

6. Reheat the skillet in which the duck breasts were cooked and add the remaining julienned duck. Over very high heat, stir them in the skillet to crisp them. To serve, spoon some stewed lentils on individual plates, or put some in a bowl or

platter and arrange some crisped duck pieces on top. Sprinkle with parsley.

Notabene:

Anyone who sells prosciutto will give you some of its fat. Just ask for it to be cut off the whole piece of prosciutto. Two tablespoons chopped fat is about ½ ounce.

TAGLIATELLE IN PARMA HAM–SAFFRON SAUCE

Tagliatelle con salsa al prosciutto e zafferano
MAKES 8 TO 10 SERVINGS

Noodles, sometimes called string pasta, come in a number of varieties and with different names by those who make and eat them. Probably the best-known Bologna noodle is *tagliatelle* and it is supposed to be as thin as possible and cut approximately ¼ inch wide. The Bolognese think there is nothing better, especially if it is homemade.

Making the pastry stars is an extra step you may wish to pass on. Paola Rossi, the chef, delighted in making this tasty garnish. One time, she added a puff pastry bow, tied.

> **FOR THE PASTRY STARS (OPTIONAL)**
> 1 sheet frozen puff pastry, thawed
> Freshly ground pepper
>
> Tagliatelle made with 3 eggs and 2¼ cups all-purpose flour (page 11) or 1 pound dried
> ¼ teaspoon saffron threads
> ¼ cup warm water
> ½ cup butter
> 4 slices prosciutto, finely chopped
> 1 cup heavy cream
> Sea salt and freshly ground pepper
> 1 cup freshly grated Parmesan cheese

1. *To make the optional pastry stars:* Preheat the oven to 400F. Butter a baking sheet. Using a small 1-inch star cutter, cut star shapes out of the puff pastry. You can make as many as the sheet will allow and freeze what you don't use, or make 2 stars per person and reserve the remaining pastry for another use. If you don't have a star-shaped cutter, use a 1-inch round shape, a crescent shape or any other small decorative shape, but do not make them larger than 1 inch.

2. Place the stars on prepared baking sheet, spacing them 1 inch apart. Liberally add freshly ground pepper over the pastry cut-outs. Bake for 10 minutes, until golden.

3. Make the pasta and set aside.

4. Combine the saffron and warm water and stir to dissolve.

5. In a large skillet, melt the butter and when it is bubbly, add the prosciutto and sauté for several minutes to crisp it. Add the cream and saffron, and stir over medium heat until the sauce is combined and hot. Add some salt and pepper.

6. In boiling, salted water, cook the tagliatelle until al dente; if it is freshly made it will take 2 minutes, if it is dried, about 8 minutes. Drain the pasta and add to the sauce in the skillet over low heat. Toss lightly but well to coat the noodles with the sauce, 1 to 2 minutes. Garnish with pastry stars, if using. If you are serving the pasta in a large platter, surround the pasta with the stars. If you are serving individual portions, lay 2 stars on top of each serving.

BRAISED PORK TENDERLOIN WITH MARSALA SAUCE

Maiale arrosto con salsa al marsala
MAKES 8 TO 10 SERVINGS

Most pork tenderloins sold in this country are packed in plastic to preserve freshness and are dated. Check the date. Inspect them after opening the package for any extra fat, and if there is any, remove it. This dish is simple and delicious; any leftovers may be served cold with the sauce reheated.

> 2 pork tenderloins (about 3 pounds total)
> 1 teaspoon coarsely ground black pepper
> 2 tablespoons olive oil
> 6 tablespoons butter
> Sea salt
> 4 large bay leaves
> ½ cup red wine vinegar
> 1 cup Marsala wine
> 1 cup chicken broth

1. Trim the tenderloins, if necessary, and wipe with a damp paper towel. By hand, pat the black pepper all over the tenderloins. In a heavy, large flameproof casserole, with a cover, heat the oil and 2 tablespoons of the butter over high heat. Sauté the tenderloins until brown on all sides, about 10 minutes. Add some salt.

2. Add the bay leaves and vinegar and cover immediately. Reduce the heat to medium-low and cook for 15 minutes. Uncover and remove the tenderloins to a plate. Add the Marsala wine and the broth and over high heat, boil until reduced by half, scraping up all the cooking residue from the bottom of the pan, 15 to 20 minutes. Remove the bay leaves. When the sauce is reduced, remove from the heat and whisk in the remaining 4 tablespoons of butter, 1 tablespoon at a time.

3. To serve, slice the tenderloins into ½-inch slices. Overlap the slices on a platter and pour the sauce to the side of the meat. Do not cover the meat with the sauce. Or, put the sauce in a serving bowl and allow each diner to take some.

INDIVIDUAL ARTICHOKE MOLDS WITH TALEGGIO SAUCE AND SAGE

Budino di carciofi in salsa di taleggio
MAKES 8 TO 10 SERVINGS

Molds, especially vegetable molds, are popular all over Italy, and here is a special one I adapted from the well-known restaurant in Parma, La Greppia. They are cooked in a water bath and will keep in the bath, once the heat in the oven is turned off, for a half hour or longer.

> 8 fresh artichoke hearts, 1 (13.75-ounce) can,
>   or 1 (10-ounce) package, frozen
> 2 cups chicken broth
> 1 cup milk, warmed
> 4 tablespoons butter, at room
>   temperature
> ½ cup freshly grated Parmesan cheese
> 3 eggs, beaten
> Dash of freshly grated nutmeg
> Freshly ground pepper
> 8 sage leaves

> FOR THE TALEGGIO SAUCE
> 2 cups Besciamella Sauce (page 168)
> 8 ounces Taleggio cheese, at room
>   temperature

1.   Preheat the oven to 350F. Butter 8 (5-ounce or
2/3-cup) timbales. If using fresh artichoke hearts,
chop them coarsely, and cook them in just
enough chicken broth to barely cover until tender, about 10 minutes. If using canned, drain and
rinse them several times in fresh water to remove
as much salty taste as is possible. If using frozen,
thaw and cook them in broth as for the fresh.
Drain artichokes and put them in the bowl of a
food processor. Add the warm milk and butter to
the processor and pulse to a count of 10. Transfer
this mixture to a bowl.

2.   Fold in the Parmesan cheese, eggs and nutmeg with the help of a rubber spatula. Add some
freshly ground pepper.

3.   Spoon into buttered timbales, leaving 1/2 inch
space at the top. Arrange these timbales in a baking pan and fill baking pan with warm water to
half of the height of the timbales. Bake for 50 to
60 minutes, until the timbales have set. These will
keep in the oven, heat off, door open for 15 minutes or so.

4.   *To make the sauce:* Over low heat, warm the
Besciamella Sauce and add one-fourth of the
cheese and stir to melt. Repeat, adding cheese
and stirring until all of the cheese has combined
smoothly into a sauce. If you think the sauce is
too thick, thin it with a little milk.

5.   To serve, run a knife around the edge of the
timbale and turn out, on individual plates. Spoon
2 tablespoons of the sauce, one on each side of the
mold, onto each plate. Place a sage leaf upward,
leaning against the mold. Serve right away.

MUSCAT SORBET

Sorbetto di moscato
MAKES 8 TO 10 SERVINGS (1 QUART)

Sweet dessert wines are made all over the boot of
Italy and they are available in the United States at
most wine shops. Since this is New Year's Day and
promises are made to start the New Year in the
right way, it seems in order to present a lighter
dessert. This sorbet can be a perfect way to end
this meal. If you feel you want to add a confection,
say a cookie, check the index for some Italian cookies. Remember that alcohol does not freeze, so the
wine must be boiled slowly; this will let the alcohol
"cook off." Later before the sorbet is finally frozen,
a little more wine will be added to reinforce the
sorbet's flavor.

> 1 1/2 cups water
> 1 1/2 cups sugar
> 4 cups muscat wine (moscato)
> 3 tablespoons fresh lemon juice (1 lemon)
> 3 tablespoons chilled moscato wine

1.   Make a simple syrup by combining the water
and the sugar in a small saucepan, bringing the
mixture to a boil, reducing the heat, and simmering until the sugar is completely dissolved, 3 to 4
minutes. Remove the pan from the heat; it is
important that this be completely cooled.

2.   Bring the 4 cups wine to boil in a saucepan
over medium heat; reduce the heat and simmer
until the wine is reduced to a little less than 3
cups, about 15 minutes. Remove from the heat
and allow to cool completely.

3.   Put both the syrup and reduced wine in the
container of an ice cream maker. Add the lemon

juice and freeze according to the manufacturer's instructions. When the sorbet develops a thick, smooth consistency, about 20 minutes, add the 3 tablespoons chilled wine. Continue to operate the ice cream maker until the sorbet has formed. Transfer to a plastic container with a lid and put in the freezer, if not using immediately. To serve, transfer the frozen sorbet to the refrigerator about 1 hour before needed; this will make it easier to scoop.

GREEN TOMATO JAM TART WITH ZABAGLIONE AND WHIPPED CREAM

Crostata di marmellata (pomodori verdi) con zabaglione

MAKES 8 TO 10 SERVINGS

If you have ever wondered what to do with green tomatoes, here is the perfect answer, for this jam makes a perfect tart. The jam is very easy to make, but you will need green tomatoes. Importers of Italian specialty foods will be able to get jars of this jam for you from Italy.

If you want to postpone your New Year's resolutions to the next day, the following recipe will serve as an incentive.

FOR THE GREEN TOMATO JAM
2 pounds green (unripe) tomatoes
1 lemon
2 cups sugar
1/4 cup honey
3/4 cup water

FOR THE PASTRY
2 1/2 cups unbleached all-purpose flour
1/4 teaspoon baking powder
2 large eggs

1 large egg yolk
1/2 cup sugar
1 tablespoon whole milk
1 scant teaspoon finely minced lemon zest
1 stick (8 tablespoons) butter, at room temperature
Confectioners' sugar
Zabaglione (page 124)
Whipped cream

1. *To make the jam:* Core the tomatoes and cut each in half. Then cut each half into very thin slices, as thinly as you can cut them. Put them in a heavy nonreactive saucepan.

2. Cut thin strips of zest down the length of the lemon, all around, and cut each piece of zest into very thin strips, as thinly as possible. Add to the saucepan. Remove and discard as much as you can of the remaining pith, cut off the ends and slice the lemon in half. Remove all seeds and thinly slice the lemon halves, as thinly as possible. Add these to the saucepan along with the sugar, honey and water. Bring to a boil, reduce the heat and simmer, uncovered, for 1 hour, stirring frequently; the jam should be thick (it will thicken more when it cools). Be careful not to burn the bottom of the pan. Let cool.

3. *To make the pastry:* Sift the flour with the baking powder into a bowl and make a well in the center. In another bowl combine the eggs, egg yolk, sugar, milk and lemon zest. Pour this into the well. Add the butter and with a fork or with your fingers bring some of the flour into the liquid and butter mixture. Continue until all the flour is incorporated to make a dough. Turn the dough onto a work surface and knead until it is smooth. Wrap in waxed paper and put it in a cool place to rest for 1 hour. If you refrigerate it, it will become too hard and will be difficult to roll out.

4. *To assemble and bake the tart:* Preheat the oven to 375F. Divide the dough into two pieces,

one-third and two-thirds of the dough. Cover the smaller piece, and on a floured work surface, roll out the larger piece to fit a 9-inch tart pan with a removable base. Roll out as thinly as possible (even if too large for a 9-inch pan), being sure you can lift and fit it into the tart pan. Trim the pastry neatly.

5.   Spread 1½ cups of the jam on the bottom pastry. (Keep any remaining jam in a clean, sterilized jar in the refrigerator for up to 6 weeks.) On a floured work surface, roll out the smaller piece of dough as thinly as possible to make at least a 10-inch circle. Cut lattice strips, about ½-inch wide. Arrange the dough strips in a lattice pattern over the jam, trimming the edges neatly at the rim of the tart pan and sealing the dough into the bottom crust.

6.   Bake until golden, about 40 minutes. Allow the tart to cool. To serve, put 1 to 2 teaspoons confectioners' sugar in a small strainer and with the help of your finger swirling around in it, dust the tart lightly with the sugar. Serve with zabaglione and whipped cream.

Notabene:

This can be made with a pastry pie crust, such as Pillsbury, treating the pastry as in the recipe. But you must make two adjustments: 1. Use only 1 cup of jam, and 2. Bake at the same temperature for 25 minutes only.

THE FLAT BREAD OF EMILIA-ROMAGNA

Piadine
MAKES 8 SMALL ROUNDS OF BREAD

One sees *piadine* snack stands all over the region. The flat bread is eaten with meals or as snacks, often sandwiched with salami, prosciutto, Swiss chard, spinach or cheese.

> 3¼ cups all-purpose unbleached flour
> 1 teaspoon sea salt
> ⅓ teaspoon baking soda
> 4 tablespoons good lard, chilled
> ⅔ cup warm water
> 2½ tablespoons olive oil, for cooking

1.   Preheat the oven to 225F. In the bowl of a food processor, combine the flour, salt and baking soda. Process to a count of 4. Add the lard and process to a count of 25. Add the water and process to a count of 5, only to blend in the liquid; the mixture should look like cooked oatmeal. Turn dough onto a lightly floured surface.

2.   Knead 5 or 6 times to gather the dough into a ball. Cut the ball into 8 pieces and roll each piece out to a 7-inch circle.

3.   Cook on a griddle, in a heavy cast-iron skillet or in a stainless steel skillet with a copper bottom (to distribute heat evenly). First add 1 teaspoon of the oil to the selected cooking vessel and heat over medium to medium-high heat. Add a dough circle and cook for about 2 minutes. Turn over and cook the other side for 30 to 60 seconds. When done, remove the bread from the griddle, put it in a baking dish, cover with foil and place in the oven to keep warm.

4. Repeat with remaining oil and bread rounds. Serve the bread warm, whole or cut into wedges.

A MEAL FOR 6 WITH COUSIN LUCIA MARINO ON THE VIA EMILIA

MENU

Grilled Asparagus and Parma Ham Salad
Insalata di asparagi alla griglia
con prosciutto di Parma

Fresh Berries with Almond Cream
Fragole di bosco e mirtilli con
crema di mandorle

Cappuccino
Cappuccino

Walnut liqueur
Nocino

Lucia took me to lunch at a hotel and restaurant in San Donnino, a suburb of Modena, which is between Bologna and Parma on the famous Via Emilia (the road built between Piacenza and Rimini in Roman times). The restaurant is called the Baia del Re. Signor Secondo Vecchi and his wife, Maria Livia, own this rustic, earthy hotel, where they prepare their family's version of the region's dishes. Lucia and I were on our way to Piacenza, about thirty miles from her city. We stopped at the Baia del Re for a quick bite to eat—we were not very hungry, and after Lucia spoke to the owner, we were presented this lovely light meal, which seemed so appropriate for this trip in early

summer. Asparagus was in season and, combined with the Parma ham in a salad, seemed nothing short of divine. The fresh berries with almond cream confirmed our aura of divinity; we were on the road to Italian heaven.

In the vicinity of Parma, for over two centuries, the Farnese family had enriched Parma with elegant buildings and wondrous works of art. These days, some of the most elegant women in Italy, and that includes Lucia, are to be found here as supporters of lyrical music, cognescenti of antiques, and, of course, some of the most knowledgeable gourmets. This is the birthplace of Toscanini and Verdi. On this trip, Lucia talked a good deal about Parmesan cheese, and told me it was mentioned in Boccaccio's *Decameron*. She explained that three provinces claimed to have invented it, Parma, Reggio and Piacenza. To keep everyone happy, a settlement was reached to sell the cheese under the protected name of Parmigiano Reggiano. She wanted to visit a cheese warehouse, but there wasn't time. As she described the exciting aromas of cheeses in these warehouses, our appetites begged for the Parma ham and some Parmigiano Reggiano. This is when Signor Vecchi appeared.

Signore Vecchi is a *cavaliere* (knight) and also the producer of fifteen- and twenty-five-year-old balsamic vinegar, used more in cooking than in salads. When I visited the factory there was a peacock, that wouldn't shut up, on top of the building. It was as if he were placed there to add a note of local color. *Aceto balsamico* is made from fresh grape juice and not wine, as most people believe. Before the liquid is put into casks, a small amount of an older, stronger vinegar is added. It ages from ten to over fifty years in casks made of acacia, ash, cherry, chestnut, mulberry and oak. In this particular case, the casks rest on the second floor of a very large barn (the factory with the loquacious peacock on the roof), one cask after another, each raised off the ground, nesting there for many years to develop a red, mahogany color, thick and syrupy. Signor Vecchi pointed to the casks and confessed, "This is my life." The Vecchis know food and balsamic vinegar. In their kitchen, they showed me how important it is to add water slowly when making a mixed broth of beef and poultry so as not to disturb the arrangement of ingredients in the pot, and to use as little water as possible in making vegetable soup or any minestrone in order to give the soup its full vegetable flavor. There is an earthy, rustic quality to Baia del Re, proud of its heritage and happy to carry on the technique of *la cucina regionale*, in duplicating Grandmother Nonna Pina's recipes. A few years ago they were named the best restaurant in the Modena province by the *Accademia della Cucina Italliana* (Academy of Italian Cooking). In June of every year, hundreds of balsamic makers compete in a contest for the best *aceto balsamico tradizionale* in a village near Modena, Spilamberto, on the southern edge of the Po River.

Wine Suggestions

Verdicchio is a famous wine from the region known as The Marches, and as the name of the wine implies, it is of a yellowish-green color with a high alcoholic content (about 14 percent). It is made in the area of the Castelli de Jesi. The wine is ancient and very pleasant. Fazi-Battaglia is a well-known producer and the wine is available across the United States.

Preparation Advice

This is one of the easiest meals to prepare in this book, as much of it may be prepared ahead the day before.

1. Prepare the asparagus up to the blanching, drain and refrigerate in plastic wrap.

2. Make the salad dressing ahead by several hours or earlier.

3. Prepare the lettuce and arugula by rinsing, and drying and storing in plastic bags in the refrigerator, to be removed ten to fifteen minutes before using.

4. Prepare the berries and the almond cream ahead of time and assemble just before serving.

GRILLED ASPARAGUS AND PARMA HAM SALAD

Insalata di asparagi alla griglia con prosciutto di Parma
MAKES 6 SERVINGS

Italy is famous for its *prosciutto crudo* (salted and air-dried ham that needs no cooking) and the most famous is prosciutto di Parma. The cognoscenti explain that the pigs in this area are fed mostly on the whey from the Parmesan cheese–making process. This makes the flesh sweet and rather mild. The pigs never roam outdoors as they are kept in sheds to grow them fat and tasty. These hams are made from the hindquarters and dried at least one year and often up to two. Law protects the production of Parma hams to the area between the Baganza and Tara Rivers, where the air and humidity levels are considered near perfect for drying and curing. Some people think the San Daniele hams from the Friuli region (north of Venice) are as good or better, although a bit pricier because of smaller production.

Most rural families in Italy still keep a pig and cure every part of it to provide food throughout the year. Cured hams, pancetta and sausages still hang in their larders. Today, of course, many of these products are produced commercially, often using the tried and true artisanal techniques. One of the most typical antipasto dishes in Italy is a plate of sliced cured meats served with pickled vegetables to whet the appetite. When I was in Ferrara, a neighboring town of Parma, my hosts, Claudio and Evalina Bonzagni, owners of the famed Hotel Duchessa, offered tastings of their homemade salami, prosciutto and *culatello* (a small ham) in their private *salumeri* (larder for keeping their cured products), served with thick slices of yellow and red peppers in vinegar with a sprinkle of sea salt and extra-virgin olive oil—a memorable taste experience. This simple asparagus and Parma ham salad brings this part of Italy to you. There is nothing like Parma ham, but if you can't find it, use black forest ham instead.

2 pounds fresh asparagus

1 teaspoon sugar

4 tablespoons fresh lemon juice

12 tablespoons extra-virgin olive oil

2 scallions, finely chopped

1 tablespoon Dijon mustard

3 tablespoons red wine vinegar

Freshly ground black pepper

6 cups baby lettuce leaves

2 small bunches arugula

⅓ cup finely chopped fresh Italian
    parsley

6 tablespoons freshly grated Parmesan
    cheese

1 pound thinly sliced Parma ham

1. Peel the lower parts of the asparagus stems with a vegetable peeler and test for the tough part of the stem by bending the asparagus. Cut off tough ends (opposite the tips) and discard. Blanch the asparagus for about 3 minutes in a saucepan filled with enough water to cover them and into which has been added the sugar and 2 tablespoons of the lemon juice. Drain immediately to stop the cooking.

2. To make the dressing, combine 6 tablespoons of the olive oil, remaining lemon juice, scallions, mustard, vinegar and pepper. Mix well and set aside.

3. Prepare the grill or the broiler. Combine the partially cooked asparagus and the remaining oil and toss lightly to cover with oil. If using the grill, place the asparagus directly on the grill and grill for about 2 minutes per side. If using the broiler, arrange the asparagus on a baking sheet with sides and broil for 2 minutes; turn the asparagus and broil for an additional 2 minutes.

4. Just before serving, combine the lettuce, arugula and parsley in a bowl and toss with the dressing and divide among six plates. Arrange the warm asparagus over the lettuce. Sprinkle Parmesan cheese over each plate. Top with slices of ham, sprinkle with pepper and serve.

FRESH BERRIES WITH ALMOND CREAM

Fragole di bosco e mirtilli con crema di mandorle
MAKES 6 SERVINGS

Another perfectly simple Italian dessert. Adding almond extract to whipped heavy cream is like a whiff of an exotic perfume and adding this to fresh berries is heaven sent. Do not overwhip the cream; keep it light and fluffy. Try to get wild strawberries; they are filled with flavor and worth the extra cents.

2 cups strawberries, preferably wild

2 cups fresh blueberries, stems removed

1 cup heavy cream

1 teaspoon almond extract

1. Remove the stem ends of the strawberries but do not wash them. Check them over and wipe with a damp kitchen towel if necessary. Put the blueberries in a colander, after removing their tiny stems, and run under cool water, tossing with your hand to freshen all the berries. Drain well and dry. Set both berries aside.

2. Whip the cream with the almond extract until some cream can stand on the beater when it is lifted. Do not overwhip.

3. To serve, apportion the berries to each plate and spoon some of the whipped cream next to the berries. Do not cover the berries with the sauce; they should be seen.

CAPPUCCINO

Cappuccino
MAKES 6 SERVINGS

Not many people own an espresso coffee machine, but it is possible to brew a fairly decent cup of cappuccino without one. Espresso coffee is sold in bean, ground and granule form in most supermarkets across the United States. Choose one of these, heat and whip some milk, sprinkle with cocoa powder and you will produce an exciting cup of homemade cappucino.

> 6 espresso-size cups brewed espresso
> 2 cups whole milk
> 1 tablespoon quality cocoa powder

1. Make the espresso by one of the methods mentioned above and keep warm.

2. Heat the milk in a small saucepan over low heat, and whip with a wire whisk until it becomes frothy. This will take constant whipping and may take up to 5 minutes.

3. Pour the hot espresso into regular coffee cups, filling about two-thirds full. Immediately add the frothy milk to each cup. Dust with cocoa powder, by putting the cocoa in a small sieve, tapping it lightly to dust over each cup, and serve immediately.

LUCIA'S MOTHER'S FRUIT VINEGARS

Aceto insaporito alla frutta

When I was visiting my cousins in Modena, after the lunch with Lucia, I paid a visit to her mother, Angela, at their home. Lucia's mother is my mother's niece. She teaches cooking in Modena. When I entered, the smells of vinegar and fruit were everywhere. Because I love anything vinegary, I thought, "What a way to greet me!"

Angela was knee-deep in fruit: peaches, oranges and raspberries. She crushed each one separately, and had to cut some of the peaches and oranges into smaller bits, plus making some zest of the orange peel, and she put each different fruit in a large nonreactive bowl and covered the peaches with red wine vinegar, the raspberries and the oranges, separately, in white wine vinegar, enough to cover the fruit. She carefully covered each bowl with plastic and left them in her kitchen to marinate for three days. She then boiled each mixture for four or five minutes, removed them from the heat and sieved the vinegar into bottles. She wanted me to take some of them home to the United States, but I said I was happy just to know how she did it, and this is the way I learned to make and enjoy fruit vinegars. They are, at times, a pleasant relief from the constant use of balsamic, which seems to have taken over the United States.

DINNER FOR 4 AT A FRIEND'S HOME IN PARMA

MENU

Parma Ham, Mortadella and Pickled Vegetables
Prosciutto di Parma, mortadella
e verdure sott'aceto

Tagliatelle with Buttery Tomato Sauce
Tagliatelle al sugo di pomodoro e burro

Curly Endive and Fennel Matchstick Salad with Fresh Herb Dressing
Insalata di indivia ricci con finocchi
a fiammifero

Pears Cooked in Wine with Mascarpone
Pere cotte al vino bianco

To better understand this area, one has to imagine a cook who can be inspired by the hair of a beautiful bride. So it was, in 1487, that Mastro Zafirano, created *tagliatelle*, the string pasta, for the occasion of the marriage of Lucrezia Borgia to the Duke of Ferrara. To complement the golden strands of pasta, the Bolognese conceived ragu, the rich pasta sauce of beef, pork, vegetables, white wine, butter and cream. Tagliatelle is featured in this menu without the ragu. A simple butter-tomato sauce is used instead.

This menu reflects the art of cooking in Parma to which creators and consumers are equally devoted. Parma, a city reflective of this art, is one of the most interesting and unusual towns in Emilia-Romagna. Maria Louisa, the daughter of an Austrian emperor, was granted this Italian Duchy, where everything bore the seal of good taste.

Wine Selection

The best-known Emilian wine is sparkling Lambrusco, made popular in the United States by Riunite. Another, of a better quality, is from around Modena, the DOC Lambrusca di Sobrara.

Preparation Advice

1. Almost everything can be made ahead. The first course requires no cooking, and if the ingredients are on hand, the plate(s) can be arranged fifteen or twenty minutes ahead of time.

2. Homemade pasta, such as tagliatelle (or even fettuccine or other flat type and unfilled pasta) will keep in a cool place for up to a month. Be sure it dries out after making it, then carefully transfer it to a platter or an uncovered flat box lined with waxed paper and store it, uncovered. Use some or all of it as you wish. In any case, this recipe calls for cooking it all, to feed four. If you wish, you may use regular spaghetti with this sauce. It will detract from the spirit of Via Emilia, but you will have a very good pasta dish. The sauce may be made the day before and refrigerated and reheated when ready to use.

3. The salad greens and dressing may be prepared ahead. Refrigerate the salad greens, and the dressing may be kept at room temperature most of the day. Pears can be cooked in wine a day ahead and refrigerated, but bring them to room temperature before serving.

PARMA HAM, MORTADELLA AND PICKLED VEGETABLES

Prosciutto di Parma, mortadella e verdure sott'aceto
MAKES 4 SERVINGS

Mixed pickled vegetables are sold packed in olive oil and vinegar, both in Italy and across the United States. Often, the name on the jars in the United States is *giardiniera* and include an assortment of vegtables: zucchini, eggplant, onions, artichokes, carrots, celery and peppers.

4 thin slices Parma ham
4 thin slices mortadella
¾ cup pickled vegetables

1. Lay a slice of Parma ham, without folding it in, across one-half of each of 4 plates. Fold the mortadella slices in halves or quarters (depending on its size), as you would a crepe, and place it alongside the ham.

2. Put a spoonful of the vegetables where the meats meet.

TAGLIATELLE WITH BUTTERY TOMATO SAUCE

Tagliatelle al sugo di pomodoro e burro
MAKES 4 SERVINGS

This pasta sauce is a simple combination of butter and tomatoes, flavored with an onion and carrot. No garlic, no olive oil, no tomato paste, no long cooking; it is fresh and light and may be considered the ultimate Italian pasta sauce for anyone's taste. The freshness, tenderness and crispness of the curly endive and fennel matchsticks give balance to the texture side of the meal, and provide a needed counterpoint in taste to the buttery sauce.

2 pounds ripe plum tomatoes or 2 cups canned Italian plum tomatoes
1 stick (8 tablespoons) butter, cut into 8 pieces
1 medium onion, peeled and quartered
1 medium carrot, peeled and quartered
½ teaspoon sugar
1½ teaspoons sea salt
Two-Egg Pasta (page 11), cut ¼ inch wide for tagliatelle
¼ cup finely chopped fresh Italian parsley
½ cup freshly grated Parmesan cheese

1. If using fresh tomatoes, wash them well, cut each in half, and cook over low heat in a covered pan for 15 minutes. Put them through a food mill to make a fine puree. If using canned tomatoes, measure 2 cups into a food mill along with about ½ cup liquid from the can and process to a fine puree.

2. Add the butter, onion and carrot pieces, sugar and salt to a medium saucepan over low heat. Add the tomato puree. Simmer for 40 minutes, partially covered. Stir frequently, checking that the simmer does not turn to a boil.

3. While the sauce is cooking, cook the pasta until al dente and drain.

4. To serve, remove the onion and carrot pieces from the sauce, and taste for salt. Add the cooked pasta to the sauce, toss well and divide among individual plates. Add a piece of cooked vegetable, if you wish, and sprinkle with the parsley. Pass the cheese.

CURLY ENDIVE AND FENNEL MATCHSTICK SALAD WITH FRESH HERB DRESSING

Isalata di indivia ricci con finocchi a fiammifero
MAKES 4 SERVINGS

Curly endive is another name for chicory, a very popular Italian green; it is a head of ragged-edged dark green leaves, which have a bitter, assertive taste. The inner leaves are yellow and white and have a milder taste. For this salad, use only the inner yellow and white leaves and keep them crisp. The fresh fennel imparts a licorice or anise flavor. Note the dressing is simple Italian: oil, fresh lemon juice, heightened with lemon zest, some dill and snipped fennel fronds. Add the dressing at the last minute and if the greens are refrigerated, remove them fifteen minutes or so before serving.

3 tablespoons fresh lemon juice
1 teaspoon grated lemon zest
Sea salt and freshly ground pepper
1/3 cup extra-virgin olive oil
2 small bunches fresh curly endive, rinsed and
  dried

1 small fennel bulb, trimmed and sliced into
  matchstick shapes
1 teaspoon finely chopped fresh dill
1 teaspoon finely chopped fresh fennel fronds

1. Combine the lemon juice, zest, some salt and pepper in a bowl. Slowly add the oil, whisking until emulsified. Keep at room temperature until ready to dress the salad.

2. Place the endive and the fennel pieces in a large bowl. Add the dill, fennel fronds and dressing; toss well and divide among four salad plates.

PEARS COOKED IN WINE WITH MASCARPONE

Pere cotte al vino bianco
MAKES 4 SERVINGS

Mascarpone is a fresh cheese, originally from Lombardy in the north of Italy, but now it is found all over Italy and in most supermarkets in the United States. Often it is served as a dessert cheese with fresh fruit and sugar. Here is a dessert I like to make utilizing mascarpone. Pears are baked all over Italy, also in red wine but white wine is used here since it doesn't compete as much with the mascarpone as the red might. Mascarpone is added to the center of each cooked pear and served warm.

4 pears for cooking, peeled, stems intact
1 1/2 cups dry white wine
1/3 cup sugar
4 whole cloves
Ground cinnamon
4 tablespoons mascarpone cheese, at room
  temperature

1. Preheat the oven to 350F. Put the pears, stem ends up, in a small baking dish (the pears should be able to stand up in the pan). Pour over the wine. Sprinkle with the sugar. Add the cloves and sprinkle cinnamon over the pears.

2. Bake for about 30 to 35 minutes, until the pears are tender. Test for doneness with a wooden skewer. If the skewer penetrates easily, the pears are cooked. The liquid should be syrupy. Remove from the oven and cool a bit.

3. Cut each pear in half and scoop out the seeds with a melon baller. Lay 2 halves on each of four dessert plates and add ½ tablespoon of the mascarpone to each center. Spoon the syrup in the baking dish over each pear. Add another pinch of cinnamon and serve while the pears are warm.

ONE-DISH MEALS

LASAGNA BAKED WITH MEAT SAUCE, BOLOGNA STYLE

Lasagna al forno alla Bolognese
MAKES 8 TO 10 SERVINGS

The Italians begin to cook in the market, selecting the freshest ingredients for a meal that will be a triumph of colors and flavors, because Italian food must be as beautiful as it is delicious. Combining tomato sauce and grilled red peppers to create an opulent scarlet-colored dish is as uncanny as the seventh Italian sense. They combine spinach and egg pasta in *paglia e fieno,* straw and hay, because

Italians love color. Take the beautiful spinach gnocchi in Tuscany or the *lasagne verde* in Bologna with their delicate sauces and you begin to imagine the Italian feeling for their food. This is why it is said that if there is one dish that sums up the essence of Italian cooking, it must surely be pasta and its sauces.

Lasagna, which is made in broad sheets, is claimed by the Bolognese to be a pasta of their own; actually it is a pasta of olden times, as far back as the Roman Empire where it was called *laganum,* and possibly derived from the word for a cooking vessel, *lasanum.* In Calabria today, lasagna is called *lagana.* What makes this particular dish of lasagna Bolognese is the use of a rich, green spinach pasta. The preferred way to cook lasagna is baking in an oven after it has been parboiled, transferred to cold water, drained and dried. In Italy, depending on where you are, fillings for lasagna are as varied as one can imagine. One of the most frequently used fillings include mozzarella and Parmesan or pecorino cheeses, ricotta and tomato sauce. But then there are also pesto fillings, sausage, vegetables such as asparagus, artichokes and I recently cooked a delightful one with radicchio and besciamella sauce. The classic Bologna version insists on fresh spinach pasta, the Bolognese ragu tomato and meat sauce, besciamella sauce and of course, Parmigiano Reggiano cheese. And in this case, it can be served as a main dish in Italy, and it is ideal on the American table.

Few pasta dishes are as luxurious and opulent as this lasagna dish, immersed in ragu Bolognese, masked with a nutmeg-flavored besciamella, and gratinéed with a golden crust of freshly grated Parmigiano cheese.

1 teaspoon sea salt
5 fresh spinach lasagna sheets, about 5 × 24
    inches each (see below)
5 cups Ragu, Bologna Style (see below)

1¼ cups fresh grated Parmesan cheese
Besciamella Sauce (page 168)

1. Before starting to assemble, be sure the spinach pasta, ragu, and besciamella are made and ready. Fill a large bowl with cold water for cooling the pasta. Preheat the oven to 450F.

2. Bring water to a boil in a large saucepan. Add 1 teaspoon salt. Put one sheet of the pasta in the boiling water and let it cook briefly. It will float to the top in less than 1 minute. Remove right away to the bowl of cold water. When it has cooled for about 1 minute, remove it to a damp cloth towel and cover with another damp towel. Repeat this procedure until all 5 pasta sheets are cooked, cooled and dried. If one of the strips should break, don't fret, just piece it together.

3. Liberally butter a 10-inch-square baking dish that is at least 2 inches deep. Fit in a single layer of spinach pasta, covering the bottom of the dish. Use a sharp knife or scissors to help cut and fit the pasta, patching where needed.

4. Layer the lasagnas in this way: Spread about 1⅔ cups of the ragu over the bottom layer of pasta and sprinkle with ¼ cup of the cheese; add another layer of pasta, spread it with about ⅔ cup of the besciamella and sprinkle with ¼ cup of the cheese; add another layer of pasta, spread it with 1⅔ cups of the ragu and sprinkle with ¼ cup of the cheese; add the fourth layer of pasta, spread with about ⅔ cup of the bescisamella and sprinkle with ¼ cup of cheese; lastly, add a layer of pasta, spead with the remaining ragu and top with the remaining besciamella and cheese.

5. Bake the lasagna for 20 to 30 minutes, until it bubbles around the edges. Insert a wooden skewer in the center of the lasagna and feel the tip of the skewer to see if it is hot. If so, remove the lasagna from the oven and let it rest for 10 minutes or so before serving.

RAGU, BOLOGNA STYLE

Ragu Bolognese
MAKES 6 TO 7 CUPS

With its base of chopped prosciutto, onion, celery, carrots and the beef, pork and chicken livers, all slowly simmered in beef broth and wine, this classic Bologna sauce has the vigor and character to stand up assertively to any heavy pasta in addition to its use in lasagna. To soften its impact somewhat, the Bolognese will enrich the ragu with heavy cream or use it in tandem with besciamella sauce.

This will make more than the five cups needed for the lasagna, so keep the remainder for another use. It will keep in the refrigerator for three days and may be frozen for up to two months.

2 cups chopped onions (about 2 medium onions)
1 cup chopped celery (about 2 medium ribs)
½ cup chopped carrot (about 1 medium carrot)
¼ pound prosciutto, chopped
6 tablespoons butter
1½ pounds ground meat: 1 pound lean beef chuck and ½ pound lean pork, ground finely by the butcher or in a food processor
1 cup dry white wine
1½ cups milk, warmed
3 cups light beef broth
3 cups canned plum tomatoes, without juice, put through a food mill
2 tablespoons finely chopped fresh Italian parsley
½ pound fresh chicken livers, fat removed, livers cut into ¼-inch dice
Sea salt and freshly ground pepper
Freshly grated nutmeg

1. On a chopping board, combine the onions, celery, carrots and prosciutto and mince them together as finely as you can with a large sharp knife. Melt 4 tablespoons of the butter in a large saucepan, and sauté the vegetable mixture over medium heat until the vegetables and ham are lightly browned, 8 to 10 minutes.

2. Add the ground meat and increase the heat to medium-high. Break up the meat with a large wooden spoon and cook until lightly browned. Add the wine, stirring all the time, and cook until it evaporates, about 5 minutes. Add the milk and cook until it evaporates, stirring frequently, about 10 minutes.

3. Stir in the beef broth, tomatoes and parsley, and bring to a boil. Reduce the heat to a simmer and cook, half covered, for 2 hours.

4. Melt the remaining butter in a small skillet and sauté the chicken livers. When they are browned, transfer them to the saucepan. Taste the sauce for seasoning, adding salt, freshly ground pepper and nutmeg as needed. Cook 5 minutes longer.

5. If not used immediately, the sauce can be cooled and refrigerated or frozen.

BESCIAMELLA SAUCE

Salsa besciamella
MAKES 2 CUPS

This sauce has been in use in Italian kitchens for hundreds of years. It is used to bind many pasta and vegetable dishes and when it is used also as a topping, as in the lasagna, it helps to prevent it from drying out.

> 3 tablespoons butter
> 4 tablespoons sifted flour
> 2 cups milk, warmed
> Sea salt and freshly ground pepper
> Freshly grated nutmeg

1. Melt the butter in a saucepan over medium heat. Add the flour and cook, whisking constantly for 2 minutes, without letting it brown.

2. Add the warmed milk slowly, whisking all the time. Add some salt and pepper and nutmeg and cook, whisking for 10 minutes or longer, until the mixture looks like heavy cream.

CANNELLONI FROM PEPPINO'S IN PIACENZA

Cannelloni alla Peppino (Piacenza)
MAKES 4 TO 6 SERVINGS

Piacenza is a city in the food-rich region of Emilia-Romagna. It is an important center built by the Romans at the end of the Via Emilia on the south bank of the Po River. Piazza Cavalli is the center of the old city, named for its pair of bronze horse statues (*cavalli* means "horses") of the dukes Alessandro and Ranuccio Farnese. In the same square is the fine Gothic Palazzo del Comune, begun in 1280. The remarkable twelfth century Lombard-Romanesque Cathedral (Il Duomo) is down the street from the square. This charming city is only thirty-five miles from Parma and about fifty from Milan. Food there is exquisite. Look for the restaurants Antico Osteria del Teatro, Via Verdi 16, Il Gotico in Piazza Gioia, 3, and Peppino's on Via Roma, 183, where you can delight in cannelloni and other pasta specialties of the area.

Serve with sliced tomatoes and cucumbers tossed in extra-virgin olive oil and fresh lemon juice, with a sprinkle of finely chopped fresh basil.

FOR THE PASTA
1¾ cups all-purpose flour
Sea salt
2 medium eggs, lightly beaten
2 egg yolks, lightly beaten
4 tablespoons butter, melted
1¼ cups whole milk

FOR THE FILLING
2 pounds fresh spinach, large stems removed, washed well and cooked, squeezed dry and finely chopped
⅔ cup each fresh ricotta and freshly grated Parmesan cheeses
½ cup mascarpone cheese, at room temperature
2 small eggs, lightly beaten
¼ cup loosely packed finely chopped fresh Italian parsley
Sea salt
Freshly grated nutmeg
½ cup freshly grated Parmesan cheese
4 tablespoons butter, cut into 4 squares each

1. *To make the pasta:* Sift the flour and a pinch of salt into a bowl. Add the eggs, egg yolks and 1 tablespoon of the butter. Slowly stir in the milk, and stir until a smooth batter is formed. Let stand for 20 to 30 minutes.

2. Heat a 6-inch nonstick skillet over medium heat. Add a little of the butter, cover the bottom of the skillet with the butter by swirling with a paper towel. Stir the batter thoroughly and add 3 tablespoons of it to the skillet. Tilt the pan to cover the bottom of the skillet with the batter. Cook for 2 or 3 minutes, until lightly golden. Turn over and cook 1 minute longer and empty onto a plate. Continue making the circles until all the batter is used. Trim each circle into a square. These squares will be the packages to receive the cannelloni filling.

3. *To make the filling:* Combine all the filling ingredients in a bowl and delicately stir until thoroughly mixed.

4. Lay the pasta squares on a flat surface and divide the filling among them by placing spoonfuls of it in the middle of each square. Fold the squares into parcels by folding over one side, folding over the other, then folding both ends over. Place the parcels, seam sides down, in one layer in a heavily buttered baking pan.

5. *To bake the cannelloni:* Preheat the oven to 375F.

6. Sprinkle with the Parmesan cheese and dot with the butter pieces. Bake in the center of the oven for 20 to 30 minutes, until the tops turn golden. These are best served piping hot.

PASTA WITH MASCARPONE, SAGE AND TOASTED BREAD CRUMBS

Pasta con mascarpone, salvia e pane macinato
MAKES 4 TO 6 SERVINGS

This is a favorite way I prepare spaghetti. It makes a great one-dish meal and needs only a green salad topped with a tomato slice. Be sure the mascarpone cheese is at room temperature and that the bread crumbs are made fresh. You will love this dish.

> 2 tablespoons butter
> ½ cup fresh bread crumbs
> 1 tablespoon finely chopped fresh sage leaves
> Sea salt and freshly ground pepper
> 8 ounces mascarpone cheese, room temperature
> 1 cup freshly grated Parmesan cheese
> 1 pound thin spaghetti

1.   In a large skillet, heat the butter and sauté the bread crumbs and sage with some salt and pepper until lightly browned, about 3 minutes. Set aside.

2.   In a large bowl, combine the mascarpone and Parmesan cheeses.

3.   Cook the pasta and drain, reserving about 1 cup of the pasta cooking water. Add the pasta to the bowl with the cheeses. Toss lightly and well. Taste for salt and add pepper. If sauce is too thick, thin with some of the hot water.

4.   To serve, divide the pasta among individual plates and sprinkle each with 1 tablespoon or more of the bread crumb mixture or put the pasta into a large platter and sprinkle bread crumbs on it.

TAGLIATELLE BAKED WITH TWO CHEESES

Tagliatelle al forno con formaggi misti
MAKES 6 TO 8 SERVINGS

It is difficult to be in Emilia-Romagna and not eat pasta every day. I go there because of *la sfoglia* (the sheet), referring to the delicious, thin, almost transparent pasta made with eggs and cut into tagliatelle, a star of the kitchen there, as are all the pasta, whether a string variety or not. I've had a dish similar to this in Rome and elsewhere.

Combining pasta with cheese and baking them is popular all over Italy, but in Emilia-Romagna, it is the quality of the pasta that makes the difference.

Serve this with a large green salad filled with fresh tomatoes, cucumbers, curly endive and cooked julienned beets batons (add these at the very last minute).

> 1 teaspoon sea salt
> 1 pound tagliatelle, preferably homemade (Three-Egg Pasta, page 11)
> 6 tablespoons butter, at room temperature
> ¼ cup freshly grated Parmesan cheese
> 1 cup heavy cream
> 1 pound fontina cheese, cut into small cubes, less than ½ inch each
> Freshly ground pepper
> ½ cup fine bread crumbs
> 1 egg
> ¼ cup finely chopped fresh Italian parsley and scallions (white and light green parts only), for garnish

1.   Preheat the oven to 350F.

2.   Bring at least 4 quarts of water to a rolling boil. Add the salt, and then the pasta, and cook

until the pasta is al dente. Drain the pasta well and return it to the pan in which it was cooked. Add the butter and toss lightly but well.

3. Add the Parmesan cheese, heavy cream, fontina and a liberal amount of pepper. Toss lightly but well.

4. Butter an oval, 9 × 13 × 2-inch glass baking dish. (Use glass, as it is helpful to be able to see through the dish during baking.) Add $1/4$ cup of the bread crumbs to the buttered dish and turn it around to coat the entire inside. Turn out any extra crumbs onto a piece of waxed paper.

5. Beat the egg in a small bowl until lemon colored. Pour it into the crumbed dish and swirl it around by tilting to cover the inside of the dish (that is, over the bread crumbs). Add the remaining $1/4$ cup bread crumbs and turn the dish again to coat with the crumbs. Turn out to empty any excess crumbs.

6. Transfer the pasta with the help of a rubber spatula into the double-crumbed baking dish. Bake for 15 minutes or until the crumbs turn golden brown. If nicely browned, remove the dish from the oven and allow to rest for at least 10 minutes. Choose a beautiful platter, preferably one with an interesting border, or a plain white one, and turn out the molded dish after loosening the edges all around the inside of the baking dish. You will need oven mitts or potholders to do this, and be careful! I lay the inside of the platter on the top of the baking container and turn over in one full sweep, but I have to be very careful doing this.

7. When the molded dish is turned out, add the chopped greens in a decoration to your liking; I usually center it in the middle or try to get a little all around the edge of the dish.

VII

UMBRIA AND THE MARCHES

LAND OF THE MYSTERIOUS AND SPELLBINDING

CITIES OF SPOLETO, TODI AND PERUGIA

Gothic in its beauty, Umbria's valleys narrow to ribbons where farm buildings hang corn to dry for polenta-making. Below the mists that rise from Lake Trasimeno are trout, pike and crayfish. The oak forests hide truffles. Umbria competes with Rome for porchetta, Florence for Chiana beef, Milan, Rome and Venice over their cathedrals, as with Assisi and Orvieto. The flatbread is called *schiacciata,* the soup is lentil, the omelet is truffled, the carp is baked, the cheese is *caciotta* (sheep), the chocolates are Perugina and everyone eats the pine nut cookies *pinocchiate*. Oh yes, the pottery is DeRuta.

One hears often that the food in Umbria is as good as it is in the adjacent region of Tuscany, which is renowned for its culinary prowess. But perhaps because the Umbrians themselves prefer a low profile and seem shyer than their Tuscan neighbors, Umbria has remained rather unknown to, and significantly less explored by, Americans. This has resulted in restaurants that are less crowded and often less costly than those of their higher-profile Tuscan neighbors.

Umbrian food is regional and traditional, paying no mind to the trendier *cucina nova* that may have passed through these parts during the past decade or two but left little or nothing behind. Go to the restaurant Coccorone in the town of Montefalco for old-fashioned cooking and you'll see almost everything prepared over a grill in an old fireplace, from sage-scented swordfish to roasted pork with rosemary. The food is good because of its earthiness, simplicity and fine flavors.

SPOLETO: HOME OF THE MUSICAL FESTIVAL OF TWO WORLDS: MENU FOR 4

MENU

The Pasta Stars of Italy with Two Sauces
Stellette d'Italia con due salse

Salmon in Parchment with Spinach and Carrots
Salmone al cartoccio con spinaci e carote

Apollinare's Chocolate Roll with Zabaglione Sauce
Salame di cioccolata con salsa allo zabaglione

Once one enjoys Spoleto, one wants to return. Although music brought Spoleto to the attention of the world in the 1950's, the splendor of the Festival of Two Worlds lasts only a few weeks. Yet, people come in and out of this historic Roman town all year long to see its antiquities and to enjoy its cuisine. Visitors and townspeople walk all the time, except at mealtimes. Looking from a window at the Hotel Gattapone, a hotel consisting of two cliffside villas with a garden built into the hill and overlooking the Ponte dei Torre, one can see this parade of bodies against a background that recalls the best of the past, in history and in food. I always want to return to Spoleto, because I enjoy it every time I'm there. It is only seventy-five miles from Rome. The Apollinare restaurant, in the old Aurora Hotel on Via S. Agata, is a ten-minute walk from the Gattapone; one has to go by foot. Andrea Scotacci, the young restaurant owner and his mother, Giovanna Gradassi, both charming hosts, have a staff of half a dozen young, hardworking "foodies" who help create the atmosphere and exceptionally good food there. The distinctive architectural features there are the original walls of a twelfth century convent and church of the Franciscan monks, on which are canvases of scenes of that period in Spoleto's history.

In Spoleto, paradise is going on foot in and out of the shrines of history, in and out of the many old *trattorias* eager to share the taste and refinement of centuries of Umbrian cooking. One realizes something else here: All generations are represented, from a brazen teenager chewing *focaccia*, to the grandfather, leaning on his cane, sipping espresso in the Piazza del Mercato, holding court with many others, young and old. Everything competes for one's attention: the eighteenth-century fountain in the square, the bright curly endive greenery in one of the stalls, the gentle tap of the grandfather's cane on the old stone floor. Suddenly, you realize it's time to leave. The late morning sky is clear, turning to golden with the noon sun. You should be on the road, but you decide a quick two-hour lunch at the Taverna dei Duchi, just a few steps away, is in order. As you sip the local wine, you recall the fresco you saw yesterday at the Duomo: *Life of the Virgin,* by Fra Filippo Lippi, who portrayed himself and an assistant among the mourners in the scene of the Virgin's death. And you want to return yourself to that fresco to paint yourself in the scene to become a permanent part of Spoleto.

Wine Selection

Select an Orvieto, a dry, light wine that is perhaps the most famous DOC wine from Umbria. There are several good producers, among them: Antinori, Barberani, Brugnoli, Decugnano dei Barberi and Palazzone. If the occasion is special, add a Spumante to go with the dessert.

Preparation Advice

1. Prepare the dessert ahead by several days but if frozen, it will take almost a full day to thaw in the refrigerator.

2. The two sauces for the pasta may be made one day ahead.

3. The salmon packages can be made three hours ahead and refrigerated and brought to room temperature before baking.

THE PASTA STARS OF ITALY WITH TWO SAUCES

Stellette d'Italia con due salse
MAKES 4 SERVINGS WITH EXTRA SAUCE

This is the light and charming pasta dish enjoyed in the Spoleto restaurant Appollinare, described above. It is served as a *primi piatto*. This dish has been adapted from the original recipe given to me by Andrea Scotacci, owner of the restaurant and a very creative cook. A fresh pasta called *frascarelli* is made using two pounds of white flour with five eggs and salt (this is enough for twelve people, but Andrea prefers making it in large quantities as he can use it over several days). He combines these ingredients, as in making pasta, and puts the dough into a large, flat, stainless steel pan called an *acciaio*, whose bottom has small holes in it. The dough is rubbed by the palm of the hand in a circular movement to make ricelike shapes. These are cooked in boiling water and will rise to the top rather quickly. They are removed with a slotted spoon and put into cold water for several minutes. They are drained and stirred with a little oil. What is unusual about this dish is that the pesto sauce is put on the plate first, then covered with pasta, then topped with tomato sauce, Parmesan and a light sprinkle of Umbrian olive oil. As the pasta is eaten and parted by a fork, the vivid green pesto at the bottom comes as a pleasant surprise of colors in celebration of the Italian flag. The taste is divine. In winter, lamb is an added ingredient in the tomato sauce. "We are greatly influenced by the cooking of Rome," explains Andrea about adding lamb. One needs special equipment for this pasta but the same end result can be achieved by using a very small-type pasta such as stellette, a pasta sold in boxes in most supermarkets in the United States; it is a popular pasta for children who like it in chicken broth, here and in Italy.

½ cup Umbrian pesto (see below)
½ cup tomato sauce (see below)
½ pound pasta stars, cooked al dente
⅓ cup freshly grated Parmesan cheese
¼ cup finely chopped scallions
Umbrian olive oil

FOR THE PESTO
1 cup fresh basil leaves, tightly packed
⅓ cup pine nuts
2 large cloves garlic, coarsely chopped
¼ cup Umbrian extra-virgin olive oil
Salt

FOR THE TOMATO SAUCE
⅓ cup Umbrian extra-virgin olive oil
3 tablespoons butter
¼ cup finely chopped onion
⅓ cup finely chopped celery
⅓ cup finely chopped carrot
2 pounds ripe plum tomatoes, or 2 cups canned
    Italian plum tomatoes, put through a food mill
¼ teaspoon sugar

1. *To make the pesto:* Combine the basil, pine nuts, garlic and 4 tablespoons of the oil in the bowl of a processor. Process while counting to six. With the motor running, add the remaining oil. Add some salt to prevent discoloration of the pesto. If too thick, thin with 1 or 2 tablespoons hot water. (No cheese is used in Umbrian pesto.) This entire process should not take more than a couple of minutes. Transfer to a small bowl and set aside, at room temperature.

2. *To make the tomato sauce:* In a large skillet, heat the olive oil and butter until bubbly. Add the onion, celery and carrot and sauté 10 min-

utes, over medium heat, until the onion is opaque and the other vegetables begin to turn color. If the vegetables begin to scorch, reduce the heat to low.

3. Add the tomatoes to the skillet with the sugar and add about 1 teaspoon salt. Cook, uncovered, at a low simmer for 30 minutes. Remove from the heat.

4. *To assemble the dish:* Place 4 plates on a work surface and on each, in the center of the plate, put 2 tablespoons of the pesto. Spread the pesto with the back of a spoon to create a 4-inch circle.

5. Spoon the drained pasta over the pesto. Then top with 2 tablespoons of the tomato sauce; sprinkle with some cheese and sliced scallions. Drizzle with a little olive oil, and serve right away.

SALMON IN PARCHMENT WITH SPINACH AND CARROTS

Salmone al cartoccio con spinaci e carote
MAKES 4 SERVINGS

This is a fantastic presentation and a very tasty dish. Don't be put off by the use of parchment paper packages, or as the Italians say, *al cartoccio;* it is quite easy to make and easy to cook if you don't mind precooking the carrots.

FOR THE SAUCE
¼ cup sour cream
1 tablespoon fresh lemon juice
Freshly grated or prepared horseradish to taste
    (see Notabene, below)
Sea salt and freshly ground pepper

1 (about 1¼-pounds) salmon fillet, skinned and
    boned, cut crosswise into 4 pieces

10 ounces fresh spinach, washed well and large
    stems removed
12 baby carrots, each about ¼ × 2 inches long
3 tablespoons butter
¼ cup good Lungarotti white wine, such as Torre
    di Giano Riserva
1 teaspoon crushed dried fennel seeds
Sea salt and freshly ground pepper

1. *To make the sauce:* Combine all the ingredients, starting with a small amount of horseradish and increasing the amount, if you wish, to get the desired pungency. Refrigerate until ready to use.

2. Cut 2 (16 × 24-inch) pieces of parchment paper. Bring the shorter ends of the parchment sheets together, fold, and cut in half; this will give you four sheets, each 12 × 16 inches in size. Fold each of these sheets and with scissors, cut the fattest, roundest heart-shape you can on the folded sheet. Start at the folded side about 2 inches from the top and cut a curve around the corner. Do this, in similar fashion, on each of the next two corners (this means cutting only three corners).

3. Prepare the salmon or ask your fishmonger to do this for you. If you have to bone the salmon yourself, simply run your fingers down the center and you will feel the bones. Use tweezers to pull out the bones. It is easier to do this before cutting the fillet into four pieces. Refrigerate, covered, until ready to use.

4. Be sure the spinach is well rinsed and dried. Put a number of leaves together and slice the spinach thinly, less than ¼ inch wide. Store in a plastic bag, tied, in the refrigerator until ready to use.

5. Trim the baby carrots if needed, cut in half lengthwise and keep cutting lengthwise to make matchstick like "batons." Steam them until crisp-tender. Do not fully cook, as they will cook further in the packets in the oven.

6. Lay open the hearts; you will need lots of counter space to do this. Arrange a handful of spinach shreds in the center on the right side of the paper heart. Lay a piece of salmon on top of the spinach. Surround the salmon with some pre-cooked carrot sticks. Add 1 tablespoon of butter on top of each salmon piece. Carefully spoon some of the wine over the salmon; use 2 spoonfuls without letting the wine run off the packet. Sprinkle with some fennel seeds, salt and pepper. Fold over the other half of the paper heart and bring the edges together. Starting at the top of the heart, crimp the edges and go all the way around to the end of the third side (it is not necessary to crimp the folded side) until the salmon and its contents are fully enclosed. These may remain at room temperature for about 1 hour.

7. Preheat the oven to 475F. Place two packets each on two baking sheets. Be sure none of the parchment package overlaps the outer edge of the baking sheets. Put both baking sheets in the oven and bake for 12 minutes.

8. Remove the packets and carefully transfer each one to a serving plate. The packets are opened at the table by each of the diners. Tear apart, with your hands, the top paper of the packet and spread wide, or cut it open with scissors. The salmon and vegetables are eaten from the packet. Once the packet is opened, pass the horseradish sauce. A spoonful of it may also be put next to each cooked piece of salmon.

Notabene

Horseradish, a relative of the radish, is a cylindrical root with a light skin, which when removed, is usually grated and served as a condiment, fresh or cooked, and often combined with mayonnaise, sour cream, yogurt, and so on. In Italy, it is seen in the markets in the spring to coincide with the Jewish holiday of Passover, when it is used as part of a celebratory meal. The user of fresh horseradish must be aware that the fresh product is considerably stronger than a bottled version. It makes an excellent accompaniment to salmon.

APOLLINARE'S CHOCOLATE ROLL WITH ZABAGLIONE SAUCE

Salame di cioccolata con salsa allo zabaglione
MAKES 10 SERVINGS

Andrea Scotacci says he changes his menus frequently but this dessert remains on all of them. It is very rich but very delicious. Massimo and Simone, two of Andrea's assistants made a number of suggestions. "Use tea biscuits *(biscotti da te),*" said one. "Or use short pastry biscuits (*biscotti di pasta frolla*), to make it even richer," said the other. They both agreed that butter cookies called *frollini* or cat's tongue cookies (*lingue di gatto*) would be good choices. These young men were making this dessert for 100 wedding guests the next day.

> 4 ounces plain cookies, such as vanilla wafers
> ²/₃ cup slivered almonds, toasted
> 9 ounces very good bittersweet chocolate, such as Val Guanaja, broken into 1-inch chunks
> 1½ sticks (6 ounces) butter
> 3 tablespoons rum
> 2 small egg yolks, at room temperature
> Zabaglione (page 124)

1. Put the cookies into the bowl of a food processor and process until the cookies look like uncooked oatmeal (count to 10). Transfer to a bowl; you need 1 cup. Process half of the almonds until finer than oatmeal. Transfer to another small bowl and set both bowls aside.

2. Place the chocolate in a metal bowl over a saucepan of simmering water, filled no more than ¹/₃ full and not touching the bottom of the bowl by several inches. Add ½ stick of butter and the rum. Stir until the chocolate melts. Remove the bowl from the heat and cool slightly.

3. Fold the egg yolks and remaining butter, a tablespoon at a time, into the chocolate mixture. Reserving a scant ¼ cup ground cookies, fold the remaining cookies into the chocolate mixture. Fold in the toasted almond slivers. Cover and refrigerate for about 1 hour, until the chocolate mixture becomes almost firm, but still malleable.

4. Lightly oil a large piece of parchment or waxed paper, at least 12 × 16 inches. With the help of a rubber spatula, transfer the chocolate mixture to the paper and form a log, 9 to 10 inches long. Mold each end to appear salami-like and wrap tightly and securely. Put into a large plastic bag folded over one or two times and freeze for about 5 hours, until solid.

5. The chocolate roll must come out of the freezer a full hour before serving. To serve, combine the ground almonds and the remaining crushed cookies on a fresh piece of parchment or waxed paper. Roll the chocolate log to cover completely. When the log has stood at room temperature for about 1 hour, serve either the whole log on a large white platter with garnishment of your choice, or serve ¹/₂-inch-thick slices on individual plates. Pass the sauce separately. Rewrap any leftover log and refrigerate if to be used in a day or so, or refreeze and use much later.

FEASTING ON SEA BASS SOUTH OF ANCONA, ON THE ADRIATIC COAST: MENU FOR 4

MENU

Poached Sea Bass in Wine with Saffron as Prepared by Fishermen's Wives in Porto Recanati
Bronzino e gamberetti alla Marchigiana
affogati in vino bianco con zafferano

Classic Broccoli: Cooked in Garlic-Flavored Oil
Broccoli saltati in padella
con aglio e olio (classico italiano)

Bruschetta (page 6)
Bruschetta

Ricotta and Honey with Thyme
Ricotta al miele con timo

Porto Recanati is about twenty-nine kilometers south of Ancona on the Adriatic, a small town of about ten thousand people. It is well known because it is one of two places (the other is Ancona) for excellent *brodetti,* considered by many to be the best fish soups in Italy. These towns are in a region called The Marches. No visitor to Porto Recanati should miss the delicious *brodetto* or local fish soup. Although Ancona uses red mullet and squid coated with flour, with a touch of vinegar added, the Porto Recanati eliminate the flour and vinegar, and use saffron to give the dish an attractive color and aroma.

The following recipe is an adaptation of such a dish. I use sea bass, because it is easy to buy (or you can use red mullet, sole or skate). The white wine, saffron and extra-virgin olive oil are essential as is the bruschetta.

Wine Suggestion

Orvieto, a white wine, has been famous in and outside Italy for centuries. There are two types of Orvieto: One is slightly sweet and should be used as a dessert wine; the second is dry and is perfect with this fish dish.

Preparation Advice

This is easy Italian if you have the ingredients at hand.

1. Prepare the fish "sauce" ahead by three or four hours and add the fish just before mealtime.

2. The bread can be made ahead by one hour and reheated.

3. The dessert can be made after the fish has been served. It takes about five minutes to prepare.

POACHED SEA BASS IN WINE WITH SAFFRON AS PREPARED BY FISHERMEN'S WIVES IN PORTO RECANATI

Bronzino e gamberetti al Marchigiana affogati in vino bianco con zafferano
MAKES 4 SERVINGS

Saffron, originating in Persia, is one of the many foods introduced into Europe by the Arabs. At the time of the Crusaders, it was so popular that a special Office of Saffron was set up in Venice to handle its trade. Its history, however, as a condiment and medicine, goes far back to Egyptian, Greek and

Roman times. It is cultivated today in France, Greece, Iran, Italy, Russia, South America, Spain and the United States. In Italy, it is grown in Sicily, Sardinia and Abruzzo and used in a variety of ways all over the boot. In Sardinia and Sicily, saffron is used in couscous dishes, obviously a connection to the Arabs. You cannot make the Sicilian dish of *pasta con le sarde* without it. The same is true for the *risotto alla milanese* of Milan. One would think it would be used in the many Abruzze fish soups, but it is not, although it is used in that way by the neighboring province of Marche.

It is best to buy saffron in strands, threads or filaments rather than powdered, as it is more difficult to know whether the powder has good strength. Although a small amount of saffron is used here, it is important to the dish, as is the final touch of olive oil.

²⁄₃ cup dry white wine
½ cup chopped, seeded tomatoes
²⁄₃ cup fish broth or clam juice
⅓ cup finely chopped onion
1 teaspoon saffron threads
Sea salt and freshly ground pepper
4 sea bass fillets or any snapper, about
    1½ pounds
½ pound shrimp (about 8 large ones), peeled,
    deveined and butterflied
2 tablespoons thinly sliced scallions
2 tablespoons extra-virgin olive oil

1. Over high heat, bring the wine to a boil in a large skillet with a cover, to reduce wine by half, 2 to 3 minutes.

2. Add the tomatoes, fish broth and onion, bring to a boil and cook for 1 minute.

3. Stir in the saffron, some salt and pepper and simmer for 2 minutes to allow the saffron to dissolve into a lovely lemony-orange color.

4. Carefully place the fish fillets in the skillet. Do not overlap the fish. Cover the skillet and poach the fillets for 3 minutes. Remove the cover, add the shrimp, re-cover and cook for 2 minutes. Do not overcook the shrimp or they will toughen.

5. Serve immediately. Bring the covered skillet to the table. When you have everyone's attention, remove the cover. The escaping steam and the fresh fish aromas are breathtaking. (A woman in the village of Vasto, farther south on the Adriatic, served it to me this way and I have never forgotten the joy she showed in her presentation.) Transfer the filets and some sauce to individual flat-type bowls, preferably with rims. Sprinkle the scallions over each filet and spoon olive oil over each portion of fish.

CLASSIC BROCCOLI: COOKED IN GARLIC-FLAVORED OIL

Broccoli saltati in padella con aglio e olio (classico italiano)
MAKES 4 TO 6 SERVINGS

Italians love broccoli and although this is considered a classic way to cook it all over Italy, there are many variations. For example, in Rome, they are not parboiled but added to the skillet with the oil and garlic. The leaves take longer to cook than the florets, so they are added first. Two cups white wine are added to the skillet and the broccoli cooks until tender. This method does have the extra step of parboiling, but that means less time in the skillet. Finishing off a vegetable in a skillet with olive oil and garlic is a popular and preferred way to cook vegetables, the Italian way.

2 pounds broccoli
Sea salt

5 tablespoons extra-virgin olive oil
2 cloves garlic, peeled

1. Prepare the broccoli by discarding the coarse leaves, retaining the tender ones, cutting off the bottoms of the stems, peeling and slicing the tender parts of the stems, and cutting off the florets. If not cooking them immediately, keep them in lightly salted cold water and drain for cooking.

2. Boil some water in a pan large enough to hold the cut broccoli, and add some salt. Add the broccoli; as soon as the water returns to a boil, remove the broccoli and drain well.

3. In a large skillet, heat the oil and lightly brown the garlic cloves. With a fork, carefully press down on the cloves to break them a little. Remove the garlic before it turns dark brown. Add the drained broccoli and cook until tender, 4 to 6 minutes, stirring lightly. The broccoli should retain its bright green look, and be cooked until crisp-tender. Add more salt before serving if you wish.

RICOTTA AND HONEY WITH THYME

Ricotta al miele con timo
MAKES 4 SERVINGS

Ricotta is widely used in Italian cooking for both savory and sweet dishes. It is considered a fresh cheese and does not have the depth of other Italian cheeses in spite of its excellent texture. It therefore is a candidate for seasoning such as honey, as in the following recipe, or pepper, nutmeg, fresh chopped herbs and in fact, other cheeses such as Parmigiano-Reggiano, in lasagnas and ravioli. In sweet dishes, it is perhaps best known for its use in cheesecakes (Italians love cheesecakes and every Italian cook has a recipe) and it is often combined with fruit.

Ricotta is a cheese most Americans like because it only has a fat content of 20 percent. Almost all supermarkets carry ricotta, in whole, skim or fat-free versions, but unfortunately none of them have the taste or texture of those sold as fresh ricotta in special Italian markets. Look for an Italian food store in your neighborhood; it will be worth the search, especially if it is to be used in this dessert. The honey and fresh thyme with the ricotta here is an unusually good combination of food, and a poetic touch of Italian ingenuity.

2 cups fresh ricotta
1 cup wildflower honey
2 teaspoons fresh thyme leaves, including small flowers
4 small sprays of thyme

1. Divide the ricotta onto 4 dessert plates.

2. Heat the honey in a small saucepan until it liquifies, about 4 minutes. Spoon or pour some honey on each of the 4 servings.

3. Sprinkle the thyme leaves and flowers over the honey, arrange a thyme spray on each plate alongside the ricotta and serve.

A POSTCARD PICTURE OF COLORFUL FISHING BOATS IN RIMINI: "WISH YOU WERE HERE": MENU FOR 4

MENU

Hot Anchovy, Mortadella and Fontina Canapes
Stuzzica apetito (o assaggini)

Grilled Swordfish with White Wine and Sage
Pesce spada grigliata con vino bianco e salvia

Glazed Celery in Mustard Sauce
Sedano glassato alla crema di mostarda

Grand Galliano Cake (see page 66, using juice of 2 lemons and ⅓ cup Galliano for the orange liqueur)
Torta al Liquore Galliano

On the Adriatic, at the end of the Via Emilia, is the Riviera of the Sun in which sits the pleasant resort town of Rimini, a town in the center of a twelve-mile-long stretch of beach. The sea cuts deeply into Rimini through a canal, which is also a port, with its postcard picture of fishing boats with brightly colored sails and their large square nets to catch fish. You shouldn't miss the morning fish market in the Piazza Cavour, where every fish taken out of the Adriatic Sea is on display for sale. This beach is very crowded in July and August; one can feel hypnotized by the discos

and the crowds. About a half mile from the resort is the old city, birthplace of the famous film director Federico Fellini. In it is the Tempio Malatestiano, a masterpiece of early Renaissance design with a not-so-innocent past. Originally consecrated as a church, in 1450 it was self-servingly converted into a personal shrine by the tyrannical Sigismondo Malatesta, a patron of the arts and a debauched sensualist descended from the town's ruling family. Filled with paintings and sculptures of Malatesta by famous artists, the renovation was also a testament to his passion for his mistress (and later wife) Isotta degli Atti. Their entwined initials appear as a recurring design motif. It was all too much for Pope Pius II, who excommunicated Malatesta and condemned him to hell. Every time I think of Rimini, I see in my mind the entwined initials *S* and *I*.

I also remember that in spite of all the eels caught in these waters, eels are not one of the fish they put in their fish soup. All kinds of fresh seafood may be enjoyed at the restaurant Acero Rosso. This grilled swordfish recipe was inspired by a visit there.

Wine Selection
A white wine from Torgiano, Torre di Giano, made from the Trebbiano and Grechetta grapes, is dry, fresh and fruity.

Preparation Advice
1.   The cake may be made one day ahead and the celery dish may be assembled ahead and cooked just before mealtime.

2.   The first course and the swordfish should be prepared before dining.

HOT ANCHOVY, MORTADELLA AND FONTINA CANAPES

Stuzzica apetito (o assaggini)
MAKES 4 SERVINGS

This appetizer's common name, *stuzzica apetito*, comes from the expression *stuzzicare a'appetito*, which means "to stimulate the appetite" and it does that exactly. These are really fun to make and you can serve them as family and friends are enjoying a pre-dinner glass of wine.

> 8 thin slices white bread, preferably Pepperidge Farm's very thin white bread
> 6 anchovy flat fillets packed in oil, drained and sliced lengthwise
> 4 thin slices fontina cheese
> 4 thin slices mortadella
> Freshly ground pepper
> 3 eggs
> 3 tablespoons heavy cream
> 1 tablespoon water
> 3 tablespoons freshly grated Parmesan cheese
> ¾ cup olive oil

1.   Place 4 slices of bread on a flat surface and arrange 3 anchovy strips on each. Cover the anchovies with a slice of fontina and then add a slice of mortadella. Don't fret if the meat and cheese overhang the bread a bit (if they overhang too much, fold over the meat or cheese into the "sandwich"). Liberally add some pepper and cover with the 4 remaining slices of bread.

2.   With a sharp knife, trim the edges of the bread. Cut each sandwich into 4 triangles, easily done by cutting from southeast to northwest corners, then reversing and cutting from southwest to northeast corners.

3.   Whisk the eggs, cream, water and Parmesan cheese in a bowl and whisk to combine them. Heat half of the oil in a large skillet.

4.   Dip each small sandwich into the egg batter and fry them, in batches, until browned all over. If you want to test for the proper heat of the oil, add a drop or two of the batter into it; if it sizzles quickly, the oil is hot enough. Move quickly to dip the sandwiches into the batter and to add them to the skillet. As they brown, remove them to paper towels to drain. Heat remaining oil and fry the remaining sandwiches.

5.   These should be served soon after cooking. They may be passed during a cocktail or refreshment, or 4 sandwiches can be plated and served at the table with a parsley sprig in the center of each plate as a first course.

GRILLED SWORDFISH WITH WHITE WINE AND SAGE

Pesce spada grigliata con vino bianco e salvia
MAKES 4 SERVINGS

Swordfish is available in the United States as it is in Italy, where it is enjoyed in a variety of ways, so you won't have to look far for swordfish. The fishermen of Bagnara (in Calabria) harpoon swordfish as did the ancient Greeks, and swordfish is a specialty of Messina also (in Sicily) where it is fried in olive oil with marjoram, or coated with bread and cheese and fried, or sautéed with tomatoes, onion and celery in olive oil. In this menu, the fish is as simple as a recipe can be.

> 2 (1-pound) swordfish steaks, about 1 inch thick
> ½ cup dry white wine
> ⅓ cup extra-virgin olive oil

2 tablespoons finely chopped fresh sage or 2
   teaspoons dried, crushed
2 tablespoons finely chopped fresh Italian parsley
Sea salt and freshly ground pepper

1. Combine all the ingredients, except salt and pepper, in a large shallow glass or ceramic dish or platter and marinate at room temperature for 1 hour, or marinate longer in the refrigerator but not overnight. If refrigerated, allow the fish to return to room temperature, about 30 minutes.

2. When the grill is ready, grill the fish on one side by searing close to the heat and then raising the grill farther from the heat to complete cooking. Use the marinade to keep the fish moistened by brushing some of it onto the fish directly. Turn and grill the other side, searing first as before. Brush on some of the marinade. Total cooking time should be 8 to 10 minutes. Remove from the grill and add some salt and pepper.

GLAZED CELERY IN MUSTARD SAUCE

Sedano glassato alla crema di mostarda
MAKES 4 SERVINGS

Most people in the United States do not cook celery, but they may be interested in this cooked celery dish that combines the vegetable with cream and mustard. The dish can be cooked and sauced ahead and then broiled just before serving.

10 celery ribs
1½ cups Chicken Broth (page 8) or canned
2 tablespoons butter
2 teaspoons sugar, plus extra for sprinkling
¼ cup plus 2 tablespoons heavy cream
2 teaspoons Dijon-style mustard
Sea salt and freshly ground pepper

1. Rinse the celery and remove any coarse strings with a vegetable peeler. Cut off the leaves, chop finely, and reserve. Cut the ribs into ½-inch-thick diagonal slices and place in a large skillet.

2. Add the broth, butter and sugar and bring to a boil. Cook, stirring, until the liquid is reduced to a glaze, about 10 minutes.

3. Combine the cream and mustard and add to the skillet. Reduce the heat and cook until the sauce is thickened, about 5 minutes. Season with salt and pepper.

4. Preheat the broiler. Divide the mixture among four individual ramekins. Sprinkle a little more sugar over the top of each. Broil until the top is flecked with brown. Sprinkle with the reserved celery leaves and serve.

AN UMBRIAN ORGY FOR 12 IN PERUGIA: CITY FOR ASSASSINATIONS AND GOOD FOOD

MENU

Bread Toasts with Truffles
Crostini al tartufo

Marinated Salmon with Rhubarb
Salmone marinato con rabarbaro

Penne Pasta with Cognac from Citta di Castello
Penne al cognac
(Trattoria dalla Lea in Citta di Castello)

Whole Roasted Suckling Pig, Umbrian Style
Porchetta alla Norciana

Vegetable Rainbow of Carrots, Zucchini, Asparagus and Broccoli Rabe
Arcobaleno di ortaggi

Cheese Tray with Mostardo, Parmigiano-Reggiano, Smoked Mozzarella and Robiola
Formaggi misti con mostarda

"What a town for assassination!" wrote the English writer H. V. Morton about Perugia. He meant that two popes had been poisoned there. Perugia, a bustling and cosmopolitan city with a population of 160,000 sits high over the Tiber. They call it a city with three faces: the first, a beautifully preserved historic medieval city; the second, an art city that rivals Florence; third: the capital of Umbria, a serene and pastoral paradise of a region in the heart of Italy. I recall with ease fabulous food at the restaurants La Taverna and at La Locanda degli Artisti and also the delicious items one can buy in the shops. You owe it to yourself, if you are there, to splurge on a small jar of black truffles *(tartufi nero)* to take back home. Truffles are a specialty of the region and the prices are less than you might imagine. A slight hint of truffle in a pasta sauce or in a frittata is a sybaritic pleasure. In addition to truffles, there are wonderful cheeses especially the *caciotta*; chocolates—this is the home of the world-famous Perugina chocolates; pastries; breads, most bakeries use ovens fueled by wood; lentils, the ones from Castelluccio; lovely golden, green extra-virgin olive oil, so important in Umbrian cooking; and of course, *porchetta* is everywhere, as prepared in the following menu which springs from other places in Umbria, as well as Perugia.

Wine Selection

This is the land of Lungarotti wines, so serve a white and a red. Lungarotti is a well-known wine producer with an exquisite inn in Torgiano, and down the street from the inn is his wine museum. The white could be a Chardonnay di Miralduolo; the red can be a Cabernet Sauvignon di Miralduolo.

Preparation Advice

1.　The bread toasts should be made at the last minute, but the salmon may be marinated ahead by several hours. The rhubarb sauce can be made one day ahead.

2.　The sauce for the penne and the vegetables may be made one day ahead. The cheeses should be at room temperature for several hours.

3.　The suckling pig requires a long cooking time so make it the morning of the day it will be served.

BREAD TOASTS WITH TRUFFLES

Crostini al tartufo
MAKES 12 SERVINGS

Probably the most noteworthy food produced in Umbria is the truffle. Most people think of truffles as white (since white truffles are only found in Italy). However, the Umbrian truffle is black and very tasty. It is for sale all over Umbria, mostly packed in brine in small and larger jars. They are an easy item to carry home. Spoleto and Norcia are the two major producers of Umbrian truffles. In Italian, the word for truffles is *tartufi* and this is often confused with another Italian term, *trifolati*; this is a term applied to any dish that is quite rich, such as kidneys or mushrooms or a combination of both. The derivation of the term is simply a tribute to the truffle, meaning richness. Here is a simple way to get the essence of Umbria's truffle, and still keep the cost within the family budget.

⅓ cup extra-virgin Umbrian olive oil
2 cloves garlic, halved
1 anchovy fillet
2 small black Umbrian truffles (about 1 ounce), about 1 inch diameter, grated (see Notabene below)
2 tablespoons fresh lemon juice
8 slices fine enriched white bread, toasted and crusts removed

1. Heat the oil in a small skillet over medium heat with the garlic. When the garlic begins to turn color, mash it a bit with the tines of a fork and then discard the garlic. Add the anchovy and stir to dissolve.

2. Take the skillet off the heat. Stir in the grated truffle. Reduce the heat to as low as possible and heat the skillet for 30 to 35 seconds. The oil must not boil or the truffles will lose their aroma. Remove the skillet and add the lemon juice.

3. Brush the oil and truffle mixture over the bread slices. Cut each slice in fourths, to make squares, and serve.

Notabene:

Truffles are grown underground, white in northern Italy and black in Umbria. With pungent aromas and irregular, knobby round shapes, they are eaten raw or cooked, and are used to flavor olive oil. One or two drops of truffle oil will enhance the flavors of salads, pastas and sauces.

MARINATED SALMON WITH RHUBARB

Salmone marinato con rabarbaro
MAKES 12 SERVINGS

Le Tre Vaselle is a posh inn in Torgiano, not far from Perugia, owned and operated by the well-known Lungarotti family, famous for their wines and wine museum. The inn's dining room is one place in Umbria that attracts elite tourists. The food there is remarkable and somewhat expensive. Along with Japanese and German patrons, I remember this particular dish, perhaps because of the rhubarb condiment. The tartness and sharpness of the rhubarb reduces the oiliness of the salmon.

3 pounds salmon fillet
½ cup extra-virgin Umbrian olive oil
6 tablespoons fresh lemon juice
Sea salt and freshly ground pepper
1 cup half-and-half
Tabasco sauce to taste

FOR THE RHUBARB SAUCE
1 pound rhubarb stalks, trimmed and cut into 1-inch pieces
2 large pieces of lemon zest, each 1 × 3 inches
½ cup sugar
½ cup water
½ cup diced (¼-inch) red radishes

1. Ask your fishmonger to skin and bone the salmon. If he won't, here's how: Place the salmon skin side down on a flat surface. Hold the tail end securely with a cloth towel in your fingers (this makes it less slippery). Place the knife at a 15-degree angle and cut gently under the skin with a sawing motion. As you cut, pull the skin toward you and against the knife. Continue this motion toward the front, making sure you do not cut through the skin. To bone: Keep the salmon flat and run your hand and fingers carefully over the inside side of the fillet; you'll feel the bones. Use a pair of tweezers and pull out each bone.

2. Slice the fillet crosswise as thinly as you can. It's easier to do this if the salmon is very cold; put it in the freezer 30 minutes and then slice. Arrange slices in a single layer on a large platter with a little depth. Spoon the oil over the slices; spoon 4 tablespoons of the lemon juice over the salmon. Add some salt and pepper. Cover with plastic and refrigerate for 4 hours.

3. Combine the half-and-half with 2 table-spoons of the lemon juice. Add salt and Tabasco sauce. Refrigerate until needed.

4. One hour before serving, transfer the salmon slices to a fresh platter, draining them well. Discard the original marinade of oil and lemon. Spoon the cream sauce over the salmon and bring it to room temperature.

5. *To make the sauce:* Combine all the ingredients in a large skillet and bring to a simmer. Cook, uncovered, stirring frequently, until the rhubarb is tender, about 20 minutes.

6. Serve the salmon either on individual plates with a dollop of rhubarb sauce and a sprinkle of radishes, or serve on the platter and add a sprinkle of radishes over the salmon. Serve the sauce on the side.

PENNE PASTA WITH COGNAC FROM CITTA DI CASTELLO

Penne al cognac (Trattoria dalla Lea in Citta di Castello)
MAKES 8 TO 12 SERVINGS

Citta di Castello, a town of about forty thousand inhabitants that happens to be the most northern city in Umbria, is not in every guidebook. That can be a fortunate thing. The last time I was there, I met only two tourists from Scotland; I joined them for a noonday drink at a local bar. We agreed that we liked the streets and architecture without teeming tourists and that the service in the restaurants was ideal. Friends of mine who live and work there (they own the Trattoria dalla Lea), Lea and Anontonio Giambanelli and their son, Cristiano, made this pasta dish for me one evening. With the help of Cristiano, I was able to get them to share this recipe.

> 2 cups Tomato Sauce (page 175)
> ¼ cup cognac
> Salt
> 2 pounds penne pasta
> ½ cup half-and-half
> Freshly ground pepper
> ¼ cup finely chopped fresh Italian parsley
> 1 to 2 cups freshly grated pecorino cheese

1. In a heavy saucepan (large enough to hold 2 pounds cooked pasta), heat the tomato sauce. Add the cognac and simmer for 10 to 15 minutes to cook off the alcohol.

2. Put the pasta water to boil. Before adding the pasta, add 1 teaspoon salt to the water. Cook the pasta until al dente according to package directions.

3. Add the half-and-half to the tomato sauce and simmer for 10 minutes without bringing the sauce to a boil. Taste for salt, adding more if necessary. Add some pepper.

4. Drain the pasta well and add it to the saucepan with the tomato-cream sauce. Toss well and transfer to a large serving bowl. Sprinkle with the parsley and pass the pecorino cheese.

WHOLE ROASTED SUCKLING PIG, UMBRIAN STYLE

Porchetta alla Norciana
MAKES 12 SERVINGS

Umbria's food is special because of its pork products, in particular, those found around Norcia, where Umbrian pigs feed on chestnuts, mushrooms and truffles. The pork and salami of Norcia are so celebrated that almost all meals in Umbria include a sampling.

The cooking of Umbria is honest and natural, somewhere between the extroverted gusto of nearby Lazio (Rome) and the refined simplicity of Tuscany (Florence). Condiments are used discreetly with an exception here and there, for example, like this tasty, peppery *porchetta*. In Perugia, as in Rome, one's culinary life starts with *porchetta*; in both places, the suckling pig is liberally salted and peppered and seasoned with a variety of herbs, not always including rosemary, which is a must in Rome. In Perugia and elsewhere in Umbria, wild fennel is always used in *porchetta*. The pig is either spit-roasted or baked. Wherever one goes in Umbria, *porchetta* is in shops, in stalls, on streets—everywhere—waiting to be sliced and put between two pieces of bread.

This suckling pig preparation was roasted with the help of a great chef and friend, Linwood Boone of Wingdale, New York.

> 1 (18- to 20-pound) whole suckling pig, readied for oven-roasting (remove kidney, if present, before roasting)
> 1½ cups olive oil
> Sea salt and freshly ground pepper
> 4 large or 8 small branches of fresh rosemary
> Cloves from 1 whole garlic bulb, peeled, ⅔ left whole, ⅓ minced
> 1 fennel bulb with leaves, coarsely chopped
> 3 teaspoons dried fresh fennel seeds, crushed
> ¾ cup red wine vinegar
> 1 whole apple and 1 raspberry or 1 thin lime slice

1. Preheat the oven to 350F. Put the pig in a 17 × 25 × 3½–inch roasting pan (commercial size) with ½ cup oil. Liberally salt and pepper the pig, inside and out. Place 3 of the large or 6 of the small rosemary branches in the cavity of the pig along with the whole garlic cloves, the chopped fennel and 2 teaspoons of the crushed fennel seeds. Lay the pig on one side in the baking pan.

2. Combine the remaining oil and vinegar, minced garlic and the remaining fennel seeds and use this mixture to brush all over the pig before putting it into the oven. Use the remaining oil mixture and any pan drippings as a baste during cooking.

3. Bake for 5 hours, basting every 20 minutes or so. To test for doneness, insert a long wooden skewer into the roast; if it meets no resistance upon entering, the roast is done. Remove from the oven and cool for 10 minutes or so. Insert the apple in its mouth and place a raspberry or lime slice into or over the visible eye socket.

How to carve the roasted pig

1. Make a big cut at the rear leg joint, to remove the rump, thighs and the rear legs.

2. Slice the thighs.

3. Cut straight along the back.

4. Slice the ribs into 1-, 2- or 3-rib portions (there is not much meat on a rib).

5. Cut off at front leg joint and slice front thighs.

6. If you want to serve the pig without a head, cut it off after roasting and discard.

Notabene:

If the pig is to be spit-roasted, sew up belly with needle and thread or use tiny steel stainless skewers (three will suffice) before affixing to the spit. Cook about 3½ hours.

VEGETABLE RAINBOW OF CARROTS, ZUCCHINI, ASPARAGUS AND BROCCOLI RABE

Arcobaleno di ortaggi
MAKES 12 SERVINGS

These vegetables can be cooked and left at room temperature until you are ready to make the rainbow arrangement. The sauce should be hot and added at the last minute. The lemon wedges are important to the taste of this dish, so don't try to skip them.

6 fresh zucchini, each about 1 × 6 inches long
1½ pounds fresh asparagus spears
6 large carrots
2 bunches fresh broccoli rabe
Salt
8 tablespoons extra-virgin olive oil
6 large cloves garlic, minced
Good pinch red pepper flakes
3 lemons, cut into wedges, seeds removed

1. Wash and dry the zucchini; cut off the ends and pare any blemishes. Leave on as much skin as you can. Hold a zucchini upright and cut a ¼-inch-thick slice straight down the full length of the zucchini. Do this on the three remaining sides. Discard the pulpy center. Cut the zucchini pieces into more strips, about ¼ inch wide. Steam them until crisp-tender and set aside.

2. Take one asparagus spear in hand and bend it, far enough so it will snap and break (it breaks at the tenderest point). Discard the tough end. Repeat with all other spears. Wash the spears and steam until crisp-tender. Set aside.

3. Trim the carrots by cutting off the stem ends and paring lightly with a vegetable peeler. Cut in half lengthwise and cut again to get lengths about ¼ inch wide. Steam until crisp-tender and set aside.

4. To prepare the broccoli rabe, wash it well and trim the ends. Remove the strings on the larger stalks as on large celery. Cut the larger leaves in half and let them stand in cool water until ready to cook them. Cut the rabe in 2-inch pieces. Heat 2 or 3 cups of water in a large saucepan. Add 1 teaspoon salt and bring the water to a rapid boil. Add the rabe and cook until just tender; depending on size and freshness of stalks, this may take 5 to 10 minutes. Drain well.

5. Heat 3 tablespoons of the oil in a large skillet. Add one-fourth of the minced garlic and cook for 1 minute. Add the rabe and move it around in the oil and garlic. Cook for 2 or 3 minutes. Remove from the heat.

6. Arrange a rainbow of vegetables on a large platter as follows: Place wide side of platter in front of you. On the left side, place the zucchini strips in a tight fan shape, spreading more at the top than the bottom. Do the same with the carrots in the center of the platter and then add the asparagus on the right side. Add the rabe to

the bottom across all vegetables. Add salt to taste.

7. In the same skillet, heat the remaining oil and remaining garlic and sauté the garlic briefly, just enough to take on a little color, 1 to 2 minutes. Remove the pan from the heat. Add the pepper flakes, stir and spoon over the zucchini, carrots and asparagus. Serve with lemon wedges.

CHEESE TRAY WITH MOSTARDO, PARMIGIANO-REGGIANO, SMOKED MOZZARELLA AND ROBIOLA

Formaggi misti con mostarda

Mostardo di cremona is considered one of the most remarkable of Italian preserves. It is a fruit mustard made of whole fruits, such as pears, little oranges, cherries, apricots, plums, figs, melon and pumpkin pieces; they are preserved in a sugar syrup flavored with mustard oil. This is surely an original combination of ingredients with a delicious flavor. A spoonful of it may be served with a piece of Parmigiano as a separate course.

Parmigiano-Reggiano: Most cognoscenti agree that there is nothing more delicious than a piece of aged, pale straw–colored Parmigiano. It is the perfect cheese to end any meal with bread or fruit, especially pears, or with a taste of mostardo.

Smoked Mozzarella: This cheese is delicious if it is made from buffalo's milk, but also because it is smoked. The color of it is pale beige to a light reddish-brown. It is extra special when freshly grated black pepper and a dash of olive oil are added to the sliced cheese.

Robiola: Wrapped in paper to protect its freshness, this cheese is actually a stracchino made from creamy milk. It is matured for a short time, usually less than two months. It is often mistaken for Taleggio (not a bad mistake, by the way). Robiola is a small, square-shaped stracchino, weighing between 3 and 4 ounces.

IN ABRUZZI, REGION OF SPICE, SAFFRON AND SCAMORZA: MENU FOR 6

MENU

Spicy Polenta with Cheese, Broccoli Rabe and Sausages
Polenta piccante con formaggio, rapini e salsicce

Fresh Fennel with Parslied Oil and Vinegar
Insalata di finocchi con olio al prezzomolo

Pineapple Ice with Strawberry Sauce
Sorbetto al pompelmo con salsa alle fragole

Abruzzi is high mountain country where the tallest peaks are covered with snow most of the year, yet it has miles of Adriatic coastline with few good harbors, except for Pescara, its main city on the sea. Abruzzi by latitude ought to be part of the north, but the physical height, almost ten thousand feet, of the Great Rock of Italy (*Gran Sasso d'Italia*) created a wall against the north and has put Abruzzi into the south. Cows and sheep graze on the high plateaus, and their milk is made into *latticini,* milk products, and the best known is the scamorza cheese, now sold in the United States. There are definitely two cuisines in this area, one based on fish along the coast, and the other one on pork (and also lamb, veal and poultry) for inland communities. The Abruzzese like spicy food and use hot peppers and wild herbs, and this is the only place in mainland Italy that grows saffron. As elsewhere in Italy, every village has its own food specialties such as the lentils of Santo Stefano, the polenta of Pettorano sul Gizio, the white beans of Capestrano and the pork products of Campotosto. Vegetables are plentiful in this region and most of the population will eat them with little or no meat. There is a famous polenta dish called *polenta sulla tavola*, polenta on the table, where the polenta is literally poured on the table, served with a sauce, usually made with small pieces of hare. In this menu, I combine polenta, with broccoli rabe and sausages—three foods that are enjoyed in this part of Italy.

Abruzzi has a harsh climate. In spite of the mountains, its basins are sheltered from the wind; vineyards and olive and almond groves prosper there. The food in Abruzzi is hearty and here is a polenta dish that uses considerable cheese. The dish is lightened by cooking greens with it. It is a famous dish enjoyed on Saint Anthony's Feast Day in January. Traditionally it is made with scamorza cheese, but you can use a good imported provolone if you can't find the scamorza. If you can't get Italian polenta, use Arrowhead Mills' organically produced yellow corn grits; it is widely available in the United States and makes an excellent polenta.

Wine Selection

Select another good Lungarotti red, San Giorgio, rich and full-bodied, made in Torgiano of Sangiovese grapes, enriched by Cabernet Sauvignon.

Preparation Advice

The dessert may be made well ahead, and so can the polenta dish. Refrigerate it for a day or two or freeze it for up to a month, The fennel can be

prepped and put in a plastic bag overnight, and dressed just before mealtime.

SPICY POLENTA WITH CHEESE, BROCCOLI RABE AND SAUSAGES

Polenta piccante con formaggio, rapini e salsicce
MAKES 12 SERVINGS

This will make more than enough for six people, but it is delicious reheated and served the next day. It will keep in the refrigerator for five or six days. This dish can be made ahead and frozen for up to a month.

3 quarts water
1 medium potato, peeled and cut into 4 pieces
1 pound broccoli rabe, trimmed, washed and cut into 2-inch lengths
2 teaspoons salt
2 ½ cups polenta or yellow corn grits
1 tablespoon olive oil
4 Italian pork sausages (about 1 pound)
5 cups Pork Tomato Sauce (page 204)
¼ teaspoon red pepper flakes
1 cup freshly grated provolone, scamorza or Auricchio cheese
½ cup freshly grated pecorino cheese
2 tablespoons butter

1.   Combine the water and the potato in a large soup pot and cook the potato until tender, about 10 minutes. Remove and mash the potato and return it to the boiling water.

2.   Add the broccoli rabe and salt and cook for 2 minutes. Add the polenta in a steady flow, stirring constantly to avoid lumping. Reduce the heat and cook for about 25 minutes, until the

polenta comes away from the sides of the pot. Do not let it stick to the bottom of the pot and beware of burning. Pour the cooked polenta into 2 oiled glass loaf pans. Let cool for 2 to 4 hours, or overnight.

3. Heat the olive oil in a skillet and sauté the sausages until browned, about 8 minutes. Remove the sausages, cool them, and slice as thinly as possible.

4. Preheat the oven to 375F. Butter a 12 × 9-inch baking dish, and pour a thin layer of the tomato sauce on the bottom. Turn out the cooled polenta and slice thinly, about ⅓ inch. Lay one-third of the polenta slices over the sauce, adding half of the sliced sausages, half of the pepper flakes and the cheeses as follows: half of the provolone and one-third of the pecorino. Make another layer like the first, using a total of 2½ cups tomato sauce. Make a third layer with the remaining polenta slices and sprinkle the remaining one-third of the Pecorino on the top. Dot with the butter.

5. Bake for about 1 hour, until bubbly. Cool for 5 minutes before serving. Serve with the remaining tomato sauce.

●FRESH FENNEL WITH ●PARSLIED OIL AND ●VINEGAR

Insalata di finocchi con olio al prezzomolo
MAKES 6 SERVINGS

Fresh fennel is now on view in every supermarket I've been in, but that wasn't always the case. During my college days, friends who visited me at home would look at a fennel head and say, "What a strange piece of celery." Fresh fennel, Florence fennel, sweet fennel or *finocchio*—call it what you

will, will dry out more quickly than celery, so always cut off the stalks (they are great in soups and to flavor roasts), and store the bulbs in plastic in the crisper sections of the refrigerator until ready to use.

3 large heads fresh fennel
½ teaspoon sugar
2 tablespoons red wine vinegar
6 tablespoons extra-virgin olive oil
Sea salt and freshly ground pepper
¼ cup finely chopped fresh Italian
    parsley

1. Wash and dry the fennel, removing any blemished outer leaves. Cut each fennel in half. Lay cut side on cutting board and slice each half as thinly as possible.

2. Combine the sugar, vinegar and oil in a small bowl and whisk until blended. Add some salt and pepper. Sprinkle the parsley over the fennel and then pour the dressing over the salad. Toss lightly to distribute the parsley and dressing over the fennel.

●PINEAPPLE ICE WITH ●STRAWBERRY SAUCE

Sorbetto al pompelmo con salsa alle fragole
MAKES 6 SERVINGS

Sorbets are always welcome desserts when a main course is hearty enough and there just isn't room for a rich dessert. This is the case in this menu, as the polenta dish is very rich, made with cheese, broccoli rabe and sausages. Fresh fruit make delicious sorbets, although you will need an ice cream maker. When sorbet is made ahead and frozen, it needs time out of the freezer to "soften" a bit.

3¾ cups unsweetened pineapple juice
1½ cups sugar
1 tablespoon unflavored gelatin, softened in
   ⅓ cup water
1½ tablespoons fresh lemon juice

FOR THE STRAWBERRY SAUCE (ABOUT 3 CUPS)
2 (12-ounce) bags frozen unsweetened
   strawberries, thawed
½ cup sugar
¼ cup strawberry preserves
12 (1-inch) squares fresh pineapple

1. In a nonaluminum saucepan, bring 1½ cups of the pineapple juice to a boil. Reduce the heat to low. Add the sugar and the gelatin mixture and cook until both the sugar and gelatin are dissolved. Remove from the heat and let cool.

2. Add the lemon juice and the remaining pineapple juice. Refrigerate until well chilled. Transfer to an ice cream maker and process according to the manufacturer's directions.

3. *To make the sauce:* Puree all the ingredients in a processor and strain through a fine sieve.

4. Spoon some strawberry sauce onto individual plates or into goblets. Top with a scoop of sorbet and 2 pieces of fresh pineapple.

ONE-DISH MEALS

A FISHERMAN'S CHOWDER FROM FANO ON THE ADRIATIC

Brodetto casalingo
MAKES 8 SERVINGS

The *brodetto* of The Marches, the old and rich fish chowder said to have been created in Athens, was spread by the Greeks throughout the Mediterranean. There is the *ciuppin* of Liguria, the *cacciucco* of Livorno, the *ghiotto* of Sicily and the *cassola* of Sardinia as living examples of this Greek influence. Julius Caesar is supposed to have eaten a version of this chowder in Forli, a province that is home to Rimini. The Italians say to make a good *brodetto* you need a good sense of smell; that you have to go to the seaside, take a breath of the sea air to determine whether it is a good fish day. Well, that's not exactly practical always, is it? The rules are given that this fish and that fish are essential to a good *brodetto,* but that doesn't hold up either, as each cook seems to have an idea about which kinds of fish are necessary. The one consistency is one of the fish used must be the *scorpena* or *scorfano,* a hogfish, which is the French *rascasse.* In the United States there is an American *rascasse* from Maine, and elsewhere there are varieites of rose fish (black-bellied, white-bellied) and either of these would make a good substitute for the scorpena. If you can't get these, then be sure to include the sea bass listed in the ingredient list below as the one essential fish to use.

3/4 cup extra-virgin olive oil

2 leeks, white part only, carefully cleaned and
thinly sliced

2 ribs celery, trimmed and thinly sliced on the
diagonal

4 cloves garlic, minced

4 pounds various fish such as flounder, any kind
of snapper, non-Chilean sea bass, trout and
tilapia, cleaned and scaled, preferably with
bone in, cut into large chunks, ready for
cooking, with heads reserved

1 pound cleaned squid, left whole

1/4 cup white wine vinegar

Sea salt and freshly ground pepper

Water

2 small onions, thinly sliced

2 cinnamon sticks

4 bay leaves

2 tablespoons finely chopped fresh
Italian parsley

16 slices bruschetta (page 6)

1. In a large saucepan, heat half of the olive oil and sauté the leeks and celery until the leeks become opaque, about 5 minutes. Add the garlic and sauté 1 minute longer. Add the fish heads, the squid and the vinegar; turn up the heat to cook off the vinegar, 3 or 4 minutes. Add some salt and pepper and enough water to cover the heads. Bring to a boil, reduce the heat to a simmer, and cook for 45 minutes, partially covered.

2. Remove the squid and set aside. Strain the sauce and set it aside. Discard the heads and other solids. Do not rinse the saucepan in which the sauce cooked. When the squid have cooled, slice them across the body to make 1/3-inch-wide slices.

3. Heat the remaining oil in the same saucepan and sauté the onion until it is opaque, about 5 minutes. Add the fish pieces, cinnamon sticks,

bay leaves, and 1 1/2 tablespoons of the parsley. Stir and add the cooked squid and strained liquid. Cook the fish over medium heat until it begins to flake, about 15 minutes. Remove the bay leaves and the cinnamon sticks.

4. Put 2 bruschetta slices in each of eight bowls, spoon the fish over the bread, and add the liquid. Dot with a little fresh parsley and serve a side dish of freshly steamed broccoli with olive oil and fresh lemon juice.

FRITTATA WITH PANCETTA, PASTA AND PEAS

Frittata con pancetta, pasta e piselli
MAKES 4 TO 6 SERVINGS

Pancetta is the Italian equivalent of unsmoked bacon. It is rolled slices of cured pork belly, which is cured in salt and spices to give it a mild flavor. Pancetta can be eaten raw but it is too fatty for most people's taste. It is probably best known as a key ingredient for the famous *spaghetti alla carbonara*, a pasta dish made famous by the Romans. There is a smoked version of pancetta and it is sold in thin strips rather than being rolled. This frittata is utterly charming and delicious. It can be prepared ahead and transported to a picnic. A beet salad with this dish makes a lovely lunch.

1 cup spaghetti, broken into 2-inch pieces and
cooked until al dente

4 eggs, lightly beaten

Sea salt and freshly ground pepper

1 cup freshly grated mozzarella cheese

6 very thin slices pancetta, cut into small pieces
and cooked until crisp

1 cup fresh or frozen green peas, lightly cooked

⅓ cup freshly grated Parmesan cheese

3 tablespoons extra-virgin olive oil

2 small cloves garlic, minced

1. In a medium bowl, combine the cooked pasta, eggs, mozzarella, salt and pepper. Mix well and set aside. In another small bowl, toss the pancetta, peas and Parmesan cheese until well combined.

2. In a 9- or 10-inch nonstick skillet, heat the oil over medium heat until hot but not smoking. Add the garlic and sauté for 1 minute. Pour half the egg and spaghetti mixture into the skillet and top with the pancetta, peas and cheese. Cover with the remaining egg and spaghetti mixture. Turn the heat to medium-high and cook, pressing the frittata down lightly with a spatula, for about 8 minutes, until the underside is golden brown.

3. Invert the frittata onto a plate, add a few more drops of oil to the pan, and slide the frittata back into the pan. Cook for 5 minutes or until golden brown. (If you are hesitant to turn over the frittata or think the contents are still too "runny," put the skillet under the broiler for 2 to 3 minutes. (Beware if the handle is made of wood; if so, wrap a piece of foil around it.) Serve warm or let cool for later.

LAMB, PEPPER AND PASTA CASSEROLE

Ragu di agnello e peperoni col pasta all'Abruzzese

MAKES 4 SERVINGS

Paolo Scipioni is a food authority in L'Aquila; he is a charming man and the owner of a prestigious restaurant called Tre Marie on the street of the same name in his city. He is the fifth generation in ownership of the restaurant, which is claimed by many to be the temple of Abruzzi cookery. In addition to the murals on the walls of the three dining rooms, I remember the chairs that were antique, not one of them had a nail in them, each part of the chair was held together by pegs. One mid-morning, lingering over a Campari and soda and sitting on one of these chairs, Paolo described some interesting local dishes such as liver cooked with honey, *fegato dolce,* and liver cooked with hot peppers, *fegato pazzo,* meaning "crazy liver." He also described how the locals enjoy lamb and he described this sauce as one of the most popular, especially when it is served with their *chitarra* pasta (squarish spaghetti that are cut by wires strung across a board). I have substituted another pasta similar in feeling and texture as it is easier to make or buy here.

1 pound lean lamb for stewing, preferably top round

4 tablespoons olive oil

2 cloves garlic, minced

2 bay leaves

½ cup dry white wine

3 large or 4 small ripe plum tomatoes, cored and diced

1 red and 1 yellow bell peppers, cored, ribs
    removed, sliced as thinly as possible
Sea salt and freshly ground pepper
1 cup broth or water
1 pound fresh *macheroni alla chitarra* or tagliarini,
    preferably homemade

1. Remove excess fat from the lamb and dice into 1/4- to 1/2-inch pieces.

2. Heat the oil in a large skillet and add the garlic, bay leaves and diced lamb and sauté over medium heat, uncovered, until browned, 15 to 20 minutes.

3. Add the wine and cook until reduced by half, 5 to 7 minutes. Stir in the tomatoes. Add the bell peppers, salt and a liberal amount of pepper. Cover the skillet, reduce the heat to low and simmer for about 2 hours, checking to see if a litle broth may be needed. Remove and discard the bay leaves. Set aside or keep warm over very low heat.

4. In a large pan, bring 4 quarts of water to boil. Once it is boiling add 1 tablespoon salt. Then add the pasta and cook until al dente. Drain well and transfer it to the skillet with the lamb. Toss well with the sauce and transfer it to a bowl if ready to serve now. To hold, transfer to an ovenproof bowl and keep it warm, covered, in a low oven until ready to serve.

5. Serve this with a salad made of fresh baby spinach leaves with thinly sliced red or white onions with a slice of scamorza cheese on the side of the salad plate.

VIII

NAPLES AND ITS BAY

BARI AND THE ADRIATIC SOUTH

In Naples, you can eat any time of the day or night, and in a hurry, for speed is the essence of Neapolitan cooking. Food between the saucepan and stomach is a direct line. All over Naples, at shops with open windows, at pushcarts or collapsible tables, the small plates of vegetables, seafood and pizzas are eaten in a hurry, standing up. The crowded old streets in the heart of Naples are filled with laundry hanging on clotheslines, children crying out of windows, on balconies and in the streets next to old people arguing, younger people working, eating and drinking, laughing, giggling and sometimes looking sad, priests scurrying about, nuns, always in pairs, trying to keep the pace and beat of the city to *adagio,* their shadows flickering in the candles before the shrines, and everyone turning their heads to smell the oil from the frying fish, the burnt pizza edges and the perfume released from the excessive use of oregano.

The Neapolitan soil is extraordinarily fertile and has been for many years, especially between Naples and Rome. This soil nourishes so many crops that the growing season seems to be year-long. It is not uncommon to see vegetables planted between fruit and olive trees and then up the hillside to heights of five and six hundred feet. The planted plains begin to disappear south of Naples and the appearance of rising cliffs give beauty to the Amalfi Drive where vines still cling to the cliffs and citrus trees grow in abundance.

Native Italians and Americans think Naples' food is all pizza and pasta. I think a third dimension should be added: vegetables, for tomatoes, peppers, cabbages, beans, broccoli and zucchini cover the earth there. The fourth dimension is fish; meat is not eaten as much as it is elsewhere, although beefsteak *alla pizzaiola* is popular eating, probably because the sauce is thick with tomatoes, garlic and wild marjoram. Mussels, clams, squid, octopus, sole, hake, red mullet, shrimp and everything else the Mediterranean delivers are in their fish preparations. Desserts are extravagant, especially pastries. Just as the breads are embellished with glazes and decorative designs, so are the pastries. *Sfogliatelle,* puff pastry of many layers in fan shapes, are filled with cream, jams or chocolates are flavored with lemon and orange essences; little balls of pastry with citrus peels are honeyed and called *strufoli;* and then there are the *zeppole,* fritters flavored with brandy. Who would disclaim the divinity of Neapolitan ice cream? These foods are but brief examples of the vast Neapolitan cuisine, which is extended by the specialties of Capri and Ischia and other nearby areas.

CHRISTMAS EVE DINNER FOR 8 TO 12 IN NAPLES

MENU

Special Provolone from Bari
Burratina di Andria

Peppery Shrimp, One-Two-Three
Gamberi piccante, uno-due-tre

Traditional Cauliflower Salad in Naples
Insalata di rinforzo alla napoletana

Spaghettini with Clams, Carrots and Wine
Spaghettini alle vongole

Fish Fillets, Neapolitan Fisherman's Style
Pesce alla pescatora

Spinach with Oil and Lemon
Spinaci all'agro

Hearts of Escarole with Red Pepper Confetti
Insalata di scarola con peperoni

Panettone Bread Pudding
Budino di panettone

For Catholics everywhere, not just in Italy, Christmas Eve is the last day of Advent, a month-long period of preparation for the birth of Christ. Catholics traditionally abstain from eating meat, and in olden days, the Christmas Eve fish meal, known as *Il Cenone,* was sparse and humble. However, over many centuries, this humble meal has grown into a fabulous feast, still meatless, but opulent in the number of fish courses. Even today, the meal usually consists of seven fish preparations, one for each of the sacraments, and sometimes, it is twelve, one for each of Christ's apostles. Taking the American table into consideration, I have reduced the number of fish dishes to three, symbolically, I suppose, for the Holy Trinity, but essentially because of costs and saving in preparation time, and of course, one's ability to consume twelve different fish preparations. When I cook this meal, I feel it's Christmas Eve. I hope you will feel the same. A lavish dessert is offered here, as it might be in Italy but remember, Italians on this evening continue a succession of delights to eat all night long: fresh pears, oranges and persimmons, roasted chestnuts, hazelnuts and almonds and platefuls of all kinds of cookies and pastries. Christmas Eve in Italy is a serious affair. Some years ago I was in Naples on this eve of eves and I was fortunate to have friends who prepared a delicious meal. But I recall how silent the evening became in Naples itself, as the shops closed, lights went out, gates to the shops slammed shut, a few people in the streets scurrying home for the big evening. Most restaurants were closed. I realized Christmas Eve in Italy was celebrated by everyone.

Wine Selection

If you can, select a Capri white wine, which goes well with fish and shellfish. It is clear, fragrant, refreshing and dry and pale straw-yellow in color. If you can't, go for a Sicilian white: Capo Bianco from Messina, a Taormino Scelto, or an Albanello di Siracusa. Be sure the latter is the dry variety.

Preparation Advice

1. Spinach may be cooked in advance and sautéed before serving. This does not have to be served hot. The cauliflower salad may be made one or two days ahead. Lettuces and vegetables can be prepped and refrigerated in plastic bags.

2. The pudding can be prepped the day before. Cover and refrigerate, bring to room temperature before baking and cool to room temperature before serving after it is cooked.

3. The fish should be cleaned, readied for cooking, refrigerated, but all cooked shortly before mealtime.

SPECIAL PROVOLONE FROM BARI

Burratina di Andria
MAKES 8 SERVINGS

This cheese is basically a member of the southern Italian cheese provolone, straw-white in color with a smooth texture and an oval or cylindrical shape. Regular provolone comes in many sizes and you've probably seen them hanging from the ceilings in Italian delicatessens. However, this is quite small and comes from the village of Andria, near Bari on the Adriatic coast. It is made with a lump of butter buried in the center of the cheese, so that when it is cut, it looks like a hard-cooked egg yolk. It is available in specialty cheese food stores. If you can't find this, use the small cylindrical shaped fresh mozzarellas kept in brine; each weighs about 1/3 pound. Because the mozzarella does not have the "neck" like the provolone, you cannot tie the chives around it.

> 3 small provolone burrinos (*burrantinas*) or
>   mozzarella, each weighing about
>   1/3 pound
> 10 long chive leaves
> 8 very small Italian parsley sprigs
> 1 large carrot, cut into very thin, 1 1/2-inch-long
>   strips
> Sea salt and freshly ground pepper
> 8 teaspoons extra-virgin olive oil

1. Carefully cut off the 2 rounded sides of each small cheese so the slices will lay flat after slicing. Cut each cheese lengthwise through the neck into 3 equal slices.

2. Wrap the chive leaves in a moist paper towel and microwave on high for 10 seconds. This makes the chive flexible. Tie a chive leaf around the neck of each of 8 cheese slices (you will have 1 left); knot and cut off the ends to trim. Place each cheese slice in the center of a plate, preferably a white one.

3. Arrange a parsley sprig next to each along with 3 or 4 pieces of carrots, crisscrossing them. Add some salt and pepper and sprinkle 1 teaspoon of the oil over each plate. Do not refrigerate. This should be served at room temperature.

PEPPERY SHRIMP, ONE-TWO-THREE

Gamberi piccante, uno-due-tre
MAKES 8 TO 12 SERVINGS

Once the shrimp are cleaned, this is one of the easiest dishes to make. It is also one of the best tasting. It is important to use fresh shrimp for the best results. Adding the pepper flakes to the shrimp after they come out of the skillet keeps them red; otherwise, they darken if sautéed with the shrimp. Also, the reason not to cook the garlic with the shrimp is to emphasize that the garlic should just turn color (or it gets bitter); cooking the cloves separately and then adding them to the already cooked shrimp provides better assurance that the garlic will be cooked properly.

2 pounds fresh shrimp (16 to 20 count per pound)
½ cup extra-virgin olive oil
Salt and freshly ground black pepper

Sprinkle red pepper flakes
3 cloves garlic, minced
⅓ cup finely chopped fresh Italian parsley

1. Shell and devein the shrimp. Rinse them carefully in cold water. Pat them dry with paper towels.

2. Heat the oil in a large skillet and sauté the shrimp over high heat, uncovered, until they turn pink, about 5 minutes, stirring all the time. Season them with some salt and a liberal amount of pepper. Remove the shrimp from the skillet and put them in a large platter. Sprinkle with the red pepper flakes.

3. Add the garlic pieces to the remaining oil in the skillet and sauté over high heat briefly, 1 to 2 minutes, stirring all the time. Do not darken the garlic pieces; they should come off the heat as soon as they begin to turn color. Immediately pour this over the shrimp in the platter and sprinkle with the parsley. These should be served as soon as they come off the stove. If the shrimp sit around too long, they begin to toughen.

TRADITIONAL CAULIFLOWER SALAD IN NAPLES

Insalata di rinforzo alla napoletana
MAKES 8 TO 12 SERVINGS

Rinforzo means to "reinforce"; what actually happens is this: A cauliflower salad is made with several other ingredients, but as it is eaten, more of the same vegetables, or even other leftover cooked vegetables, may be added to "keep the salad going." It is considered a holiday salad in Naples. It can be made ahead by a couple of days;

in fact, it is better to do so to allow the flavors to develop.

6 tablespoons extra-virgin olive oil
2 tablespoons white wine vinegar
6 anchovy fillets, minced
2 tablespoons dried oregano, crushed
3/4 cup coarsely chopped cured black olives
    (do not use canned California variety; these
    must be cured, either in oil or brine)
1/4 cup capers, drained, dried and chopped
1 1/2 cups roasted red bell pepper strips
2 cloves garlic, minced
1/4 cup finely chopped fresh Italian parsley
Salt
Juice of 1 1/2 lemons and zest of 1/2 lemon
1 large cauliflower head, trimmed of stem and
    tough outer leaves, cut into 1-inch florets

1.   In a large bowl, combine the oil, vinegar and anchovies. Whisk to make a smooth sauce. Add the oregano, olives, capers, bell peppers, garlic and parsley and stir so the olives and peppers are well coated. Set aside.

2.   Bring a large pot of water to boil, add salt, lemon zest, one-third of the lemon juice and the cauliflower florets. Cook for 5 or 6 minutes until the cauliflower is tender, drain immediately, and run cold water over them to stop the cooking. Drain well and pat dry with paper towels.

3.   Add the cauliflower, some salt and pepper and the remaining lemon juice to the salad. Toss lightly but well. Leave at room temperature for several hours to allow flavors to develop. If made one or two days ahead, refrigerate, but bring the salad to room temperature by removing from refrigerator 1 hour before serving.

SPAGHETTINI WITH CLAMS, CARROTS AND WINE

Spaghettini alle vongole
MAKES 8 TO 12 SMALL SERVINGS

There is no single way to prepare spaghetti or linguini with clam sauce except to use the best ingredients you can get and to respect the traditions of the dish, which comes from Naples and the Amalfi coast. This is where the real *vongole veraci* clams are to be found; they are tender, tiny and sweet. But I have tasted *arselle* clams in Genoa, called *vongole* in Rome, and it's difficult for me to see or taste the difference. Manila clams or small clams, such as littlenecks, cockles or Cedar Key (Florida), sometimes called littleneck pasta clams, work best in the United States. Purists may take me to task for using canned or jarred clams, minced, but they make a tasty substitute. The carrot adds color, and a touch of sweetness as in *vongole veraci*.

5 dozen Manila or littleneck clams, or
    3 (7 1/2-ounce) cans minced clams
2 cloves garlic, minced
8 tablespoons extra-virgin olive oil
4 tablespoons butter
1 carrot, trimmed, cut lengthwise into 6 pieces
    and finely chopped
1/2 cup finely chopped scallions
1 cup clam juice in addition to cooking liquid from
    fresh clams or liquid from canned clams
1 cup dry white wine
1/4 cup finely chopped fresh Italian parsley
1 pound spaghettini (thin spaghetti)
Freshly ground pepper

1. If using fresh clams, scrub the clams thoroughly with a stiff wire brush, rinsing them several times. Soak clams in cool, fresh water 30 minutes or longer to remove any sand that may be in them. Remove the clams by hand from the bowl or pan in which they soak. The sand will have settled in the bottom and removing by hand prevents stirring the sand. Place the clams in a heavy saucepan with a cover, along with half the garlic and 3 tablespoons of the olive oil. Cover and cook over medium heat until the clams open, 10 to 15 minutes. Discard any clams that have not opened. When you separate the clams from their shells, do so over a bowl so you can catch all the juices, which will be used later. Chop the clams and set the clams and the juice aside.

2. In a large skillet, heat the remaining oil (if you used some with the fresh clams, or all of it if you used minced, canned clams) and the butter over medium heat. Add the carrots and sauté for 5 minutes. Add the scallions and remaining garlic (or all of the garlic if you are using canned clams) and cook for 3 minutes. Add all the juice from the cooked clams (or from the canned clams), the additional 1 cup clam juice and the white wine. Cook to reduce the wine, 10 to 15 minutes. Season with salt.

3. Cook the pasta in boiling salted water until al dente and drain well. While the pasta is cooking, heat the sauce to be sure it is hot. As soon as the pasta is done, add the chopped clams to the sauce and cook until the clams are heated through, 2 to 3 minutes.

4. Add the cooked pasta to the sauce, and over heat, toss to bring the pasta and sauce together. Taste for salt and liberally add pepper. Transfer to a large platter and sprinkle with parsley. This can rest for a few minutes.

FISH FILLETS, NEAPOLITAN FISHERMAN'S STYLE

Pesce alla pescatora
MAKES 8 TO 12 SERVINGS

In Naples, the fishermen cook chunks of fish with skin and bones in this fashion. This has been adapted to use fish fillets instead. Cooking this the Neapolitan way will give more flavor, but I am convinced that Americans do not want to sit across from each other picking small bones out of their mouths; besides, it reduces the risk of swallowing small fish bones.

> 2 pounds fish fillets (sole, flounder, snapper, bass)
> Juice of 1 lemon
> 4 tablespoons extra-virgin olive oil
> 2 cloves garlic, minced
> 1 onion, finely chopped
> 3 cups fresh tomatoes, cored, blanched, peeled, seeded and chopped, or 3 cups canned plum tomatoes, put through a food mill
> 1/3 cup finely chopped fresh basil and Italian parsley
> 1 teaspoon dried oregano, crushed
> Salt
> 1/2 cup dry white wine
> Freshly ground pepper
> 8 to 16 pieces crostini or bruschetta (page 6)

1. Rinse the fillets in cool water, dry them with paper towels and put in a bowl with the lemon juice. Let marinate for 15 minutes. Cut them into 3-inch pieces and set aside.

2. In a large skillet, heat the oil, add the garlic and onion, and brown lightly, about 8 minutes.

Add the tomatoes, herbs and some salt, and cook over medium heat, uncovered, 15 minutes. Add the wine, and cook for 7 or 8 minutes.

3. Add the fish fillets and a liberal amount of freshly ground pepper, cover the skillet and cook over medium heat until the fish is opaque, 5 minutes. Serve over small or large crostini, but do not put the fish and its sauce over the bread until they are ready to be served and eaten.

SPINACH WITH OIL AND LEMON

Spinaci all'agro
MAKES 8 TO 12 SERVINGS

This is probably the most common way spinach is served in Italy. It is an excellent partner with fish of almost any kind and it doesn't have to be eaten hot. Take my advice about several rinsings of the spinach to rid it of sand; there is something un-American about grit on cooked spinach.

> 3 pounds fresh leaf spinach
> Salt
> 6 tablespoons extra-virgin olive oil
> 2 cloves garlic, sliced lengthwise
> 4 tablespoons fresh lemon juice (1½ lemons)

1. Cut off the stem ends of the spinach and trim any leaves needing it. Also remove any especially long stems. Rinse the spinach at least three times; it is best to soak it in a sink with a drain plug or a very large basin of water. Shake the spinach leaves in the water to dislodge any foreign matter. It is usually necessary to do this even with packaged fresh spinach sold as ready-to-use. Remove the spinach by hand, trying not to disturb the bottom of the sink or basin. Drain dirty water and start anew.

2. Transfer the spinach to a large saucepan. No water is necessary; the water clinging to the spinach leaves is adequate. Add some salt, cover the pan, and cook over high heat, for 6 or 7 minutes, stirring several times. Remove from the heat, drain and press as much liquid out of the spinach as is possible. Chop it coarsely.

3. In a large skillet, heat the oil over medium heat and sauté the garlic. When the cloves brown lightly, remove and discard them. Add the spinach and cook it over medium heat, uncovered, for 6 to 8 minutes, stirring several times. Transfer to a serving platter and sprinkle with fresh lemon juice. Add more salt, if needed.

HEARTS OF ESCAROLE WITH RED PEPPER CONFETTI

Insalata di scarola con peperoni
MAKES 8 TO 12 SERVINGS

The hearts of escarole are white and pale yellow and quite tender. Although it's difficult to buy just the hearts (they are available sometimes), you will have to buy regular heads of escarole and peel away the green leaves, which can be used in other dishes, such as soups. This is a refreshing, tender salad and so pretty to look at. A classic dish in Naples is cooked escarole with raisins and pine nuts, called *scarole natale*, and I have adapted that idea to form this salad.

> 4 heads escarole, green leaves removed and
>   reserved for another use
> 1 red bell pepper, cored, seeded, ribs removed, cut
>   into tiny dice
> ¼ cup golden raisins, soaked in warm water
>   30 minutes and then drained and dried
> ¼ cup pine nuts, toasted

⅓ cup finely chopped chives
⅓ cup extra-virgin olive oil
2 tablespoons herb-flavored white vinegar
1 teaspoon capers, drained
½ teaspoon sugar
Sea salt and freshly ground pepper

1. Trim the stem end of the escarole. Use only the tender leaves, white and pale yellow, with a tint of green. Pull these tender leaves apart. Rinse them and dry with paper towels or spin dry. Put the leaves into a large bowl. Add the bell pepper, raisins, nuts and the chives.

2. In a smaller bowl, combine the oil, vinegar, capers, sugar and some salt and pepper. Mix well and pour the dressing over the escarole. Toss lightly but well.

PANETTONE BREAD PUDDING

Budino di panettone
MAKES 8 TO 12 SERVINGS

Panettone, a rich buttery bread, supposedly first made in Milan, is the most popular holiday bread in Italy. It is a household staple at Christmastime and in this country, it is available all year long in many supermarkets. Bread pudding, made with panettone, is made all over Italy, and each area, city, village and town, claims the origin of this buttery, sweet, brioche-type bread.

16 slices panettone, 2 inches wide × ½ inch thick
    × 6 inches high
1½ sticks (6 ounces) butter, cut into 6 pieces
¾ cup honey
½ cup dark rum
6 large eggs
¾ cup sugar

1½ cups heavy cream
4½ cups milk
1 cup heavy cream, whipped (optional)

1. Preheat the oven to 375F. Butter a 12½ × 11 × 2½-inch oval glass or ceramic baking dish. Cover the bottom of the dish with slices of panettone, overlapping as necessary.

2. In a small saucepan, melt the butter over low heat; add the honey and rum. Increase the heat and cook, stirring constantly, until the mixture bubbles and thickens. Remove from the heat and pour over the bread, spreading it as evenly as you can.

3. Beat the eggs and sugar in a large bowl until well combined. Slowly mix in the cream and then the milk. Be sure the mixture is well mixed. Pour over the bread.

4. Bake for 20 minutes, reduce the heat to 325F and bake for 20 minutes, until the bread has a golden color and the pudding is set. Let rest for 10 minutes before serving with a dollop of whipped cream, if desired.

Notabene:
A bowl of fresh pears, a bowl of oranges and persimmons, a small basket of roasted chestnuts, another small basket of hazelnuts and almonds and platefuls of all kinds of candies (especially *torrone*), cookies and pastries can also be served with this menu.

The Neapolitans and Their Love of Macaroni: Menu for 6

MENU

Penne with Pork Tomato Sauce
Penne al ragu di maiale

Sliced Pork (part of sauce for penne)
Maiale Cotto

Carrots with Marsala
Carote al marsala

Romaine Lettuce, Watercress and Snow Peas with Lemon
Lattuga romana crescione e taccole al limone

Cousin Giuseppe's Meringue Cookies
Croccante di meringa, pinoli e mandorle

Naples is the land of macaroni, that of machine-made tubular pasta, for we are now south of the land of fresh, soft sheet or ribbon pasta, as it is called up north; sheet being the name given for pasta when it is rolled out before cutting, ribbon pasta meaning when it is cut into fettuccine, tagliatelle and so on. Dried pasta has been manufactured in Naples since the fifteenth century, and today, there is no question that Naples is the capital of this form of Italy's national staple food. In the south, there is *pasta lunghe* (spaghetti, linguini and so on) and *pasta corte* (short pasta, which includes farfalle, rigatoni, penne and many others). The sauces served in the south do not have the restraint of those in the north for we

are now in the land of the Greeks, the Byzantines, the exuberant, the colorful; the repertoire of pasta sauces is constantly being extended.

In this area, we see dark green palms and blue-gray olive trees, oleander blooms in multiple shades of pink, field after field of San Marzano tomatoes and fields of eggplant, celery and broccoli. There are fields of red poppies. In the kitchens are strings of red-hot dried peppers and hanging provolones. And wherever there is a family, one will see the eight-quart vessel filled with rapidly boiling water, waiting to receive the *pasta lunghe* or *pasta corte*. This is precisely the image for anyone preparing this menu for the American table.

Wine Selection

Choose a Gragnano, most popular with the Neapolitans, one of the wines of the Colli Sorrentini.

Preparation Advice

1. This is a simple meal to prepare. The sauce, cooked with the pork, should be made ahead.

2. The lettuces can be prepared ahead and dressed at mealtime. The carrots and pasta can be cooked shortly before eating.

PENNE WITH PORK TOMATO SAUCE

Penne al ragu di maiale
MAKES ABOUT 6 CUPS

This sauce should be made ahead and the fat should be removed. The pork shoulder can be served separately with a vegetable and salad. If you decide against the pasta and just want to use some of the sauce with the pork, refrigerate the remaining sauce for several days or freeze for several weeks. It is very tasty and hearty and wonderful over pasta.

> 3½ pounds boned pork shoulder (may be in 1 or
> 2 pieces)
> 2 medium cloves garlic, minced
> 1 cup finely chopped fresh Italian parsley
> 6 tablespoons olive oil
> 1 large onion, finely chopped
> 7 cups pureed plum tomatoes (after putting them
> through a food mill)
> ½ teaspoon red pepper flakes
> Sea salt
> 1 pound penne pasta

1. Lay the meat flat on a work surface and spread with the garlic and parsley. Roll it and tie with string. If two pieces of meat are used, do this for both, dividing the amount of garlic and parsley equally.

2. Heat the oil in a large heavy pot and sauté the rolled pork over medium heat, uncovered, until it is browned all over, about 10 minutes. Add the onion and sauté for 2 or 3 minutes, stirring several times. Add the tomatoes and pepper flakes and cook, covered, over low heat for about 2 hours. Taste for salt and add some if it is needed.

3. Remove the pork and set aside for later serving. If sauce appears thin, cook down to desired thickness, for up to 20 minutes.

4. Cook the pasta according to package directions, drain well, and add 1 to 1½ cups tomato sauce.

5. Serve the penne with the sauce first. Then slice the pork to serve as a separate course. If you are omitting the pasta course, add 2 tablespoons sauce to each portion of meat when serving with the carrots and salad.

CARROTS WITH MARSALA

Carote al marsala
MAKES 6 SERVINGS

Carrots cooked in classic Italian style require them to be sautéed in butter with salt, pepper, sugar and flour, and then some broth is added; this results in a vegetable with a slightly thickened sauce. The newer Italian chefs are abandoning the flour-thickening technique and going for a bit more flavor by adding a wine, such as Marsala. The result is most satisfying.

> 4 tablespoons extra-virgin olive oil
> 6 medium carrots, trimmed and sliced on the bias
> Sea salt and freshly ground pepper
> ½ to 1 cup chicken broth
> 1 tablespoon sugar
> ¼ cup Marsala wine
> ¼ cup finely sliced scallions

1. Heat the olive oil in a large skillet over medium heat and add the carrot slices. Sauté for 3 or 4 minutes, adding some salt and pepper. Add 2 tablespoons of the chicken broth.

2. Cover and simmer over low heat until the carrots are tender, about 20 minutes; add more broth by tablespoons to keep the carrots from sticking to the pan.

3. Increase the heat, and sprinkle the sugar over the carrots. Stir until the sugar caramelizes and the carrots turn light brown. Add the Marsala, and cook until it evaporates, 3 or 4 minutes. Garnish with scallions.

ROMAINE LETTUCE, WATERCRESS AND SNOW PEAS WITH LEMON

Lattuga romana crescione e taccole al limone
MAKES 6 SERVINGS

The hearts of this lettuce as a rule do not need to be rinsed. However, check carefully before dressing them. Romaine lettuce is named for the Romans, who cultivated many varieties of lettuce. Although Americans often prefer the hearts of romaine, we should be aware that the outer, darker leaves of romaine have as much as six times more vitamin C and up to ten times more beta carotene than iceberg lettuce. (The same is true for arugula.) The addition of watercress and thinly sliced snow peas add interest to the salad.

    2 small heads romaine lettuce
    1 bunch watercress, rinsed and
        dried
    24 snow peas, about ⅓ pound, trimmed
    ½ cup extra-virgin olive oil
    Juice from 1 lemon (about 3 tablespoons)
    Salt and freshly ground pepper
    2 tablespoons finely chopped mint
    1 clove garlic, minced

1. Remove outer green leaves from the heads of lettuce and discard or reserve some leaves for another use. Cut the hearts of this lettuce lengthwise, in half, and then again lengthwise in thirds to make 6 pieces. Repeat with the second head of lettuce.

2. Put the watercress and the snow peas in a large mixing bowl.

3. In a smaller bowl, combine the oil, lemon juice, some salt and pepper, mint, and garlic. Mix well.

4. Arrange 2 wedges of lettuce on each of six plates. Spoon a little of the sauce over each lettuce wedge. Add the remaining dressing to the bowl with the watercress and snow peas. Toss lightly but well. Add some of this to each plate over the lettuce wedges and serve.

COUSIN GIUSEPPE'S MERINGUE COOKIES

Croccante di meringa, pinoli e mandorle
MAKES ABOUT 24 COOKIES

This is a delicious, crunchy cookie that keeps well if stored in an airtight container, so they can be made days ahead. It is a variation of the famous Sienna cookie, as the flavor is somewhat similar, but the crunch makes the cookie a totally different confection. They can be eaten by themselves, or with some fresh berries, or used as a base for ice cream. I am the cousin Giuseppe who made these cookies for cousins in Caserta, the city northeast of Naples, famous for the *Reggia di Casertaa*, the eighteenth-century Bourbon palace with gardens, often called the Versailles of Italy. The palace has 1,200 rooms and the gardens are spread over 250 acres. This is a grand place for this cookie.

    2 cups almond slivers
    ½ cup pine nuts
    1½ cups granulated sugar
    ½ cup confectioners' sugar, plus extra for dusting
    1 teaspoon finely grated orange zest
    3 egg whites, at room temperature
    ½ teaspoon cream of tartar
    ½ teaspoon almond extract

1. Put the almonds and pine nuts in the bowl of a large food processor and process them until they look like a very fine sand. Transfer the mixture to a large bowl.

2. Add ¾ cup of granulated sugar, the confectioners' sugar and orange zest to the bowl with the nuts and combine them well with the help of a rubber spatula.

3. In a very clean bowl of an electric mixer, add the egg whites and start to whip, preferably with a balloon whisk. When the egg whites are frothy, add the cream of tartar. When they have tripled in volume but are still somewhat soft, add the remaining ¾ cup sugar, a heaping tablespoon at a time. When the whites are reasonably stiff and shiny, add the almond extract. Transfer to the bowl of dry ingredients and fold in the egg whites, slowly, carefully and thoroughly.

4. Fit parchment paper into 2 baking sheets (jelly roll pans work well here). By teaspoonfuls, place mixture onto parchment leaving 1½ inches between cookies. Arrange 12 or 15 cookies in each baking pan. Flatten each with the back of a clean, wet teaspoon; each should be about ½ inch thick.

5. Preheat the oven to 350F. Bake one pan of cookies at a time, for 8 to 10 minutes. Do not brown them. Remove from the oven, let cool on the pan before removing them. Dust with confectioners' sugar before serving.

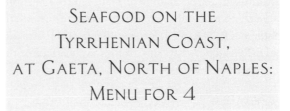

SEAFOOD ON THE TYRRHENIAN COAST, AT GAETA, NORTH OF NAPLES: MENU FOR 4

MENU

Grilled Fennel Slices with Fresh Lemon
Finocchi ai ferri

Sole, Shrimp and Squid, Deep-Fried, Gaeta Style
Fritto misto di mare alla moda di Gaeta

Sliced Potatoes with Oil and Herbs
Insalata di patate con olio alle erbe

Caramelized Oranges
Arance caramellizzate

The town of Gaeta is almost midway between Rome and Naples and it has a gorgeous bay, incredible views, and a great seafood restaurant, Antico Vico, which are three good reasons for being there. The Gulf of Gaeta is proud of its scampi, called *mazzancolle* locally, and claim it is better than those of Venice. Like most coastal Italian towns and villages, Gaeta prepares fish in a number of ways: In fish stews and soups, they combine cuttlefish with artichokes and their *fritti misti di mare,* is based usually on shrimp, sole, squid and sometimes mullet. Here is a version, also made in Bari, without the mullet, although you could well add it if you wish.

Wine Selection

Reach for an Apulian white such as Castel del Monte Bianco, or look for a Tenuta Frassitelli Epomeo IGT Bianco, produced by D'Ambra (of Ischia), a wine with fruit aromas, well suited with the fish.

Preparation Advice

1. The dessert may be made ahead, and the fennel can be prepped ahead and dressed at mealtime.

2. The main-course fish should be prepared at mealtime.

GRILLED FENNEL SLICES WITH FRESH LEMON

Finocchi ai ferri
MAKES 4 SERVINGS

Fennel bulbs and their feathery leaves both impart a mild, sweet flavor similar to licorice or anise. Because of its taste, fennel is also called anise in many markets, but actually, it is quite a different plant from the herb anise. In Florence, it is known as sweet fennel or *finocchio*. Italians have been enthusiastic about fennel for many years, and cultivate it more than anyone else. The vegetable now appears in many U.S. markets.

> 2 large fresh fennel bulbs
> 6 tablespoons extra-virgin olive oil
> ½ cup chicken or vegetable broth
> 2 tablespoons fresh lemon juice
> Pinch dried fennel seeds
> Sea salt and freshly ground pepper

1. Trim the fennel by trimming the bulb end and cutting the bulb from any branches. If possible, reserve 4 small sprays of the feathery green leaves for garnish. Cut both bulbs into thin slices, leaving each slice attached at the bulb end. Do not fret if some slices are loose and unattached.

2. Heat 1 tablespoon of the oil in a large skillet and arrange the fennel slices in one layer. If this is not possible, cook in batches. Add enough broth just to cover the slices. Simmer, uncovered, for 20 minutes, until tender. Remove and drain the slices.

3. Brush a little more oil on the slices and transfer the slices to a heated grill or warmed broiler pan. Grill to achieve grill marks, or broil to brown the slices. Remove them to a large plate or platter.

4. Combine the remaining oil and lemon juice. Add the fennel seeds and some salt and pepper. Mix well. Pour over the fennel slices and let marinate, at room temperature, for up to 1 hour. If longer, refrigerate, but remove at least 30 minutes before serving. Transfer the fennel to 4 plates, with sauce over each portion. Add a spray of fennel leaves to each and serve.

SOLE, SHRIMP AND SQUID, DEEP-FRIED, GAETA STYLE

Fritti misto di mare alla moda di Gaeta
MAKES 4 SERVINGS

Many people know the town of Gaeta for its great black olives, but it is also known for its fish dishes. Scampi from the Gulf of Gaeta are bigger than those in the Adriatic, and everyone has a special recipe for preparing them. One of the best dishes of the area is *fritti misto di mare*, a mixed fish fry and here is one of the best recipes from the area.

> TO MAKE A BATTER
> 2 tablespoons olive oil
> 1 tablespoon white wine vinegar

2 egg whites

¾ cup all-purpose flour

7 tablespoons cornstarch

2 teaspoons baking soda

1 cup water

To deep-fry and serve the fish

About 4 cups vegetable oil for deep-frying

1 pound sole fillets, rinsed, dried and cut into
  fingerlike pieces

1 pound cleaned squid, cut across the body into
  ⅓-inch-wide rings

1 pound shrimp (16 to 20 count), shelled,
  deveined, rinsed and dried

1½ cups all-purpose flour

Sea salt and freshly ground pepper

3 lemons, cut into wedges, ends cut off and seeds
  removed

1. *To make the batter:* In a large bowl, combine the oil, vinegar and egg whites with a whisk. Whisk until well blended.

2. Add the dry ingredients, whisking lightly but well. Add the water, a little at a time, until well mixed. Cover the bowl with plastic and let rest for 20 minutes.

3. *To fry:* Have the well dried fish and shellfish, the flour in a flat dish and the batter near the deep-fryer.

4. It is best to do this in a deep-fryer with a basket, but if you don't have one, use a deep, medium saucepan and a strainer or a slotted spoon to retrieve the fish. Heat the oil until a piece of bread sizzles as soon as it is put in the oil (about 350F).

5. Dip each piece of fish or shellfish first into the flour, shake off any excess, then into the batter and place carefully into the oil. Fry in batches as the pieces tend to stick together. Use a long fork to stir the pieces in the oil to keep them apart. Fry for 1 minute and remove the basket or

the strainer. Repeat this process until all the fish and shellfish are fried, flouring and battering just before putting the pieces into the oil. Be sure the temperature of the oil comes back to the bread-sizzle stage for each batch.

6. As the fried pieces are removed, place them on paper towels to drain. Add some salt and pepper and serve with several wedges of lemon.

SLICED POTATOES WITH OIL AND HERBS

Insalata di patate con olio alle erbe
MAKES 4 SERVINGS

Another classic because of its simplicity and taste, make this ahead by several days to allow the potatoes to absorb the flavor of the oil, vinegar and herbs. Be sure to take out of the refrigerator at least one-half hour before serving. They are best at room temperature.

1½ pounds potatoes, boiled with skins and then
  peeled and sliced about ¼ inch thick

4 tablespoons extra-virgin olive oil

1 tablespoon white wine vinegar

2 cloves garlic, minced

¼ cup finely chopped herbs: fresh oregano, fresh
  basil and fresh parsley

1 tablespoon chopped capers, drained and dried

1. As soon as the potatoes are put to boil, combine the remaining ingredients in a bowl and let sit until the potatoes are boiled, peeled and sliced. Put the potatoes in a bowl.

2. While the potatoes are still warm, add the dressing. Toss lightly and well. The warm potatoes will absorb the dressing more so than if the potatoes were cold. If the potatoes appear dry, add a little more oil and vinegar. This may be made ahead and left at room temperature for about 3 hours, or refrigerated if made earlier.

●

●

●CARAMELIZED ORANGES

Arance caramellizzate

MAKES 6 SERVINGS

There are many versions of this dessert and most of them call for slicing the oranges. I like them left whole, dipped in the syrup before it caramelizes the orange strips, and served whole with caramelized orange strips on top. This is a special dessert.

6 oranges
1 cup plus 1 tablespoon sugar
2/3 cup water
2 tablespoons kirsch or brandy

1. Remove the zest (orange part only) from 3 of the oranges with a knife; slice the zest as thinly as possible. Peel all 6 oranges, removing the bitter white pith. Set aside.

2. Stir together the sugar and water in a large saucepan and bring to a boil over medium heat. If the sugar mixture reaches to the top of the saucepan, quickly remove the saucepan from the heat source and as the syrup recedes, put it back on the heat. Boil for 7 minutes.

3. Add the kirsch, cook for 1 minute and remove from the heat. Dip each orange in the syrup for 2 minutes. Remove and place on a plate. Reserve the syrup in the saucepan.

4. Put the strips of orange peel in a saucepan and cover with water. Bring to a boil, reduce the heat and simmer for 10 minutes. Drain well.

5. Cook the drained zest in the reserved syrup until caramelized.

6. To serve, place an orange on a plate and top with the candied zest.

BARI AND THE ADRIATIC SOUTH

The imprint of Greece seems far greater in Apulia (Bari) than in Campania (Naples) and its effect on food in this area can be felt in its fish soups and lamb stews. Its coastline, over four hundred miles, is the longest of any region in Italy. Bari, Italy's second most important port (the first is Genoa), spreads across a fertile plain and most of the region's produce comes from here. It leads the province in wine and olive oil production, has about one hundred flour mills and pasta factories; many canneries for *marmellata* (jams and preserves), fish and vegetables; and distilleries for liqueurs. Today, one of the two great fairs of Italy is the Fiera del Levante in Bari (the other is in Milan).

The food here is oysters from Taranto, see page 221, exquisite lobsters from the Tremiti Islands, off the coastline, see page 219, clams, mussels (the black cozze from Taranto), and the many pastas cooked with cauliflower and the *spaghetti alla zappatora* (ditch-digger's spaghetti) cooked with lots of garlic and red-hot pimiento. Garlic is used sparingly in Apulia, but not in this dish. And there are a variety of baked pasta, *maccheroni al forno*, dishes that make excellent one-dish meals.

MENU

Potato and Zucchini Soup from Franco Ricatti
Zuppa di patate e zucchine alla pugliese

Shrimp in Olive Oil and Lemon Juice with Rosemary
Gamberi in salsa d'olio, limone e rosamarino

Red Bell Peppers Stuffed with Pine Nuts and Golden Raisins
Involtini di peperoni

Roasted Figs with Almonds and Chocolate
Fichi Mandorlati

Franco Ricatti is the owner of the restaurant Ristorante Bacco in Barletta, north of Bari on the Adriatic coast of Italy. He once said, wisely, "cooking in the style of Puglia is very easy because it is so simple." For example, the straightforward combination of potatoes, zucchini and pasta in this soup comes together beautifully, and the addition of extra-virgin olive oil, freshly ground black pepper and Parmigiano-Reggiano at the finale certainly reflect the clear, distinct Puglian flavors.

Wine Selection

A great deal of wine is grown in Apulia, but much of it goes north to be blended into the Piedmont, Tuscan and other wines. Instead, seek the Terradora Di Paolo wine, Fiano Di Avellino DOC from Campania (Naples), made of 100 percent Fiano grapes. This comes alive two years after harvest. It's a delightful wine with the shrimp dish.

Preparation Advice

1. The roasted figs and chocolate may be made a week ahead and stored in an airtight container. The stuffed peppers may be made ahead, in the morning of the day on which the meal is to be served.

2. Much of the shrimp dish may be made ahead by several hours.

3. The soup ingredients may be prepped well ahead but this soup is at its best when it is freshly made.

POTATO AND ZUCCHINI SOUP FROM FRANCO RICATTI

Zuppa di patate e zucchine alla pugliese
MAKES 6 SERVINGS

When I first described this soup to a good friend, the response was, "Potatoes, zucchini and water—where is the flavor?" I made the soup anyway because I had enjoyed it with Franco Ricatti, who at the time was in Rome, and I knew it would be delicious. My friend now claims it is one of her favorite soups. Again, sheer simplicity. The little bit of pasta is the binder and let me warn you not to overcook and disintegrate the potatoes or zucchini; they should be cooked to the point of perfection (tender and keeping their shapes) and when eaten as a soup, they will simply dissolve in your mouth.

This recipe makes more than enough for four persons; any leftovers are absolutely delicious reheated to lukewarm, as they like their soup in Italy.

4 cups water

Salt

6 medium potatoes, peeled and cut into
  ½-inch dice

6 small zucchini, scrubbed and cut into
  ½-inch dice

2 tablespoons plus 6 teaspoons extra-virgin
  olive oil

4 ounces dried vermicelli, broken into 2- to
  3-inch pieces

Freshly ground pepper

6 tablespoons freshly grated Parmesan cheese

1.   Bring the water to boil in a large soup pot over medium high heat. Add some salt and the potatoes. When boiling again, reduce the heat to a very slow but steady simmer, and cook, covered, for 5 minutes.

2.   Add the zucchini and return to a boil.

3.   Add 2 tablespoons olive oil and the pasta. Stir well, and cook, uncovered, until the pasta is al dente and the vegetables are tender, about 10 minutes.

4.   To serve, ladle the soup into warmed bowls, adding 1 teaspoon of the olive oil to each bowl along with freshly ground pepper and 1 tablespoon of the grated cheese.

SHRIMP IN OLIVE OIL AND LEMON JUICE WITH ROSEMARY

Gamberi in salsa d'olio, limone e rosamarino
MAKES 4 SERVINGS

Fresh lemon juice has the ability to quicken the intoxicating scent of rosemary on shrimp and some other fish. We all know what rosemary can do to lamb and other cuts of meat, but in this recipe the unusual touch is rosemary, with the help of lemon, on shrimp.

Salt

1 pound large shrimp (16 to 20 count)

½ cup extra-virgin olive oil

Juice of 1 lemon (about 3 tablespoons)

½ teaspoon finely chopped fresh rosemary

Freshly ground pepper

4 sprigs of rosemary, 3 or 4 inches long

1.   Bring water with some salt to boil in a large saucepan. Add the shrimp and cook until pink, 2 to 3 minutes after the water returns to a boil. Drain and rinse under cold water. Peel and devein the shrimp. Dry them well with paper towels and put them into a glass bowl to cool.

2.   Combine the oil, lemon juice, chopped rosemary and some salt and pepper. Mix well and pour over cooled shrimp. Allow to marinate for 20 to 30 minutes. Toss again.

3.   Place a rosemary sprig on each of four plates. Carefully arrange 4 or 5 shrimp on each plate, slightly overlapping the rosemary and with each shrimp hugging another, side by side. Spoon some of the dressing over the shrimp and serve immediately.

RED BELL PEPPERS STUFFED WITH PINE NUTS AND GOLDEN RAISINS

Involtini di peperoni
MAKES 4 SERVINGS

Roasted and peeled bell peppers, a mainstay in almost every Italian kitchen, is prepared in as many ways as there are cooks, as least as far as the embellishments go. The inspiration for this filling comes from a cousin who once had a restaurant in Caserta, near Naples. They can be made ahead and are delicious a day or two later, as long as they are brought to room temperature before serving.

2 large red bell peppers
½ cup freshly made bread crumbs (page 7)
4 anchovy fillets, minced
1 tablespoon capers, rinsed
¼ cup pine nuts
¼ cup golden raisins
2 tablespoons finely chopped fresh Italian parsley
Sea salt and freshly ground pepper
2 to 4 tablespoons extra-virgin olive oil

1. Broil or grill the red peppers until their skins blacken. Cool enough to handle. Remove charred skin, stems, ribs and seeds. Cut each pepper in half lengthwise.

2. Preheat the oven to 350F. Mix all the remaining ingredients except the olive oil. Add salt, if needed, and pepper. Add enough olive oil, by tablespoon, to moisten the mixture.

3. Divide the filling among the centers of each pepper half, and enclose the filling by raising the pepper sides to go over the filling. Carefully arrange the filled pepper halves in a pie dish or other a baking pan, drizzle a little oil over the peppers and bake for 30 minutes.

ROASTED FIGS WITH ALMONDS AND CHOCOLATE

Fichi Mandorlati
MAKES 25 PIECES

In Bari and Calabria, neighbors of Naples, desserts are associated with ancient traditions and contain many delicious ingredients, such as figs and honey, almonds and dried fruits, which are exported to places all over the world. Some people say the dried figs of Bari, packed in square straw boxes, are the best from anywhere. They are large, dark and moist, packed with a faint roasted flavor. Fennel seeds and almonds are added for additional flavor. Bay leaves are added to the boxes, also for flavor. Typical of these desserts is the one presented here, but only the best-quality figs should be used. These can be made several days ahead of the time of serving.

25 whole unblanched almonds
25 moist dried figs
½ cup diced candied peel
2 ounces bittersweet chocolate, broken into small pieces
2 tablespoons dried fennel seeds
⅔ cup unsweetened cocoa powder
⅔ cup confectioners' sugar
25 bay leaves

1. Preheat the oven to 350F. Bake the almonds for 12 minutes. Set aside.

2. Trim off any stalks on the figs and carefully cut the figs on one side to create a pocket. Stuff

each fig with a roasted almond, a couple of pieces of peel, 2 fennel seeds and a small piece of chocolate. Close the pocket by pressing it shut with your fingers. Transfer each fig to a baking sheet and bake until they darken a bit, about 15 minutes.

3. Meanwhile, combine the cocoa powder and confectioners' sugar in a shallow dish. As soon as the figs are removed from the oven, roll them in the cocoa mixture and place each fig on a bay leaf. Pack the figs with the bay leaves in an airtight container. Serve 2 or 3 per person and pass more of them if you wish. The figs will keep in an airtight container for a week.

NESTLED IN A SEA OF OLIVE TREES AT THE INN AT MONOPOLI, SOUTH OF BARI: MENU FOR 6

MENU

Marinated Cannellini Beans with Oregano and Crisp Salami
Cannellini con origano

Grilled Eel with Wine, Brandy and Thyme
Anguilla arrostita al timo (in gratella)

Zucchini Pudding
Budino di zucchine

Assorted Melon with Caprini Cheese
Melone e caprini

Il Melograno, now an outstanding inn with magnificent food, was a seventeeth-century fortified farmhouse, built originally as a defense against Saracen and Byzantine invaders. It is nestled in a sea of olive trees bent by breezes from the Adriatic, and gnarled by the passing centuries. *Melograno* means pomegranate. It's a great location from which to visit bustling markets in old cities, explore Byzantine ruins or baroque cathedrals, or drive leisurely through the countryside. Here is a menu inspired by the foods sampled in the area.

Wine Selection

Get a lovely white wine from Avellino (actually in Campania, but close enough to Apulia), such as Fiano di Avellina or a Taurasi. Or go for a 100 percent Greco di Tufo grape made into wine by the great producer Mastroberardino called Vignadangelo.

Preparation Advice

1. The bean dish may be made ahead by one day; crisp the salami at the last minute. The zucchini dish can be brought together ahead and baked an hour or so before mealtime. The melon can be prepped in the morning, covered and refrigerated until needed.

2. The fish can be marinated a couple of hours ahead, but they are best just off the grill.

MARINATED CANNELLINI BEANS WITH OREGANO AND CRISP SALAMI

Cannellini con origano
MAKES 6 SERVINGS

If you are in Italy in summer or fall, you will surely see all kinds of beans in their pods. But you will also see dried beans as you do in this country. When you buy them dried, always check the date of sale on the package; if dried beans are old, they're hard, shriveled and generally not good to look at (and this is after cooking them). I find canned cannellinis most acceptable (especially if you don't have time for the presoaking of dried beans); be sure to rinse them in a colander before using them.

2 (16-ounce) cans cannellini beans or
    1½ cups dried
Sea salt and freshly ground pepper
1 teaspoon finely chopped fresh oregano or
    ½ teaspoon dried
⅓ cup extra-virgin olive oil
½ teaspoon aged balsamic vinegar
6 very thin salami slices
3 small celery hearts, root ends trimmed, cut in
    halves lengthwise

1. If using canned beans, drain them well and put them in a bowl. (If using dried beans, put them in a bowl and soak them overnight in lukewarm water, or for at least 8 hours before cooking. Drain, put them in a saucepan with water to cover by several inches and bring the contents to a boil, covered. Reduce the heat, and simmer until the beans are done, 50 to 60 minutes. Drain the beans and transfer to a bowl. Dried beans can always be cooked a day ahead and refrigerated in the cooking liquid until ready for use.)

2. To the beans, add some salt and pepper; if using canned beans, you may not need to add any salt. Stir in the oregano, ¼ cup of the olive oil and the balsamic vinegar. Stir well and leave at room temperature for 1 hour, or longer in the refrigerator. (If refrigerated, the beans must be served at room temperature.)

3. To crisp the salami slices, arrange the slices on 3 layers of paper towels and microwave on high for 30 seconds, or put them on a baking pan and bake at 350F for 3 to 5 minutes, depending on thickness of the salami slices.

4. To serve, place 3 tablespoons of dressed beans in the center of a serving plate. Add a celery heart piece alongside the beans. Sprinkle the remaining olive oil over each serving, being sure to get some on the celery. Take a crisped salami slice and stick it upright into the beans.

GRILLED EEL WITH WINE, BRANDY AND THYME

Anguilla arrostita al timo (in gratella)
MAKES 6 SERVINGS

Italians treat eel as a delicacy and it is cooked all over Italy, especially in towns and villages along the hundreds of miles of coastline. It may be stewed, baked or grilled, or left in the sun to cook. In this part of Italy, townspeople enjoy the practice of cooking in ancient ways. Brindisi and Galipoli both compete for the most ancient fish chowders, Greek style. One ancient way to cook eels (only newborn tiny eels are used) is to put them in large basins of seawater, and leave them in the sun until all the water has evaporated. A dash of vinegar is added and an eel dish is ready. Mostly, it is complemented by a variety of herbs such as bay leaves, rosemary, sage or basil as in the following recipe. When grilled this way, the flesh is sweet and firm. Eel must be freshly killed and skinned at once, and a fishmonger will do this. In the United States, conger eel, also known as sea eel, is common on the Atlantic coast.

6 (3-inch-long) eel pieces (about 3 pounds)
1 cup dry white wine
3 tablespoons brandy
4 tablespoons extra-virgin olive oil
Juice of 1 lemon
1 tablespoon chopped fresh thyme or 1 teaspoon dried
Sea salt and freshly ground pepper
2 tablespoons chopped fresh basil or 1 tablespoon dried

1. Rinse and dry the eel pieces and place them in a glass or ceramic dish in one layer.

2. Combine the wine, brandy, 2 tablespoons of the oil, lemon juice, thyme and some salt and pepper. Mix well and pour over the fish. Marinate in the refrigerator for 2 hours; bring to room temperature, about 30 minutes before grilling.

3. Prepare a grill. Split each piece of eel lengthwise and pat the basil in between the halves. Thread on 3 skewers, and when the fire is ready, grill for 15 minutes, turning carefully and basting with the remaining oil. The eel is done when it turns white and a wooden skewer can be inserted with no resistance. Serve hot.

ZUCCHINI PUDDING

Budino di zucchine
MAKES 6 TO 8 SERVINGS

Puddings are quite popular everywhere in Italy, and zucchini lends itself well to this type of dish as it is somewhat bland (and surely inexpensive when compared to other foods) and picks up the flavor of other food easily—in this instance, cream, butter, basil and red peppers. As simple as this dish may be, the trick is to let the salted zucchini shavings stand in a colander for the required time, and being sure that most of the watery liquid is squeezed out of them. Once you prepare this dish, you will want to cook it again.

About 4 medium zucchini
Sea salt
½ large red bell pepper, trimmed and cut into small dice
¼ cup finely chopped fresh basil, plus 1 sprig for garnish
3 eggs, at room temperature
¼ cup all-purpose flour
2 tablespoons butter, melted
2 cups half-and-half

1. Wash the zucchini and cut off the ends, but do not peel. If the zucchini are small, grate the whole vegetable; if they are large, grate only the outside portion (cut them in half lengthwise, and remove the seeds). Grate the zucchini using the shredding side of a grater. There should be 2 cups. Transfer the grated zucchini to a colander, sprinkle lightly with some salt and let the liquid drain from the zucchini for 30 minutes. Press down on the gratings with your hands to extract as much liquid as possible. Transfer the zucchini to a bowl. Add the bell pepper and the basil.

2. Preheat the oven to 325F. Beat the eggs well, and stir them into the zucchini mixture. Add the flour and stir again. Add the butter and half-and-half. Pour this mixture into a buttered 1½-quart glass or ceramic baking dish, and place the baking dish into a larger pan of hot water, forming a water bath, or what the Italians call *a bagno-maria*.

3. Bake for 1 hour, until set. It will form a custard delicately flavored with fresh zucchini. Garnish with the basil sprig and serve from the baking dish within 10 minutes.

ASSORTED MELON WITH CAPRINI CHEESE

Melone e caprini
MAKES 6 SERVINGS

Caprini is a goat cheese from southern Italy. It does not travel well and will be difficult to find. However, it is found in bottles of flavored Italian olive oil (usually with herbs and chilies). If you have trouble finding it, try some fresh ricotta on the side of the melon slices. Here is a chance to have a fruit and cheese dessert.

    6 thin wedges cantaloupe, trimmed, seeds
        removed
    6 thin wedges honeydew melon, trimmed, seeds
        removed
    6 thin slices watermelon, trimmed, seeds removed
        and cut into 3-inch triangles
    Sea salt and freshly ground pepper
    6 small wedges caprini (goat cheese)
    ¼ cup finely chopped fresh mint
    12 to 18 small bread squares, toasted

1. Arrange the cantaloupe and honeydew melon, side by side, on a large, shallow dessert plate and place the watermelon triangles against them. Add some salt and pepper. Place the cheese to one side, but touching the melons.

2. Sprinkle the mint over the melons and pass a plate of crisped bread squares to be eaten with the cheese.

ALONG THE ADRIATIC, NEAR BRINDISI, IN THE VILLAGE OF ALBEROBELLO: MENU FOR 4

MENU

Peppers with Almonds, Basilicata Style
Mandorlata di peperoni

Lobster with Spicy Herbed Tomatoes
Aragosta fra diavolo

Baked Caramelized Onions
Cipolle al forno

Tangerine Sherbet with Lemon Liqueur
Sorbetto al mandarino con liquore di limone

A turn at Monopoli, twenty miles or so south of Bari, will lead you to the area of the *trulli* houses, stone buildings shaped into cones, usually whitewashed and topped with crosses. They are grouped together as farmhouses (and granaries), and single *trullos* as residences with cool interiors. There are tens of explanations as to why they were built. The one interesting and amusing explanation is that they could be disassembled in a hurry (they are built with no mortar) at tax time, thereby avoiding the taxes. Alberobello's main street is made up of *trulli* town houses of shops, hotels and even a church. The drive from here to Martina Franca, a charming wine and *trulli* town, and on to the Locorotundo is a reason to see the magnificent view of the Valle d'Istria. There is fine cooking in these towns, in homes and restaurants. The quality of olive oil compares favorably to those produced in Tuscany and Liguria; it is a bright golden color with streaks of green and an aroma of bitter almonds.

Wine Selection

A more expensive wine will be Campanaro Fiano di Acellino DOC from the Naples area, produced by Feudi di San Gregorio. If that is not available ask for the Greco di Tufo DOC, Vignadangelo, produced by Mastroberardino.

Preparation Advice

1. Make the dessert ahead by one week.

2. The peppers may be made one day ahead, the caramelized onions the morning of the meal.

3. This leaves the lobster for last-minute baking.

PEPPERS WITH ALMONDS, BASILICATA STYLE

Mandorlata di peperoni
MAKES 4 SERVINGS

This southern Italian pepper dish, because of the sugar and vinegar ingredients responsible for creating the *agrodolce* (sweet-sour) taste, gives credibility to the school of thought that the origins of Italian cooking are Greek and Roman. The foods of those days were salty, probably because of preservation needs, so in their cooking they resorted to disguising the saltiness by adding vinegar and wines, honey, dried fruit and so on. The *agrodolce* sauces are still popular in Italy, especially with venison, wild boar and hare, but also with vegetables, as is evident here.

> ½ cup golden raisins
> 6 bell peppers, 2 each red, yellow and green
> 2 tablespoons extra-virgin olive oil
> ½ cup slivered almonds
> ⅓ cup red wine vinegar
> 2 tablespoons sugar
> Sea salt and freshly ground pepper
> 2 tablespoons finely chopped fresh Italian
>   parsley

1. Put the raisins in warm water to cover and let steep for about 15 minutes. Drain well.

2. Rinse and dry the bell peppers. Remove the stems, ribs and seeds and slice them lengthwise into ½-inch strips. Set aside.

3. Heat the oil in a large skillet and add the bell peppers. Sauté them over the lowest heat possible, stirring frequently, for 20 minutes.

4. Add the raisins, almonds, vinegar and sugar. Stir to combine. Add some salt and pepper. Over very low heat, sauté the mixture, uncovered, for 20 minutes. The peppers should be very tender but should hold their shapes. This may be served warm or at room temperature. Sprinkle with the parsley before serving.

LOBSTER WITH SPICY HERBED TOMATOES

Aragosta fra diavolo
MAKES 4 SERVINGS

Italian lobsters have no claws and are different from Maine lobsters in other ways. The Italian ones are really spiny lobsters, more like those found on the Pacific Coast and in the Caribbean. From a basic cooking point of view, they can be treated alike. The Italian preparations are usually simple, some olive oil, lemon, herbs, salt and pepper. The preparation given here is quite simple also but cooking it *fra diavolo* means adding hot peppers, tomatoes and cheese.

> 2 (about 1½-pound) live lobsters
> 1 tablespoon each extra-virgin olive oil and butter
> 1 clove garlic, minced
> 2 large tomatoes, peeled, seeded and chopped
> 3 tablespoons chopped fresh Italian parsley
> 2 teaspoons finely chopped fresh oregano or
>   ½ teaspoon dried
> ¼ teaspoon red pepper flakes
> Sea salt and freshly ground pepper
> 2 tablespoons freshly grated Parmesan cheese

1. Put a lobster on a cutting board and plunge the tip of a large, sharp knife between the eyes (this kills the lobster instantly and humanely). Immediately, cut down sharply in the direction of the tail, splitting the whole lobster in half. With a paring knife, remove the intestinal tract; it looks like a thin vein running the length of the lobster. Also, remove the sandy sac just underneath the eyes. The coral is edible and delicious, so retain it for extra flavor. Repeat this procedure with the second lobster. Place them, cut side up, in a large baking dish. Set aside.

2. Preheat the oven to 350F. Heat the oil and butter in a skillet and sauté the garlic until it turns light brown, 1 to 2 minutes. Add the remaining ingredients through the cheese. Simmer, stirring occasionally, over low heat until blended into a thick sauce, about 15 minutes.

3. Pour the sauce over the lobster halves and bake until they are tender, about 20 minutes. Sprinkle with the Parmesan cheese and return to the oven for 2 or 3 minutes, just until the cheese melts. Serve right away.

BAKED CARAMELIZED ONIONS

Cipolle al forno
MAKES 4 SERVINGS

This is a prime example of the simplicity of Italian cooking, so easily duplicated in American kitchens. The onions, once cooked this way, will simply melt in your mouth.

> 4 medium onions, peeled
> 4 tablespoons extra-virgin olive oil
> Sea salt and freshly ground pepper
> 8 teaspoons dry bread crumbs,
>   unseasoned

1. Preheat the oven to 325F.

2. Cut each onion crosswise to make 8 halves. Using about 1 tablespoon of the oil, rub the halved onions all over and set them in an oiled shallow baking pan in a single layer, cut side up. Season liberally with salt and pepper.

3. Using half of the remaining oil, spoon some onto each half. Bake for 40 minutes. Remove from the oven and sprinkle 1 teaspoon of the bread crumbs over each onion half. Add more oil, and bake until caramelized, about 40 minutes. These should be served warm.

TANGERINE SHERBET WITH LEMON LIQUEUR

Sorbetto al mandarino con liquore di limone
MAKES 4 SERVINGS

A wonderful combination of citrus flavors. Most sherbets, when made ahead and frozen, become hard (almost too difficult to scoop). Be sure to remove from the freezer ten minutes or so before ready to serve.

> ½ cup water
> ¾ cup sugar
> 1 cup fresh orange juice
> 1 tablespoon fresh lemon juice
> 1 teaspoon grated tangerine zest (about 2 small tangerines)
> ¼ cup lemon liqueur, such as Ramo d'Oro
> 1 cup Asti Spumante

1. Stir together the water and sugar in a saucepan and bring to a boil over medium heat. Transfer to a bowl and cool.

2. Add all the remaining ingredients and mix well. Cover and refrigerate until chilled.

3. Pour into the container of an ice cream maker and follow the manufacturer's directions. When the sorbet has reached the desired consistency, transfer into freezer containers and freeze until needed.

IN TARANTO, ON THE INSIDE OF THE BOOT HEEL, ON THE IONIAN SEA: DINNER FOR 4

MENU

Baked Oysters, Taranto Style
Ostriche in forno, alla Tarantina

Grilled Red Pepper Shrimp
Gamberi piccanti alla griglia

Whipped Potatoes with Olive Oil
Patate schiacciate con olio di oliva

Zucchini in a Hot Sauce, Farm Style
Zucchine piccanti alla contadina

Blueberry Ice with Melon Ball Spears
Granita di mirtilli con palline di melone

Taranto has a great advantage over other tourist towns because seafood abounds, it's good and inexpensive. Spaghetti with clams and mussels cooked with basil and olive oil are treats in Taranto. Seafood is the specialty, such as mixed seafood pasta and tubetti pasta with mussels at the Trattoria Gatto Rosso, a well-known local eatery. A very old city (founded in the seventh century B.C.), it became one of the most important Magna Graecia cities. The Old Quarter, in need of considerable repair, is tied to the new town by a swing bridge. People go to Taranto to visit its famous National Museum, which shows Magna Graecia history better than anywhere else. But they also go for the seafood, and especially for oysters.

Wine Selection

Rosa del Golfo is a rosé wine made in Apulia. Mr. Calo, the owner of the vineyard is often called the king of *rosato*. It is a bright pink color with coral accents and an aroma of fresh berries.

Preparation Advice

1. The dessert may be made ahead by one week.

2. The potatoes and zucchini can be made early in the day of the meal.

3. The oyster and the shrimp preparations should be cooked shortly before mealtime.

BAKED OYSTERS, TARANTO STYLE

Ostriche in forno, alla Tarantina
MAKES 4 SERVINGS

The oldest oyster beds in the world are those of Taranto. The foot of Italy was colonized by the Greeks, who established the oyster beds, later taken over by the Roman Empire. They seem to be grown today as they were in ancient times. These are oysters shipped all over Italy for home and restaurant use, and as you may imagine, are prepared in a variety of ways. In Taranto, they are mainly eaten fresh with a squeeze of lemon juice.

But they also have a simple way to bake them, and here it is.

> 2 dozen fresh oysters
> ½ cup finely chopped fresh Italian parsley
> ½ cup freshly made bread crumbs (page 7)
> 2 cloves garlic, minced
> Freshly ground pepper
> Extra-virgin olive oil for sprinkling
> 2 lemons, cut in wedges, seeds removed

1. Shuck the oysters as described below. Arrange the half shells carefully (do not spill any of the juices) in one layer in one or two large baking pans.

2. Preheat the oven to 350F.

3. Sprinkle some of the parsley over each oyster. Combine the bread crumbs and the garlic. Mix well, and sprinkle over the oysters. Liberally sprinkle with pepper.

4. Carefully spoon about ¼ teaspoon olive oil into each shell. Bake for 10 to 12 minutes. Serve 6 per person with 2 or 3 lemon wedges.

Notabene:

Oysters should be tightly closed and odorless. Fresh oysters should be consumed as soon as possible after buying them. If you need to keep them a short while, store them in plastic bags in the refrigerator, making small openings in the bag (snip with a scissors after tying the bag) to let air inside.

HOW TO SHUCK OYSTERS

Hold each oyster in your hand, which should be protected by a thick kitchen towel. The flat side of the oyster should be up and the hinge side should face out. Put the tip of an oyster knife into the hinge; twist carefully to free the top shell. To help do this, run the knife along the underside of the top shell. This will cut the muscle. Do not cut the small muscle that holds the edible oyster to the bottom shell as it will cause the oyster to curl and lose its flavor. Discard the top shell.

Try to do this slowly and carefully to avoid losing the juices inside the shell.

GRILLED RED PEPPER SHRIMP

Gamberi piccanti alla griglia
MAKES 4 SERVINGS

A really delicious and easy dish, because it is prepared ahead and marinated, the grilling of the shrimp takes only a few minutes, and it is best to cook them just before you need them. It is always best to slightly undercook shrimp for they have a tendency to toughen if overcooked.

> 1½ pounds medium shrimp (about 24 count) in the shell
> 4 cloves garlic, minced
> 1 teaspoon salt
> 4 small, dried red pepper chilies, crushed
> 1 cup extra-virgin olive oil
> 3 lemons, cut into 8 wedges each
> 12 large bay leaves, halved, or 24 small bay leaves

1. Wash and dry the shrimp, leaving the shells and tails intact. Place in a large glass or ceramic bowl.

2. In a small bowl, combine the garlic, salt, chilies and ½ cup of the oil and mix well. Blend in the remaining oil and pour over the shrimp, turning to coat all sides. Marinate in the refriger-

ator for 4 hours; remove 1 hour before grilling. Drain, reserving the marinade.

3. Preheat a grill. Thread the lemon wedges, bay leaves and shrimp alternatively on four metal skewers.

4. When the fire is ready, grill the shrimp about 3 minutes on each side, brushing with the reserved marinade. Serve on the skewers. It is best to serve these directly from the grill.

WHIPPED POTATOES WITH OLIVE OIL

Patate schiacciate con olio di oliva
MAKES 4 SERVINGS

Do not mash these potatoes in a blender or food processor for they will get gummy. Americans add cream and butter; this Italian preparation adds good-quality olive oil and pecorino cheese with some cream. This can be made ahead, kept refrigerated, and then reheated in a warm oven.

> 3 pounds boiling potatoes, Yukon Gold preferred, scrubbed
> ¾ cup half-and-half
> ½ cup extra-virgin olive oil
> Sea salt and freshly ground pepper
> ¼ pound pecorino cheese

1. Boil the potatoes in a large pot up to 1 hour, or until tender. To test for doneness, pierce a potato with a wooden skewer. If it goes through easily, the potatoes are done; if it meets resistance, the potatoes need further cooking. Drain and set aside to cool slightly.

2. Peel the potatoes and return them to the pot in which they were cooked. Mash them with a potato masher, incorporating the half-and-half. Put over low heat to keep warm.

3. Stir in the oil, 1 tablespoon at a time, stirring until the oil is incorporated before adding more. Continue until all the oil is used. Season with some salt and pepper.

4. Using the large holes on a cheese grater, grate enough of the cheese to make ½ cup. Add half of this amount to the potatoes and stir until the cheese is melted. Keep the potatoes warm, and just before serving, add the remaining ¼ cup of the cheese to individual servings.

ZUCCHINI IN A HOT SAUCE, FARM STYLE

Zucchini piccante alla Contadina
MAKES 4 SERVINGS

It is unItalian to peel zucchini, so don't give in to this American aberration. The peel adds color to the dish, but also adds a more defined form to the vegetable. Wash the vegetable well and, if you wish, scrape only a few lengths of the skin, so the zucchini appears striped; otherwise leave completely unpeeled.

8 small zucchini, 1 × 5 inches
Sea salt
1 cup freshly made bread crumbs (page 7)
2 tablespoons red wine vinegar
6 tablespoons extra-virgin olive oil
2 anchovies, minced
1 tablespoon each capers, chives and finely
    chopped fresh Italian parsley
Pinch of red pepper flakes

1. Rinse the zucchini well and trim the ends. Leave them unpeeled except for any small blemish. Bring a pan of water to boil, add the whole zucchini and cook until tender, 10 to 15 minutes, depending on size. Add some salt to the water for the last 1 to 2 minutes of boiling. Drain and set aside.

2. Add the bread crumbs to a bowl and sprinkle with the vinegar. Toss lightly but well. Let stand for about 5 minutes. Add the olive oil, anchovies, capers, chives, parsley and red pepper flakes. Mix lightly but well. Taste for seasoning and add salt if needed. Serve the zucchini whole, two per person, with a spoonful of the sauce over the zucchini. The zucchini should be warm and the sauce at room temperature.

BLUEBERRY ICE WITH MELON BALL SPEARS

Granita di mirtilli con palline di melone
MAKES 4 SERVINGS

In addition to its beauty as a dessert, this blueberry ice and melon combination is delicious. All of it can be made ahead. Bring the ice out of the freezer 10 minutes or so before ready to serve, to soften it a little.

1½ cups water
1 cup plus 2 tablespoons sugar
1½ pints fresh blueberries, picked over, rinsed
    and drained
3 tablespoons fresh lemon juice

FOR THE MELON BALL SPEARS
20 melon balls (from cantaloupe, honeydew
    melon or any other melon of your choice)
¼ cup grappa

16 fresh blueberries

4 mint sprigs

1. Stir together the water and sugar in a saucepan and bring to a boil over medium heat. Reduce the heat and simmer until the sugar is dissolved. Transfer to a nonaluminum bowl and set over ice water to chill for 1 hour, stirring occasionally.

2. Meanwhile, put the blueberries through a food mill, in batches. Add the puree to the cooled syrup. Stir in the lemon juice. Cover with plastic wrap and refrigerate for several hours.

3. Freeze in an ice cream maker according to manufacturer's instructions. When the ice cream has reached the desired consistency, transfer to a freezer container and freeze until ready to serve. Remove from the freezer about 30 minutes before serving to make scooping easier.

4. Marinate the melon balls in the grappa for about 30 minutes. Drain. Thread on 4 long bamboo skewers alternating melon balls and blueberries, using 5 melon balls and 4 blueberries on each.

5. To serve, place a scoop of the ice on each plate and lay a melon ball spear alongside. Garnish with a mint sprig.

ONE-DISH MEALS

THREE PIZZAS:

Sweet Pepper Pizza with Ricotta Salata
Pizza con peperoni e ricotta salata

Broccoli Rabe and Goat Cheese Pizza
Pizza con broccoli rapa e formaggio di capra

Artichoke, Mortadella and Fontina Pizza
Pizza con carciofi, mortadella e fontina

Pizza reached the height of its popularity during the *Borboni* (Bourbon) rule in the Kingdom of the Two Sicilies, of which Naples was the capital. It was the food of the *lazzeroni* (the people). Pizza is a simple food in that it has no mystical or religious meaning as do many other Italian foods. It does not represent money, power or fertility. It is the ultimate fast food, ancient for sure, but with such appeal in modern times. It has grown in popularity outside Naples and Italy for these reasons and also because anyone can add anything to it, once the dough is made. No other food is so egalitarian.

Making and serving a pizza can seem like an easy task and it is, but there are some preparation steps to pay attention to. For example, to achieve a crisp-cooked pizza, it is best to use a pizza stone and pizza paddle. They are available in shops that sell kitchen equipment. See Sources (page 269). In adding toppings to the dough, be sure liquids and juices have been strained out. For example, if using ricotta or fresh mozzarella cheese, put them in a colander lined with cheesecloth and let them drain for 30 minutes to one hour before using. If applying tomato sauce, use just a thin coating of it on the dough and always brush some oil on the top of the dough before adding anything else. Pizza should be eaten as it comes out of the oven (after a few minutes' rest), and the best way to cut it is with a pizza wheel. If the pizza has to be reheated, put some slices on the pizza stone, which has been preheated in the oven at a temperature of 400F. Do not cover it as it will become mushy.

PIZZA DOUGH

Impasto per Pizza
MAKES 1 (14- TO 15-INCH) PIZZA

If a pizza dough fails, it is more likely because the water added was too hot. It is better to err on the cool side as kneading the dough will help it rise later. Also, kneading the dough should be thorough. In other words, knead the dough until it is smooth and satiny. The dough, while kneading, needs to rest every once in awhile, so knead and rest, knead and rest.

> 3 cups unbleached all-purpose flour
> 1 scant tablespoon sea salt
> 1 tablespoon sugar
> 1 (¼-ounce) envelope quick-rising yeast
> 1¼ cups lukewarm water, no warmer than 105F
> 2 tablespoons Garlic-Flavored Oil (page 226)
> Cornmeal

To make the dough in the food processor:

1. Put the flour, salt, sugar and yeast in the bowl of the processor. Pulse to a count of 4.

2. Combine the water and the oil and pour it into the bowl through the feed tube. Stop as soon as a ball of dough is formed. Let the dough rest for 2 minutes.

3. Process the dough for a total of 1 minute, but stopping the machine every 15 seconds for a few seconds. (This 1 minute of processing takes the place of manually kneading the dough).

4. Turn the dough out on a lightly floured surface and form a ball. Put the dough into a lightly oiled bowl. Turn the dough over to coat it, cover

with with a moist cloth kitchen towel and let it rise in a warm, draft-free place for 40 to 60 minutes, until double in size. To test for rising, put two fingers into the dough; if the indentations remain, the dough is properly risen. If the indentations disappear, the dough needs more time to rise properly.

5. Turn out the dough, form it quickly into a ball, and return it to the bowl and let rise again until double in size (this is important, do not eliminate this step).

6. Turn the dough out into a 14- to 15-inch pizza pan with some cornmeal to loosely cover the bottom, and use your hands and fingers to fit the dough into the pan. If properly risen, it will stretch into place easily. If the dough resists, let it rest for 1 or 2 minutes and continue fitting it into the pan.

To make the dough by hand:

1. Combine the dry ingredients in a mixing bowl, add the water and oil and mix with a wooden spoon. When it becomes difficult to move the spoon, start kneading with your floured hands on a lightly floured surface.

2. Knead for 5 minutes, rest for 2 minutes, knead for 5 minutes and rest for 2 minutes until a smooth, satiny dough is achieved. Let rise and shape as above.

GARLIC-FLAVORED OIL

Olio all'aglio
MAKES 1 CUP

Minced garlic, or even thinly sliced garlic put on top of the pizza before baking will usually darken or burn and become bitter. Some pizza makers like to add finely minced fresh garlic to the topping of a pizza after it has come out of the oven but raw garlic dominates the other flavors in the topping, and will "burn" the inside of one's mouth. The best way to get a good garlic flavor is by adding some drops of garlic-flavored oil to the topping.

> 15 large cloves garlic, peeled
> 1 cup extra-virgin olive oil

1.   Add the garlic and oil to a small saucepan. Over very low heat, cook at the lowest simmer possible until the garlic turns golden; this could take up to 20 minutes. If not ready to use, cool and then put into a small jar just large enough to hold the garlic and oil and refrigerate. If ready to use, drain and use the oil. If refrigerated, the oil must always be brought to room temperature.

SWEET PEPPER PIZZA WITH RICOTTA SALATA

Pizza con peperoni e ricotta salata
MAKES 4 SERVINGS

Just add a fresh green salad with your favorite salad dressing.

> 2 tablespoons extra-virgin olive oil
> 1 red and 1 yellow or orange bell pepper, cored, seeded, ribs removed and cut into thinnest slivers possible
> ¼ pound grated ricotta salata
> 1 tablespoon finely chopped fresh oregano (or 1 teaspoon dried, crushed
> 1 tablespoon chopped fresh Italian parsley
> 1 tablespoon chopped fresh chives
> About 2 tablespoons Garlic-Flavored Oil (above)
> 1 (14- to 15-inch) pizza dough (page 225), ready to receive the topping
> Freshly ground pepper

1.   Heat the olive oil in a large skillet over low heat and add the bell peppers. Toss lightly but well. Cover, and gently cook until the peppers become soft, about 15 minutes.

2.   In a small bowl, combine the grated cheese and herbs, and toss lightly but well.

3.   Preheat the oven to 450F. Brush some of the Garlic-Flavored Oil over the dough. Arrange the peppers on top, covering the pizza, and sprinkle with the herb-flavored cheese. Spoon 1 table-spoon of the Garlic-Flavored Oil over the topping. Liberally sprinkle with pepper.

4.   Bake until golden and crisp, about 15 minutes. Cut into wedges and serve hot.

BROCCOLI RABE AND GOAT CHEESE PIZZA

Pizza con broccoli rapa e formaggio di capra
MAKES 4 SERVINGS

This is a favorite of mine. The combination of flavors is divine. The proper way to prepare broccoli rabe is described on page 34; please take a minute to read this.

¼ pound goat cheese, crumbled
¼ pound mozzarella cheese, cut into smallest dice or grated through the large teeth of a cheese grater
1 tablespoon finely chopped fresh rosemary
Freshly ground pepper
About 2 tablespoons Garlic-Flavored Oil (page 226)
1 (14 to 15-inch) pizza dough (page 225), ready to receive topping
1 bunch broccoli rabe, trimmed, steamed, and cut into ½-inch pieces, including stalks, drained and dried
Pinches of red pepper flakes (optional)

1. Combine the two cheeses, the herbs and a liberal amount of pepper. Toss lightly but well. Set aside.

2. Brush some of the Garlic-Flavored Oil over the pizza dough and carefully arrange the cooked and cut broccoli rabe over the surface of the pizza.

3. Preheat the oven to 450F. Sprinkle the cheese over the broccoli and drizzle with more Garlic-Flavored Oil. Add the red pepper flakes, if you wish. Bake until golden and crisp, about 15 minutes. Cut into wedges and serve hot.

ARTICHOKE, MORTADELLA AND FONTINA PIZZA

Pizza con carciofi, mortadella e fontina
MAKES 4 SERVINGS

Canned artichokes work well here, and it is not necessary to buy those packed in olive oil. If they are packed in water, rinse them several times to wash away the saltiness, and dry them well before combining with the other topping ingredients. If they are packed in oil, simply drain them well; do not rinse them.

1 (13.75-ounce) can artichoke hearts, finely chopped
¼ pound thinly sliced mortadella, finely chopped
½ cup finely shredded fontina cheese
2 tablespoons Garlic-Flavored Oil (page 226)
1 teaspoon sea salt and freshly ground pepper
1 (14- to 15-inch) pizza dough (page 225), ready to receive the topping

1. Preheat the oven to 450F.

2. Combine all the ingredients, except the dough, and spread the topping over the pizza dough.

3. Bake until golden and crisp, about 15 minutes. Cut into wedges and serve hot.

FRESH ANGEL HAIR PASTA IN CUSTARD MOLD FOR LUNCH

Sformato di pasta in besciamella
MAKES 8 SERVINGS

This is a delightful preparation; it is tasty, easy to prepare and serve. Just add a salad of asparagus, green beans or a variety of green lettuces with sliced plum tomatoes in wine vinegar and extra-virgin olive oil.

- 1½ cups fresh ricotta cheese
- 3 large eggs, beaten
- 3 tablespoons finely chopped chives, plus extra for garnish
- 1 teaspoon finely chopped fresh rosemary
- 1½ cups milk
- Pinch red pepper flakes
- Sea salt
- 6 ounces fresh angel hair pasta (if nested, use 3 of them)
- 4 tablespoons butter
- Freshly ground pepper

1. Preheat the oven to 350F. Mix the ricotta, eggs, chives, rosemary, milk, red pepper flakes and some salt in a large bowl. Combine well and set aside.

2. Cook the pasta in boiling salted water until al dente. (Fresh pasta cooks in less time than dried, so this should take about 3 minutes.) Drain well and return the pasta to the saucepan in which it was cooked. Add 3 tablespoons of the butter and toss to coat. Transfer the pasta to a well-buttered 1½-quart baking dish.

3. Cover the cooked pasta with the ricotta mixture, season with pepper and dot with the remaining 1 tablespoon butter. Bake for 1¼ hours. Remove from the oven and let cool for 10 to 15 minutes. Loosen the edges with a small knife and cut into squares and serve. Sprinkle some more chopped chives over each serving.

MOZZARELLA MEAT LOAF

Polpettone di mozzarella
MAKES 8 SERVINGS

This is a moist, delicious meat loaf that can be served in many ways. It is an ideal one-dish meal in that it can be served warm or cold, in slices, with a composed green salad (include some cooked broccoli). Slice it and make sandwiches of it between thin slices of Italian bread, or use it to top a bruschetta and serve it with a warmed tomato sauce.

- 2 pounds ground beef chuck
- 2 links Italian sausage, casings removed
- 2 eggs, beaten lightly
- 2 small onions, peeled, finely chopped
- 2 tablespoons finely chopped fresh Italian parsley
- 1 clove garlic, minced
- ½ cup grated pecorino cheese
- 2 cups ¼-inch cubes fresh mozzarella
- 5 slices Italian bread, soaked in ¾ cup milk, squeezed dry
- ¼ cup chopped canned tomatoes
- Sea salt and freshly ground pepper

1. Preheat the oven to 350F. Combine the ground chuck with the sausage in a large bowl. Add the eggs, onions, parsley, garlic, pecorino and mozzarella cheeses, bread and the tomatoes.

Add a generous sprinkle of salt and pepper. With splayed fingers, toss the mixture lightly but blending well.

2. Transfer the mixture to a flat surface and with your hands, shape it into a loaf (like a long loaf of Italian bread) and put it on an oiled baking sheet with a rim (such as a jelly roll pan to keep the meat juices from overflowing).

3. Bake for 1½ hours. Remove from the oven and allow to cool for about 10 minutes before slicing, or allow it to cool completely if serving it cold.

IX

THE DEEP SOUTH OF THE MAINLAND

BASILICATA AND CALABRIA; SARDINIA

AND THE PORT CITIES OF SICILY

BASILICATA AND CALABRIA

Calabria is the toe of the Italian boot and probably the most Greek Italian area; there are more Greek ruins there than elsewhere in Italy except for Sicily. In spite of the Greek influence on Sicily, it was the Arabs who left a greater impression. The Sicilian kitchen is essentially Saracen. Sicily excels with crops of lemons, oranges, tangerines, figs, olives and olive oil, almonds, cauliflower (purple), wheat (the granary of Italy) and honey. It sends its first vegetables to the north in spring. Seafood is everywhere: *pasta con sarde* (with sardines), stuffed sardines, Palermo and Catania style, *l'aragosta* (lobster), *triglia al cartoccio* (red mullet in paper), *calamari ripieni* (stuffed squid), *tonno* and *pesce spada* (tuna and swordfish) *infornato* (oven-baked), along with caponata, cauliflower, fennel and many fried vegetables and sweet desserts.

Calabria is a region of many mountains and almost no roads until the relatively new superhighways were built. For the innocent beholder, it would seem that Italian civilization ended at Naples. This can't be so, because the first colonies founded by the Greeks in the eighteenth century B.C. were where present Calabria is situated. Cities, such as Sybaris, had a great wealth and a resplendent lifestyle (thus the derivation of the word *sybarite*). Calabria was quite Greek, even today, some Greek words are in the dialect spoken in Reggio-Calabria and the swordfish fishing techniques are about the same as those used by the ancient Greeks.

In the third century B.C. the Romans took over, and after that, the Lombards, Saracens, Byzantines and the Normans, when finally in 1860, the area became part of unified Italy.

In spite of the mountains, there are numerous fruit-bearing trees along the coastal plains, olive trees, bearing for centuries in the seaside resort of Gioia Tauro (Reggio-Calabria has second place in all of Italy for olive oil production, and grows every known citrus fruit). Vegetables take a key place in the cuisine there, as does fish; tuna is caught in many Calabrian ports and one of them, Bagnara, specializes in swordfish.

It was difficult for the Greeks and other invaders to leave a strong imprint on Basilicata, in spite of its two small coastlines, because of the mountains. It was off the beaten path then, and still is today. Waverly Root reported that tribes of the mountain region of central Italy moved into this area before either the Greeks or Romans.

Olive oil is an important product here as are oven-dried olives, citrus fruits and most of all, their preserved meats, *lucanica* or *luganega*, and

soppressata pork sausage (flavored with ginger), and the highly smoked sausage, *capocollo*. Their cheeses are provolone, caciocavallo, mozzarella, cream and cottage cheeses, and a pecorino cheese made with sheep and goat milk. All of these foods are combined with pasta. The food is hot here because of the addition of ginger and tiny, hot red pimientos. You'll find salt cod with hot peppers, oven-baked trout with oil and parsley or cooked in bouillon and sprinkled with olive oil and lemon juice. Pastas are similar to those in Apulia and include *panzerotti,* ravioli filled with ricotta.

LUNCH FOR 4 WITH NICOLA BELMONTE, AN ITALIAN-AMERICAN IN RUOTI, A SUBURB OF POTENZA, IN THE SOUTH OF ITALY

MENU

Grilled Peppers in Anchovy Sauce with Roasted Olives
Peperoni alla griglia con salsa all'acciuga

Eggs in Purgatory with Grilled Sausages
Uova in purgatorio e salsicce arrostite

Fried Zucchini Slices
Zucchine in padella

Chocolate Soufflé with Fig Preserves
Budino di cioccolato con marmellata di fichi

"Nick", as I called him, worked in the United States for about twenty years and returned to his birthplace to spend the rest of his life. Ruoti is a small village where the streets are still of cobblestone. It is a place where time has stood still. When I first entered his home, women, clad in black, were working in the courtyard putting new raffia on the seat of an antique chair. This is the area of *mezzogiorno,* part of which was called Lucania by Mussolini and now called Basilicata. Different peoples invaded this area over hundreds of years and perhaps that is why the men of Lucania built their villages on high ground. In this town, as in many others around it, the main event of the year is the killing of the pig. Ancient Romans knew and appreciated the local sausage, which Cicero called *lucanica.* This sausage is known throughout Italy, and in the Veneto and Lombardy, it is still called *luganega.* The pork in the sausage is spiced with chili peppers and it's used in probably more than half of the dishes made in the area. This meal is simple but as tasty as it can be. The food is typical to the area, but Nick did confess that the dessert was inspired by one he ate at the Hotel Caruso-Belvedere in the not-so-distant town of Ravello, on the Amalfi coast.

Wine Selection

In this area, near the extinct volcano of Vulture, a red wine is made called Agliatico. It is a fairly heavy wine with a high alcoholic content, but it is good with spicy and grilled or broiled foods. It is available in the United States.

Preparation Advice

1. The grilled pepper dish may be made ahead, refrigerated and then reheated.

2. The tomato sauce may be made ahead by a day, refrigerated, and then reheated before adding the eggs.

3. The zucchini may be made a little ahead but shouldn't sit around longer than a half hour.

4. It is best to make the dessert shortly before mealtime.

GRILLED PEPPERS IN ANCHOVY SAUCE WITH ROASTED OLIVES

Peperoni alla griglia con salsa all'acciuga
MAKES 4 SERVINGS

In Ischia, an island in the Bay of Naples, a well-known fish dish is *alici all'ischiana* (anchovies, Ischia style). Fresh anchovies are sprinkled with olive oil, fresh lemon juice and marjoram and then baked. Anchovies in Apulia appear in tart form with bread crumbs, parsley and olive oil. Anchovies are appreciated in the north of Italy, especially in Liguria, where they stuff the little fish with bread moistened in milk, cheese, eggs, olive oil and herbs and baked. At times, they deep-fry the stuffed anchovies after dipping them in egg and bread crumbs. Other times, they don't stuff them at all, they are scaled, beheaded, their tails and fins cut off and just deep-fried. Many Americans are not as enthusiastic about anchovies as their Italian friends. Here is a good way to get started.

FOR THE BELL PEPPERS
2 bell peppers, preferably red and
    yellow
½ of a 2-ounce can of anchovy fillets,
    drained
2 cloves garlic
2 tablespoons chopped mixed fresh herbs:
    oregano, basil and chives
4 tablespoons extra-virgin olive oil
Freshly ground black pepper

FOR THE OLIVES
½ pound Gaeta olives
2 cloves garlic, sliced
2 small sprigs fresh rosemary
¼ cup dry white wine
Pinch of red pepper flakes

1. *To prepare the bell peppers:* Grill or roast the peppers as directed on page 258. Let cool. Peel and remove the seeds. Cut the peppers into long strips about 1 inch wide. Refrigerate until ready to use, but bring to room temperature before serving.

2. Combine the anchovies, garlic, herbs and oil in the bowl of a food processor and blend well. Arrange the peppers on individual plates, and spoon some of the sauce over them. Sprinkle with black pepper. These may remain at room temperature for about 30 minutes.

3. *To prepare the olives:* Preheat the oven to 400F. Place the olives in a small ceramic baking pan large enough to hold them in one layer. Add the remaining ingredients and bake for 15 minutes. Cool before serving.

4. Add 3 or 4 olives to each plate alongside the bell peppers. Put remaining olives in a jar with a cover and refrigerate for another use, but always bring to room temperature before serving.

EGGS IN PURGATORY WITH GRILLED SAUSAGES

Uova in purgatorio e salsicce arrostite
MAKES 4 SERVINGS

This is a simple, peasant type dish that is easy to prepare. Its roots are from southern Italy. The sausage used for this dish is traditionally called *luganega*; it is long and thin and made of pure pork. If you cannot find this type of sausage, a perfectly acceptable substitute is link-style Italian sausage.

1½ pounds *luganega* or 8 links Italian pork
     sausage
2 tablespoons extra-virgin olive oil
½ cup finely chopped onion
¼ cup finely chopped green bell pepper
2 tablespoons chopped fresh Italian parsley
2 cloves garlic, minced
1 (16-ounce) can Italian plum tomatoes, chopped
Sea salt and freshly ground pepper
4 eggs, at room temperature
4 large slices bruschetta (page 6)

1. If using the *luganega*, cut the long, thin sausage into 4 pieces, about 6 inches each and form each piece into a coil. Secure with toothpicks that have been soaked in water for 20 to 30 minutes. Set aside. Preheat a grill or broiler.

2. Heat the oil in a large skillet and sauté the onion and bell pepper until softened, 5 minutes. Add the parsley and garlic and sauté for 2 minutes.

3. Add the tomatoes, and season with some salt and pepper. Bring the mixture to a boil, reduce the heat and simmer for 15 minutes.

4. While the tomatoes are simmering, grill or broil the coils of sausage for about 5 minutes per side, or until well cooked.

5. Break the eggs, one at a time, into a saucer and slide them into the tomato mixture. Increase the heat slightly, cover the skillet and poach the eggs until the whites are formed and the centers are semihard. If you wish, cook the eggs longer to a more solid state.

6. To serve, place a bruschetta in a large luncheon plate, and spoon an egg with some of the sauce onto each piece, adding more of the sauce to the side of the eggs. Add a coil of cooked sausage to each plate.

FRIED ZUCCHINI SLICES

Zucchine in padella
MAKES 4 SERVINGS

In padella (cooked in the skillet) is a popular way to cook many things in Italy, especially vegetables; zucchini are a favorite cooked this way. Be sure to dry them well (use paper or cloth towels) after they are sliced; zucchini are so filled with water that you see the liquid even as they are sliced and if they are not dried well, they will not fry well. As an extra touch, you can add a few drops of quality balsamic vinegar to the slices after they are salted and fried.

> 4 small zucchini (about 1 pound)
> 1/2 cup all-purpose flour
> 4 tablespoons extra-virgin olive oil
> Sea salt

1. Wash the zucchini and trim the ends. Slice into 1/4-inch rounds. Dry them well.

2. Dredge them with the flour, removing excess.

3. Heat the oil in a skillet, and sauté the zucchini on both sides, leaving plenty of space between each slice. Brown them lightly and transfer with a slotted spoon to paper towels to drain. Sauté until all the slices are done. Salt the slices lightly before serving.

CHOCOLATE SOUFFLÉ WITH FIG PRESERVES

Budino di cioccolato con marmellata di fichi
MAKES 4 SERVINGS

This "soufflé" is baked in a shallow dish rather than the traditional deep mold. This is a bit of magic, and is a delightful dessert. Different jams and preserves may be used, although in this part of Italy, figs are preferred. Be careful and follow the directions when beating the egg yolks and whites.

> 1 to 2 tablespoons butter, at room temperature
> 4 eggs, separated, at room temperature
> 1/4 cup sugar
> 1/4 cup Dutch process cocoa powder
> 2 tablespoons orange liqueur
> 8 tablespoons fig preserves
> 1 tablespoon confectioners' sugar

1. Position the baking rack in the upper third of the oven and preheat to 375F. Butter a 9 × 14 × 2-inch glass oval gratin or baking dish (which may also be metal or enamel).

2. Beat the egg yolks in a large bowl of an electric mixer until pale yellow and slowly dissolving ribbons form when the beaters are lifted, 6 to 8 minutes. Beat the egg whites in another bowl until soft peaks form. Slowly beat in the sugar, about 1 tablespoon at a time. Add the cocoa powder to the egg whites, about 1 tablespoon at a time, and beat until stiff but not dry. Gently fold the egg yolks into the egg white mixture, then fold in the liqueur.

3. Spoon the fig preserves into the prepared baking dish in mounds, spacing evenly. Pour the egg mixture over and smooth with a spatula. Bake until the "soufflé" is puffy, about 15 minutes.

4. Sprinkle with confectioners' sugar and serve immediately, including two portions of preserves with each serving.

LUNCH FOR 4 IN POTENZA WITH PEPPERONCINI AND GINGER

MENU

Pasta with Ginger and Garlic
Pasta allo zenzero e aglio

Chicory Salad Mimosa
Mimosa di cicoria

Sliced Oranges with Marsala
Fette di arance al Marsala

Enriched and Crisped Vanilla-Almond Cookies
Bocconcini alle mandorle

Potenza is in Basilicata, a southern Italian province between Apulia and Calabria. Much of the region is barren, steep mountain land, where in the past, feudalism and excessive taxation impacted the population. The style of cooking there is one of making the most of humble ingredients. This is done with the help of hot peppers, especially pepperoncini (chili peppers) and with ginger, a legacy of the Saracens who formerly invaded and occupied the area. The main part of this lunch is a pasta dish with an Asian accent. My father cooked it religiously and swore it was an old ancestral recipe from Potenza, Italy, but I often accused him of inventing it, for he was born on Mott Street in New York City, a street that quietly "divided" Little Italy from Chinatown. My father's youth was spent in Italy and my research leads me to concur with him in that ginger is used in southern Italian cooking. Waverly Root's *Herbs and Spices, The Pursuit of Flavor,* (McGraw-Hill, 1980), says "Almost all of the dishes of Basilicata are hot with pepper, and ginger is so ubiquitous in Calabria that its presence is taken for granted even when it is not named. A strong dish there is understood as one dominated by ginger." A preparation also appears in Umbria—spaghetti with olive oil, garlic and ginger—strange as this may seem.

This is a simple menu and easy to prepare. The pasta, salad and fruit course are typical of the region for they depend on simple and affordable ingredients. Times seem to have changed in many villages and towns of the *mezzogiorno* area, and the area is beginning to open up to tourism largely because of agritourism and the willingness of northern capital to invest in the south. Butter, as a rule, is not a common ingredient in the south except one will find its increased use in the many fancy pastry shops, *I pasticcerie,* so I have taken the liberty of adding very rich, buttery almond cookies.

Wine Selection

Use a Calabrian red wine such as Ciro, which has been made there since ancient Greek times. It is said that this is the wine given to returning atheletes from the Olympic Games. There is also a white Ciro, made from the Greco Biano grape, grown "ad alberello," as a little tree, and is one of the best table wines of the region, with a marked bouquet, and a full, flowery, yet dry taste. There is also a Chardonnay by Planeta (Sicilia IGT).

Preparation Advice

1. The pasta is so simple, it can be prepared before serving. Be sure to have all the ingredients set aside, ready to be used as needed.

2. The lettuce greens may be trimmed, washed and dried and refrigerated in a plastic bag. The eggs may be cooked ahead and set aside. The dressing can be made ahead and set aside until ready to use.

3. The oranges may be made ahead by several hours. The cookies may be made early in the day to serve later, or the day before, cooled and packed in an airtight container.

PASTA WITH GINGER AND GARLIC

Pasta allo zenzero e aglio
MAKES 4 SERVINGS

Ginger and garlic suit each other as bacon and eggs. I have substituted candied ginger for the fresh ginger and get good results. This dish is a conversation piece. It is important to "marry" the sauce and the cooked pasta; you do this by keeping both over heat for 2 or 3 minutes, tossing all the time.

> ½ cup extra-virgin olive oil
> ½ cup finely diced carrot
> 1 tablespoon minced fresh garlic
> 2 tablespoons finely chopped fresh ginger
> 2 tablespoons finely chopped fresh scallions
> 1 teaspoon dried oregano, crushed

> ¼ to ½ teaspoon dried red pepper flakes
> ½ cup dry vermouth
> Sea salt
> 1 cup water
> 1 pound pasta, spaghettini, vermicelli or spaghetti
> 4 tablespoons butter
> ¾ cup freshly grated Romano cheese

1. Heat water in a large saucepan for the pasta. Meanwhile, heat the oil in a skillet and add the carrot. Cook for 3 minutes, stirring occasionally. Add the garlic, ginger, scallions, oregano, red pepper flakes and vermouth. Add some salt, if you wish. Cook for 5 minutes. Add the 1 cup water to thin the sauce, bring to a boil, reduce the heat and simmer for about 10 minutes.

2. Cook the pasta in salted, boiling water until it is al dente. Drain the pasta, return it to the pan in which it was cooked, add the butter and stir. Add three-fourths of the sauce and toss again. Serve in warm plates or bowls, adding another 1 tablespoon of the sauce to the top of each serving. Pass the cheese separately.

CHICORY SALAD MIMOSA

Mimosa di cicoria
MAKES 4 SERVINGS

Chicory is also known as curly endive. The flavor is slightly bitter. The head forms a loose bunch of ragged-edged leaves on long stems. The outer leaves are deep green whereas the leaves in the center are yellow and milder tasting. Use only the center leaves for this salad. If you can't find chicory, use arugula.

> 2 heads chicory, outer leaves removed for another use

2 tablespoons extra-virgin olive oil

2 tablespoons fresh lemon juice
   (½ lemon)

1 clove garlic, minced

Sea salt and freshly ground pepper

2 hard-cooked eggs

1. Separate, wash and dry the inner chicory leaves and put into a bowl. Add the oil, lemon juice, garlic and some salt and pepper. Toss the salad.

2. Shell the eggs and discard the whites. Mash the yolks finely and sprinkle over the salad. Serve right away.

SLICED ORANGES WITH MARSALA

Fette di arance al Marsala
MAKES 4 SERVINGS

Marsala is an important dessert wine with a particular virtue; it does not deteriorate after the bottle has been opened, so that one can be sure in any Italian cafe, restaurant or home of having a glass of Marsala in decent condition. Marsala is Sicily's most famous wine. Like sherry and port, it is a fortified wine and it bears some resemblance to Madeira in that one of its constituent parts is heated. Virtually all the production of Marsala is in the hands of big companies, of which Florio is probably the most distinguished Italian producer. All bottles of the real thing bear a numbered neck-label showing the outline of the Island of Sicily in red.

4 to 6 large eating oranges

⅓ cup Marsala wine

2 tablespoons sugar

8 small fresh mint leaves

1. Peel the oranges and remove all the white pith. Thinly slice in rounds and discard any seeds. Arrange in a large dish, preferably a platter with a little depth to hold the wine.

2. Sprinkle first the Marsala, then the sugar, over the oranges. Allow to macerate for several hours at room temperature. Just before serving, garnish with the mint leaves.

ENRICHED AND CRISPED VANILLA-ALMOND COOKIES

Bocconcini alle mandorle
MAKES ABOUT 80 COOKIES

There are probably more cookies made with almonds in Italy than any other one ingredient; these cookies explain why. They are sort of like American "icebox" cookies as the ingredients can be pulled together, rolled as in the directions, wrapped and stored in the refrigerator until ready to be sliced and baked.

½ pound blanched almonds

½ pound butter, at room temperature

1 cup sugar

2 large eggs, room temperature

½ teaspoon pure vanilla

2½ cups all-purpose flour

1. Put the almonds in the bowl of a food processor and process until finely chopped. If the food processor is small, chop the almonds in batches. Do not overprocess. Set aside.

2. Cream the butter and add the sugar by tablespoons. It is best to do this in an electric mixer with a paddle; if not, do this by hand with a wooden spoon.

3. Add the remaining ingredients and form a dough. Divide the dough in half and roll each into 2-inch-thick logs. Wrap them carefully in waxed paper and refrigerate them overnight, or 2 nights if you wish.

4. Liberally butter 2 large baking sheets. If you use both logs of cookie dough, you will have to repeat this twice. If you decide to bake only once, keep the unused dough in the refrigerator for a day or two or freeze. Before baking, preheat the oven to 350F. Remove the dough logs from the refrigerator and slice as thinly as possible and place the slices on cookie sheets leaving a 1-inch space between them. Bake until edges crisp, 12 to 15 minutes, depending on thickness of the cookies.

ALONG THE CALABRIAN COAST, WAITING FOR A GREEK GALLEY TO APPEAR OVER THE HORIZON: MENU FOR 4

MENU

Calabrian Onion Soup with Potatoes
Minestra Licurdia

Skewered Tuna, Grilled with Lemon and Oregano
Tonno, alla griglia con salsa di olio, limone e origano

Spaghetti with Garlic and Chili
Cifutti

Baked Zucchini Slices with Mozzarella
Zucchine e mozzarella al forno

Roasted Grapes with a Slice of Caciocavallo
Uva cotta in forno con caciocavallo

A meal in a region of dramatic landscapes, unspoiled wilderness and spicy, simple food: Calabria, and this will be the feeling you get as you look at the indescribably beautiful blue sea and at the cliffs and rocks, bleached of all color by the powerful sun. You will imagine that time stands still and that a galley might actually drop anchor. Little of the land can be cultivated, but where it is, it yields worthy crops, such as in the fertile land surrounding Reggio Calabria. Most of the world's production of bergamot comes from this area but it also produces beautiful vegetables, especially eggplants, sweet peppers, citrus fruits, olives and many flowers important to the perfume industry. This is the land of the famous *luganega* sausage, famous since Roman times, and the killing of the pig is still a main event. The making of capocolla is essential here, as is soppressata, both are cured by smoking. They are not high on desserts, but figs and cheeses, honey and almonds are exported to places all over the world. This land and that of its neighbor, Basilicata, are probably the least known areas of Italy, although there is evidence that tourism to these parts is growing.

Wine Selection
Choose Nozze d'Oro, Bianco Sicilia IGT, produced by Conte Tasca d'Almerita to honor the fiftieth anniversary of his marriage to Franca.

Preparation Advice
1. Make the soup and roast the grapes for dessert one day ahead.

2. The rest of the meal is simple enough to be prepared at mealtime.

CALABRIAN ONION SOUP WITH POTATOES

Minestra Licurdia
MAKES 4 SERVINGS

This soup is typical of the Cosenza district and the term *licurdia* refers to both a soup and a sauce. It is a peasant dish, as is most of the cooking in this region, and here it has been uplifted by the use of butter and chicken broth; originally, the butter would not be used and water would have been used in place of the broth. As the region slowly opens up to tourism, the restaurant and some home cooking are seeing changes. This is especially true in the area of Reggio Calabria, where people seem to eat better, probably because the economy is better (thanks to the production of bergamot used in perfume production), and surely because it's closer to Messina, just across the strait where the art of preparing food is more developed.

> 6 tablespoons butter
> 1½ pounds onions, thinly sliced
> 1 pound potatoes, peeled, diced ½-inch
> 1 tablespoon sugar
> 6 cups chicken broth, heated to boiling
> ¼ cup grappa or brandy
> 4 slices bruschetta (page 6)
> ¾ cup freshly grated Pecorino
>   cheese
> 4 teaspoons extra-virgin olive oil

1. In a large saucepan, heat the butter and sauté the onions and potatoes until they take on some color and the onions become translucent, 8 to 10 minutes. Add the sugar, stir and cook for 2 minutes.

2. Add the boiling broth and when it has returned to the boil, reduce the heat to a steady, slow simmer and cook, covered, for 25 minutes.

3. Add the grappa and cook for 5 minutes over medium heat, uncovered.

4. To serve, add a piece of bruschetta to a soup bowl, pour in some soup, add a spoonful of cheese to the top, and pour 1 teaspoon of the oil over the cheese. Most Italians do this by writing the initial of their first name in oil.

SKEWERED TUNA, GRILLED WITH LEMON AND OREGANO

Tonno, alla griglia con salsa di olio, limone e origano
MAKES 4 SERVINGS

Although most of the food in Calabria is based on pasta and vegetables, there are a number of places along the coast where fish is a specialty. Fish here is best when it is prepared simply, the way the natives do. One special way of preparing tuna is to boil it in chunks and flavor it with oil, parsley, garlic and hot pepper. Another way is to grill it; this is as simple as cooking can get and it is delicious because of its simplicity.

> 2 pounds fresh tuna, at least 1½ inches thick
> ⅓ cup extra-virgin olive oil
> Juice of 1 lemon (about 3 tablespoons)
> 2 cloves garlic, minced
> ⅓ teaspoon red pepper flakes
> Freshly ground black pepper
> 1 teaspoon sea salt
> ¼ cup finely chopped fresh Italian parsley
> 1 large sprig oregano (large enough to use as a
>   brush during grilling)

1.   Prepare a wood fire, if possible; if not, charcoal will do. Ready the fire and let it reach the ashen stage. The goal is to get a red-hot fire with gray coals.

2.   Cut the tuna into large chunks, preferably 1½ inches square. Wipe them dry and place them in one layer in a flat dish.

3.   Combine the remaining ingredients in a small bowl and spoon over all the chunks of tuna, turning to cover all sides. Allow to marinate for 15 minutes. Arrange the tuna on skewers just before grilling; reserve the marinade.

4.   Put the skewers on the grill and cook them quickly on all sides, always brushing or basting them with the oregano sprig dipped in the reserved marinade. The total grilling time will take 5 to 10 minutes depending on how rare you wish the tuna to be. Serve on individual plates with some spaghetti (below).

SPAGHETTI WITH GARLIC AND CHILI

Cifutti
MAKES 4 SERVINGS

Cifutti is a dialect name given to this dish by the Calabrians because they say the word sounds like the noise the cooked spaghetti makes when it is added to the skillet with the hot oil and chili pepper.

> Sea salt
> ½ pound spaghetti
> 4 tablespoons extra-virgin olive oil
> 2 cloves garlic, minced
> ½ teaspoon red pepper flakes
> Freshly ground pepper (optional)
> ½ cup freshly grated pecorino cheese
> Finely chopped fresh Italian parsley, for garnish

1.   Bring water to a boil in a large saucepan. Add 1 teaspoon salt, then the spaghetti. Cook the spaghetti until al dente, 8 to 10 minutes. (It is always best to consult the pasta manufacturer's instructions about cooking time, but it is also important to test along the way by forking a strand of pasta from the pot and tasting it. It should have "bite" between the teeth.) Drain the pasta, reserving ½ cup of the cooking water.

2.   Heat the oil in a large skillet. Add the garlic and sauté for less than 1 minute. Remove from the heat; add the red pepper flakes. Stir and add the spaghetti. Toss lightly but well, putting the skillet back on the heat. Add 1 tablespoon or more of the cooking water to the skillet while tossing the pasta. Add salt and freshly ground black pepper, if you wish.

3.   Serve on individual plates, topping with some freshly grated pecorino cheese and a sprinkle of parsley. Pass more cheese.

BAKED ZUCCHINI SLICES WITH MOZZARELLA

Zucchine e mozzarella al forno
MAKES 4 SERVINGS

Small zucchini work best here; they have fewer seeds and less water. The oil and mozzarella will add plenty of flavor.

> 4 small zucchini, 1 × 4 or 5 inches long
> 4 tablespoons extra-virgin olive oil
> Sea salt and freshly ground pepper
> ½ cup shredded mozzarella cheese

1.   Rinse and dry the zucchini. Cut off the ends. Hold each zucchini up on one end and slice off

some of the outer skin. Do the same with the other side of the zucchini. Then slice the zucchini down the middle to get 2 slices, about ¼ inch thick by 4 or 5 inches long. Repeat with the other zucchini. Wipe slices dry.

2. Preheat the oven to 350F.

3. Heat 2 tablespoons of the oil in a large skillet, add the zucchini slices and sauté until nicely golden. Turn over, adding more oil, if necessary, and sauté the other side. Oil a flat baking pan to hold the zucchini in one layer. Arrange them side by side, sprinkle with some salt and pepper and carefully put the mozzarella over the slices. Bake until the mozzarella melts, about 5 minutes. Serve as a vegetable side dish, on individual small plates. Do not be tempted to save on dishes and add the zucchini to the plate with the spaghetti and grilled tuna.

●ROASTED GRAPES
●WITH A SLICE OF
●CACIOCAVALLO

Uva cotta in forno con caciocavallo
MAKES 4 SERVINGS

There are several places in Calabria, notably Catanzaro and Verbicaro, where they bake grapes in a preparation called *panicielli d'uva passa*, which means that small bunches of grapes are wrapped in cedar or chestnut leaves and are then baked. My friend and mentor, Georgianna Orsini, has given me an idea that works really well here. I like it because it eliminates the difficult task of finding cedar or chestnut leaves.

> 1 pound red grapes, rinsed and drained
>   well
> 4 slices caciocavallo cheese

1. Preheat the oven to 350F. Remove the grapes from their stems and put them on an oiled baking pan or pizza pan. Bake the grapes for 1 hour or until they begin to caramelize (the grapes will begin to collapse).

2. To serve them hot or lukewarm, simply spoon some on individual plates and add a slice of cheese next to the grapes.

SARDINIA

D. H. Lawrence once said of Sardinia, ". . . not a bit like the rest of Italy." In spite of the ever-increasing number of condominiums along some parts of the north coast, much of the island is still rustic. It is an island of hills, with rolling plains and a coastline that is rocky. There are wild horses (like the pure-blooded ones the Arabs rode in the ninth century), pink flamingos, deserted beaches and hundreds of antique *nuraghi,* cone-shaped fortified towers made of huge blocks of stone without mortar. In a way actually, it is like some parts of Italy because of its spectacular landscapes. The distance from the mainland helped keep the island's customs and food culture intact. The Sardinians themselves are not seagoing people, and most of their settlements were inland, making it more difficult for invaders to hold sway over them.

Most Sardinians are either farmers or shepherds. They thrive on spit-roasted pork, lamb and goat (sometimes barbecuing them in the ground). Fish, although plentiful, is not as popular as meat. Local cheeses are pecorino and ricotta; pasta is mostly spaghetti, ravioli and macaroni. Vegetables and legumes are prepared in many fashions but are not as popular as elsewhere in Italy. However, beans, artichokes, cauliflower, tomatoes and eggplant, usually combined with other foods, do appear.

One popular resort area is the Emerald Coast

(*Costa Smeralda*) in the northeastern part of the island known as Gallura—it has one of the most indented coastlines. The development of this area was promoted by a group of people headed by the Aga Khan; one of the main resorts is Porto Cervo. Nearby is the town of Arzachena, located at the foot of a mountain range. As an agricultural market town, it is surprising to find hotels, inns and two especially good restaurants: Grazia Deledda and the Casablanca, both featuring international and mainland cooking.

DINNER FOR 6 IN THE LITTLE PORT TOWN OF ALGHERO AMONG OLIVE TREES, EUCALYPTUS AND PARASOL PINES

MENU

Snapper or Trout in Vernaccia Wine
Triglie al Vernaccia

Baked Cauliflower with Sardinian Pasta
Cavolfiori al forno con fregola

Grilled Hot Cherry Peppers
Peperoni rossi cotti alla griglia in sott'aceto

Ricotta Cheese Fritters
Fritelle di ricotta

In the fourteenth century Alghero was occupied by the Catalans and because of its Spanish air, some people refer to it as the Barcelonetta of Sardinia. Its citizens still wear Catalan costumes and many speak Catalan. The following menu is not from one specific area, but more generically Sardinian.

Wine Selection

The Barbera and Dolcetta of Piedmont, and the Sangiovese from Tuscany have all been transplanted to Sardinia, but have not yet reached the acclaim of the originals (nor the price). The big change in Sardinian wines has to do with the geometric growth of wine cooperatives, which are now producing the major portion of the wine. The most popular is Vernaccia (very similar to sherry) and although it is drunk before and after meals in Sardinia, it would be difficult to serve as a dinner wine. However, serve the Vernaccia with the fritters. For the pasta dish, serve a Chianti from Tuscany or a Dolcetta from Piedmont.

Preparation Advice

1.   The cauliflower dish can be made early in the day and baked just before eating.

2.   The fritter mixture can be made ahead, even the day before and refrigerated, and the cheese rolled and crumbed, ready to be fried shortly before eating.

3   It is best to cook the fish ½ hour or so before mealtime.

4.   The peppers can be prepared ahead of time, but they are best if grilled just before eating.

SNAPPER OR TROUT IN VERNACCIA WINE

Triglie al Vernaccia
MAKES 6 SERVINGS

In Sardinia, the fish called for in this preparation is red or gray mullet and sometimes, trout. Mullet can be purchased in major cities and for most readers, this fish may be difficult to find. So snapper, red or most other kind of snapper, does well. If you have difficulty finding Vernaccia wine from Sardinia, substitute equal portions of sherry and dry white wine.

> 3 whole snappers, about 1½ pounds each, or
>   6 trout
> 3 tablespoons extra-virgin olive oil
> 1 medium carrot, trimmed, and finely chopped
> 2 cloves garlic, minced
> 1 teaspoon each finely chopped rosemary and
>   oregano
> ¼ cup finely chopped fresh Italian parsley
> 2 tablespoons grated lemon zest
> Sea salt and freshly ground pepper
> 4 cups Vernaccia wine, or 2 cups sherry plus 2
>   cups dry white wine

1. Ask your fishmonger to prepare the fish for cooking. The heads of the fish should stay on; snapper tails may be clipped.

2. In a very large skillet or large sauté pan in which the fish will fit in one layer, heat the oil. Add the carrot and cook for 3 or 4 minutes, until the carrot pieces are tender. Add the garlic and cook for 1 minute.

3. Add the rosemary, oregano, parsley and lemon zest and lay the fish on top of them. Add some salt and a liberal amount of pepper. Pour the wine carefully into the skillet to cover the fish.

4. Cook, over medium heat, for 10 to 15 minutes on each side, until the fish begins to flake (use a wooden skewer and put it through the body of the fish, if it penetrates easily, the fish is cooked). Most of the wine should have evaporated. One snapper will serve 2 people; or if using trout, serve 1 per person. Serve the fish with whatever sauce is left in the skillet.

BAKED CAULIFLOWER WITH SARDINIAN PASTA

Cavolfiori al forno con fregola
MAKES 6 SERVINGS

It would be best to make this with Sicilian pasta, known as *greula Sarda* or *fregola*, if you can; but it is difficult to find in the supermarkets, so the best substitute would be small pasta such as tubettini, ditalini or small shells, available in every grocery shop.

> 1 cup small pasta such as tubettini, ditalini or tiny
>   shells or Sardinian pasta
> 2 large heads cauliflower, trimmed and cut into
>   florets
> 4 tablespoons butter
> 4 tablespoons all-purpose flour
> 3 cups milk, heated to the boiling point
> 3 tablespoons finely chopped fresh oregano or
>   1½ teaspoons dried, crushed
> Pinch red pepper flakes
> Freshly ground pepper
> 1½ cups freshly grated pecorino cheese
> Sea salt
> ½ cup freshly made bread crumbs (page 7)

1. Cook the pasta in boiling water for 3 minutes, drain immediately, and put into a bowl of cool water.

2. Preheat the oven to 375F. Butter an 11 × 7 × 2-inch baking pan. Drain the pasta and spread in the prepared pan. Arrange the cauliflower florets over the pasta.

3. Melt the butter in a medium saucepan over medium heat, and when it bubbles, stir in the flour. Reduce the heat, and cook, stirring constantly with a whisk or wooden spoon for 2 to 3 minutes. Slowly add the hot milk, and cook, stirring most of the time, until the mixture thickens, 4 to 5 minutes. Remove from the heat.

4. Add 2 tablespoons of the oregano and red pepper flakes. Add a liberal amount of ground pepper. Stir in 1 cup of the pecorino cheese, and stir to blend into the sauce. Check for salt and add it, if needed. Pour the sauce over the cauliflower, then sprinkle the bread crumbs over the top.

5. Bake in the lower part of the oven for 40 minutes (if the crumbs darken too much, cover the dish with foil). Remove the pan from the oven and sprinkle the remaining ½ cup of cheese over the top. Continue cooking until the cauliflower florets are tender, 30 to 40 minutes. To test for doneness, pierce a floret with a wooden skewer; if it penetrates easily, the florets are cooked, if it meets with resistance, cook a bit longer. Let stand for 5 to 10 minutes, sprinkle with the remaining oregano and serve.

GRILLED HOT CHERRY PEPPERS

Peperoni rossi cotti alla griglia in sott'aceto
MAKES 6 SERVINGS

This preparation is more of a condiment than it is a vegetable, and will, therefore, go with many other dishes in this book, especially grilled meats and poultry. They are spicy, so beware. They can be made with fresh cherry peppers, but the pickled peppers called for in the recipe are delicious.

12 pickled hot cherry peppers (red, green or a mixture both)
2 or 3 (1-inch-thick) slices Italian bread
Salt and freshly ground pepper
⅓ cup extra-virgin olive oil

1. Cut out stems of peppers, as if coring tomatoes for filling. Opening should be wide enough to receive a 1-inch bread cube. Discard stems and seeds.

2. Brush both sides of bread slices with some of the oil, then cut the bread into 1-inch cubes. Toss peppers in remaining oil. Add some salt and pepper. Toss well. Place one bread cube into each pepper. Thread 6 peppers on each of 2 skewers, from top to bottom, leaving almost no space between the peppers.

3. Preheat grill. When the grill is hot, grill the peppers for several minutes on each side, rotating until all sides show grill marks. Serve 2 per person.

RICOTTA CHEESE FRITTERS

Fritelle di ricotta
MAKES ABOUT 16 FRITTERS

There are many dessert fritters in Italy and this comes from Sardinia, where they are usually dipped in flour, egg and crumbs and then deep-fried. I have eliminated that step and gone directly from tablespoons of batter to hot oil for browning both sides. The ricotta, ginger and rosemary are essential although any plain cookie can be finely crushed and substituted for the vanilla cookies used In this adaptation.

1 pound fresh ricotta cheese
½ pound amaretti, finely ground
¼ cup sugar
2 cups ground vanilla cookies
¼ cup finely chopped candied ginger
1 tablespoon finely chopped rosemary
2 tablespoons unbleached all purpose flour
2 eggs, beaten
6 tablespoons honey
Vegetable oil for frying
Confectioners' sugar for dusting
Small sprays of rosemary for garnish

1. Wrap the ricotta in several layers of cheese-cloth (or a cloth towel) and put into a colander. Allow to drain for several hours. Unwrap and put into a large bowl.

2. Add the ground amaretti, sugar, ground vanilla cookies, ginger, rosemary, flour and eggs. Mix well to make a fine paste.

3. Heat ½ inch oil in a skillet over medium-high heat. Carefully place 8 individual tablespoons of batter into the skillet and fry until they turn golden, 2 to 3 minutes. As they brown, transfer to paper towels. Repeat until all the fritters are made.

4. To serve, place 2 fritters on each of 6 plates, dusting them lightly with the confectioners' sugar. It is easiest to put some sugar in a small sieve, place the sieve over the fritter and tap the sieve lightly and some sugar will fall through. Add 1 tablespoon of honey, on the side, to each plate, and a small sprig of rosemary. These should be served as soon as possible after frying.

SICILY

When I think of Sicily I think of the letter M: marzipan, manic Spanish Baroque, mountains, Moorish cupolas, market-bazaars, *melanzana*, the Magna Graecia, Marsala, Monreale, Mondello, Messina, and of course, the Mediterranean, the Mafia. If you've been to Sicily, you'll know it as a land of oranges and almonds, sandy beaches and the hot *sirocco*, rolling hills and castle-crowned promontories. It is the land of legends where the goddess of the harvest, Demeter, dropped her scythe and cut the harbors of Trapani and Messina; a land where the Phoenicians built their ports and the Greeks their temples. For more than a thousand years, the Sicilians spoke Greek, for hundreds more Arabic and not until the 1200's did they speak Latin, as did the rest of Europe. In spite of many conquests, Sicily was a flourishing Mediterranean power, a seat of great culture and an island of exciting food.

This is the land where common criminals became Mafioso as Vikings took on Muslim airs (and harems, too). Waverly Root in his *The Foods of Italy* (Vintage Books, 1971), suggests that the name Mafia may come from the Arabic "manfa," place of exile, referring to the Saracens who, after they lost control of the island, became "exiles" on their own former territory, taking refuge in an occult government parallel to the official one.

Garibaldi landed in Marsala, Sicily, in 1860 and only then did the island become part of a unified Italy. Sicily today lives off the land and the sea, as it has in the past. It produces vast quantities of fruit, wine and olives and its fishing fleet is one of the largest in Italy. Its mild climate produces vegetables all through the year. Eggplant, in many guises, finds its way into pasta dishes, antipasti, on grills, in ovens, and in the sublime caponata. It is true that when you think of Sicilian food, you have to think Saracen, for the Arabs brought the pine nuts and currants that flavor almost everything, stuffings in squid, swordfish and risotto; they brought the sesame seeds on bread, the almonds in marzipan (from the many almond trees in Agrigento), the various oranges, especially the blood orange, now called the Sicilian orange. The Arabs brought sherbet to Sicily and the love for ice cream, cannoli and *cassata siciliano,* a cake with a ricotta and cream filling, lots of candied fruit, and green pistachio icing. Only the Marsala wine, from the town of the same name, has a different origin. It was created in the eighteenth century by an Englishman.

The Greeks impregnated Sicily, more so than anywhere else in Italy. Yet, it was the Saracens in the end, in spite of the ancient Greek influence, who left their impression on Sicilians—especially in their food culture. There is a trace of Greek cooking still there—the fish chowders and lamb with vegetables (see page 254), but what we consider typical Sicilian food is usually typically Saracen.

In the Year 1250, Sicilian Pasta was *Maccaruni*: Menu for 6

MENU

Rigatoni with Eggplant in a Creamy Curry Sauce
Rigatoni con melanzane in salsa al curry

Salad of Assorted Lettuces with Capers and Tarragon
Insalata di lattuga con capperi e dragoncello

Peach Soup with Raspberries and Toasted Panettone Fingers
Zuppa di pesche e lamponi con fette di panettone tostate

There is a legend about *maccaruni* at the time it was served to one of Sicily's foreign rulers by a Sicilian nobleman, the pasta was stuffed with earth instead of ricotta; when the food was blessed and by a miracle, the earth became ricotta. According to folklore, this was the *cannelloni alla catanese,* (Catania style) still served today. The filling is ricotta and meat, with a rich tomato sauce and topped with grated cheese. The first written record of pasta in Sicily is in a twelfth-century manuscript. But it is believed that it existed prior to that time and was one of the many foods the Arabs introduced to Sicily. Most of the pasta eaten these days is machine-made and it is of a very good quality. Pasta in Sicily is often combined with eggplant, as in the famous dish *alla Norma.* Here is an updated version of this combination of food, which adds a touch of curry.

Wine Selection

Look for the Sicilian IGT Rosso del Conte, produced by Conte Tasca d'Almerita; this is a wine identified with Regaleali, the huge feudal domain acquired by the Tasca family in 1830, which has become a vast winery, and producer of famous Sicilian wines.

Preparation Advice

1. The dessert may be made ahead, except for toasting the panettone fingers.

2. The lettuces may be prepped and stored in plastic bags, refrigerated, until needed. The dressing may be made ahead.

3. The rigatoni should be made before mealtime.

RIGATONI WITH EGGPLANT IN A CREAMY CURRY SAUCE

Rigatoni con melanzane in salsa al curry
MAKES 6 SERVINGS

In Sicily, Naples and other parts of Southern Italy, round hollow pasta is used more often than the other pastas. Generally, this kind of pasta is called macaroni. Bucatini or perciatelli is a thick version of spaghetti (with a hole through it). Ziti, also hollow like the rigatoni and bucatini, are only two inches in length, whereas rigatoni are longer and larger tubes with *rigati* (grooves) on the outside. Rigatoni seem popular elsewhere in Italy. I recall a dish I had up north called *rigatoni del Curato*, rigatoni in the style of the rustic priest.

Rigatoni are sold dried, made of durum wheat and are on all Italian supermarket shelves. In this recipe, they are prepared with a hint of curry, which found its way into Italy through early spice routes, especially located in southern Italy. This is also true of ginger.

> Sea salt
> 1 (1-pound) eggplant, diced
> ½ cup extra-virgin olive oil
> ¾ pound zucchini, diced
> 1 medium onion, diced
> 2 cups tomato puree (not paste)
> Freshly ground pepper
> 1½ cups heavy cream or half-and-half
> 1 tablespoon curry powder
> 1 pound rigatoni
> 1 cup fresh finely chopped basil
> ½ cup freshly grated Parmesan cheese

1. Sprinkle salt over the eggplant and drain in a colander for about 1 hour. Dry the eggplant with kitchen towels. Heat ¼ cup of the oil in a large skillet over medium heat, add the eggplant and sauté until tender. Drain on paper towels and set aside.

2. Sauté the zucchini in the remaining oil until softened, drain on paper towels and set aside.

3. Sauté the onion in the same skillet until transparent, 6 to 8 minutes. Add the tomatoes and some salt and pepper. Cover and cook for 8 minutes over medium heat. Remove from the heat and stir in the cream and curry powder.

4. Boil the rigatoni until al dente, drain, and add it to the skillet. Add the eggplant, zucchini, and the basil. Mix well over high heat for several minutes to bring the sauce and pasta together. Serve right away with the Parmesan on the side.

SALAD OF ASSORTED LETTUCES WITH CAPERS AND TARRAGON

Insalata di lattuga con capperi e dragoncello
MAKES 6 SERVINGS

Many Italians pick dandelions from the wild before they start to flower. They love their peppery-tasting leaves, leaves that are long and indented, and they look like lion's teeth; this is why they are called *dente di leone* and also often called *cicoria di campo*, field chicory. Cultivated dandelion are available in many greengrocers and some supermarkets.

Arugula grows wild in the Italian countryside and it is cultivated, too, and appears in every supermarket in the United States. Lamb's lettuce, called *valeriana* in Italy grows wild there, too, and it is a must ingredient in *misticanza* (a salad of mixed wild greens). You will see it in some shops as rounded leaves bunched together in a rosette shape, the smaller and rounder the leaves, the fuller the taste. If you are in an Italian market at the right time, you will see at least a dozen or more fresh salad greens. Italians like their salad greens simply dressed with olive oil and either vinegar or lemon juice, and serve the salad after the main course, to cleanse the palate.

   2 bunches fresh dandelion
   1 large bunch fresh arugula
   2 bunches lamb's lettuce
   1/4 cup finely chopped red onion
   1 tablespoon chopped capers
   1 teaspoon finely chopped fresh tarragon or
     1/2 teaspoon dried
   4 tablespoons extra-virgin olive oil
   2 tablespoons fresh lemon juice

   Pinch sugar
   Sea salt and freshly ground pepper

1. Trim the lettuces from their roots and put them in several changes of cool water to clean them. Handle them with care, as they are fragile, especially the lamb's lettuce. Dry them carefully and well. Put them in a large salad bowl, adding the red onion, capers and tarragon.

2. In a small bowl, combine the olive oil, lemon juice and sugar. Add some salt and pepper. Stir well and pour over the lettuces. Toss lightly and well. Serve right away.

PEACH SOUP WITH RASPBERRIES AND TOASTED PANETTONE FINGERS

Zuppa di pesche e lamponi con fette di panettone tostate
MAKES 6 SERVINGS

This is a modern touch, brought about by young restauranteurs who want to preserve the old flavors, but present them in new light. The good news is that the "soup" can be made with frozen peaches, which are available in every United States supermarket. And these days, I find panettones in the same markets.

   2 1/2 pounds ripe peaches or 2 (10-ounce)
     packages frozen peaches
   3/4 cup sugar
   3 tablespoons fresh lemon juice
   1/4 cup good-quality Marsala wine
   1 orange, peeled, pith removed, sliced across the
     segments to make wheels
   1 pint fresh raspberries

12 (½ × ½-inch-thick) slices panettone, toasted

1. If using fresh peaches, peel them and remove the pits. If using frozen peaches, thaw them and drain in a colander. When fully drained, cut them into 1-inch pieces. Cut them into coarse pieces and put either frozen or fresh in the bowl of a food processor.

2. Add the sugar to the fresh peaches (add only ¼ cup if using sweetened frozen peaches). Add the lemon juice and the Marsala. Process to thoroughly puree the mixture. Transfer to a bowl. Refrigerate until ready to use.

3. When ready to serve, spoon the puree into rimmed soup plates. Arrange an orange slice in the middle of each bowl and arrange some raspberries over each serving. Pass the panettone slices.

DINNER FOR 4
AT THE RESTAURANT
LEON D'OR IN
AGRIGENTO, SICILY

MENU

**Scallops and Pancetta on
Chicory Hearts and Radicchio**
Capesante e pancetta fritte su cuori
di cicoria e radicchio

Sautéed Fresh Tuna with Aromatic Herbs
Tonno agli aromi

Roasted Potatoes with Crushed Fennel Seeds
Patate arrosto con semi di finocchio

Selection of Italian Cheeses
Selezione di formaggi: asiago, provolone
affumicato, e pecorino siciliano (canestrato)

Sicily is the largest region of Italy, and the largest province in Italy is Palermo. Nine provinces make up Sicily, and Agrigento is one of them. It is on the southern side of Sicily between Trapani and Siracusa. It is the site of the famous Valley of the Temples, an unbelievable collection of temples built in the fifth and sixth centuries B.C., or what remains of them. An almond festival is held there every February when the almond trees are in full bloom. Food here, as elsewhere in Sicily, is based on bread, pasta, fish and vegetables. This menu features fish as both the appetizer and main course.

Wine Selection

Choose either the Sicilian IGT Chardonnay produced by Plancta or the Nozze d'Oro Bianco Sicilia IGT, one of the Regaleali wines.

Preparation Advice

1. The cheeses should be set out several hours ahead to reach full room temperature, and the potatoes can be roasted several hours ahead.

2. The scallop and tuna dishes (other than marinating) should be prepared just before mealtime, but all the prep work can be done earlier by several hours.

SCALLOPS AND PANCETTA ON CHICORY HEARTS AND RADICCHIO

Capesante e pancetta fritte su cuori di cicoria e radicchio
MAKES 4 SERVINGS

Pancetta and bacon are the same cut of pork, except that pancetta is not smoked as is bacon; it is cured in salt and spices, and it is shaped like a salami. As a rule, it is thinly sliced to order. It is available in some supermarkets and almost always available in specialty food shops. If you can't get pancetta, use thinly sliced prosciutto, or as a last resort, thinly sliced bacon.

3 tablespoons raisins
½ cup *vin santo* or white wine
2 small heads radicchio
2 small heads chicory
16 large fresh sea scallops
Sea salt and freshly ground pepper
16 small slices of pancetta (or 8 cut in half, lengthwise), to fit around the curved side of each scallop
4 tablespoons extra-virgin olive oil
½ teaspoon finely chopped fresh rosemary
⅓ cup walnut pieces, toasted
4 fresh lemon wedges, seeds removed

1. Combine the raisins and the *vin santo* in a small bowl and allow to stand for one hour to plump the raisins. Drain, reserving the wine, and set the soaked raisins aside. Trim the radicchio heads of their first layer of outer leaves, core the heads and cut them in half. Slice each half very thinly. Remove the green leaves from both heads of chicory to reach the yellowish-white inner hearts. Cut off the stem ends and finely slice the hearts. Set aside.

2. Rinse and dry the scallops. Season with some salt and pepper and wrap a piece of pancetta around each scallop, securing with a toothpick.

3. Heat 3 tablespoons of the oil in a large skillet. Add the rosemary and sauté for about 1 minute, stirring. Add the scallops and cook until the pancetta begins to brown. To do this, put the scallops in the skillet on their sides, rotating every now and then, to brown evenly. Turn the scallops on their flat sides and sauté. Sautéing the scallops should not exceed 5 minutes and it is necessary to stay at the stove during this procedure. Transfer the scallops to a dish and set aside. Do not clean the skillet.

4. Add the remaining oil to the same skillet. Add the radicchio and chicory slices, the walnut pieces and the raisins to the skillet. Toss constantly, over medium-high heat, to wilt the greens. If the mixture seems too dry in the skillet, add 1 or 2 teaspoons of the reserved wine. Sautéing the greens from start to finish should take about 3 minutes.

5. To serve, remove the toothpicks from the scallops. On each of 4 plates, add a portion of the sautéed greens. Arrange 4 scallops in each plate, on top of the greens. Add more salt and pepper and serve with a lemon wedge.

SAUTÉED FRESH TUNA WITH AROMATIC HERBS

Tonno agli aromi
MAKES 4 SERVINGS

The sauce here is tasty and flavorful and there will be more than you need to serve with the sliced tuna. Use any leftover sauce (it will keep refrigerated up to a week) as a delicious topping for small crostini or to be mixed with cooked (one pound) pasta, such as penne or small rigatoni.

> 1 thick tuna steak, about 1 to $1\frac{1}{2}$ pounds
> 1 cup dry white wine
> 4 tablespoons extra-virgin olive oil
> 2 tablespoons each chopped parsley, basil and mint
> Freshly ground pepper
> 2 tablespoons butter
> 1 small onion, minced
> 1 large clove garlic, minced
> 1 carrot, trimmed, scrubbed and finely diced
> 2 large tomatoes, peeled, seeded and diced
> 1 tablespoon tomato paste
> Sea salt

1. Rinse the fish and pat dry with paper towels. Put the steak in a glass or nonmetal container holding the steak in one layer and pour in $\frac{1}{2}$ cup of the wine. Sprinkle 2 tablespoons of the oil overall, pinches of the parsley, basil and mint, and a liberal sprinkling of freshly ground black pepper. Turn the steaks over and let marinate, at least 1 hour. Remove from the refrigerator 10 to 15 minutes before sautéing.

2. Heat the remaining olive oil and the butter in a skillet, and sauté the onions about 3 minutes. Add the garlic and sauté 1 minute longer.

Add the carrots, parsley, basil, mint, tomatoes, tomato paste, the remaining $\frac{1}{2}$ cup of wine and some salt and pepper. Cook over low heat until the sauce combines and thickens, about 12 minutes.

3. Drain the tuna steak and, in a second skillet, sauté on both sides over very high heat, 2 minutes per side. Pour the onion and herb mixture over the fish and cook for 3 to 6 minutes depending on how rare or well-done you like tuna. Remove from the heat, let stand a couple of minutes, slice and serve with some of the vegetable mixture.

ROASTED POTATOES WITH CRUSHED FENNEL SEEDS

Patate arrosto con semi di finocchio
MAKES 4 SERVINGS

Usually, regular medium to large boiling potatoes are used; they are cut lengthwise in half and then again lengthwise three or four times. However, the fish dish has a busy, complex sauce, so it seems more appropriate here to use small whole new potatoes, which will make a better presentation on the plate.

> 16 small new potatoes, uniform in size with clear skins
> 4 tablespoons extra-virgin olive oil
> 4 cloves garlic, sliced in halves
> 1 teaspoon dried fennel seeds, crushed
> Sea salt and freshly ground pepper

1. Pare the potatoes, rinse them in cool water and dry completely with paper or cloth towels. Preheat the oven to 375F.

2. Heat 3 tablespoons of the oil in a skillet large enough to hold the potatoes in one layer. Add the garlic halves and sauté them until they turn light brown, about 1 minute. Immediately discard them. Add the potatoes and sauté them until they lightly brown all over, 5 to 10 minutes, depending on the size of potato. Shake the skillet often to rotate the potatoes so they will form crusts on all sides.

3. Transfer the potatoes and any oil remaining in the skillet to a baking dish large enough to hold the potatoes in one layer. Add the remaining 1 tablespoon oil and the crushed fennel seeds. Season with salt and pepper. Cover the baking dish and bake for 30 to 45 minutes, until the potatoes are tender when pierced with a wooden skewer.

SELECTION OF ITALIAN CHEESES

Selezione di formaggi: asiago, provolone affumicato e pecorino siciliano

The most attractive way to serve cheese is to buy good-size chunks of it, meaning at least one-half pound per piece, and arranging them on an attractive flat tray, each cheese with its own knife. There are numerous garnishments one can use to catch the eye, such as a low bed of long, freshly cut chives as a base for the cheeses, or a large leaf, washed, dried and oiled, and so on.

Asiago. This splendid cheese gets its name from the small, pine tree–filled village of Asiago in northern Italy. Originally, this cheese was made solely with sheep's milk, but the rocky terrain of Asiago could not provide adequate land for the sheep to graze, thereby making the herds unable to keep up with the tremendous demand for this village's prize cheese. These days, Asiago is produced with pasteurized cow's milk in the neighboring village of Veneto, which has brought forth several different versions, the most popular being Asiago d'Allevo. Made partly from skim milk and either salted dry or immersed in brine, this "aged" Asiago has a buffed yellowish appearance, unmistakable sweet smell, and tiny, evenly distributed holes with a deep, dark colored rind. It is often eaten as a dessert cheese if it is not too mature. After six months, the semi-matured cheese *(Asiago da taglio)* develops a more piquant, saltier flavor and can still be eaten on its own. If the cheese is more than twelve months old, it is really only suitable for grating and cooking.

Smoked Provolone (*Provolone affumicato*). Straw-white in color with a smooth, supple texture, an oval or cylindrical shape, provolone is a southern Italian cheese. It can be found hanging from the ceiling in almost all Italian food stores and in many in the United States. In the south of Italy, buffalo's milk is often used, and the cheeses are also smoked. But it can be made from different types of milk and rennet; the strongest versions use goat rennet, which produces a spicy flavor. One interesting variety of provolone is called *provolone burrino* and it comes from Calabria. It is made by enclosing a lump of unsalted butter in the center of the cheese, so when sliced, it appears as a large, hard-boiled egg. If smoked provolone is not available, then look for a mild, fresh, unsmoked one for once it becomes strong, it is better to be used in cooking as in pizza and pasta preparations.

Pecorino Siciliano (*Canestrato*). All cheeses in Italy made with sheep's milk are called pecorino. They vary considerably in flavor and texture, all the way from soft and mild, to hard and strong. The pecorino made in Sicily is also known as *canestrato* and is available all year for eating because of the stabilized nature of the cured cheese. In

Sicily, it is usually sold unwrapped and the cheese itself bears traces of the draining basket (*canestrato* is the name of the draining basket). There is an interesting variety of it in Sicily that is studded with whole black peppercorns called *pecornio pepato;* you can imagine the peppery jolt in taste.

ON A CLEAR DAY, A VIEW FROM A TAORMINA TRATTORIA STRETCHES AS FAR AS MOUNT ETNA: MENU FOR 6

MENU

Eggs with Tuna Mayonnaise
Uove sode tonnate

Lamb and Vegetables, Greek Style in Southern Italy
Spezzatino d'agnello

Apricots with Amaretti Crumbs and Cream
Albicoche agli amaretti sbriciolati

At a height of 820 feet above sea level, Taormina (Sicily) is a natural balcony overlooking the sea and facing Etna. The small city is known for its beautiful monuments (especially the Greek theatre), gardens (with exotic plants and views of the coast and Sicilian Sea), tourists (of every description), and places to get a good meal. Next to the Greek theatre is the new Timeo (hotel and restaurant) where minced garlic is sautéed in butter with cream, tomatoes, shredded zucchini, finely chopped pistachio nuts, and then wedded to cooked small penne (*pennette*). On Taormina's main street, Corso Umberto, is La Griglia, an utterly charming eatery, where thinly sliced fresh artichoke hearts are mixed with fresh chicory in oil and lemon and served with perfectly grilled local fish. At the end of this dining room, there is a large window that shows the city's rooftops and beyond. In preparing this meal, think of looking through the Greek theatre, all the way to Etna.

Wine Selection

A fairly new DOC red wine, Primitivo di Manduria, made in southern Italy (Apulia) by Felline has received some praise and good notice. It should be drunk after the first two or three years of bottling.

Preparation Advice

1. The first course and the dessert may be made ahead by five or six hours.

2. The packets for the lamb and vegetables can be made early in the day; it is best to grill them a little before mealtime.

EGGS WITH TUNA MAYONNAISE

Uove sode tonnate
MAKES 6 SERVINGS

This is a simple, classic Italian appetizer or first course, which by itself will make an excellent light luncheon dish if served with a freshly made green salad. The flavors are very Sicilian: tuna, capers, anchovies and lemon juice. Yes, you can use prepared mayonnaise, but the dish is noticeably different, and significantly better, if homemade is used.

FOR THE MAYONNAISE (ABOUT ¾ CUP)
1 egg yolk, at room temperature (see Notabene on raw eggs, page 48)
1 teaspoon fresh lemon juice
1 teaspoon prepared mustard, preferably Dijon
⅔ cup vegetable oil

FOR THE TUNA SAUCE
1 (6-ounce) can Italian tuna, packed in olive oil
3 anchovy fillets, plus extra for serving
2 tablespoons fresh lemon juice
1 tablespoons capers, rinsed, well drained, and dried, plus extra for serving
Sea salt and freshly ground pepper
6 large eggs, at room temperature

1. *To make the mayonnaise:* In a small bowl, whisk the egg yolk and whisk in the lemon juice and mustard until well combined. Whisk in the oil, 1 tablespoon at a time, until ⅓ of the oil is incorporated, then add the remaining oil all at once, whisking all the time. Whisk until smooth, cover with plastic wrap and refrigerate until ready for use, up to 1 day ahead.

2. *To make the tuna sauce:* Put the tuna and its oil in the bowl of a food processor. Add the anchovies, lemon juice and capers and process until smooth. Transfer to a medium bowl.

3. Fold in the mayonnaise and add some salt and pepper. Refrigerate for 1 hour or longer, but remove from refrigerator 15 minutes before using.

4. Simmer the eggs until they are hard, about 12 minutes. Cool them by running under cold water. Peel the eggs and slice in half lengthwise. Arrange them on a serving dish and spoon the sauce over them. If you wish, add more anchovies by cutting some in half, lengthwise, and placing

them on top of the egg, and sprinkling more capers on top.

LAMB AND VEGETABLES, GREEK STYLE IN SOUTHERN ITALY

Spezzatino d'agnello
MAKES 6 SERVINGS

It has been said that the food of Italy is a function of its history. Over a period of thousands of years, invaders came and went and some stayed. Each brought its customs, traditions and eating habits; three, in particular, laid the foundation for Italian cooking: the Etruscans, the Greeks and the Saracens. The Etruscans and the Greeks were there before the Saracens and divided the whole peninsula between them, with the Etruscans taking over the north, the Greeks the south. In addition to the many Greek ruins that punctuate the southern Italian countryside, there are also remnants of Greek cooking. Here is an adaption of a lamb stew, Greek style; instead of baking it in the oven, this is wrapped in foil and cooked on a grill.

2 pounds lean boneless shoulder of lamb, cut into 6 pieces
3 large cloves garlic, halved
6 small new potatoes, scrubbed and halved
6 whole mushrooms, stems trimmed and wiped clean
6 Italian frying peppers, stems, seeded, ribs removed and halved
6 medium onions, halved
6 (1-inch-thick) eggplant slices skin on, each slice cut into 3 pieces
12 canned plum tomatoes, drained, seeded and coarsely chopped

3 tablespoons finely chopped fresh oregano or
   3 teaspoons dried
Sea salt and freshly ground pepper
12 tablespoons chicken broth
6 tablespoons extra-virgin olive oil

1. Cut 6 pieces of heavy-duty foil about 18 inches square, large enough to envelop the lamb and vegetables.

2. Place one piece of lamb on each piece of foil and top with a garlic half. Add 2 pieces of potato, a mushroom, 2 pieces of pepper, 2 pieces of onion, 3 pieces of eggplant and some tomatoes.

3. Sprinkle the oregano over the mixture, adding some salt and pepper. Also add 2 tablespoons of the chicken broth and 1 tablespoon of the oil. Wrap the foil by picking up 2 sides, the one closest to you and the one away from you. Bring them together and fold 2 or 3 times, leaving some air space in the packet. Fold in the ends tightly, to avoid spills when the packets are turned over.

4. Preheat a grill. Place all the packets on the grill, about 3 inches above the heat source. Cover the grill and cook for 25 minutes. Carefully turn the packets over and cook for 20 minutes (if using a grill without a cover, cook for a total of 55 to 60 minutes). Before serving, it is always best to open one packet to test for doneness.

APRICOTS WITH AMARETTI CRUMBS AND CREAM

Albicoche agli amaretti sbriciolati
MAKES 6 SERVINGS

This is a dessert that will fit almost any occasion. If the apricots are fresh, it will be sublime. But jarred or canned apricots also fare well here with the help of the liqueur and wine. If you cannot get amaretti cookies, crush a few vanilla cookies as a substitute.

12 apricots, preferably fresh, cut in halves, stones
   removed, or 12 canned apricot halves, drained
1/2 cup hazelnut liqueur
1/2 cup white wine
2/3 cup sugar
1/2 cup heavy cream
12 amaretti (Italian macaroons), crushed with a
   rolling pin

1. Place the apricots cut side down in a skillet. Add the liqueur, reserving 1 tablespoon, and wine. Sprinkle with the sugar and cook over medium heat until the fresh apricots are cooked through, 8 to 10 minutes, or the canned ones are heated through, 3 or 4 minutes, and the sauce has become syrupy. Remove the apricots and cook down the sauce to about half its original volume. Let cool.

2. Add the reserved 1 teaspoon liqueur to the cream and whip to soft peaks.

3. Arrange 4 apricot halves on each dessert plate, spoon over the sauce, add whipped cream to the side overlapping one apricot and sprinkle with the amaretti crumbs. Serve right away.

AL FRESCO MEAL FOR 12 IN SICILY FOR THE AUGUST CELEBRATION *FERRAGOSTO* OF THE FEAST OF THE ASSUMPTION OF THE BLESSED VIRGIN

MENU

Caponata
Caponata

Tuna in Roasted Red, Orange and Yellow Peppers
Tonno in peperoni arrostiti

Rotelle Pasta Salad with Cucumber Sauce
Insalata di pasta (rotelle)

Sicilian Meat Loaf
Falsomagro

Swordfish Steaks with Two Sauces: Blood Orange and Caper/Anchovy
Pescespada grigliato con due salse

Sicilian Cream Cake
Cassata alla siciliana

August 15th is a religious holiday celebrating the Feast of the Assumption of the Virgin Mary, in honor of her death and ascension to heaven. It is also the beginning of vacation time when almost every Italian, or so it seems, leaves work and home to holiday by the sea or in the mountains. The larger cities close down, and traffic on the roads is bumper-to-bumper. The religious holiday is observed all over Italy and each town provides its own spectacle. Because this comes at a time when vegetables and fruit are ripe, meals look more like feasts, with plenty of flowing wine. The following menu is appropriate for eating al fresco, buffet style, and takes advantage of Sicilian foods such as eggplant, tuna, swordfish and pasta, ending with a famous Sicilian dessert.

Wine Selection

For red, choose a Vino da Tavola di Sicilia wine, Duca Enrico-Rosso, produced by Duca di Salaparuta. Or select a Corvo Rosso, one of Sicily's most popular wines. For a white wine, look for Vignadangelo, Greco di Tufo DOC, produced by Mastroberardino, in Avellino, near Naples.

Preparation Advice

1. Everything in this menu can be made ahead. The caponata, tuna and pasta salad may be made the day before and refrigerated. The cake may be made one day ahead.

2. The sauces for the swordfish may also be made ahead and kept in the refrigerator. Grill the swordfish just before mealtime.

3. The meat loaf is best made earlier in the day of the meal.

CAPONATA

Caponata
MAKES 12 SERVINGS

I am always amazed when by accident I learn something new. Such is the case with the Sicilian specialty dish of caponata, one of my favorite things to eat. Each Sicilian friend in the United States and in Italy claims to have the best way of preparing this dish. I have enjoyed it in each of their fashions, until one day in Palermo, I took a wrong turn while walking and stumbled upon a small trattoria, Al Cancelletto Verde, the green gate. It is located north of Via Vittorio Emanuele in a tony shopping area known as Ruggiero-Settima. This caponata was light and fresh, not dark and heavy as some people prepare it. I was told by the owner that the "secret" is to sauté the eggplant cubes and set them aside. The onion, celery (after pre-cooking), capers, tomatoes, oil, vinegar, sugar are then sautéed and combined with the eggplant after all the cooking is done.

It may be served as an appetizer, (especially delicious on small pieces of toast) or as a condiment to chicken, pork, beef, lamb or scrambled eggs.

2½ pounds eggplant, peeled and cut into 1-inch
    squares
Sea salt
Vegetable and olive oils
1 large onion, chopped
6 ribs celery (do not use outer ribs), cut into 1-inch
    pieces and steamed to pre-cook them
3 cloves garlic, minced
2 cups Tomato Sauce (page 175)
1⅓ cups green olives, pitted and halved
½ cup capers, rinsed and drained
½ cup finely sliced basil leaves, plus extra for
    garnish
Freshly ground pepper
1¼ cups red wine vinegar
3 tablespoons sugar

1.   Put the eggplant pieces in a large colander and sprinkle with salt. Allow to drain for at least 30 minutes. Using paper or cloth kitchen towels, dry the eggplant pieces.

2.   Add ½ inch vegetable and olive oil (¾ vegetable oil and ¼ olive oil) to a heavy skillet, and

heat over medium heat. Add the eggplant and fry for 10 to 15 minutes, until browned on all sides, stirring frequently. Transfer to paper towels to drain and set aside.

3.   In the same skillet used to cook the eggplant, add the onion and celery and sauté over medium heat for 8 minutes, stirring frequently. Add more oil if needed. Add the garlic, stir, and cook for about 2 minutes.

4.   Stir in the tomato sauce, olives, capers and basil. Add some salt and pepper. Bring to a boil and add the vinegar and sugar. Simmer over low heat for about 15 minutes. The vegetables should be cooked through but not be mushy. Drain off as much liquid as you can. Stir in the eggplant, adjust the seasoning and allow to stand at room temperature for up to 2 hours, or refrigerate. When ready to serve, leave at room temperature for 30 minutes and sprinkle a little more finely chopped fresh basil over the top.

TUNA IN ROASTED RED, ORANGE AND YELLOW PEPPERS

Tonno in peperoni arrostiti
MAKES 12 SERVINGS

Canned tuna is stored in most Sicilian (and other Italian) pantries. Some people still can fresh tuna at home, but this seems to be a household chore of the past; one of the reasons being that delicious and high-quality canned tuna packed in olive oil is available. I noted in the introduction to this book that new cooks and others in Italy are defining the future by celebrating the past. They are creating small revolutions by redefining their own regional tastes. An example of this has to do with the traditional grilled pepper and tuna antipasto one finds in Sicily and all over Italy. I enjoyed a half roasted pepper wrapped around an ethereal tablespoonful of tuna mousse at the splendid restaurant Gener Neuv in Asti, a short distance from Turin, in the northern part of Italy that I think works wonders at this Sicilian buffet, which would ordinarily have had roasted peppers and canned tuna with other antipasti.

6 bell peppers, 2 each red, orange and
   yellow
4 tablespoons extra-virgin olive oil
4 cloves garlic, halved lengthwise
1 teaspoon red wine vinegar
Sea salt and freshly ground pepper
3 (6-ounce) cans Italian tuna packed in olive oil
2 sticks (1 cup) butter, at room temperature
1 tablespoon cognac or brandy
2 tablespoons finely chopped fresh oregano or
   2 teaspoons dried

1. With a damp cloth, wipe the peppers clean. Place them on a baking sheet, and broil them slowly, under low heat, until the skins are charred on all sides. Then put the peppers in a brown paper bag, and set them aside to cool for 10 minutes. Shake the bag back and forth to help loosen the skins. When the peppers are cool enough to handle, remove the cores, peel off the skins and remove the seeds. Cut them in half and put them in a flat glass dish, like a pie dish. Pour the olive oil over the peppers, and add the garlic and vinegar. Add some salt and pepper. Toss lightly but well. Cover with plastic wrap and leave at room temperature for up to 2 hours. Refrigerate if not served within that time and bring to room temperature before serving.

2. Drain the tuna, reserving the oil. Add the tuna to the bowl of a food processor. Add the butter and cognac. Add some salt and pepper. Process to make a smooth puree.

3. Take a bell pepper half and lay it flat, inside side up. Put a heaping tablespoon of the tuna mousse to one side of the pepper half. Bring up the other side to cover the tuna, yet showing just a little of the tuna. Transfer to an attractive platter, one large enough to hold all the peppers in 1 layer. Repeat with remaining peppers and tuna mousse. Pour some of the leftover oil from the pepper dish or the canned tuna over the peppers and sprinkle with the oregano. Add more salt and pepper. This is to be served at room temperature and may stand at room temperature for up to 1 hour, or refrigerate and bring to room temperature before serving.

ROTELLE PASTA SALAD WITH CUCUMBER SAUCE

Insalata di pasta (rotelle)
MAKES 12 SERVINGS

Rotelle are little pasta wheels that look like the wheels on antique Sicilian carts. It is a popular pasta throughout Italy and it appears on most supermarket shelves. This particular way to cook it was talked about by Giuseppe Calafiore, a man with a taxi who drove me from Palermo to Marsala, on to Mazara del Vallo, and then on to Agrigento. Giuseppe would return home to Palermo and his family after each of my stops and come back to drive me on to the next location. In addition to being a good driver, he knew a good deal about food and the Mafia. In the middle of a sentence about preparing pasta or tuna he would interrupt himself to show me a statue, from the taxi window, built in memory of one or more citizens who were gunned down by the Mafia. I did not want to part with Giuseppe, but I thought it was short of ridiculous for him to come from Palermo each time, especially so when it was halfway across Sicily. The idea for this pasta salad is his.

> 4 small cucumbers, preferably Kirby, peeled and pureed (if using other cucumbers, seed them after peeling)
> ¼ cup white wine vinegar
> ½ cup extra-virgin olive oil
> 1 cup diced red onion (about 1 medium onion)
> 1 cup diced red bell pepper
> ¾ cup finely chopped fresh basil
> 3 cloves garlic, minced
> 4 plum tomatoes, peeled, seeded and chopped
> 1 tablespoon sugar, or to taste
> Sea salt and freshly ground pepper
> 1 pound rotelle pasta
> 1 tablespoon crushed, dried oregano

1. Combine all the ingredients, except the pasta and the oregano, in a large bowl and stir with a fork until well mixed. Add a bit more sugar if the sweet-sour taste is not to your liking.

2. Cook the pasta in boiling salted water until al dente. Drain in a colander and immerse the colander in ice-cold water to stop the cooking. Drain the pasta really well by shaking the colander to remove as much liquid as possible.

3. Add the pasta to the sauce and stir to coat it with the sauce. Sprinkle with the oregano and serve. This is excellent served at room temperature.

SICILIAN MEAT LOAF

Falsomagro
MAKES 12 SERVINGS

In Sicily, this "meat loaf" is called *farsumagru* or *falsomagro alla Bellini*, after the great nineteenth-century Sicilian composer Vicenzo Bellini. Both the house in which he lived and the church in which he was baptized still exist on the picturesque, barrue Cruciferi Street in Catania. The meat loaf is really a stuffed beef roll and versions of it exist elsewhere in Italy, so I have to believe that Signor Bellini did not create it; perhaps this is the way he liked it prepared.

> 2 pounds lean beef, in 1 piece, such as a top round steak
> 2 small to medium onions, finely chopped
> 2 cloves garlic, minced
> 1 pound ground beef and veal
> 2 links Italian sausage, out of casing
> 3 slices bacon, cut into small pieces
> 2 eggs, beaten
> Good pinch freshly grated nutmeg
> Sea salt and freshly ground pepper
> ¼ pound Parma ham, finely chopped
> ¼ pound pecorino cheese, grated on large teeth of cheese grater
> ½ cup each finely chopped fresh mint and fresh Italian parsley
> 2 hard-cooked eggs, sliced
> 3 tablespoons olive oil
> 1 cup Sicilian red wine
> 2 cups beef broth

1. Ask your butcher to pound the slice of beef until ¼ inch thick or less for you, to make it rectangular in shape and to make small cuts along the edge to keep it from curling as it cooks. Explain to him what you plan to do with it, that is, stuff and roll it. It is easy enough to do this at home and a meat pounder will facilitate the process. Set the beef aside.

2. Combine half of the chopped onions, the garlic, ground meat, sausage, bacon, eggs and nutmeg in a bowl. Add some salt and pepper. With splayed fingers, mix the ingredients until blended.

3. Spread the ground meat mixture over the beef, leaving about ½ inch free at the edges. Sprinkle the ham and cheese over the ground meat mixture and do the same with the mint and parsley. Arrange the egg slices over the ground meat mixture. Roll the beef from the larger side, like a jelly roll, and tie securely with kitchen string.

4. In a Dutch oven large enough to hold the beef roll, heat the oil over medium heat and sauté the remaining chopped onion for 3 to 4 minutes, until the onion begins to brown. Carefully place the beef roll in the pan, and cook over medium heat to brown all sides. Add ½ cup of the wine and cook, uncovered, until the wine evaporates. Add some salt and pepper. Add the remaining wine and the broth, cover and cook over low to medium heat for 1½ to 2 hours, until the beef is tender. This can be served warm or at room temperature. Remove the strings and slice.

SWORDFISH STEAKS WITH TWO SAUCES: BLOOD ORANGE AND CAPER/ANCHOVY

Pescespada grigliato con due salse
MAKES 12 SERVINGS

The Strait of Messina (Calabria-Sicily), prized for its abundant swordfish and tuna, provides these fish that are prepared in many ways. Often, the simplest preparation is the one most seen, a slice of it grilled simply with oil, lemon and a selected herb. Italian gourmets will add special sauces, as provided here. If you don't have time to make both sauces, choose one. The swordfish takes little time to grill, so grill it just before serving.

The bloodred color of the flesh of the blood orange gives these sweet, juicy oranges their name. They are mostly imported from Mediterranean countries. Italy, particularly Sicily, is a major producer. They are small to medium-size fruits with smooth or pitted skin that is sometimes tinged with red. If you can't find the blood oranges, use navel or Valencia and add a touch of tomato paste to the sauce to achieve the red color.

The caper and anchovy sauce is excellent over fish, cooked vegetables, meat and poultry, all hot or cold.

FOR THE BLOOD ORANGE SAUCE
1 blood orange, or 1 sweet orange
2 recipes Mayonnaise (page 254)
1 teaspoon tomato paste, if using
　　sweet orange

FOR THE CAPER/ANCHOVY SAUCE
2 anchovy fillets
½ cup white wine vinegar

3 tablespoons capers, rinsed, dried and chopped
  (see Notabene, below)
½ cup extra-virgin olive oil
Sea salt and freshly ground pepper
2 tablespoons finely chopped fresh
  Italian parsley

3 (1½-pound) swordfish steaks (one steak
  should serve 4 people)
6 tablespoons extra-virgin olive oil
3 tablespoons finely chopped fresh oregano,
  or 3 teaspoons dried, crushed
½ teaspoon red pepper flakes
Sea salt and freshly ground black
  pepper

1. *To make the blood orange sauce:* Grate the orange for zest and set aside 2 tablespoons. Squeeze the orange for juice and set aside ¼ cup.

2. Add 1 tablespoon of juice at a time to the mayonnaise, mixing until you get a consistency like lightly whipped heavy cream. If using a sweet orange, blend in the tomato paste, a little at a time, to color it. Fold in the orange zest.

3. *To make the caper/anchovy sauce:* Place the anchovies and vinegar in the bowl of a food processor and process to a count of 10. Transfer the mixture to a large nonstick skillet.

4. Add capers and bring to a boil. Reduce the heat, cover the skillet and cook for 5 minutes over low heat. With the help of a rubber spatula, transfer the mixture to a bowl.

5. Add the oil and beat with a wire whisk. Add some salt and pepper and the chopped parsley.

6. *To grill and serve the swordfish:* Ready a wood or charcoal fire for grilling. Be sure the coals turn gray (the coal inside is red-hot).

7. Combine the olive oil, oregano and pepper flakes. Brush some of this on both sides of the fish.

8. Grill the fish steaks for 3 or 4 minutes per side, brushing on more of the oil mixture several times during the grilling period.

9. Remove from the grill, brush lightly with more of the oil mixture and add some salt and pepper. Cut each steak into 4 portions. Put each of the sauces into bowls and serve with the fish.

Notabene:

Capperi, as they are called in Italy, are the flower buds of a wild, Mediterranean, thorny climbing shrub and have been used as a condiment for thousands of years. They are preserved in brine or pickled in white wine vinegar. In Sicily, they are packed in salt, which should be rinsed off before using. Their use in Italy is widespread, as they are added to fish and seafood dishes, salad and vegetable sauces, pizzas and to pastas, such as in the famous Sicilian pasta dish *pasta colle sarde.* Try using pickled, brine- or salt-packed capers and your taste will prevail as to which type you will buy in the future. Rinsing them before use softens their piquant, sharp flavor. They should also be dried before adding them to a preparation. The larger capers are cheaper than the smaller ones. There is no difference in taste, but the smaller ones seem to make a better garnish. Italians buy their packed-in-salt capers by the *etto,* which simply means they are sold loose; one *etto* equals three and a half ounces. Once opened, capers packed in liquid should be kept refrigerated; they will last indefinitely, as will the ones packed in salt.

SICILIAN CREAM CAKE

Cassata alla siciliana
MAKES 12 SERVINGS

The two main Sicilian desserts are *cannoli* and *cassata*. There are many versions of both, and as many as there may be of cassata, each variation always includes candied fruit. I have enjoyed many good eating experiences in Sicily and one I remember especially well has to do with desserts in the town of Erice, a town that rises 2,500 feet above the Trapani Harbor. The Antica Pasticceria del Convento concocts sinfully good sweets. In addition to the cassata presented here, I remember eating a free sample of a cookie called *brutti ma belli,* ugly but oh so good. If I remember correctly, I was told they are made all over Italy, different versions, of course. Erice has a medieval character. The streets are very narrow and cobblestoned. The walls are thick stone. In winter, the town is enshrouded in mist and cold. In the summer months, on a clear day, the view reaches all the way south to North Africa. It is one of the best places for views, cookies and *cassata*.

1½ pounds fresh ricotta or cottage cheese
2 cups sugar
1 teaspoon vanilla extract
2 tablespoons tangerine or orange
    liqueur
5 squares (5 ounces) bittersweet chocolate,
    crushed into small bits
½ cup finely diced candied fruit
¼ cup whole pistachio nuts
Sponge Cake (page 121)
Confectioners' sugar, for sprinkling

1.   Put the ricotta, sugar, vanilla and liqueur in the bowl of a food processor and process until smooth, about 15 seconds. Transfer to a bowl and fold in the chocolate, fruit and pistachios. Mix well.

2.   Cut the sponge cake into ½-inch slices and line a 10-inch round glass bowl with some of the slices. Add the creamed ricotta mixture over the sponge cake pieces and pat it down with a rubber spatula. Cover with the remaining slices of sponge cake. Make a cardboard cutout the same size as the top of the cake inside the bowl. Cover with plastic wrap and press the plastic side of the cutout on top of the cake. Weight it with one or two cans of food. Put in the refrigerator for at least 4 hours, or overnight.

3.   When ready to serve, remove the cake from the refrigerator and turn it over onto a large platter or plate, holding the cardboard and bowl steady and securely. Remove the bowl and sprinkle it with confectioners' sugar and serve. I like to be able to see the pattern of the turned-over cake slices through the confectioners' sugar.

ONE-DISH MEALS

SPICY SEAFOOD STEW IN SYRACUSE

Frutti di mare in umido alla Siciliana
MAKES 8 SERVINGS

The famous geometrician Archimedes was born in 287 B.C. at Syracuse, one of Sicily's most prestigious cities of Magna Graecia, rivalling Athens at the time. Archimedes would forget to eat and drink, he was so absentminded. While taking a bath, he realized that any body immersed in water loses weight equivalent to that of the water it displaces. He was so delighted with his new finding, he jumped out of the tub and ran naked through the streets, bellowing "Eureka!" ("I found it!"). Italian cities are rich in such stories. This one was told to me by the owner of the Archimede restaurant on Via Gemellaro in Syracuse where I enjoyed fish dishes similar to the one given here.

The old town of Siracuse is on the island of Ortygio (right in the middle of the city), whose streets are rich with medieval and baroque palaces. When I was there last year, many of these buildings were covered with scaffolding; Sicilians are as eager to restore their heritage as others in Italy. On these narrow streets, there is restaurant after restaurant, and more of them are in the piazzas and squares, whose menus are filled with tuna and swordfish dishes. These fish are prepared as they are elsewhere along the coast—cooked in oil, tomatoes, onions, celery, olives, capers and potatoes.

The addition of potatoes is a nice touch, especially for a one-dish meal, as it readily provides the starch. Here is a version of one of them that uses shellfish. Syracuse raises shellfish, including oysters, and its large delicious shrimp are crayfish are well known. Other cities in Sicily, notably Ragusa, Agrigento, Palermo, Messina and Trapina, cook shellfish and crustaceans in a similar manner.

This particular seafood stew is my adaptation.

2 pounds shrimp (16 to 20 count per pound), shelled, deveined (reserve the shells for making broth)
2 medium to large Idaho potatoes (about 1 pound)
1/2 cup extra-virgin olive oil
2 medium onions, finely chopped
4 cloves garlic, minced
2 tablespoons finely chopped fresh basil or 4 teaspoons dried
2 teaspoons finely chopped thyme
2 teaspoons saffron strands, crumbled
1 teaspoon red pepper flakes
4 whole cloves
Sea salt and freshly ground pepper
2 (28-ounce) cans plum tomatoes, seeded, cut into small pieces and drained
1 1/2 cups dry white vermouth, preferably Martini and Rossi
4 lobster tails with shells (about 2 pounds), each cut into 4 pieces with the shell on
2 pounds fillets of bass, grouper, cod or other white fish, cut into 2-inch squares
2 tablespoons Sambuca, or to taste
1 to 2 cups Seafood Broth (below)

1. Rinse the shrimp well and dry them in paper towels. Set aside.

2. Peel the potatoes, cut in half lengthwise and then cut them in 1/2-inch slices. Put them in a bowl of cold water until needed.

3. In a very large Dutch oven, heat the oil. Add the onions and cook for 5 minutes. Add the garlic, basil, thyme, saffron, red pepper flakes, cloves and some salt and pepper.

4. Add the tomatoes and vermouth and bring to a boil. Drain the potatoes and add them. Simmer over low heat, covered, for 20 minutes.

5. Add the shrimp, lobster and fish. Stir, bring to a simmer and cook for 25 minutes, partly covered.

6. Add the Sambuca and cook for 5 minutes. Spoon the seafood mixture into individual large bowls and top each serving with a piece of the lobster in shell, or serve in the Dutch oven with the lobster pieces on top.

Notabene:

This stew is not a soup and therefore should not have too much liquid. It will make its own juice from the vegetables and fish. However, if you feel it is too dry for your taste, add a ½ cup at a time of the Seafood Broth to increase the amount of liquid you wish to have.

SEAFOOD BROTH

Brodo di pesce
MAKES ABOUT 2 CUPS

> Reserved shells from the peeled shrimp
>   (See page 263)
> 1 fish bouillon cube, chopped

Put the shells into a small saucepan and add cold water just to barely cover them. Add the bouillon cube. Bring to a boil over medium heat. Reduce the heat to get a steady simmer, cover the pan and cook for 30 minutes. Drain, squeezing as much juice as you can from the shells.

TIMBALE OF EGGPLANT AND PASTA

Timballa di pasta e melanzane
MAKES 6 SERVINGS

Sicilians are very fond of timbales and it doesn't matter whether the container is made of pastry, vegetables or pasta. I particularly like this one, a pasta filling with an eggplant shell, as it reminds me of the macaroni pie that was served to selected citizens of Donnafugata in Lampedusi's *The Leopard*. Try to include the grated *caciocavallo* to make the dish authentically Sicilian. *Caciocavallo* is bound with a cord as is provolone, and bottle-shaped. It is inclined to be salty, so watch the amount of salt you use otherwise.

Mala insana, meaning the raging apple, was the name given to eggplant *(melanzane)* for hundreds of years because of its bitterness. People thought it had poisonous drippings. This is the reason it is necessary to salt and let it rest for thirty minutes or so. This is especially the case with the larger-size eggplants. Buy smaller-size ones, with lovely green, capelike bracts and stems firmly attached. Loose bracts are an indication of aging and spoiling. The eggplant should be firm.

> 1 (about 1-pound) eggplant
> Vegetable oil for frying
> 1½ cups Tomato Sauce (page 175)
> ½ pound small pasta such as penne, elbows or
>   shells, cooked until al dente
> 4 large hard-cooked eggs, coarsely
>   chopped
> 1 tablespoon finely chopped fresh oregano or
>   1 teaspoon dried
> ¾ cup combined grated caciocavallo and
>   pecorino cheeses

Sea salt and freshly ground pepper
2 tablespoons butter

1.   Remove the top and bottom of the eggplant, leaving the skin on. It should be able to sit upright. Slice lengthwise into very thin slices. Salt each slice and put them in a colander to drain for 30 minutes. Set the colander over a plate and discard any liquid. Pat each slice dry and set aside.

2.   Preheat the broiler. Liberally brush each eggplant slice with oil, arrange them in a jelly roll pan and broil on both sides about 6 inches from the heat source until they take on some color, about 4 minutes per side. Broil in batches if necessary. Remove the slices when cooked to paper towels to drain.

3.   Preheat the oven to 375F. In a large bowl, combine the tomato sauce, pasta, eggs, oregano, all but 2 tablespoons of the cheese and some salt and pepper.

4.   Butter a 2½-quart ceramic soufflé dish or a rounded glass ovenproof bowl and line it with half or more of the eggplant slices, standing them up so they can later be turned over to close in the top side, overlapping each slice and making an attractive arrangement (imagine this as it will be when turned out). Transfer the pasta mixture to the eggplant-lined dish, and fold over the over hanging eggplant slices and add any remaining slices to fully cover the pasta mixture.

5.   Bake for 30 to 40 minutes, until heated through and bubbling. Remove from the oven, allow to rest for 6 to 8 minutes, loosen the edges with a sharp knife, lay a flat plate over the dish and turn it over. Carefully remove the baking dish. Dot the mold with the butter and sprinkle with the remaining cheese.

PORK, CABBAGE AND BEAN CASSEROLE

Favata

MAKES 6 SERVINGS

Sheep, goats and pigs are numerous in Sardinia. Pigs graze on acorns and this feed makes the pork tasty. Acorns are plentiful because oak trees are the most common tree on the island, and they drop many acorns. Much of the pig is preserved, which is easy to do, as salt is plentiful (half or more of Italy's salt supply comes from the Cagliari coastal flats). I have no way of making the comparison but I've been told that the saltworks at Cagliari are the largest in Europe. Sardinians make excellent sausages and hams. One part of the pig, namely its foot, is featured in a well-known dish, *favata*, or *fava e lardu*, cooked with cabbage, fennel and fava beans. Dried favas, limas or butter beans require overnight soaking. If you have the time, this is the preferred way to prepare this dish. If not, there is an American shortcut of using canned or frozen beans, drained or thawed. Pork sausages and spareribs are used in this updated version of the dish.

This should be served with Bruschetta (page 6).

1½ pounds dried fava, lima or butter beans,
     3 (16-ounce) canned beans, or 3 (10-ounce)
     packages frozen
⅓ cup extra-virgin olive oil
6 Italian pork sausages, about 1½ pounds
6 pork spareribs, in one piece, 1 to 1½ pounds
6 thin slices pancetta or bacon, finely chopped
2 medium fresh fennel bulbs, trimmed and
     chopped, including some of the pale green
     leaves

1 medium head Savoy cabbage, trimmed, core
    removed and thinly sliced

2 medium onions, trimmed and thinly sliced

1 cup finely chopped canned or fresh plum
    tomatoes, seeds removed

Sea salt and freshly ground pepper

1 cup freshly grated pecorino cheese

1.   If using dried beans, run your hands through them to be sure there are no stones or other foreign matter. Soak the beans overnight in cold water to cover. Drain in a colander, and rinse again by holding the colander under the faucet. Set aside. If using canned beans, drain and rinse in cool water. Set aside. If using frozen beans, thaw and set aside in a bowl.

2.   Heat the oil in a large Dutch oven over medium heat. Add the sausages and spareribs and brown them, uncovered, moving the meat about in the pan as each side browns. If using dried beans, add them now with enough boiling water to cover the meat and beans. Add all the remaining ingredients, except the cheese, including some salt and a liberal amount of pepper. Bring to a boil and reduce the heat to achieve a steady simmer. Cover the pan and simmer for 2 hours. After 1 hour of cooking, check to see if more water is needed.

3.   If using canned or frozen beans, brown the sausages and spareribs as in Step 2. Add all the remaining ingredients, except the cheese and beans, with 6 cups water. Bring to boil, and reduce the heat to achieve a steady simmer. Cover the pan and simmer for 1½ hours. Add the canned or frozen beans to the casserole and cook for 30 minutes. Check to see if more water is needed after 1 hour of cooking.

4.   Remove the pan from the heat. Transfer the spareribs to a cutting board and cut into individual ribs. Put one rib in each of six shallow rimmed soup plates. Add a sausage to each and a spoonful of the bean mixture. Sprinkle some of the pecorino over each dish and pass the remaining cheese.

BIBLIOGRAPHY

Anderson, Burton. *Best Italian Wines*. London: Little, Brown and Company, 2001.

Artusi, Pelligrino. *L'Arte di Mangiare Bene*. Bologna: Libritalia, 1999.

Battifarano, A.J. and Alan Richardson. *The Four Seasons of Italian Cooking*. New York: Time-Life Books, 1998.

Boni, Ada. *Italian Regional Cooking*. New York: Bonanza Books, 1969.

Caggiano, Biba. *Modern Italian Cooking*. New York: Simon & Schuster, 1987.

Capalbo, Carla et al. *The Italian Cooking Encyclopedia*. New York: Hermes House, 1997.

Cardella, Antonio. *Sicilia e le Isole in Bocca*. Palermo, Italy: Edikronos, 1981.

David, Elizabeth. *Italian Food*. New York: Harper & Row, 1963.

de'Medici, Lorenza. *The de'Medici Kitchen*. San Francisco: Collins Publishers, 1992.

Esposito, Mary Ann. *Mangia Pasta*. New York: William Morrow and Company, 1998.

Famularo, Joe. *Italian Soup Cookbook*. New York: Workman Publishing, 1998.

————. *The Joy of Grilling*. New York: Barrons, 1988.

Famularo, Joe and Louise Imperiale. *The Festive Famularo Kitchen*. New York: Atheneum, 1977.

————. *The Joy of Pasta*. New York: Barrons, 1983.

————. *Vegetables*. New York: Barrons, 1985.

Ferrari, Ambra. *Emilia in Bocca*. Palermo, Italy: Edikronos, 1981.

Field, Carol. *Celebrating Italy*. New York: William Morrow and Company, Inc., 1990.

————. *The Italian Baker*. New York: HarperCollins Publishers, Inc, 1985.

Grimaldi, Gianni. *Liguria in Bocca*. Palermo, Italy: Il Vespro, 1972.

Hazan, Marcella. *The Classic Italian Cookbook*. New York: Alfred A. Knopf, 1980.

Kasper, Lynne Rossetto. *The Italian Country Table*. New York: Scribner, 1999.

————. *The Splendid Table*. New York: William Morrow and Company, 1992.

Lanza, Anna Tasca. *The Flavors of Sicily*. New York: Clarkson Potter Publishers, 1996.

Mallo, Beppe. *Calabria e Lucania in Bocca*. Palermo, Italy: Il Vespro, 1978.

Martini, Fosca. *Romagna in Bocca*. Palermo, Italy: Il Vespro, 1979.

Mayes, Frances. *Bella Tuscany*. New York: Broadway Books, 1999.

Piazzesi, Elisabetta. *Tuscan Cookery Book*. Florence, Italy: Bonechi, 1999.

Ray, Cyril. *The Wines of Italy*. New York: McGraw-Hill Book Company, 1966.

Roden, Claudia. *The Book of Jewish Food*. New York: Alfred A. Knopf, 2001.

Romagnoli, Margaret and G. Franco. *The Romagnoli's Table*. Boston: Little, Brown and Company, 1974.

Root, Waverly. *The Food of Italy*. New York: Atheneum, 1971.

————. *Herbs and Spices*. New York: McGraw-Hill Book Company, 1980.

Sada, Luigi. *Puglie in Bocca*. Palermo, Italy: Edizione de Il Vespro, 1972.

Santolini, Antonella. *Roma in Bocca*. Milano: Editrice de Il Vespro, 1976.

Viazzi, Alfredo. *Italian Cooking*. New York: Random House, 1979.

Willinger, Faith Heller. *Eating in Italy*. New York, William Morrow and Company, Inc., 1998.

SOURCES

INGREDIENTS AND EQUIPMENT

Agata & Valentina
1505 First Avenue, New York, NY 10021
Telephone: 212-452-0690
Salt-packed anchovies, salted capers and a wide variety of Italian products including San Marzano tomatoes

The Baker's Catalogue
P.O. Box 876, Norwich, VT 05055-0876
Telephone: 800-827-6836; Fax: 800-343-3002
www.bakerscatalogue.com
Unbleached all-purpose flour, flour-storage buckets, whole wheat flours and artisanal bread flours

Bel Canto Foods
1300 Viele Avenue, Bronx, NY 10474
Telephone: 718-497-3888
Pastas, oils, vinegars, olives, cheeses, grains, flours and polenta

Bridge Kitchenware
214 East 52nd Street, New York, NY 10022
Telephone: 212-838-6746
Cooking ware of all types plus cutlery

Broadway Panhandler
477 Broome Street, New York, NY 10013
Telephone: 212-966-3434
Pizza stones and wooden pizza peels

Butte Creek Mill
P.O. Box 1, Eagle Point, OR 97524
Telephone: 541-826-3531; Fax: 541-830-8444
Buckwheat flour, unbleached white bread flour and semolina

Chef's Catalogue
P.O. Box 620048, Dallas, TX 75262
Telephone: 800-338-3232; Fax: 800-967-3291
Kitchenware, appliances and cutlery

"Club delle Fattorie"
Piazza dei Martiri della Liberta, 2, Pienza, Italy
Fax: 0578-748-150
Dried porcini mushrooms, capers, balsamic vinegars, extra-virgin olive oils, pasta, preserves, candied fruit, cookies and chocolates and honey

D'Artagnan
280 Wilson Avenue, Newark, NJ 07105
Telephone: 800-DARTAG or 973-344-0565;
Fax: 973-465-1870
www.dartagnan.com
Pâtés, sausages, smoked delicacies, foie gras, organic game and poultry and mushrooms

Dean and Deluca (New York store)
Telephone: 800-999-0306 (see extensions below)
www.deandeluca.com
Extension 221 for oils, spices, truffle oil, vinegars, coffees, olives, preserves, nuts, saffron, truffles; extension 247 for cheeses (scamorza, taleggio, caciocavalla for grating)

A. G. Ferrari Foods
14234 Catalina Street, San Leandro, CA 94577
Telephone: 877-878-2783
www.agferrari.com
Oils from Lazio, Tuscany, Liguria and Sicily; wide selection Italian pastas (from Naples, Marche, Gragnano, in Campania, Lombardy, Emilia-Romagna, Sardinia, Abruzzi, Piemonte, Puglia, Basilicata); and flavored oils, herbs from Italy; San Marzano tomatoes, saffron, rice, beans, polenta, stone-ground flours, salamis, cheeses, honey, cherry and other jams and torrone

Formaggio Kitchen
244 Huron Avenue, Cambridge, MA 02138
Telephone: 888-212-3224; Fax: 617-547-5680
www.formaggiokitchen.com
Cheeses and oils from all over Italy; flavored oils; pastas

and rices; biscotti; Mostarda di cremona and others; cherry and other fruit jams; and honey from Sardinia

Mackenzie
1027 Wilso Drive, Baltimore, MD 21223
Telephone: 800-858-7100; Fax: 800-858-6547,
www.mackenzieltd.com
Leg and rack of lamb, salmon, lump crabmeat, soft-shell crabs, artisanal balsamic vinegar, Ravida Sicilian olive oil, Cerignola olives, whole bean espresso coffee and coffee grinders

Manganaro Foods
488 Ninth Avenue, New York, NY 10018
Telephone: 800-472-5264 and 212-563-5331;
Fax: 212-239-8355
Wide assortment of Italian products including cured meats

NapaStyle, Inc.
801 Main Street, St. Helena, CA 94574
Telephone: 866-776-6272
www.napastyle.com
Preserves, pasta flour, cocoa powder, honey, rice, spices, polenta, coffee and herbs

Todaro Brothers
555 Second Avenue, New York, NY 10016
Telephone: 878-472-2767, 212-532-0633;
Fax: 212-639-1679
www.todarobros.com
Wide variety of Italian specialty food items

Viansa
P.O. Box 35, Vineburg, CA 95487-0035
Telephone: 888-875-5057; Fax: 707-935-4731
www.viansa.com
Oils, vinegars, sauces, spices, condiments, mustards, preserves and nuts

Vinny's Deli and Pasta
14 East Main Street
Pawling, NY 12564
Telephone and fax: 845-855-1922
www.freshgratedcheese.com
Pastas, imported cheeses, oils, vinegars, olives, cured meats and fresh mozzarella

John Volpi & Co.
5254 Daggett Avenue, St. Louis, MO 63110
Telephone: 800-288-3439, extension 3332
www.volpifoods.com
Prosciutto, pancetta, salamis, pepperoni, coppa, bresaola, mortadella and panettone.

Zingerman's
422 Detroit Street, Ann Arbor, MI 48104
Telephone: 888-636-8162; Fax: 734-477-6988
www.zingermans.com
Oils, chocolates, vinegars, spices, artichokes in oil, lemon oil, truffle oil, salamis, salt-packed anchovies and olives and wild cherry jams

INDEX